BALKAN BABEL

SECOND EDITION

BALKAN BABEL

———————— ◆ ————————

The Disintegration of Yugoslavia
from the Death of Tito
to Ethnic War

Sabrina Petra Ramet

Westview Press
A Member of the Perseus Books Group

Published in 1996 in the United States of America by Westview Press, Inc., 5500 Central Avenue, Boulder, Colorado 80301-2877, and in the United Kingdom by Westview Press, 12 Hid's Copse Road, Cumnor Hill, Oxford OX2 9JJ

Library of Congress Cataloging-in-Publication Data
Ramet, Sabrina P., 1949–
    Balkan babel : the disintegration of Yugoslavia from the death of
Tito to ethnic war / Sabrina Petra Ramet. — 2nd ed.
        p.   cm.
    Includes bibliographical references and index.
    ISBN 0-8133-2558-7 — ISBN 0-8133-2559-5 (pb)
    1. Yugoslavia—History—1980–1992. 2. Yugoslav War, 1991–
I. Title.
DR1307.R36   1996
949.702'4—dc20   95-25078
                                                                                         CIP

The paper used in this publication meets the requirements of the American National Standard for Permanence of Paper for Printed Library Materials Z39.48–1984.

10   9   8   7   6   5   4

To Susan McEachern,
my editor, my friend

Contents

List of Tables   xi
Foreword, Ivo Banac   xiii
Preface to the Second Edition   xix
Preface to the First Edition   xxi
List of Abbreviations   xxiii
Credits   xxv
Map of Yugoslavia   xxvii
Map of Bosnia-Herzegovina   xxviii

Introduction   1

Part One
Politics, 1980–1991

1 Political Debate, 1980–1986   7

Political Decay, 8
Crisis and Polarization, 10
The Search for Solutions, 11
The Serbian Solution, 14
The Constitution and the System, 16
Notes, 18

2 The Gathering Storm, 1987–1989   21

The Mobilization of Slovenia, 24
Serbian National Revival and Its Effects, 26
Political Fragmentation, 31
Issues on the Agenda, 33
Notes, 35

3 Brotherhood and Disunity, 1989–1991   37

Sources of Discord, 37
Serbs and Non-Serbs, 40
The Spread of Civil Turmoil, 42
The Disintegration of the Economy, 44
The Federal Budget, 45
The Republics Awaken, 46
On the Brink, 49
War, 52
Notes, 55

Part Two
Culture and Society

4 The Press   63

The Purpose of the Press and the Application of Censorship, 64
Nationalism and the Republicanization of the Press, 67
A New Law on the Press, 70
The Youth Press, 72
Life of a Journalist, 76
A Critical Press, 77
The Struggle for the Press, 80
The Media and the Dissolution of the SFRY, 81
Notes, 86

5 Rock Music   91

The Early Years, 92
Rebellion or Conformity, 95
Yugoslav Rock Comes of Age, 96
The Ethnic Impulse, 99
Politicians and Rock, 101
Censorship—Now You See It, Now You Don't, 104
New Primitivism, 108
The Support System, 109
The End of Yugo-Rock, 110
Notes, 112

6 Women and Men   117

Serbian Pastoralism and the Male Complex, 119
Prostitution, 122
Agriculturalist Society: Slovenia and Croatia, 123
The Broader Picture, 124

Yugoslav Women in Troubled Times, 127
Phallocracy and War, 128
Notes, 129

Part Three
Religion, Up to 1991

7 The Catholic Church   135

The Symbology of the Church in Yugoslavia, 135
The Dawn of Communist Rule, 136
The Trial of Archbishop Stepinac, 140
The Priests' Associations, 143
Phases in Church-State Relations, 145
Internal Divisions, 150
Belief and Unbelief, 153
The Miracle at Medjugorje, 156
The End of Yugoslavia, 157
Notes, 159

8 The Serbian Orthodox Church   165

The Soul of the Church, 165
The Great Catastrophe, 170
The Communist Assault and the Effort to Rebuild, 171
Whittling the Church Down, 174
Church-State Relations, 1970–1986, 177
Rehabilitation, 180
Conclusion, 181
Notes, 182

9 Islam   185

Basic Facts and Resources, 186
The Social Presence of Islam, 189
Women and Islam, 191
Recent Developments, 192
Notes, 193

Part Four
Dissolution and Ethnic War

10 Serbia and Croatia at War Again   197

Serbia at War, 200
An Independent Croatia, 208

Ethnic Peripheries, 213
Conclusion, 214
Notes, 215

11 On Their Own: Slovenia and Macedonia Since 1991   223

Slovenia's Troubled Path to Prosperity, 225
Macedonia—Reluctantly Independent, 230
Conclusion, 237
Notes, 238

12 The Struggle for Bosnia   243

The Bosnian War, to April 1993, 245
The Diplomacy of Accommodation—Second Phase, 251
U.S., Russian, and Other Foreign Responses, 253
The European Union Plan of June 1994, 256
War Crimes, 258
Belgrade's Friends in the West, 259
The End of the Embargo? 261
Conclusion, 267
Notes, 268

13 Repercussions of the War in Religion, Gender Relations,
and Culture   275

In the Name of God, 276
The Politics of Serbian Orthodoxy, 279
A Papal Visit, 280
The New Patriarchy, 282
The Cultural Sector, 286
Notes, 293

Epilogue   299

For Further Reading   331
About the Book and Author   335
Index   337

Tables

4.1 Which periodical do you respect the most? (1989) 82
4.2 Which periodical do you read most frequently? (1989) 83
4.3 Yugoslav newspapers with circulations larger
  than 10,000 in rank order (1990, with
  comparative figures from 1983) 84

6.1 Number of prostitutes arrested and charged in Serbia
  proper, 1968–1975 123
6.2 Women in leadership organs of the LCY (1984) 124

7.1 Proportions of believers and nonbelievers
  in Yugoslavia, 1953–1984 153
7.2 Responses to the question, "Do you accept marxism?" (1969) 154
7.3 Responses to the question, "How often do you participate in
  public meetings?" (1969) 155
7.4 Proportion of population reporting religious belief
  (November 1985), by federal unit 155

9.1 Proportion of ethnic Muslims, Serbs, Croats, "Yugoslavs,"
  and other nationalities in Bosnia-Herzegovina, 1948–1991 187

11.1 Military strength of Macedonia and Greece (1993) 232
11.2 Population of Macedonia, by nationality (1991, 1994) 233

12.1 Ethnic composition of Bosanska Krajina (1991, 1994) 263
12.2 Troop strengths of the rival forces (November 1994) 264
12.3 Armaments possessed by the combatants in Bosnia
  (November 1994) 265
12.4 Composition of UNPROFOR troops stationed in Bosnia
  (December 1994) 266

Foreword:
The Politics of Cultural Diversity
in Former Yugoslavia

THE COLLAPSE OF SOVIET AND EAST EUROPEAN communism has upset all the political and ideological conventions in the countries concerned. One noticeable consequence has been the revival of nationalism—that much misunderstood mutant ideology whose many faces have tested a legion of analysts. The nationalisms of Eastern Europe, in particular, have long been a stumbling block for U.S. observers. The example of a stable civil society like the United States, where an assimilationist political culture mitigated the effects of ancestry, really cannot inform the "ethnic" relations of East European multinational states. The latter—and Yugoslavia was a prime example—are really conglomerates of historical nations, each with its own internal subnational—or, if you prefer, ethnic—problems. Yugoslavia has not survived the pressures of its component parts and no longer exists as a state. For insight into why this has happened, it might be wise to look at the political implications of cultural diversity in what used to be Yugoslavia and in its successor states. It is to Sabrina Ramet's great credit that she understood the cultural context of South Slavic nationality relations at a time when most of her colleagues promoted entirely unrealistic readings of the subject.

The cultural diversity *among* the nationalities of Yugoslavia has frequently been so acute that there is a tendency to underestimate the elements of diversity *within* each single nationality. Take the Serbs, for example. Vuk Karadžić (1787–1864), the foremost Serb cultural reformer, was probably not the first Serb scholar to recognize the vast cultural—not just linguistic—differences between the Serbs of the Habsburg Monarchy and those of the Ottoman Empire. Jovan Cvijić (1865–1927), a noted Serbian geographer, developed a whole system for the classification of Serb "cultural belts," having personally identified three Serb "psychological types" (really, cultural types). And, indeed, there are vast differences between the disciplined "imperial sons" from the former Habsburg Military Frontier, the exponents of urban Byzantine Orthodoxy from southern Serbia, the patriarchal and natural Orthodox highlanders of Herzegovina and Montenegro, the latitudinarian clergy and burghers from the Vojvodina, and their no less latitudinarian kinsmen from the harbors of the Montenegrin littoral, not to forget the Serbs who live in areas of predominantly Muslim influence. One could go on like this and demonstrate to what extent the perennial calls for Serb unity (including cultural unity) address the real fears of cultural fragmentation in reputedly one of the most homogeneous of South Slavic nationalities. Slobodan Milošević, currently the paramount Serbian leader, is therefore as keen as any of his non-Communist predecessors to foster the homogenization of Serbs throughout the Western Balkans, that is, beyond Serbia itself.

The extreme cultural diversity of the South Slavs stems from the fact that they are situated at the cultural crossroads of the Old World. The continental crusts of Rome and Byzantium have been colliding here for a millennium. The subcontinent of Islam dashed at the emerging landmass half a millennium ago. There is a Central European belt (Slovenia, northern Croatia, the Vojvodina) and a Mediterranean belt (the littorals of Slovenia, Croatia, and Montenegro). There is a Muslim belt and an Eastern Orthodox belt. And they used to come together. In Mostar, Herzegovina, before the warlords destroyed it, one was able not too long ago to sip Viennese coffee and read newspapers mounted on wooden frames, listening all along to a muezzin's call in the shadow of a Franciscan church (where the chant was Latinate), and then wander into a fig grove that surrounds a Byzantine-style church (where the chant was Slavonic). None of this was imported for the tourists. It raised no native eyebrows. And it did not prompt intolerance.

Because South Slavic cultural diversity is really religiously based, there have been numerous attempts to link the country's divisions to religious intolerance. In fact, South Slavic interconfessional relations never occasioned religious wars on the scale of those fought in Western Europe after the Reformation or along the banks of the Tigris for the length of the Islamic era. The tragic events of World War II and of the current conflict, when some of the massacres committed by the contending sides became religiously based, occurred in the context of occupation, not of religious or even civil war (a much misused term). The hold of religious culture is strong, but not stronger than the practicality of the usually practical South Slavs. An epic Croat folk song tells of how the war party of the Uskoks of Senj, a sixteenth-century martial community that lived on piracy and plunder, was faced with an unexpected spell of cold weather. Instead of permitting his men to freeze, the Uskok leader offered the following solution:

I do not know of a stone cave [where they presumably could hide];
But I know of Saint George's church.

> We shall break the door of the holy church,
> We shall burn fire in it,
> So that God will send us his luck,
> So that we shall warm our flesh,
> And safely return to Senj.
> We shall then build a better church,
> And secure it with a new door,
> Made of silver and purest gold.

I mention the question of cultural diversity and its misapplications because diversity, as such, is not the fuel of current national hostilities. I personally have been a strong exponent of the idea that the nationality question in Yugoslavia and other East European countries does not derive from religious differences, cultural diversity, or even from the problems of unequal economic development. Rather, I have argued that the nationality question was shaped by the dissimilar structure and goals of various national ideologies that have emerged within the political culture of each of Eastern Europe's national groups. Quite obviously, these national ideologies are historically determined, which is to say that each one of them also contains elements of historically determined cultural diversity. From that point of view, it might be useful to trace the postwar Communist experience in order to discover how Communist ideology operated within the context of Yugoslav cultural diversity, thereby reshaping the national ideologies of Yugoslavia's principal national groups.

The Yugoslav Communists promoted the interests of their respective national groups a great deal more than is usually imagined, and not just since the death of Tito in 1980. The Communists have debated the Yugoslav nationality question from the beginning of their party in 1919 and "solved" it in turns as revolutionary centralists and unitarists, separatists, federalists, and, increasingly in the 1980s, as confederalists. They emerged from World War II with the program of "new Yugoslav socialist culture," which was intended to eliminate the nationality question by eradicating its historical sources. This proved impossible from the beginning. The permitted, mainly traditional, cultural cults could not easily be harmonized and frequently expressed fundamentally irreconcilable cultural and national aspirations. Worse yet, the Communist cults of "new Yugoslav socialist culture" were no more harmonious.

Two of the foremost literary figures of socialist Yugoslavia, Nobel laureate Ivo Andrić and Miroslav Krleža, were the living embodiment of Communist cultural diversity. They were not just stylistic antipodes; their communism itself covered the diapason of Yugoslav Marxist patterns. Like most intellectuals, Krleža came to Leninism from the shipwreck and carnage of Central European civilization, which collapsed on the fields of Galicia in World War I. His principal literary motif was his profound skepticism about the historical mission of the Central European bourgeoisie. The fog that enveloped Croatia (and Eastern Europe) could only be lifted "when whole flotillas of nations and classes start sailing" toward the Leninist beacon. But that beacon, too, was fundamentally chimerical. Krleža's Lenin-types, for example his Christopher Columbus, are crucified by the mindless masses. Nevertheless, Krleža's pessimistic revolutionism brought the intelligentsia to the Communist Party. In terms of nationality programs, it was an expression of a steadfast federalist project, built on the premise, which Krleža shared with many of his non-Communist fellow Croats, that Yugoslavia's cultural diversity (the Rome-Byzantium cleavage) could not easily be filled. In Andrić we have a veteran of the nationalist and mythopoeic Bosnian Youth—the movement that cast forth the Sarajevo assassins—a Yugoslav integralist of profoundly authoritarian bent, a prewar diplomat, and an associate of right-wing cultural journals, who missed the Chetnik train by a very small margin. His postwar membership in the Communist Party was typical of the premium paid to the unitarist intelligentsia by the cultural architects of the new state.

The building of the "new Yugoslav socialist culture" also ended as a failure among the generation of literary partisans—the veterans of Tito's wartime insurgency. Members of the partisan generation failed to integrate Yugoslavia culturally. Moreover, prominent partisan writers became the ideologists of Yugoslavia's new national divisions and contributed to the collapse of Yugoslav cultural unitarism that can be dated from the mid-1960s. The changing nature of official Yugoslav ideology and statecraft, the growing delegitimation of the Communist movement (with the accompanying need to seek national underpinnings of legitimacy), and real national grievances (but also the attempts to explain and cure them) are among the other factors that contributed to the failure of cultural unitarism.

Tito's answer to this failure was a more consistent federalism that substituted democracy with formal axiomatic constructions (the rotation system of leadership, parity in leaderships, constitutional reforms, the refederation of Serbia's two autonomous provinces, and an indirect system of elections). These constructions and changes necessarily prompted resistance, which exploded after Tito's death and reached its culmination in the current war between Serbia and the two other successor states of Yugoslavia—Croatia and Bosnia-Herzegovina. It is important to note here that the content of Communist thinking in all of Yugoslavia's six territorial parties came to resemble, indeed duplicate, the national ideologies that have evolved and prevailed in the given party-state before the war. In other words, when he still espoused Communist doctrine, Serbia's leading figure, Slobodan Milošević, had more in common with the prewar Radical Party, the party of Serbian supremacy, than with Slovene or Croat Communists. Yugoslav communism, national since 1948, had become further nationalized along

internal national divisions before it collapsed. A similar process has occurred in the Soviet Union, where, for example, the pre-August 1991 discourse between Lithuanian and Russian Communists resembled the old
contention between the Lithuanian national movement and the imperial
Russian state.

The South Slavs have never been more divided than today. Never before
in their histories have they shared such deep resentment for one another.
As bitter as this assessment certainly is, it is also entirely true. The Yugoslav
project is finished, root and branches. At this late date, after Serbia unleashed a war of conquest against its western neighbors, after the destruction of Bosnia, after ethnic cleansing and strategic rape, there is little
prospect of peace, let alone reconciliation. In the future, after a semblance
of stability returns, after the project of national homogenization is recognized as criminal utopism, the successor states of Yugoslavia will be judged
by their fidelity to human rights, especially the protection of minorities. The
equality and territoriality of each of ex-Yugoslavia's nationalities must be
protected, as must the legitimacy of the links between the minority nationalities and their matrix-states. For example, the Serbs should be able to
enjoy their independent statehood without obstructing the national institutions and the democratic rights of Serbia's minorities. The protection of minorities, especially their cultural unity, could in time be extended to the
whole of Eastern Europe, thereby lessening the importance of some of the
region's more irrational borders, and perhaps even contributing to their
change. Moreover, the full legitimation of the national cultures would necessarily legitimate diversity, which must prevail if peace is to return to the
South Slavs.

Ivo Banac

Preface to the Second Edition

CHAPTERS 10 THROUGH 13 ARE NEW to this edition as is the epilogue. Chapter 3 has been extensively revised. There have also been small revisions to Chapters 5 through 8. In preparing these revisions, I benefited from two-week interview trips to Ljubljana in March 1992 and to Skopje in March 1995, and am grateful to the International Research Exchanges Board (IREX) for providing travel grants in support of those trips.

I am grateful to *Current History* for permission to use my article "The Bosnian War and the Diplomacy of Accommodation" (originally published in that journal in November 1994) as the basis for the more extended treatment in Chapter 12.

I wish to thank Susan McEachern, my editor at Westview, for encouraging me to undertake this second edition and for her wise counsel on many matters relating to this book. I also wish to thank Professor Nicholas R. Lardy, Director of the Henry M. Jackson School of International Studies, for arranging a pause quarter for me in autumn 1994, which made it possible for me to carry out these revisions. And I am also deeply indebted to Christine Hassenstab, my spouse, for giving me feedback on both the earlier chapters and the new material and for assisting with the proofreading of the new material. I also wish to thank Atsushi Saito for his helpful comments on an earlier draft of Chapter 11 and Rudi Rizman for comments throughout.

Sabrina Petra Ramet
Seattle, Washington

Preface to the First Edition

IT GIVES ME GREAT PLEASURE to be able to collect some of my previous writings on Yugoslavia and reissue them in book form. Of the nine chapters printed herein, six are revised and updated incarnations of earlier publications of mine. Three chapters (Chapters 3, 5, and 6) are new.

I took up the study of Yugoslavia in 1977 while still in graduate school—I had become excited about ethnic relations in that country while engaged in master's research on my mother's country, Austria-Hungary. Since then, I have visited Yugoslavia repeatedly and spent time in all of the republics except Montenegro. Inevitably, most of my work has taken me to the cities—above all to Ljubljana, Zagreb, and Belgrade, but also, on occasion, to Sarajevo and Skopje. I have also had occasion to visit villages in Slovenia, Croatia, and Serbia and to get some idea of the differences between city and countryside in the Yugoslav setting.

My impressions of Yugoslavia have been formed by the people I have met and interviewed in Yugoslavia and through their writings. I have tried, in my own writings, to convey something of the "spirit" of Yugoslavia—what makes its people tick, what issues concern them, and how they think. That spirit, for me, is the lifeblood of political history.

In bringing together these essays, I hope to suggest a vital interconnection and interaction among the political, cultural, and religious spheres and show how changes in one sphere are accompanied by parallel changes in the other spheres.

Chapter 1 was previously published in *Crossroads*, No. 23 (1987). Chapter 2 was previously published in *Global Affairs,* Vol. 5, No. 1 (winter 1990). Chapter 4 was previously published in John B. Allcock, John J. Horton, and Marko Milivojevic, eds., *Yugoslavia in Transition: Choices and Constraints* (Oxford and Hamburg: Berg; New York: St. Martin's Press, 1991). Chapter 7 was previously published in Pedro Ramet, ed., *Catholicism and Politics in Communist Societies* (Durham, N.C.: Duke University Press, 1990). Chapter 8 was previously published in Pedro Ramet, ed., *Eastern Christianity and Politics in the Twentieth Century* (Durham, N.C.: Duke University Press, 1988). And Chapter 9 was previously published in *Religion in Communist Lands* (a publication of Keston College), Vol. 18, No. 3 (summer 1990). I am grateful to the editors of these publications and to the respective presses for permission to reuse this material. I am also deeply grateful to Karen Walton for coding this manuscript and assisting in other ways.

Some of these essays appeared originally under my former name, Pedro Ramet. I changed my gender and my name in December 1990: Pedro and Sabrina are one and the same person.

Sabrina Petra Ramet
Seattle, Washington

Abbreviations

AVNOJ	Antifašističko vijeće narodnog oslobodjenja Jugoslavije (Antifascist Council of the People's Liberation of Yugoslavia)
CC	Central Committee
CIA	Central Intelligence Agency
CSCE	Conference on Security and Cooperation in Europe
EC	European Community
FBIS	Foreign Broadcast Information Service
FRY	Federal Republic of Yugoslavia
IMF	International Monetary Fund
JNA	Yugoslav National Army
LCY	League of Communists of Yugoslavia
NATO	North Atlantic Treaty Organization
NDH	Nezavisna Država Hrvatska (Independent State of Croatia, 1941–1945)
RL	Radio Liberty
RFE	Radio Free Europe
SAWPY	Socialist Alliance of Working People of Yugoslavia
SFRY	Socialist Federated Republic of Yugoslavia
UDBa	Uprava Državne Bezbednosti (State Security Administration, i.e., secret police)
UNPROFOR	United Nations Protection Force

Credits

Permission has been generously given to reprint material in this book that has been adapted from the following articles:

Sabrina Petra Ramet, "The Role of the Press in Yugoslavia," *Yugoslavia in Transition—Choices and Constraints: Essays in Honour of Fred Singleton,* eds. John B. Allcock, John J. Horton, and Marko Milivojević (Oxford: Berg Publishers, 1992), pp. 414–441.

Pedro Ramet, "The Catholic Church in Yugoslavia, 1945–1989," *Catholicism and Politics in Communist Societies*, ed. Pedro Ramet (Durham, N.C.: Duke University Press, 1990).

Pedro Ramet, "The Serbian Orthodox Church," *Eastern Christianity and Politics in the Twentieth Century,* ed. Pedro Ramet (Durham, N.C.: Duke University Press, 1988).

Sabrina Petra Ramet, "Islam in Yugoslavia Today," *Religion in Communist Lands* (published by the Keston Institute and now called *Religion, State, and Society),* Vol. 18, No. 3 (autumn 1990).

Sabrina Petra Ramet, "The Bosnian War and the Diplomacy of Accommodation," *Current History,* Vol. 93, No. 586 (November 1994).

Permission was also kindly given for reprinting parts of the following items:

"Child's Play" by Judi Benson, extracted by permission of the poet.

From *The Dictionary of the Khazars,* by Milorad Pavić, trans., C. Pribićević-Zorić. Copyright © 1988 by Alfred A. Knopf, Inc. Reprinted by permission of the publisher.

From *Marpingen: Apparitions of the Virgin Mary in Nineteeth-Century Germany,* by David Blackbourn. Copyright © 1988 by Alfred A. Knopf, Inc. Reprinted by permission of the publisher.

Excerpt from *South to Destiny* by Dobrica Ćosić, copyright © 1982 by Harcourt Brace & Company, reprinted by permission of Harcourt Brace & Company.

Excerpt from *Garden, Ashes* by Danilo Kiš, trans. William J. Hannaker, English translation copyright © 1975 by Harcourt Brace & Company, reprinted by permission of the publisher.

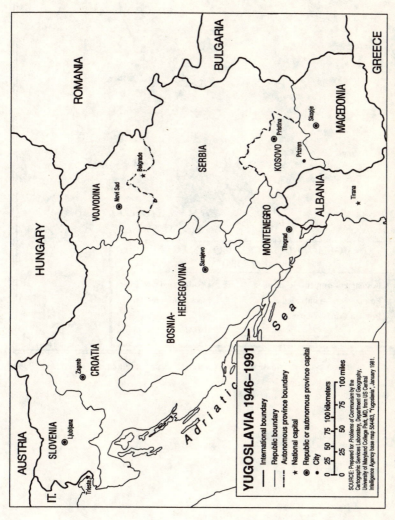

YUGOSLAVIA 1946–1991

——— International boundary

——— Republic boundary

- - - - - Autonomous province boundary

★ National capital

◉ Republic or autonomous province capital

• City

| 0 | 25 | 50 | 75 | 100 kilometers |
| 0 | 25 | 50 | 75 | 100 miles |

SOURCE: Prepared for *Problems of Communism* by the
Cartographic Services Laboratory, Department of Geography,
University of Maryland College Park, MD, from US Central
Intelligence Agency base map 504483, "Yugoslavia", January 1981.

AUSTRIA

IT.

Trieste

SLOVENIA

Ljubljana ◉

HUNGARY

CROATIA

Zagreb ◉

VOJVODINA

Novi Sad ◉

Belgrade ★

ROMANIA

SERBIA

BULGARIA

BOSNIA-
HERCEGOVINA

Sarajevo ◉

MONTENEGRO

Titograd ◉

KOSOVO ◉ Pristina

Prizren •

ALBANIA

Tirana ★

MACEDONIA

Skopje ◉

GREECE

Adriatic Sea

NOTE: The autonomous provinces of Vojvodina and Kosovo were abolished as juridical units in 1989.

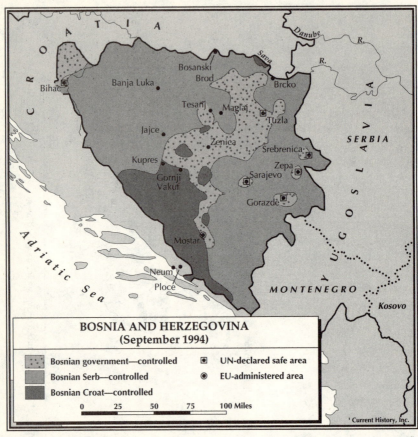

BOSNIA AND HERZEGOVINA
(September 1994)

Bosnian government—controlled   ◼ UN-declared safe area

Bosnian Serb—controlled   ◉ EU-administered area

Bosnian Croat—controlled

0   25   50   75   100 Miles

' Current History, Inc.

SOURCE: Reprinted with permission from *Current History* magazine (November 1994). © 1994, Current History, Inc.

BALKAN BABEL

Introduction

THERE WAS NO YUGOSLAVIA before 1918. Until then, Serbs and Croats had never lived in the same state. Until then, Slovenes had for centuries been attached to Austria and in cultural terms looked north to Vienna, rather than south to Belgrade, for kinship. Kosovo, remembered by Serbs today as the heartland of the medieval Serbian kingdom, was ruled by Turkey for some 500 years, and by the time Serbia regained rule over Kosovo in 1913, the province had a decisive Albanian majority. Yugoslavia's prophets (in the nineteenth century) had conceived of the state as a land in which related peoples—the South Slavs—could build a common life. Many of Yugoslavia's early rulers, however, were essentially the rulers of the former Serbian state and conceived of the new state as an extension of old Serbia.

Since 1918, there has been a constant tension between Serbs and non-Serbs in this polyglot country, as Serbs have repeatedly tried to Serbianize and/or dominate the non-Serbs, and non-Serbs have doggedly fought such domination. This struggle between Serbs and non-Serbs lies at the heart of the instability for which Yugoslavia was famous. It was never the *only* source of Yugoslav instability, but it was a crucial component in that syndrome.

Yugoslavia was a multinational country in which every national group was a minority. The Serbs, for example, were the largest group, numbering 8.1 million out of a total 22.4 million persons, representing 36.3 percent of the population in 1981. Croats were the second largest group with 4.4 million or 19.7 percent of the population. Ethnic Muslims numbered 2.0 million or 8.9 percent of the population. The fourth largest group in 1981 was the Slovenes (1.8 million, or 7.8 percent), followed by the Albanians (1.7 million, or 7.7 percent). All other groups numbered less than 1.5 million persons (i.e., less than 7 percent of the total population). These other groups included Macedonians, Montenegrins, Hungarians, Gypsies, and Turks.

Yugoslavia was also a multiconfessional country. The three largest religious groups were the Serbian Orthodox Church (which claims to have some 10 million adherents), the Catholic Church (which claims some 7.3 million adherents), and the Islamic community (which claims some 3.8 million adherents). All of these figures are inflated and do not take account of the secularization of the population. This reflects the tendency of these respective organizations to claim the allegiance of the entire membership of each national group traditionally affiliated with the given religion (as if all Serbs and Montenegrins were Orthodox or all Slovenes and Croats were Catholics). Fortunately, sociological studies have been conducted that reveal more accurately the proportion of each ethnic group reporting religious belief. These figures are given in Chapter 7. Taking these figures into account, we may estimate that in real terms there were probably about 2.5 million Catholics, 1.2 million Muslims, and 1.1 million Serbian Orthodox in Yugoslavia in 1981. Given general population growth and a modest religious revival among all groups, these figures would be somewhat larger for 1991, possibly in the range of 3 million Catholics, 1.5 million Muslims, and 1.2 million Serbian Orthodox. The Catholic Church was, by this revised estimate, easily the largest religious body in the country. There were also smaller numbers of Protestants, Jews, Jehovah's Witnesses, Hare Krishnas, and others. There were also many agnostics, atheists, and religiously uncommitted.

Yugoslavia was also a multicultural country, and in fact the cultural differences were often so wide that different groups could not understand each other at all. The difficulty that Serbs and Slovenes had understanding each other was in part a function of the vast differences separating their respective cultures.

Finally, Yugoslavia was also—if one may use the expression—a multipolitical country, by which I mean that politics in its diverse regions always differed, one to the other. This was especially true of the period since Yugoslav President Tito's death in 1980.

This book is about politics. It is also about culture and religion. I have brought these topics together because I am convinced that no country's politics exists independently of its cultures or its religions and that without an understanding of the culture and religion one can *never* understand the politics. Those Western analysts who have made the most sense of Yugoslav politics have been those who have understood Yugoslavia's culture and its religious climate.

Culture and religion are about values, about prescribed behavior, about social expectations. These components cannot but impinge on politics and infuse politics from below. I might even be so bold as to say that culture should be understood as the source of values and hence, of conflicts over values—which is to say that without culture (of which religion is a constituent part), there can be no politics. Or to put it differently, religion and politics alike were born at the same point in time as offspring of a common mother—and that mother is culture in the broad sense.

I was always pessimistic about Yugoslavia, even when I gave it credit for its achievements. By late 1989, Yugoslavia was already dying—in cultural terms. It had no more unifying energy, only divisive energy rooted in a complete and total breakdown of intercultural contact and exchange. The cultural death of a country is bound to lead to its political death, in due course, even if the Great Powers intervene to delay the moment of truth. The only escape might have been through an Ataturk, who would have had to create a new consensus on the basis of a new culture.

But for better or worse there was no Yugoslav "Ataturk" on the scene to rescue the country from disintegration. Where a united Yugoslavia once existed there are today five smaller states struggling to survive: Slovenia, Croatia, Bosnia-Herzegovina, Macedonia, and a Serb-Montenegrin union, which has taken for itself the name "Federal Republic of Yugoslavia."

PART ONE

◆

Politics, 1980–1991

CHAPTER ONE

◆

Political Debate, 1980–1986

JOSIP BROZ TITO RULED Yugoslavia for some thirty-seven years, guiding the country through a major crisis in relations with the Soviet Union, steering it through four constitutions, and creating a political formula centered on self-management (in the economy), brotherhood and unity (in nationalities policy), and nonalignment (in foreign policy). Despite the internal crises that shook the country in 1948–1949, 1961–1965, and 1970–1971, Tito created a network of institutions that many hoped would prove stable and resistant to destabilizing change. Yet, for reasons quite different from and independent of those affecting other countries in Eastern Europe, Yugoslavia's political institutions ultimately proved vulnerable to pressures for change. Such pressures built up gradually and steadily from the grass roots, from the intellectuals, from feminists, environmentalists, pacifists, and liberals. Political change was adumbrated first in the cultural sector[1] and borne along by small independent organizations set up from below.

The ruling party, the League of Communists of Yugoslavia (LCY), was aware even as Tito was dying that his political formula needed revision. The result was a political debate that raged for nearly a decade. The debate went through three broad phases: 1980–1987 (internal party debate), 1987–1989 (internal party debate pitting Milošević supporters against his antagonists), and 1989–1991 (interparty debate between the remnants of the old Communist Party and the new noncommunist parties in Slovenia, Croatia, Bosnia, and Macedonia over the future of the country). This chapter is concerned with the first phase and argues that the system was so constituted that substantive change was precluded by the very nature and structure of the system. At the core of the problem was the party's insistence on narrowing the debate by excluding discussion of pluralization; the preservation of its power monopoly was taken for granted. This proved to be an unexpected source of bottlenecks, as I shall show.

After Tito's death in May 1980, critical voices began to be heard in a way they had not been in Tito's time. Gradually, in the course of the 1980s,

Yugoslavia saw the abandonment of the party's claim to have devised an exportable model, abandonment of the central concept of the withering away of the state, abandonment of the idea that self-management was the font of the system and the key to the solution of all policy issues, redefinition of nonalignment in terms of *Realpolitik,* abandonment of the idea that the LCY had a historic or superordinate claim to rule, and rejustification on the grounds that any alternative would lead to civil war (though increasing numbers of people rejected even this rejustification in order to argue for the establishment of a two-party or multiparty system in Yugoslavia). This post-Tito disintegration of ideology in Yugoslavia followed on the heels of a devolution of powers to the constituent republics and provinces that revived, on a nationwide basis, the autonomist logic of the Cvetković-Maček *Sporazum* of 1939.[2]

POLITICAL DECAY

In the course of the years 1980–1986, leading Yugoslav party functionaries and news organs charged almost every major social institution with malfunctioning. Only the army was exempted from criticism at that time. Other organizations were variably charged with unconstitutional practices, corruption, rampant inefficiency, unresponsiveness to people's needs, etc.

Problems in the functioning of the party remained central to these concerns of course. Here the pivotal concern was the manifest inability of the eight regional party organizations of Yugoslavia's eight federal units (six republics and two autonomous provinces) to coordinate their policies or agree on strategies. This, in turn, gave birth to the realization that the LCY had already ceased to exist as an organizationally unified and politically meaningful unit: the LCY had become merely the institutional arena in which the real powers in the system—the regional party organizations—met and discussed their common concerns.

Within the party itself, the real channels of authority often diverged considerably from the formal channels: the secession of the provincial party organizations of Kosovo and Vojvodina from the effective jurisdiction of the Serbian republic party organization was only one example of this. While the party as a whole was weak and disunified, local branches sometimes showed a resilient capacity for intrusion into domains lying outside their jurisdiction. Local party members often joined out of sheer opportunism and used their positions for private gain, often, evidently, in disregard of the law.[3] Even *Socijalizam,* the party theoretical organ, admitted in summer 1984 that the LCY was having difficulties with members who ignored party directives and behaved in an irresponsible fashion.[4]

But while the federal party organization had become totally divorced from governmental functions—to the extent that it experienced considerable difficulty in making any headway in applying the 1982 recommenda-

tions of the Kraigher Commission for the Reform of the Economic System—
the regional party organizations retained a firm grasp on power, thus provoking complaints of "republican etatism." A striking illustration of the balance of power came in the second half of 1984, when the Fourteenth
Central Committee (CC) Plenum was held. Under party statutes, the eight
regional party organizations (of six republics and two autonomous
provinces) were obliged to meet to compare their own policies with the latest CC resolution (which dealt specifically with the economy and the failure to implement the Kraigher Commission's recommendations). In actual
fact, not a single regional party organization bothered to meet in this connection[5]—a sure sign of the flimsiness of central party discipline.

The self-managing interest communities likewise got out of control.
Created in late 1974 with the idea of involving citizens in monitoring public services in education, health, social welfare, childcare, employment,
sports, information, and so forth,[6] the communities (known collectively as
"SIZ," from the Serbo-Croatian *Samoupravne interesne zajednice*) quickly
mushroomed in number and scope. The resulting system, in which two
parallel structures exercised jurisdiction in the same area, was mocked as
"SIZ-ophrenia" (a pointed pun on "schizophrenia"). But under the constitution the self-managing communities were supposed to be created by local
bodies of citizens and not by republic or provincial legislation; in practice,
on the contrary, all such communities owed their existence to republic or
provincial legislation. Moreover, instead of functioning as consumer advocates—their supposed portfolio—the new institutions quickly adopted the
behavior of government agencies.

Finally—where political institutions are concerned—the Socialist
Alliance of Working People of Yugoslavia (SAWPY), a front organization designed to involve nonparty people in supportive activity, had long been little more than a marionette of party barons.

The malfunctioning of political organizations might not have become a
problem had it not been for repeated charges to that effect and for an attendant shrinkage of public confidence in the system. But neither the malfunctioning of institutions nor the shrinkage of confidence would have gar-
nered much attention had it not been for the economic mire, which
probably deserves to be credited in the first place as the chief catalyst of
the crisis of confidence. Precipitated by a combination of uncoordinated investments, unbridled trade imbalances, and overborrowing throughout the
1970s, economic problems by 1985 included spiraling inflation in excess of
100 percent annually and a growing gap between the cost of living and real
wages. The latter gap was compensated by the growth of a barter economy
and by smuggling and black marketeering.

The party's strategy in creating the Krajgher Commission was to try to
correct the economic problems without tampering with the fundamental

political institutions, which some Yugoslavs blamed for the problems in the first place.

CRISIS AND POLARIZATION

That post-Tito developments in the economic and political spheres were pushing Yugoslavia into a very real crisis was at first denied by party spokespersons. Only in 1983—four years after the economic situation began to deteriorate, two years after the provincewide riots by Albanians in Kosovo, and a year after the controversial Twelfth Party Congress—did party elders finally concede that there was a "crisis" in Yugoslavia and even that a "Polish situation" could develop in the country.[7]

This hesitation in turn constricted party participation in the political debate that started in Yugoslavia soon after Tito's death. At first, the chief participants were scholars and journalists. The Twelfth Party Congress, insofar as it opened the floodgates to debate within the party itself, was a turning point.

In the initial phase of the debate (1980–1981), the economic difficulties were not yet far advanced, and discussion therefore centered on press policy, supervision of the universities, and general political democratization. Within this context, there were two broad positions: one partial to liberalization, and one opposed. Later, as economic deterioration forced Yugoslavs to confront the sources of strain, four clear factions emerged as constituted by the dual issues of liberalization vs. retrenchment and recentralization vs. preservation of the decentralized system. While almost every constituent regional party organization was factionalized to some extent, liberal recentralizers were dominant in the Serbian party, conservative recentralizers in the Bosnian and Montenegrin parties, liberal decentralists in the Slovenian and Vojvodinan parties, and conservative decentralists in the Croatian, Macedonian, and Kosovar parties.[8] Needless to say, this double polarization prevented any broad coalition from being formed, since there were at least three parties on either side of each of the issues. The result was that while the disintegration of the center allowed the burgeoning of political debate and the generation of sundry prescriptions, it simultaneously prevented, under conditions of double polarization, the imposition of a new solution on the system, even though there was widespread consensus that *something* needed to be done. Ultimately, of course, this irresolution would contribute to breaking the Communist Party's hold in four republics (Slovenia, Croatia, Macedonia, and Bosnia) in 1989, which in turn resulted in opening up new strategies for dealing with the crisis.

The weakening of the center after Tito's death allowed the Serbian, Slovenian, and Vojvodinan parties to further liberalize their policies in the spheres of culture, the media, and even religion. Controversial plays such as Jovan Radulović's *Pigeonhole* and Dušan Jovanović's *The Karamazovs*—

which touched on politically delicate subjects—were staged in these republics, though the former play was eventually suppressed under pressure from the more conservative Croatian party organization. Serbia's most popular weekly magazine, *NIN,* actively encouraged the awakening of popular interest in Goli Otok,[9] the prison in which the Communist Party had incarcerated and tortured its political enemies in the late 1940s. The media in these federal units, and to a certain extent also in Croatia, launched a new era of investigative journalism in Yugoslavia—sometimes even to the point of muckraking.[10] Where religious policy was concerned, Slovenia and Vojvodina achieved a rare tranquility in Church-state relations, while in Serbia, the Serbian Orthodox Church was allowed (in 1984) to lay the foundation stone for a new theological faculty in Belgrade and continued its lively publication activity with the first *official* Orthodox Church translation of the New Testament into Serbo-Croatian. Since liberalization was dependent on the slackening of authority at the center, it was understandable that few liberals could be found among recentralizers at that stage.

In Croatia and Bosnia, by contrast, conservative forces remained dominant. One expression of this more conservative political climate came in the shape of a series of petty harassments of clergymen in these two republics (above all of Catholic clergymen and Muslim ulema and officials). But while Bosnian and Montenegrin conservatives were also recentralizers—with the Montenegrin Central Committee suggesting in November 1981 that regional party organizations should be shorn of their power to select their own representatives to the LCY Central Committee[11]—the internally divided Croatian party moved from a position partial to system standardization in 1982,[12] to a position of jealously safeguarding Croatian autonomy (by 1984).

In Kosovo, finally, local provincial party barons tried, in the years 1974–1981, to maximize their autonomy not merely from the federal administration but also from the Serbian Republic, to which both autonomous provinces (Kosovo and Vojvodina) were nominally subordinate. They sought to accomplish these objectives above all by restricting the publication of Serbo-Croatian accounts of party meetings and by constricting the flow of information to Belgrade. The result was that Belgrade was largely unaware of the activities of Albanian irredentist organizations in Kosovo at this time, even though the provincial government in Priština was monitoring them. The unconstitutionally broad extent of Kosovar autonomy could only be safeguarded by repressing open discussion of issues; hence, in Kosovo, devolutionary policy was wedded to cultural and political conservatism.

THE SEARCH FOR SOLUTIONS

That the political debate had, by the mid-1980s, revived certain themes first bandied about in the late 1960s suggested that the underlying problems were anything but new. As early as 1967, for instance, M. Čaldarević had urged that the principle of democratic centralism was outmoded in conditions of self-management.[13] These same sentiments were voiced by Zagreb journalist Antun Žvan in 1981, when he argued that since democratic centralism only applied to party members its effect was to make party members "less free" than nonmembers.

Again, the idea of pumping life into SAWPY and transforming it into a second party had a long history.[14] The revival of this idea in the mid-1980s was a measure of the discontent with the political status quo.

By the time party elders convened the Twelfth Party Congress in summer 1982—the first congress since Tito's passing—there were strong expectations that the occasion would prove a breakthrough in terms of the political direction of the system. But all radical proposals for organizational "reform" (most of them inspired by hopes of reconstituting the center) were blocked, including Rade Končar's rather dramatic proposal on the floor of the Congress that the republic-based federal organization of the party be scrapped and replaced with organization on the basis of lines of production.[15] The upshot was that while decentralists and liberals alike could gloat over their defeat of the sundry centralizing proposals presented at the Congress, the rivalry between the recentralizers and the decentralists in the party had not been resolved, hence the pressure for change had not been removed.

Although the Twelfth Party Congress thus accomplished little or nothing, it did signal the impotence of the center, which naturally further encouraged republican and provincial elites to ignore exhortations emanating from the center. A subsequent CC resolution (in April 1983) urging its own members not to misconstrue themselves as representatives of their respective republics or provinces was, for instance, ignored by all concerned. In early summer 1984, the party leadership made another attempt to restore resilience to the central organs. The CC Presidium drew up a report on relations between the central and regional party organizations. The report found that "decisions adopted unanimously at the national level are being carried out only half-heartedly [at the republican and provincial levels], and execution is largely limited to those aspects which suit the particular region at the moment."[16] This report was submitted to the Thirteenth Session of the Central Committee for action. But, despite the urgings of those who warned of the creeping "federalization" of the party itself,[17] the committee demurred and decided to pass the text on to the 70,000 basic organizations of the party for discussion and to delay final action until the Thirteenth Party Congress, in June 1986.

By then, recentralization was no longer rationalized in terms of the vanguard role of the party as the political instrument of the working class. Recentralization was presented, on the contrary, as a pragmatic consideration.[18] Ideologically deflated, the Yugoslavs quietly abandoned their earlier claims to greater fidelity to Lenin.[19] Former partisan general Peko Dapčević, for instance, told the Twelfth Party Congress that Leninism was outdated—a conclusion presumed by Žvan's earlier effort to scuttle democratic centralism and seconded in 1983 by Svetozar Stojanović[20] and in 1985 by sociologist Vladimir Arzešnek and party theorist Vladimir Goati.[21] Indeed, Arzenšek charged that Leninist ideas remained a serious impediment to necessary change throughout Eastern Europe. Likewise, whereas the Yugoslavs were once fond of claiming that their system was neither a one-party system nor a "bourgeois" multiparty system, but rather something unique,[22] *Socijalizam* now openly conceded that Yugoslavia had been set up as, and hence still was, a one-party system.[23]

The realization that the system had dead-ended gave birth to an astonishingly wide range of reform proposals. Famed economist Branko Horvat, for example, suggested in 1984 that "all political parties" (i.e., the Communist Party in its sundry regional organizations) be abolished and that Yugoslavia be reorganized as a "partyless" socialist system operated through citizens' associations.[24] Two political scientists from Belgrade suggested in 1983 that a multiparty system be restored[25]—an alternative specifically repudiated at the June 1984 Session of the 163-member LCY Central Committee. In reflecting upon the evident support for this remedy, Radoslav Ratković drew a distinction between "the pluralism of self-managing interests" and political pluralism, calling it erroneous to think that the legitimacy of the former could legitimate the latter.[26]

Despite the party's obvious reluctance to share power with noncommunists, sociologist Miroslav Živković did not hesitate, in spring 1985, to call for the establishment of a full-fledged "social democracy" in Yugoslavia.[27] Still others (such as Čedo Grbić) called for a more liberal attitude toward private enterprise, or for the restoration of strongarm (*Čvrsta ruka*) rule, or—more tamely—for the complete rewriting of Communist Party statutes.[28] Multi-candidate elections were also a popular idea, especially as a device to defuse support for multiparty elections.[29]

Within the context of this debate, then, SAWPY appeared as both temptation and, ostensibly, opportunity. Its advocates were able to argue, plausibly, that the organization was entitled under the constitution to a greater role in public life and that the LCY control of SAWPY was an "unnatural partnership."[30] Perhaps drawing lessons from the Polish crisis of 1980–1981, Radoš Smiljković told the Zagreb weekly magazine *Danas* in 1984 that the "marginalization" of SAWPY deprived noncommunist citizens of legitimate political channels and risked pushing them into the illicit "politicization of nonpolitical organizations and associations." Indeed, for Smiljković, "new political groups appear, and they will keep appearing" until legal structures would be offered, because "if people are not satisfied with the existing or-

ganizations, they create new ones, or [lapse into] a catastrophic political apathy."[31]

The difficulty, according to high-ranking party official Čedo Grbić, was
that SAWPY had been controlled by "semilegal coordinating groups and
commissions" that excluded the public from any voice in personnel questions and perpetuated the organization's docile subordination to party hi-
erarchies.[32] Seconding this assessment, Grličkov noted that noncommunists
had only slight chances of being promoted to republic-level leadership
posts in SAWPY. His remedy was to allow 30–50 percent of responsible
posts in the Socialist Alliance to be filled by noncommunists and to expand
its jurisdiction. Going one step further, Serbian political scientist Mihailo
Popović told a party symposium in spring 1984 that SAWPY should be allowed to reorganize itself as an independent party, in order to provide an
independent, critical voice in the role of permanent opposition. Finally,
Svetozar Stojanović outlined a program in which SAWPY would gain organizational independence from the LCY, have a separate membership, and
share power with a still dominant LCY.[33]

The radical tenor of some of these proposals was a measure of the seriousness with which the participants in the Yugoslav debate viewed the political situation. But any structural or systemic reorganization, as well as any
far-reaching revisions of the statutes of the LCY, the regional parties, or the
SAWPY, could only be achieved on the basis of a broad consensus among
the leaderships of the eight regional party organizations (or nine, if the
army's party organization was included). Such consensus was lacking. In
early 1984, for example, the Slovenian leadership took the small step of
suggesting that it might propose three candidates for its single seat on the
collective state presidency and allow a popular vote to determine the outcome. The other republican leaderships objected, and Slovenia withdrew
its proposal and simply named Stane Dolanc to the post.

THE SERBIAN SOLUTION

The most comprehensive "reform" package to be proposed by a regional
party organization in the first five years after Tito's death came in October
1984, when the Serbian party organization issued a four-part draft reform
program calling for the strengthening of the role and autonomy of economic enterprises, the strengthening of the federal government, the democratization of the electoral system, and a rollback of the prerogatives and
overall autonomy of the two autonomous provinces. The last of these
points was assured of popularity among Serbia's Serbs, who were becoming disgruntled over the provinces' power to veto legislation. Serbs complained that their republic had unique difficulties in passing important leg-

islation and blamed obstructionism on the part of the autonomous provinces. As part of the package, the Serbs also resurrected the 1981 proposal to divest republican parties of the power to select their representatives on the Central Committee.

The regional party organizations of Kosovo, Vojvodina, Slovenia, and Croatia were enraged. Kosovo and Vojvodina, in particular, had been fighting (since the April 1981 Albanian riots in Kosovo) to stay the Serbian backlash. But Slovenia and Croatia were likewise concerned about the threatened erosion of their hard-won autonomy. Slovenian–Serbian differences came into full view at the Fourteenth CC Plenum in October 1984, when Dragoslav Marković attacked the Slovenian deputies for their opposition to the Serbian package. Marković also called into question the propriety of requiring unanimity among the eight organizations before a decision could be taken. This challenge in turn impelled Slovene Andrej Marinc to take the podium, observing *inter alia* that the principle of unanimity was a longstanding procedure in the LCY and that Marković's view had been specifically repudiated at a previous session. Marinc added that continued public discussion about changing the system could lead to "a political crisis, to a crisis of society."[34] The Serbian party leader, Slobodan Milošević, replied to Marinc the following month:

> We have been threatened with a political crisis if we continue to discuss these problems. All right, let us enter that political crisis. This crisis is going to produce a great uproar about the question of unity or separatism. In such a crisis, separatism will not prevail, because the people have accepted unity. Those leaders incapable of seeing this will lose the public's confidence. If separatism is not opposed, our country will have no prospects for the future. It can only disintegrate.[35]

The equation of advocacy of the federal status quo with "separatism" was a polemical punch that had some clout in Yugoslavia at that time. But with four other regional parties antagonistic in varying degrees to the Serbian draft, and a fifth (the Bosnian) at best "restrained" in its support, the prospects for adoption of this package seemed, and indeed proved to be, slight.

In the wake of this exchange, a new term crept into Yugoslav polemical vocabulary: autonomism. Used by Serbian recentralizers as a pejorative term for the Vojvodinan party's desire to maintain the political status quo, the term was incorporated into a draft resolution of the Serbian Central Committee in April 1985, where it was placed in the same category with "Serb nationalism" and "Albanian nationalism."[36] When Vojvodina's press responded to criticism with counter-criticism of its own, some Serbian politicians grumbled that Vojvodina's newspapers were launching "an attack on the reputation of the Serbian Assembly"—a charge that suggested a desire to curb the independence of the provincial press.[37]

THE CONSTITUTION AND THE SYSTEM

In October 1984, *Borba* carried a series of articles by University of Zagreb Professor Jovan Mirić arguing that the 1974 Constitution was the source of *all* of Yugoslavia's problems and that the exaggerated decentralization had destroyed the unified market and even interfered with the market mechanism.[38] Ribičič (a Slovene), Grličkov (from Macedonia), and Hamdija Pozderac (a Bosnian Muslim) applauded Mirić's series. Others, including archconservatives France Popit (from Slovenia), Jure Bilić (from Croatia), and Dušan Popović (a Serb from Vojvodina), were antagonistic. Jovan Djordjević, a coauthor of the 1974 Constitution, himself admitted that the confederal coloration assumed by the system had not been the intention of the constitution's drafters.

Eventually, the party decided to set up a commission to review the political system and prepare recommendations for change and reform. Modeled on the Krajgher Commission for the Reform of the Economic System, this new commission was entrusted to the chairship of Tihomir Vlaškalić, a ranking Serbian party official. The Vlaškalić Commission was asked to prepare a report for submission to the Thirteenth Party Congress.

As the Thirteenth Party Congress approached, sundry party officials broached diverse proposals aimed at reestablishing central authority. The reasoning, according to Tanjug, the official news agency, was that "the orientation of the Twelfth Congress went in the wrong direction."[39] In a strikingly pointed phrase, CC member Dušan Dragosavac told the twenty-second Session of the Central Committee in November 1985 that Yugoslavia could "more easily endure a multiparty system along[side] a united League of Communists than a coalition of a number of [regional] parties within the League of Communists."[40] Strange solutions started to be proposed, such as eliminating separate status for the regional party organizations, dropping the presidents of republican central committees from ex officio membership in the LCY Presidium, suppressing local autonomy in scientific institutes, and—perhaps most surprising of all—selectively dropping the "ethnic keys," which assigned fixed quotas to specific nationality groups in sundry party and governmental bodies. In the last instance, it was argued specifically that if the LCY Central Committee was ever going to function efficiently, it would have to be reduced in size—a measure that would require some compromise with the network of ethnic, social, and age keys applied in selecting that body's membership.[41] Ultimately, the Central Committee's membership was reduced to 129.

In a related move, which simultaneously reflected the strains produced by Serb–Albanian frictions in Kosovo, the Constitutional Court of Serbia handed down a decision (in October 1985) annulling a number of decrees relating to cadres policy in Kosovo—decrees that had guaranteed ethnic representation in the leadership proportionate to the given group's presence in the province. These decrees had been the instrument whereby the numerically dominant Albanians had taken over the provincial party apparatus in the course of the 1970s. According to the court, however, "the application of proportional national representation . . . facilitates the suppression of the numerically smaller nations and nationalities, which is contrary to the principles of equality laid down in the constitution. Also, this principle endangers the guaranteed rights of citizens to have equal access to every job and function."[42]

What these and other proposals reflected was that the issue of recentralization vs. continued decentralism was steadily becoming the dominant subject of debate.

On the eve of the Thirteenth Party Congress, regional differences on the subject remained clear. The Slovenian Party Congress (held in April 1986), for instance, emphasized the "unacceptability" of approaches that used the economic crisis "to put forward centralist-unitarist solutions."[43] By contrast, the Montenegrin Party Congress—held a few days later—underlined the importance of "unity" in finding solutions, to the extent of seconding the earlier call for bringing scientific institutes throughout the country under central direction.[44]

In the course of 1986 it became clear that the decentralists were becoming more isolated and less sure of themselves—with the Slovenian party remaining the only regional party organization that continued to champion the decentralized system. Centralizers were, in short, able to put together a working consensus for a partial reconstitution of central authority. The Thirteenth LCY Congress, held 25–28 June 1986, was thus replete with calls for party unity and warnings about the effects of the conversion of local party organizations by technocratic interests into agents for purely local interests. The new party statute, adopted at the Congress, transferred the right to elect members of the Central Committee from the republics to the LCY Congress, entrusted the Central Committee with the authority to oversee the work of republic and provincial party organizations and if necessary to convoke extraordinary republic and provincial congresses to halt local deviations, and—should that fail—to convoke an Extraordinary LCY Congress to rein in a headstrong republic party organization.[45] In addition, the new statute provided a more explicit affirmation of the controversial principle of democratic centralism and strengthened the ability of the party organs to discipline wayward party members.[46] In sum, as Josip Vrhovec put it, the changes were designed to reverse the processes through which the party "was beginning to lose its vanguard role."[47]

There were those who wanted to carry recentralization further yet and a more general pressure for political change, whether in one direction or another. But as long as the party maintained its political monopoly there were some serious constraints on political change in Yugoslavia. The first and most important factor, which I have taken pains to document, was the division of the party into eight autonomous regional organizations gravitating toward four distinct and conflictual policy positions. A second factor—which strongly suggested that the decentralization of the 1970s could not be reversed easily, if at all—was the ethnic dimension. The sundry nationality groups had grown accustomed to governing their own republics, and—as would become clear at the end of the decade—any serious effort at recentralization could, in the circumstances, only carry grave risk.

Third, even aside from the regional elites themselves, the decentralized system threw up other vested interests, whether in the political-administrative hierarchy or in economic decisionmaking, interests that could be expected to fear the consequences of change in the system.

Fourth, where the "national question" was concerned, there was a more specific—if often unspoken—fear of the repercussions that curtailment of autonomy or the introduction of a "new course" would have in Croatia (the scene of a powerful nationalist movement, 1967–1971) and in Kosovo (shaken by Albanian riots throughout the province in 1968 and again in 1981). A curious symptom of party caution in this area was the omission of any reference to Albanian nationalist disorders in Kosovo from the draft platform for the Thirteenth Party Congress—an omission promptly criticized by the Zagreb daily *Vjesnik.*[48]

Fifth, there was the fact that the intelligentsia up to then had by and large accepted the premise that even the most thoroughgoing overhaul of the system should be undertaken in partnership with actors in the regime rather than in opposition to the regime and the system. At that time, thus, declarations that the system had failed tended to be translated into political debate rather than into political opposition. Yet one must register a caveat, for below the surface the process of the defection of the intellectuals had already begun, and by 1987 various intellectuals in Belgrade, Zagreb, and Ljubljana were quietly working to overhaul, and perhaps overthrow, the system.[49] Their voices, inaudible in 1985, became more and more audible, culminating in the formation of alternative political parties by some of these same intellectuals in the course of 1988–1989.

NOTES

This chapter is a revised version of an earlier article, "The Limits to Political Change in a Communist Country: The Yugoslav Debate, 1980–1986," originally published in *Crossroads,* No. 23 (1987). The author wishes to thank the editors of *Crossroads* for granting permission to reproduce the article here.

1. Pedro Ramet, "Apocalypse Culture and Social Change in Yugoslavia," in Pedro Ramet, ed., *Yugoslavia in the 1980s* (Boulder, Colo.: Westview Press, 1985).

2. The *Sporazum* established an autonomous *banovina* of Croatia, comprising roughly 30 percent of the territory and population of Yugoslavia and enjoying budgetary and administrative independence and independent authority in most spheres of domestic policy. The monarchy was in fact the sole remaining constitutional link between Croatia and the rest of Yugoslavia.

3. *Start* (26 March 1983), trans. in Joint Publications Research Service (JPRS), *East Europe Report,* No. 83734 (22 June 1983), p. 54; and *Vjesnik* (Zagreb) (6 April 1985).

4. Miroslav Stojanović, "Opštepartijska debata o ulozi Saveza komunista," *Socijalizam,* Vol. 27, Nos. 7–8 (July–August 1984), p. 996.

5. *Borba* (Belgrade) (20 November 1984).

6. Milan Dimitrijević, "Samoupravne interesne zajednice," *Opština,* Vol. 29, Nos. 5–6 (1976), pp. 116–118.

7. For particulars, see Pedro Ramet, "Yugoslavia and the Threat of Internal and External Discontents," *Orbis,* Vol. 28, No. 1 (spring 1984), pp. 104–105.

8. Evidence for these characterizations will be provided in the text.

9. Interview, Belgrade, July 1982.

10. For details, see Pedro Ramet, "The Yugoslav Press in Flux," in Ramet, *Yugoslavia in the 1980s.*

11. *NIN,* No. 1601 (15 November 1981), p. 9.

12. Ibid. *NIN,* No. 1645 (11 July 1982), p. 10.

13. M. Čaldarević, *Komunisti i samoupravljanje* (Zagreb: FPN, 1967), p. 486, as cited in Simo S. Nenezić, "Divergentne koncepcije u SKJ o demokratskom centralizmu," *Socijalizam,* Vol. 18, No. 1 (January 1975), p. 53.

14. See, for instance, "Jugoslawischer Theoretiker für Zweiparteiensystem," *Osteuropäische Rundschau,* Vol. 13, No. 12 (December 1967), pp. 19–21.

15. Rade Končar, a Serb, was at the time chair of the Novi Beograd (city) party organization and a member of the party committee of the city of Belgrade. He was forced to resign these posts soon after the Congress.

16. CK SKJ Predsedništvo, *Ostvarivanje vodeće uloge SKJ u društvu i jačanje njegovog idejnog i akcionog jedinstva* (Belgrade: Komunist, 1984), pp. v–vii, as quoted in Wolfgang Höpken, "Party Monopoly and Political Change: The League of Communists Since Tito's Death," in Ramet, *Yugoslavia in the 1980s,* p. 37.

17. See Vjekoslav Koprivnjak, "Protiv tendencije federalizacije Saveza komunista," *Socijalizam,* Vol. 28, No. 1 (January 1985).

18. See, for instance, *Politika* (Belgrade) (17 January 1985).

19. For details, see Pedro Ramet, "Self-Management, Titoism, and the Apotheosis of Praxis," in Wayne S. Vucinich, ed., *At the Brink of War and Peace: The Tito-Stalin Split in a Historic Perspective* (New York: Brooklyn College Press, 1982), pp. 169–170, 174–177, 192–193.

20. Svetozar Stojanović, "Marks i ideologizacija marksizma—kritika jedne predrasudne moći" [based on a talk given in Novi Sad in December 1983], *Gledišta,* Vol. 25, Nos. 1–2 (January–February 1984), pp. 28–33.

21. *Radio Free Europe Research* (24 July 1985), pp. 19–22.

22. Edvard Kardelj, *Democracy and Socialism,* trans. by Margot and Boško Milosavljević (London: Summerfield Press, 1978), p. 69.

23. Stipe Šuvar, "Sloboda misli—da, ideološki i politički pluralizam—ne," *Socijalizam,* Vol. 27, Nos. 7–8 (July–August 1984), p. 1129.

24. Miladin Korač, "Branko Horvat: 'Politicka ekonomija socijalizma'—kriticka analiza trećeg dela knjige," *Socijalizam,* Vol. 27, No. 10 (October 1984), pp. 1518–1519, 1526–1530.

25. Vojislav Koštunica and Kosta Čavoški, *Stranački pluralizam ili monizam* (Belgrade: Institut za društvene nauke, 1983).

26. Radoslav Ratković, "Interes nije bazična kategorija," *Socijalizam,* Vol. 27, Nos. 7–8 (July–August 1984), p. 1057.

27. *Večernje novosti* (Belgrade) (16 April 1985).

28. On the last of these points, see *Vjesnik* (19 March 1985).

29. See, for instance, *Politika* (8 January 1985).

30. *Borba* (7–8 April 1984); and *Duga* (Belgrade) (10 March 1984).

31. *Danas* (9 April 1984), trans. in JPRS, *East Europe Report,* Nos. EPS–84–076 (18 June 1984), p. 91.

32. *Borba* (7–8 April 1984).

33. For more details on these two proposals, see Ramet, "Apocalypse Culture and Social Change," pp. 19–20.

34. Quoted in Höpken, "Party Monopoly," p. 41.

35. *Politika* (24 November 1984).

36. *Dnevnik* (Novi Sad), 21 April 1985, p. 3, trans. in *Foreign Broadcast Information Service (FBIS), Daily Report* (Eastern Europe) (2 May 1985), p. 17.

37. *Politika* (20 December 1984), p. 5, trans. in JPRS, *East Europe Report,* No. EPS–85–012 (23 January 1985), p. 29.

38. *Borba* (12–15 October 1984). See the Editorial Report in JPRS, *East Europe Report,* No. EPS–84–135 (1 November 1984), p. 120.

39. Tanjug (14 November 1985), trans. in *FBIS, Daily Report* (Eastern Europe), 15 November 1985, p. 13.

40. Tanjug (18 November 1985), trans. in *FBIS, Daily Report* (Eastern Europe), 20 November 1985, p. 16.

41. Ibid., p. 17; and Tanjug (18 November 1985), trans. in *FBIS, Daily Report* (Eastern Europe), 26 November 1985, pp. 16–18.

42. Tanjug (24 October 1985), trans. in *FBIS, Daily Report* (Eastern Europe), 1 November 1985, p. 19.

43. *Politika* (20 April 1986).

44. *Politika* (24 April 1986).

45. *Vjesnik* (30 June 1986); also Tanjug (16 February 1986), trans. in *FBIS, Daily Report* (Eastern Europe), 20 February 1986, p. 13; and *Vjesnik* (29 June 1986).

46. *Vjesnik* (30 June 1986).

47. *Vjesnik* (27 June 1986).

48. *Vjesnik* (24 August 1985).

49. For details and discussion, see Pedro Ramet, "Yugoslavia 1987: Stirrings from Below," *South Slav Journal,* Vol. 10, No. 3 (autumn 1987).

CHAPTER TWO

◆

The Gathering Storm, 1987–1989

AS THE 1980s WORE ON, it became clear that the deepening economic crisis and the political inertia that characterized the system were profoundly incompatible. Rising ethnic frictions in Kosovo and, just below the surface, in Bosnia were straining the political fabric at another level, too. Increasingly, there were voices calling for a "return" to some imagined pristine centralism—calls originating largely among Serbs.

In 1987, the entire political picture changed virtually overnight. A forty-six-year-old banker-turned-politician named Slobodan Milošević had risen to the post of chair of the Central Committee of the Serbian party in 1986, when his friend and mentor, Ivan Stambolić, assumed the post of Serbian president. Milošević turned against his erstwhile mentor and by September 1987 had scored a major victory over him. In mid-December, Milošević engineered Stambolić's removal from the presidency and asserted his unilateral control of the Serbian republic.[1] Milošević quickly abandoned the long-standing strategies of the LCY and the Serbian party organization and set out to suppress the autonomous provinces (annexing them to Serbia), to recentralize the system (at the expense of the autonomy of the other republics), and to rehabilitate the Serbian Orthodox Church, coopting it to serve as the vehicle of a revived Serbian nationalism. His policies destroyed what remained of any consensus in the system, and by late 1989, for all practical purposes (legislative, economic, cultural), Yugoslavia had ceased to exist. In its place there were four emerging national environments, which claimed the primary loyalty of their citizens: Slovenia, Croatia, Serbia (including the autonomous provinces of Kosovo and Vojvodina, as well as the republic of Montenegro), and Macedonia. These four regions were increasingly self-contained and even isolated from each other, and cultural contact between them, at one time actively stimulated by the party, had become, by then, largely superficial. Serbian and Slovenian nationalism was in full blaze, while in Croatia, despite a certain passivity that could be dated to the suppression of the "Croatian spring" in December 1971, there was a marked hostility toward everything Serbian, and the traditional Western orientation reasserted itself. Only in Macedonia did one still find a real sense of "Yugoslavism," although even there increasing signs of grumbling about Macedonia's alleged second-rate status in the federation were apparent. Finally, multiethnic Bosnia-Herzegovina—43.77 percent "ethnic Muslim," 31.46 percent Serbian, and 17.34 percent Croatian (in 1991)—was internally divided and its political infrastructure shattered along ethnic lines. Bosnian officials openly described the political situation in the republic as "difficult," with some observers calling greater Serbian nationalism the greatest problem at this point and others charging that fundamentalist Islam was driving Bosnian Serbs to take flight.[2]

The Serb–Croat conflict has always been at the center of political strife, at least potentially, and in the fragile conditions associated with the rise of Slobodan Milošević in Serbia reemerged as the pivotal conflict in Yugoslavia. Serbian politicians spread stories of a "Vatican-Comintern conspiracy" (supposedly designed in part to benefit Croatia) and accused Croatian politicians of genocidal tendencies. Radio Mileva in Belgrade accused Croat Ante Marković, the chair of the Federal Executive Council, of being a CIA agent, while Serbian poet Gojko Djogo's description of the Croatian Communist authorities as "pro-Ustasha" was given publicity.[3] At the same time, Serbs talked of the Orthodox (hence "Serbian") ancestry of Croatia's Dalmatian population, revived demands for autonomy for Serbs living in Croatia, and even talked of the political rehabilitation of wartime Chetnik leader Draža Mihailović.[4]

Croatian politicians in turn accused Serbian leader Slobodan Milošević of "Stalinist" and "unitarist" tendencies and charged that Serbian politicians were trying to destabilize and neutralize Croatia.[5] Hence when economist Jovo Opačić attempted to organize a Serbian cultural society in Croatia in July 1989, Croatian leaders had him arrested and tried.

In quasi-confederal Yugoslavia, the six constituent republics already enjoyed vast autonomy and operated, to a considerable extent, as independent mini-states. This system had been developed in the course of the late 1960s and early 1970s in order to satisfy the desires of the distinct nationality groups for a measure of political self-determination, while at the same time preserving the Communist power monopoly. The alternative route— maintaining a unified political system but opening it up to alternative parties—had been rejected. Conscious of the relationship between pluralization and self-determination, the Communists substituted regional pluralization (administrative decentralization) for political pluralization (multiparty democracy) and justified the substitution by arguing that a multiparty system would only lead to fratricidal war in Yugoslav conditions. In order to maintain this fiction, Yugoslav politicians stoked the fires of interethnic distrust by constant commentaries on the ethnic genocides of

World War II. Indeed, even today, it often seems that World War II has never ended for Yugoslav politicians.

Regional pluralization quickly became a powerful force for liberalization—both because some of the leading advocates of decentralization were also liberals and because the division of power created alternatives within the system: people who were unable to publish something in one republic, for example, might turn around and publish the same text in another republic.

This system could function reasonably smoothly as long as two conditions were present. First, it was necessary to have a final arbiter who could resolve interrepublican differences if need be. President Josip Broz Tito functioned as this arbiter until his death in May 1980; but the system he bequeathed to Yugoslavia, based on collective decisionmaking at all levels and the right of veto by any republic in many areas of decisionmaking, lacked such an arbiter.

Second, the system presumed a degree of prosperity, such as existed in the later 1970s. When the economy eroded, however, the political seams were exposed to full view and the "quasi-legitimacy" of the system disintegrated. Now, with inflation roaring at more than 1,000 percent annually and incomes sagging below minimal levels, people were becoming desperate. In some cities, people decided to live without electricity, since they could not pay the bills.[6] Crime also soared, and authorities linked the increase with economic crisis.[7] In Montenegro, 30,000 desperate citizens took to the streets in August 1989 to protest against hunger and poverty and to demand effective action.[8] Increasingly, there was talk of the need to reprivatize the economy.

In this context, Ćiril Ribičič and Zdravko Tomac—the former a member of the Central Committee of the League of Communists of Slovenia and the latter a member of the Political Science Faculty of the University of Zagreb—coauthored a book in which they argued for the "de-etatization" of the economy and the strengthening of certain features of the federation in order to assure optimal conditions for the development of a modern market economy. As they argued, "a new economic system requires a new political system, a new economic system cannot be built within the framework of the old political system."[9]

There was a gathering consensus in Yugoslavia that the status quo could not endure much longer. In such conditions, solutions that only a year or two earlier would have sounded extreme were now openly discussed. In summer 1989, for example, Vladimir Rabzelj, a Slovenian writer, proposed the secession of Slovenia and Croatia and their association in a new confederal state.[10] Along parallel lines, Serbian writer Antonije Isaković, famous for his novels *Tren I* and *Tren II*, argued for the redrawing of republic boundaries and the confederalization of the system.[11]

In September 1989, in a move that would have been unthinkable only a year earlier, the Slovenian Assembly passed a series of amendments to the Slovenian constitution, unilaterally granting the Slovenian republic the right of secession and the right to approve or disapprove the proclamation by federal authorities of extraordinary measures in their republic. This highly controversial move, which excited public protest meetings in Montenegro and was immediately taken to the Federal Constitutional Court for resolution, was thus only symptomatic of the breakdown of the sense of community, of consensus on the rules of the game.[12]

THE MOBILIZATION OF SLOVENIA

The Slovenian amendments, which were hotly attacked in the Serbian press throughout September, were the outgrowth of the mobilization of the Slovenian public in the course of 1988 and 1989. This process can be dated to the publication by the Slovenian journal *Nova revija* (in February 1987) of a collection of articles devoted to the "Slovenian national program," which included, *inter alia,* a protest against the second-class status of the Slovenian language in Yugoslavia.[13] But more properly, the mobilization of the Slovenian public must be traced to the trial of Janez Janša, Ivan Borstner, David Tasić, and Franci Zavrl (the editor of *Mladina*) for publishing material about a military plan to mop up liberalism in Slovenia. The trial inflamed the Slovenian public, and the fact that the trial was conducted in Serbo-Croatian, although on Slovenian territory, only aggravated passions. There were repeated public protests, including a large demonstration by at least 40,000 people from all over Slovenia on Ljubljana's Liberation Square on 22 June 1988. It was the largest public gathering of Slovenes since World War II.[14]

In response to the trial, an independent Committee for the Protection of Human Rights was formed in Ljubljana and began issuing periodical bulletins in English.[15] More than 100,000 persons signed protest petitions drawn up by the committee, along with more than 1,000 collective organizations, including the local trade union and the Slovenian Bishops Conference of the Catholic Church. The successful creation of this committee encouraged others, and over the course of the next few months several embryonic political parties were launched, including the Social Democratic Alliance, the Slovenian Democratic Union, the Slovenian Christian Socialist Movement, and a "Green" Party. Meanwhile, a previously existing Slovenian Peasant Union experienced rapid growth and by September 1989 claimed some 25,000 members from all parts of Slovenia.[16]

This pluralization was tolerated by the Slovenian authorities, and this tolerance in turn encouraged both the vibrant Slovenian youth organization and the long stagnant Socialist Alliance—both nominally transmission belts for party policy—to begin plans to transform themselves into independent political parties and to field their own candidates in Slovenia's spring 1990 elections. Polls taken in August 1989 ranked the Slovenian youth organization as the most popular (potential) political party, with the Socialist Alliance in second place and the League of Communists trailing as a distant third. Yet although the Socialist Alliance of *Slovenia* talked about functioning independently, the Socialist Alliance of *Yugoslavia* expressed no such intention; hence, the Socialist Alliance of Slovenia would in due course have to separate from the Yugoslav organization.[17] In practice, SAWPY broke up the following year, when the regional organizations in Slovenia and Croatia did indeed transform themselves into new "Socialist" parties and the Serbian branch merged with the League of Communists of Serbia to form a supposedly new "Socialist Party of Serbia." By the end of 1990, SAWPY no longer existed.

Meanwhile, membership in the Slovenian Communist Party had been steadily declining for about five years. Party organizations at many factories and enterprises completely disintegrated.[18] To the extent that the party still commanded some prestige, it was in part attributable to the party's popular leader, Milan Kučan, who was easily the most popular politician in that republic (as demonstrated by his subsequent election as Slovenia's president in the free elections of spring 1990).

The Slovenes claimed that their republic, the richest and most efficient in the country, was being milked by the less efficient republics. As a result, they jealously guarded their autonomy and, at a minimum, hoped to preserve the quasi-confederal character of the system. In the wake of the trial of "the four" (Janša et al.), the Slovenes increasingly talked about the virtues of "asymmetric federation," under which they would enjoy certain special prerogatives not enjoyed by other republics. A key demand associated with this concept was for a special Slovenian military district, with all Slovenian recruits serving in Slovenian regiments and Slovenian as the language of command. Secession was described by essentially all Slovenes as a "last resort," if all else should fail. Furthermore, Ćiril Ribičič, in a speech to the Slovenian Central Committee on 26 September, described the new amendment sanctioning secession as consistent with the existing federal constitution.[19]

Other republics, especially Serbia, Montenegro, and Bosnia, looked with dismay at Slovenian developments. The Yugoslav collective presidency at first demanded that the proposed Slovenian amendments be discussed at one of its sessions—but the Slovenian presidency categorically rejected the suggestion.[20] Arguments were heard in Belgrade that whatever the Slovenes might say, their proposed amendments, including the amendment concerning secession, were in fact contrary to the federal constitution. When the Slovenes remained undaunted, others talked of summoning an urgent, extraordinary session of the Federal Assembly.[21] The Slovenes went ahead undaunted and passed their amendments.

SERBIAN NATIONAL REVIVAL AND ITS EFFECTS

The Serbian party championed a very different solution. As early as September 1981, Ivan Stambolić, a member of the Serbian Central Committee, had argued that a "unified and strong Serbia" was a prerequisite for a strong Yugoslavia.[22] The extension of vast autonomy to the autonomous provinces of Kosovo and Vojvodina, he argued, had resulted not merely in the federalization of Serbia but in its effective disintegration.[23] By 1984, Serbia was actively pressing for the reduction of the autonomy of the provinces, as well as for an expansion of the decisionmaking powers of the federal organs vis-à-vis the republics. The Serbs thus were once more championing a strong center—a position often tainted with the pejorative term "unitarism" in Yugoslav parlance. Slobodan Milošević, then only a regular member of the Serbian Central Committee, struck a defiant note. "We must free ourselves of the complex of unitarism," he said in November 1984. "Serbian Communists have never been champions of unitarism. On the contrary, we have throttled every attempt at such a policy. The Serbian Communists have long been saddled with a complex about unitarism, and unjustly so, and made to feel guilty for a relationship with the Serbian bourgeoisie."[24]

Despite the clarity of the Serbian position, there seemed to be little progress toward realizing Serbian objectives. Stambolić, who had served as president of the Serbian Central Committee since April 1984, was seen by many as a careerist whose commitment to the Serbian program was largely formal. Milošević, in particular, wanted a new strategy. By summer 1987, the waxing conflict between Milošević and Stambolić was in the open, and in autumn 1987 Stambolić was forced to resign.

In the ensuing months, Milošević consolidated more power than any Yugoslav leader had enjoyed since Tito—although with the important reservation that Milošević's power was limited to the republics of Serbia and Montenegro. Milošević removed a large number of party functionaries and replaced many of the journalists at the Politika publishing house. He appealed to Serbian pride and Serbian nationalism—for example, by introducing more Cyrillic in a republic that had for years been shifting more and more to the Latin alphabet. He granted the Serbian Orthodox Church permission to build new churches and to restore old ones. By summer 1989 the Serbian Assembly was weighing which of two traditional hymns to adopt as the official anthem of Serbia: the popular but militant song, "March to the Drina," composed by Stanislav Binički after a Serbian military victory in 1914; or "Tamo daleko" (There, afar), composed in 1916 by an unknown hand, while the Serbian army was in exile on the Greek island of Corfu.[25] In Tito's time, part of the text of "Tamo daleko" was banned. Above all, Milošević replaced provincial authorities in 1988 with people loyal to him and succeeded, in early 1989, in ramming through a series of changes to the constitutions of the Serbian republic and its autonomous provinces that effectively reduced the provinces to shadows of their former selves.

All of these measures were enormously popular among Serbs, and Milošević was genuinely loved by many (though not all) Serbs as no other leader had been since Chetnik leader Draža Mihailović. But the very reasons that endeared him to nationalist and traditionalist elements among the Serbs made him hated and feared in Croatia and Slovenia. Milošević was a unifying force among Serbs but a divisive factor in Yugoslavia as a whole.

In the course of 1989, Milošević tried to create a base of support among non-Serbs by talking about a program of "antibureaucratic revolution." This campaign was widely viewed with a combination of distrust and cynicism outside Serbia, however, and Croats in particular were mindful of the fact that Serbian nationalists were raising awkward issues, among them:

- Serbs began to talk about the large-scale transfer of industry from Serbia to Croatia and Bosnia in the years 1945–1951, a transfer that Serbs now said had been intended by Tito to weaken Serbia;[26]
- Serbs talked of the "Orthodox" origin of Dalmatian Croats;
- Serbs revived a long latent claim that Montenegrins were actually Serbs, and many Montenegrins responded warmly (such a claim had been taboo as long as Tito was in power);
- Serbs attacked the entire legacy of Tito, arguing that it was above all anti-Serbian in thrust, and suggested that it was time to weed out the confederal elements introduced by Tito (such as the veto system).[27]

Slovenia, Croatia, and Macedonia responded by trying to defend Tito's legacy, and Tito personally, against Serbian attacks. In the process, Tito received support in unlikely quarters. For example, Miko Tripalo, the Croatian party secretary purged by Tito in December 1971 for "liberalism," told me in September 1989, "Croatia can, at this point, be satisfied with its position in the federation. But it is gravely threatened by Milošević, who is trying to bring about a totalitarian revolution and achieve Greater Serbian hegemony. This threatens not only Croatia but the other republics as well. It is critical, in these circumstances, to defend Tito. He is the symbol of everything that has been achieved."[28]

Milošević's strategy was both populist and nationalist. In endeavoring to undermine the autonomy of the autonomous provinces (successfully) and to restore the primacy of the federal government (unsuccessfully), he restored to grace many Serbian dissidents, including Milovan Djilas and the accomplished poet Gojko Djogo. He restored the *Praxis* philosophers to positions of eminence. He allowed rumors to circulate about an eventual rehabilitation of Draža Mihailović. And, as already mentioned, he allowed the Serbian Orthodox Church to revive. Milošević's policies in Kosovo and Vojvodina made him a national hero among Serbian nationalists. As recently as summer 1987, one could speak of real opposition currents in Serbia.[29] By the end of 1989, it was essentially impossible to speak of an opposition in Serbia: most of the opposition had gone over to Milošević. For example, rock singer Bora Djordjević, elected in 1989 to the Serbian Writers' Association in recognition of his prolific poetry, was writing nationalist poems about Kosovo[30] and praised Milošević for what he had done in the provinces. Throughout Serbia, Kosovo was in the air. Serbs gloated over their reconquest of the province. Serbian bookstores filled their shelves with books about Kosovo. Musical artists dedicated their works to Kosovo.[31] There was even a new perfume, "Miss 1389"—an allusion to the Battle of Kosovo of that year, when an invading Turkish army allegedly smashed the Serbian army, leaving the Kingdom of Serbia helpless. The Orthodox Church likewise waxed enthusiastic and in June published an interesting St. Vitus Day message in its newspaper, *Glas crkve,* which said, among other things: "The recent proclamation of the Republic Constitution restored to Serbia the sovereignty of the state over the whole of its territory, while retaining the existence of the two autonomies in its composition—*which can be accepted only as a temporary solution.*"[32]

The response of the Serbian opposition to Milošević's rise had parallels in the other republics as well. It would be too much to speak of an "alliance" between regional elites and their "oppositions," but it was obvious to all concerned that there was a partial symbiosis of purpose between the Serbian political elite and the Serbian opposition, between the Slovenian political elite and the Slovenian opposition, and so on. This had consequences both for the internal politics of each republic and for the wider political climate in the country as a whole. (On the other hand, the Serbian Writers' Association boldly issued a seven-point appeal for political pluralism on 10 May, accusing Serbia's leadership of obstructing democracy.[33])

Directly related to this was the form assumed by the emergent national revival in Yugoslavia. Throughout the country there was a renewed interest in the past, especially in the national literature and national history. But in every case this revival focused on the local nationality; in no instance did this revival assume an all-Yugoslav dimension. For example, in Serbia the revival of interest in earlier Serbian writers Njegoš, Ivo Andrić, and Miloš Crnjanski, which began at least a decade and a half ago, recently deepened and became politicized, with an increase of interest as well in contemporary Serbian writers Dobrica Ćosić, Matija Bećković, and Vuk Drašković. In Slovenia, the literary revival focused on the earlier Slovenian writers Primoš

Trubar, France Prešeren, and Ivan Cankar, with strong interest in such contemporary Slovenian writers as Andrej Hieng, Rudi Šeligo, Tomas Salamun, and Drago Jančar. In both cases, the interest in the literary past was growing in direct proportion to the rise in national consciousness and, in the Slovenian case, to the growth of interest in Slovenian sovereignty.[34]

The national revival was also reflected, in part, in the growth of underground cultural groups. The cultural underground saw, in particular, the sprouting of multimedia "new art" groups in several cities: Neue Slowenische Kunst (New Slovenian Art) in Ljubljana, Novi Evropski Poredak (New European Order) in Zagreb, Autopsija in Ruma (near Belgrade), Aporea in Skopje, and Metropolie Trans in Osijek. These groups infused their art with political meanings, in multimedia "happenings" that featured avant-garde music. Neue Slowenische Kunst (with its rock group Laibach) is the best known in the West, because of its strident coquetting with totalitarianism; the group also distributed, at one point, a map showing Slovenian settlements at their greatest extent (in the seventeenth century)—which, given the quasi-Nazi effect of their music, suggested a kind of "Slowenien über Alles." Aporea, by contrast, looked to the more distant past—to the Byzantine empire—for inspiration. The result was innovative music with strong liturgical sources and overtones. But in much the same way that Neue Slowenische Kunst came across as "foreign" to most Yugoslavs outside Slovenia, even more so, Aporea appealed strictly to a Macedonian audience, for only in Macedonia does Byzantium stir the soul. Nor is it merely a question of historical imagery; it is a question of differing national values.

At the most fundamental level, the peoples of Yugoslav lost the ability to understand each other—because they do not understand each other's values and concerns or each other's perceptions. The president of the Serbian Writers' Association told me, for instance, that "the Albanians in Yugoslavia have more rights than minorities in any other country. They have their academy of sciences, their university, their institutes for language and culture, all the perquisites of cultural autonomy. The only thing they lack is their own national state on the territory of Serbia. The Serbs in Croatia do not enjoy as many rights as the Albanians in Kosovo."[35] To a Serb, this statement was perfectly clear and rational. To a Croat or a Slovene or a Macedonian, however, this statement was essentially unintelligible and came across, at best, as the emotionally charged lament of a Serbian nationalist.

Political and cultural ethnocentrism was reinforced by the tendency of Yugoslavia's nationality groups to read "their own" newspapers. Serbs read the Serbian press, Croats the Croatian press, and so on. This phenomenon extended even to Bosnia, with dramatic polarizing effects within the republic. More broadly, this signified the weakening of ties to Yugoslavia. As a prominent cultural figure told me in 1989, "the Yugoslav idea is starting to become unpopular in Yugoslavia. Nobody wants to be Yugoslav anymore. People want to be Serbian or Croatian or Slovenian. Yugoslavia doesn't mean anything anymore."[36]

Accompanying these developments, there was a revived interest in monarchy. Almost no one was seriously thinking of restoring the monarchy (although a Yugoslav opinion poll conducted in late 1988 showed that 5 percent of Slovenes would ideally have preferred a monarchical government), but in Serbia, Croatia, and Montenegro there were signs of a "pop" nostalgia for kings and queens. In Serbia, for example, Princess Jelena Karadjordjević (who normally lives in Paris and Peru) was invited by the Serbian Patriarchate to attend the 600th anniversary celebrations of the Battle of Kosovo and received permission from Milošević to do so. The Orthodox Church's nostalgia for the monarchy was also shown in its periodical, *Crkveni život,* which in 1989 featured a portrait of King Aleksandar on its front page.[37] Also in Serbia, on 10 September 1989, the remains of King Lazar were ceremoniously reinterred at the monastery of Ravanica, while local citizens hoisted a huge banner displaying the fourteenth-century king's likeness,[38] and there was talk of transporting the last remains of King Petar II back to Yugoslavia, for burial in Oplenac.[39] Meanwhile, in Montenegro, the republic presidency agreed to receive back the remains of Montenegrin King Nikola I (a Montenegrin "green") and his family, and arrangements were made for transporting them back from San Remo.[40] And in Croatia, the decision was taken to restore the equestrian statue of Ban Josip Jelačić, the nineteenth-century governor of Croatia, to the Square of the Republic (from which it had been removed in July 1947).[41] Jelačić, a loyal retainer of the Habsburgs, had been condemned by Marx for his role in suppressing the short-lived Hungarian Republic (1848–1849) and accordingly became an important symbol for anticommunist sentiment in Croatia.

As Yugoslav unity disintegrated and nostalgia for monarchy waxed, Crown Prince Alexander, heir to the throne of the Kingdom of Serbs, Croats, and Slovenes, offered himself as a potential king in a revived kingdom. He argued that he could provide an important symbol of unity and that no other symbol could do the same. Despite his Serbian blood, Alexander had lived basically his entire life in England and was, for all practical purposes, a refined English gentleman first and foremost. He was not entangled in the politics of Communist and postcommunist Yugoslavia—a fact that encouraged some Yugoslavs to consider him a viable candidate. So removed from Yugoslavia was Alexander, in fact, that as of 1991 he was trying to learn Serbo-Croatian from a tutor. But English or not, Alexander had no power base of his own, and political discussions in the country made no reference to him. With some qualifications where

Alexander is concerned (in that his popularity seemed to be greater among émigré Yugoslavs than among Yugoslavs in the country), the revival of interest in the monarchy, thus, was always nationally specific (Serbian, Croatian, Montenegrin) and thus likewise reflected the fragmentation of the country into four environments.

POLITICAL FRAGMENTATION

It is not just culturally and economically that Yugoslavia was becoming fragmented. On the contrary, the country's fragmentation was also political, to the extent that it was necessary to speak of the emergence of different political systems in the separate republics. On the *formal* level, the political systems of the republics were still, as of autumn 1989, interchangeable: each republic had the same governmental and party structures, and—the Slovenian constitutional amendments aside—the same underlying legal-constitutional framework. On the *informal* level, however, there was a widening gap between the republics, not just in the matter of what was permitted but also where basic procedures and operational strategies were concerned. Serbia, for example, had reverted to a traditional patrimonial system and saw a revival of ethnic chauvinism and male chauvinism to underpin this reversion. Slobodan Milošević was clearly the dominant figure in Serbia, and people in key positions were either admirers and advocates of his or afraid to speak out. Montenegro, run at that time by supporters of Milošević, was, for all practical purposes, a colony of Serbia (as it remains in mid-1995). Bosnia, divided into three competing ethnic groups, was riven by intra-elite conflict and distrust and mired by corruption. A local quip had it that Bosnia combined Austrian bureaucracy with Ottoman slowness and inefficiency—a deadly combination. Slovenia allowed opposition parties to organize, meet, and sell their newspapers on the street and subsequently allowed them to field candidates in the spring 1990 parliamentary elections. As in Serbia, there was a waxing rapport between the party and certain sections of the opposition, but in Slovenia it was the opposition that was taking the initiative, not the other way around. In Croatia and Macedonia, loyalty to Tito was combined with incipient liberalism—in the former taking the form of efforts to democratize the party, while in Macedonia there were strong currents within the party in favor of moving toward a multiparty system. For example, in October 1989, Vasil Tupurkovski, the Macedonian member of the Yugoslav collective presidency, called pluralization the "top priority" on the agenda.[42] The Croatian party spoke of advocating a *Jugoslavenska sinteza* (Yugoslav synthesis), by which it meant essentially preservation of the federal system in something approximating its Titoist form; but at the same time the Croatian party by then clearly favored a transition to a market economy and the establishment of a "semi-multiparty" system (in which "nationalist" parties would be proscribed).[43] At times, Croatian politicians seemed willing to go even further. For example, Marin Buble, a member of the Croatian Central Committee, told *Slobodna Dalmacija* in late 1989, "a multi-party system has become a necessity, indeed only a matter of time, because the development of a modern society presumes above all a modern economic market, as well as a developed democratic political system. You can't have one without the other. They are two sides of the same system."[44]

Ironically, the political fragmentation of the system was aggravated by Milošević's attempt to consolidate a strong center. In the case of Macedonia, for example, which in 1988 was gravitating toward Milošević's camp, the Serbs alienated Macedonians by trying to pass a measure that would have allowed Serbs who had land titles from the interwar period to reclaim their land. Although aimed at Kosovo, the measure would have had consequences in Macedonia, too. The two republics fell out. Later, in October 1989, the Serbian leadership insensitively backed a proposal to declare 1 December—the day on which Yugoslavia was first united in 1918—a national holiday. This move again inflamed the Macedonians, who recalled that in its first incarnation Yugoslavia was known as the "Kingdom of the Serbs, Croats, and Slovenes"—the Macedonians, then called "south Serbs," were excluded.[45] Almost at the same time, evidence surfaced that the Serbian security service had been operating in Bosnia without the knowledge or approval of Bosnian authorities; Ivan Cvitković, secretary of the Bosnian party presidency, denounced Serbia's actions as "an attack on the sovereignty of Bosnia-Herzegovina."[46]

Milošević's championing of "an effective, modern state" also won him enemies. The reaction to Milošević recapitulated, in some ways, the reaction sparked by eighteenth-century Habsburg Emperor Josef II, who sought to consolidate a strong center, spoke in terms of political "modernization," championed a certain kind of liberalism, and ultimately inflamed insecurity among the non-German peoples of his empire by promoting German as the single language of administration. A central demand in Milošević's program was for a reform of the Federal Assembly. Under the system bequeathed by Tito, both houses of the bicameral legislature apportioned equal numbers of delegates to each constituent republic. Milošević argued that this was inconsistent with the democratic principle of "one citizen one vote." He demanded that *one* of the two chambers—specifically, the Federal Chamber—be reorganized so that the delegates to that chamber would represent equal numbers of citizens. In effect, his proposal would have closely followed the American model. The Slovenes, however, angrily rejected this proposal as a device to undermine their sovereignty, and both Slovenes and Croats worried that the proposal might be designed to give the Serbs political hegemony within the system. The fact that Serbs were enthusiastic about the proposal only seemed to confirm Slovenian and Croatian fears.

ISSUES ON THE AGENDA

There were four pivotal issues on the Yugoslav political agenda in the late 1980s: the federal question, the economy, pluralization, and the breakdown of the sense of community.

The Federal Question

There were four alternative scenarios available that attempted to preserve the Yugoslav state: confederalization (championed by a few Slovenian intellectuals, along with Serbian novelist Antonije Isaković, and others), asymmetric federation (championed by the Slovenian party), consolidation of a strong center (championed by the Serbian party and most Serbian intellectuals), and continuation of the status quo (not really championed by anyone, although Macedonia was clearly wary of any of the alternatives being proposed). Beginning in 1988, both Communists and noncommunists tended on the whole to discuss the first two scenarios within the framework of the continuation of the post-Titoist system of regional state monopolies, that is to say, with local republic elites making the key decisions affecting economic development and political life within their republics. Taken in isolation, thus, the federal question accentuated the nationalities question, even as it distorted it. Indeed, the federal question dominated discussion and marginalized all other questions—which was dangerous insofar as all four issues were serious.

The Economy

There was a broad consensus among both economists and laymen in Yugoslavia that radical economic reform was needed. In the more developed republics, the tendency was to talk in terms of reprivatization and the establishment of a true market economy. In the less developed republics, chiefly Macedonia and Bosnia, there were those who feared that such a change would only benefit the more developed regions and that they would be net losers. More fundamentally, reprivatizing the economy was a political question. Dismantling nationalized enterprises meant that republic elites, state-appointed directors, and the self-managing interest communities would all lose power. Inevitably, there were those who resisted reprivatization.

Pluralization

There were about a dozen independent political parties in Yugoslavia as of late 1989—some legally registered, some awaiting registration, and some denied registration and thus technically illegal. Most of these were based in Ljubljana or Zagreb. There were also between one and two dozen independent social and political interest groups, devoted variously to feminist, ecological, gay rights, pacifist, cultural, or other concerns. Most of these were based in Belgrade, Ljubljana, and Zagreb, although some were to be found in other cities. Many of them were issuing bulletins or other periodicals; some of them (particularly in Slovenia) were protected through registration as an activity of the local youth organization (a legal fiction).

Political pluralization in Yugoslavia was a symptom of societal mobilization and reflected, at the same time, the breakdown of the old political order. At the same time, the question of pluralization was organically tied to the federal question, since it lay within the jurisdiction of republic, not federal, authorities to grant or withhold the registration of political associations.

Breakdown of the Sense of Community

The foregoing issues were well understood in Yugoslavia and were being intelligently, albeit sometimes polemically, debated. Surprisingly, the breakdown of the sense of community, which was intuitively clear, received almost no explicit attention in the press, and there were no serious proposals to deal with this issue—i.e., unless secession of one or another republic was counted as a "solution."

Yet this fourth dilemma threatened the stability of the Yugoslav political order. The breakdown of communication across republic borders and nationality groups is the key to the disintegration of interethnic relations in Yugoslavia in the late 1980s—a process that can be traced, on one level, to the Kosovo riots of April 1981[47] and, on another level, to the very foundation of the state. So far advanced was this process by 1989 that people spoke openly of impending civil war and compared Yugoslavia to Lebanon.

Reprivatization and political pluralization might have defused the crisis had they been carried out at the end of the 1970s, or even by 1984 or 1985. But the longer the delay, the more economic deterioration aggravated the entire political climate and contributed, in particular, to the worsening of interethnic relations.

Some Yugoslavs took to citing the Helsinki Act, which barred any change in European borders, as an impediment to Slovenian secession or to the breakup of Yugoslavia. The citation was folly. Western powers were, to be sure, ready to provide Yugoslavia with much needed credits, at least until Milošević's unconstitutional moves in spring 1991, but it was scarcely to be believed that the signatories of the Helsinki Act would use armed force to hold Yugoslavia together.

NOTES

This chapter is a revised and expanded version of an earlier article, "Yugoslavia's Troubled Times," originally published in *Global Affairs,* Vol. 5, No. 1 (winter 1990). The author wishes to thank the editor of *Global Affairs* for granting permission to reproduce the article here.

1. For details of Milošević's biography and career, see Sabrina P. Ramet, "Serbia's Slobodan Milošević: A Profile," *Orbis,* Vol. 35, No. 1 (winter 1991).

2. *Večernji list* (Zagreb) (15 September 1989), p. 2; and *Politika* (Belgrade) (8 September 1989), p. 9. Latest census figures, as reported in Tanjug (30 April 1991), trans. in *Foreign Broadcast Information Service (FBIS), Daily Report* (Eastern Europe), 1 May 1991, p. 53.

3. *Večernji list* (6 September 1989), p. 5, and (11 September 1989), p. 2; *Nedjeljna Dalmacija* (Split) (19 September 1989), p. 6; and *Večernji list* (19 September 1989), p. 6.

4. On the last point, see *Večernji list* (21 September 1989), p. 10.

5. *Večernji list* (11 September 1989), p. 2, (15 September 1989), p. 5, and (24 September 1989), p. 4.

6. *Danas,* No. 394 (5 September 1989), p. 11.

7. *Vjesnik* (Zagreb) (28 August 1989), p. 5.

8. *Intervju* (Belgrade), No. 215 (1 September 1989), p. 19.

9. Ćiril Ribičič and Zdravko Tomac, *Federalizam po mjeri budućnosti* (Zagreb: Globus, 1989), p. 183.

10. *Mladina* (Ljubljana) (1 September 1989), p. 4.

11. *Intervju,* No. 215 (1 September 1989), p. 32.

12. See *Politika ekspres* (Belgrade) (24 September 1989), p. 2.

13. Summarized in *Svet* (Belgrade) (September 1989), pp. 50–51.

14. Gregor Tomc, "The Active Society," *Independent Voices from Slovenia, Yugoslavia,* Vol. 4, No. 3 (July 1988), p. 6.

15. Interview, Ljubljana, 4 September 1989.

16. Interview, Ljubljana, 1 September 1989.

17. Interview, Ljubljana, 5 September 1989.

18. Ibid.

19. *Večernje novosti* (Belgrade,) (27 September 1989), p. 4.

20. *Večernji list* (12 September 1989), p. 6.

21. *Večernje novosti* (27 September 1989), p. 2.

22. Ivan Stambolić, *Rasprave o SR Srbiji, 1979–1987* (Zagreb: Globus, 1988), p. 49.

23. Ibid., p. 62.

24. Quoted in Wolfgang Höpken, "Party Monopoly and Political Change: the League of Communists since Tito's Death," in Pedro Ramet, ed., *Yugoslavia in the 1980s* (Boulder, Colo.: Westview Press, 1985), p. 41.

25. *Intervju,* No. 213 (4 August 1989), pp. 23–25.

26. *Duga,* No. 406 (16 September 1989), pp. 82–83; and interview, Belgrade, 23 September 1989.

27. Radoslav Stojanović, *Jugoslavija, nacije i politika* (Belgrade: Nova knjiga, 1988), p. 213.

28. Interview with the author, Zagreb, 8 September 1989.

29. See Pedro Ramet, "Yugoslavia 1987: Stirrings from Below," *South Slav Journal,* Vol. 10, No. 3 (autumn 1987).

30. Bora Djordjević, *Neću, neću, neću, neću* (Belgrade: Književna zadruga, 1989), pp. 11, 18–19.

31. E.g., Vanja Brkić's album, *Kosovo je moja domovina* (Kosovo is my homeland), released by ZKP RTV, Ljubljana.

32. *Glas crkve* (Šabac), quoted in *Borba* (Belgrade) (25 July 1989), p. 3, trans. in *Foreign Broadcast Information Service* (*FBIS*), *Daily Report* (Eastern Europe) 4 August 1989, p. 43, my emphasis.

33. Yugoslav Situation Report, *Radio Free Europe Research* (26 May 1989), pp. 33–34.

34. Interview, Belgrade, 21 September 1989; and interview, Ljubljana, 4 September 1989.

35. Interview with Matija Bečković, Belgrade, 21 September 1989.

36. Interview with Goran Bregović, leader of Bijelo dugme, Sarajevo, 14 September 1989.

37. Interview, Ljubljana, 1 September 1989.

38. *NIN,* No. 2020 (17 September 1989), pp. 42–43.

39. *Slobodna Dalmacija* (Split) (22 September 1989), p. 16.

40. *Večernje novosti* (18 September 1989), p. 3; *Večernji list* (23 September 1989), p. 12; and *Frankfurter Allgemeine* (2 October 1989), p. 1.

41. *Vjesnik* (10 September 1989), p. 5; *Slobodna Dalmacija* (22 September 1989), p. 16; and *Politika* (25 October 1989), p. 7.

42. *Slobodna Dalmacija* (10 September 1989), p. 13.

43. Interview, Zagreb, 8 September 1989.

44. *Slobodna Dalmacija* (10 September 1989), p. 10.

45. *Politika* (20 October 1989), p. 7.

46. *Danas,* No. 401 (24 October 1989), p. 15.

47. See Sabrina P. Ramet, *Nationalism and Federalism in Yugoslavia, 1962–1991,* 2d ed. (Bloomington: Indiana University Press, 1992), and Sabrina P. Ramet, *Social Currents in Eastern Europe: The Sources and Consequences of the Great Transformation,* 2nd ed. (Durham, N.C.: Duke University Press, 1995), Chapter 8.

CHAPTER THREE

◆

Brotherhood and Disunity, 1989–1991

ON 25 JUNE 1991, SLOVENIA AND CROATIA unilaterally declared their independence, making good on their threat to take matters into their own hands if interrepublican negotiations regarding constitutional reform remained deadlocked.[1] The following day, the Serb-controlled Yugoslav National Army (JNA) sent tanks and helicopters crashing across the Croatian-Slovenian border into Slovenia. Hundreds of Slovenian civilians were killed or wounded, alongside casualties among both JNA units and units of the Slovenian Territorial Militia. The JNA strafed civilian trucks, bombed private homes and farms, and shot and killed civilians sitting at cafes, working in their fields, and engaging in other peaceful pursuits. The army also wrought considerable damage to Slovenia's economic infrastructure, including roads and bridges. The army, which in late 1990 had established a special political party linked with Slobodan Milošević and pledged to restore hard-line communism throughout the country, was clearly demonstrating *its* understanding of the meaning of the old Titoist phrase, "brotherhood and unity."

After two days of fighting, the JNA controlled the Ljubljana airport and all major access roads to Italy, Austria, and Hungary. The sides agreed on a truce. The European Community signaled its refusal to recognize Slovenian or Croatian independence and sent a delegation to pressure the combatants to find a peaceful solution, while U.S. Secretary of State James Baker advised Slovenes to negotiate—a recommendation that amounted to advising the Slovenes to capitulate to Serbian hegemony and the prospect of re-communization. Do Slovenes and Croats enjoy the right of national self-determination? Slobodan Milošević, the JNA, the European Community, and the U.S. Department of State all joined in giving a resounding "no" to this question. That was not the end of the story, however.

SOURCES OF DISCORD

Yugoslavia had been beset with problems from the time of its establishment in 1918, of course, and one may quite accurately say that no sooner was the multiethnic state constituted than it started to fall apart. Over the course of its seventy-year history, Yugoslavia lurched from crisis to crisis, abandoning one unstable formula for another. Finally, in the course of 1989–1991, the unifying infrastructure of the country largely dissolved. Slovenia and Croatia first declared that their local laws took precedence over federal laws. The republics subsequently withheld budgetary contributions to the federal government, throwing the federal budget into crisis. Three republics (Slovenia, Croatia, and Bosnia) issued declarations of sovereignty in 1990 and threatened to secede (albeit under rather different conditions). A fourth republic—Macedonia—issued a similar declaration in January 1991. Economic, cultural, and social relations among the republics were largely frozen, if not cut altogether. For all practical purposes, Yugoslavia had already broken up, even before the crises of 1991. The question was whether its squabbling politicians could manage to piece this Humpty Dumpty together again. To do so, they would have needed to find a radically new political formula.

Yet any peaceful dismantling of the union would have required some meeting of minds, some willingness on the part of all concerned to recognize that the status quo was untenable and that the problem could not be resolved by force. As an anonymous Slovene wit put it at the time, though, Yugoslavia was in such a mess that it could not even disintegrate properly. Serious nationality-based conflicts and disagreements had marred Yugoslav politics from the beginning, and the intractability of differences had often encouraged extremist solutions, which predictably crashed on the shoals of opposition.

The years 1918–1945 saw a series of experiments with pseudo-democratic Serbian hegemony, royal dictatorship, Serb-Croat settlement with other groups neglected, and fascism. None of these formulas worked.

Josip Broz Tito's partisans started out as run-of-the-mill Stalinists. But their expulsion from the Cominform by Stalin in June 1948 forced them to find their own formula and, in the process, gave them a new image. Tito became the new David to Stalin's Goliath and was seen as a hero in the West. In the 1960s and 1970s, it even appeared that Yugoslavia had finally found the key to solving its most important problems. The constitution of 1974 seemed to provide political stability (using cautiously crafted practices of ethnic quotas, strict rotation of cadres, and the universal enjoyment by constituent republics of the right to veto federal legislation). The economy was enjoying a boom. And then there was Tito—who played a crucial role as arbiter in the system, pulling it back from deadlock when all else failed. Even the nationality question seemed—in the years 1971–1981—to have been laid to rest.

Between 1979 and 1982, however, several things changed, causing Yugoslavia's leaders to reach the point, by 1983, of openly admitting for the first time since the 1948 expulsion that the country was in crisis. First, the economy began to deteriorate—largely as a result of internal dynamics; the process was sharpened and quickened by the steep increase in oil prices after 1973. Second the deaths of Vice President Edvard Kardelj in 1979 and President Tito in 1980 deprived the country not only of unifying symbols but more importantly of strong leaders capable of imposing unity. A third factor contributing to the disintegration of the old order was the outbreak, in April 1981, of widespread anti-Serbian rioting among the Albanian population of the then-autonomous province of Kosovo. These riots proved to be the clarion call of a new phase, in which underground groups of Albanian nationalists proliferated and Serb–Albanian frictions intensified. And fourth, there was the disastrous prime ministership of Branko Mikulić, whose mismanagement contributed to a general plummeting of public confidence in government officials and whose term of office was blemished, in particular, by the damaging Agrokomerc financial scandal in the summer of 1987.

Yet for all that, it required a catalyst to take Yugoslavia from "mere" crisis to the brink of civil war. That catalyst was Slobodan Milošević. As already noted, Milošević ended the policy of balance identified with his predecessor, Ivan Stambolić, and adopted a program of bare-faced Serbian nationalism. Milošević took politics to the streets, mobilizing large crowds of angry peasants (mostly middle-aged males) in a move to topple the local governments of the Republic of Montenegro and the provinces of Vojvodina and Kosovo. Sweeping his rivals out of power in these federal units, he installed his own supporters. Meanwhile, in a series of measures, he dismantled the autonomy of the provinces, subordinated them to the Serbian legislature and court system, shut down the provincial assembly in Kosovo (an illegal move on his part), ordered the arrest of the duly elected members of the now banned Kosovo Assembly, and, finally, suppressed Kosovo's major Albanian-language daily newspaper, *Rilindja*.[2]

After dealing with Montenegro, Vojvodina, and Kosovo, Milošević turned his eyes to Bosnia and Macedonia, as outlined in the preceding chapter. Even Slovenia and Croatia came to fear that Milošević aspired to be a new Tito and watched with horror as he promoted his "reform" plan, which aimed at reducing the powers of the republics and strengthening a central government that he obviously planned to control. Earlier allies in 1970–1971, Slovenia and Croatia had become politically estranged in the early and mid-1980s, at a time when party liberals prevailed in Slovenia, while party conservatives held sway in Croatia. Now, sharing a common apprehension of Serbia's nationalist regime, Slovenia and Croatia forged a new alliance, which encouraged talk of the formation of the aforementioned Slovenian-Croatian confederation (should the joint talks with the other republics fail).

SERBS AND NON-SERBS

Yugoslavia did not arise on on the basis of self-determination. It was created by Serbian bayonets, which installed the Serbian king as King of Yugoslavia. To impose unity, Serbian armies had to put down armed resistance in several parts of the country, including in Montenegro and Kosovo.[3] The interwar regime was a Serbian regime to which Croats never assented and in which Albanians, Muslims, and Macedonians were deprived of their national rights. Macedonians were treated as "south Serbs" and offered education in the Serbian language. Albanians were expelled wholesale to Albania; the Belgrade regime confiscated their land, some 154,287 acres, turning much of it over to Serbian settlers.[4] The government propagated a theory of the "tri-named people," which held that everyone in the kingdom, except the Albanians, was "really" a Serb, even if some people might not agree. Croats, for example, were viewed as "Catholic Serbs," while Slovenes were considered "alpine Serbs." The Slovenes' distinctive language was declared to be "poor Serbian."

All of this created problems that culminated in the splintering of the country in World War II, and the installation of a fascist regime in Croatia. Large numbers of all nationalities died in Yugoslavia during the war, but when the war ended, instead of subsiding, interethnic hatreds hardened, feeding on bitter recollections of the interwar kingdom and the war. Shortsighted party leaders stoked these hatreds by dwelling endlessly on the atrocities of the war and blaming many of them (in Croatia) on the Catholic Church and its functionaries.

The past has never been laid to rest in Yugoslavia. By contrast with the United States, where historical memory is quite short, peoples in the Balkans talk about events in 1389, 1459, 1921, 1941, 1948, 1970–1971, as if they were fresh. The wounds of the past have never healed. In a recent illustration of the way the past haunts the present, tens of thousands of anticommunist demonstrators assembled on 27 March 1991, to mark the fiftieth anniversary of the military coup that overthrew a pro-Nazi Serbian government and to draw a parallel to the present Serbian regime, which many accused of "fascism." Or again, the Party of Democratic Action in Kosovo included in its program a demand for autonomy for the Sandžak of Novi Pazar, on the argument that the Sandžak was a part of Bosnia in 1459.[5]

The past has also figured actively in the lively polemics between the pro-Milošević and anti-Milošević camps, most especially in the arsenal of anti-Croatian rhetoric spewed out by Serbia's controlled press. For Yugoslavs, World War II seems never to have ended. Serbs continue to assail the Catholic Church for alleged complicity in wartime atrocities—provoking the Church, at one point, into publishing a wartime Vatican decree in which the Holy See had explicitly forbidden its clergy to collaborate in any way with the Croatian fascist authorities (the Ustasha). Croatian historian and political activist Franjo Tudjman devoted his 1989 *Absurdities of Historical Reality* to debunking Serbian myths about the past.[6]

Of course, different nationalities remember the past in different ways. The Serbs remember the Tito era as an anti-Serbian era and cite Tito's transfer of large numbers of industrial plants from Serbia to Croatia and Slovenia in the late 1940s, which Serbs say was motivated by the desire to weaken and despoil Serbia. But Serbs forget that while Tito restored the old Ottoman-Habsburg boundary between Serbia and Bosnia without alteration, he aggrandized Serbia in the north by transferring to her jurisdiction a slice of eastern Croatia, Srem, which had never before belonged to Serbia.[7] Serbs also complained that the creation of the republics of Montenegro and Bosnia was artificial and that those territories, along with the territories established as autonomous provinces, should have been placed under strict Serbian control. Croats and Albanians, by contrast, are apt to remember Tito's many concessions to the Serbs, in particular in the first twenty years to communism. The 1946 trial of Croatian archbishop Alojzije Stepinac, on trumped-up charges of collaboration with the Ustasha, was, in Croatian eyes, a concession to Serbian hatred (especially among Orthodox clergy and believers) of Catholics and Croats alike. Likewise, Croats, Macedonians, Albanians, and ethnic Muslims alike remember that until July 1966 Tito worked closely with Aleksandar Ranković, head of the secret police, in pursuing a centralist policy injurious to the interest of non-Serbs.

These different memories, set atop unhealed wounds, provided the seedbed for deep bitterness, resentments, and recurrent desires for revenge.

The Tito era need not have ended as it did. In the late 1960s and the dawn of the 1970s, Tito allowed liberals in Slovenia, Croatia, Macedonia, and Serbia to chart a new course. The result was the growth among people of a sense of control over their own destiny. In particular, Croats vested great hope in the Croatian republic's leaders at that time—Miko Tripalo and Savka Dabčević-Kučar—who came to be seen as legitimate leaders. Tripalo told me in 1989 that as a result of the loosening up of the power structure, "there developed a rather broad democratic popular movement, which started to publish a large number of its own newspapers and magazines, thus creating forums in which people could speak freely. And the whole political life, which had been closed to the public, now opened up, and people started to speak their minds, both about the way things were then and about how things had been in the past."[8]

In December 1971, Tito removed Tripalo and Dabčević-Kučar from power. He subsequently also fired liberals in the other republics. As a result, these liberals were mythologized in the public consciousness and even gained in stature as late Titoism cracked and crumbled. By late 1990, Tripalo and Dabčević-Kučar had emerged from a kind of internal exile and were once again taking part in political discourse. In Macedonia, Kiro Gligorov, one of the liberals of the 1970–1971 era, returned to politics as president of Macedonia. In Slovenia, the memoirs of the late Stane Kavčič, the leading liberal of the early 1970s, were published and widely read. In Slovenia, Croatia, Bosnia, and Macedonia, it was the dissidents of yester-year who took hold of the reins of power in 1990. The current presidents of Croatia and Bosnia, in fact—Franjo Tudjman and Alija Izetbegović—both spent time in prison in the early 1980s after being tried on charges, re-spectively, of Croatian nationalism and Islamic fundamentalism.

THE SPREAD OF CIVIL TURMOIL

During the years 1989–1991, civil turmoil, which had overtly afflicted Kosovo since 1981, spread through much of the country, giving rise to se-rious fears of impending civil war. Civil turmoil often figures as a prelimi-nary phase that ultimately gives rise to civil war. Yugoslavia was clearly in a state of civil turmoil by summer 1989. The question was, could it avert the final descent to civil war? As of the end of June 1991, however, a peace-ful *and harmonious* (and hence, stable) solution appeared to be utterly im-possible. Despite the erosion of interrepublican ties, beginning with the Slovenian–Serbian relationship, Yugoslav-minded politicians in the squab-bling republics were not yet prepared to give up the "Yugoslav idea." Throughout much of 1990, they pinned their hopes on democratization, privatization of the economy, and, in particular, on Ante Marković's pro-gram of economic stringency, which, it was hoped, would finally restabi-lize the Yugoslav economy. Ultimately, they were disappointed. The intro-duction of multiparty elections proved insufficient because, despite the election of noncommunist liberals in Slovenia, Croatia, Bosnia, and Macedonia, Slobodan Milošević clung to power in Serbia and continued to advocate a policy aimed at maximizing Serbian hegemony, talking even of Serbia's desire to annex Montenegro as well as large portions of Croatia and Bosnia.

Neither the destabilization of Kosovo nor the alienation of Slovenia was sufficient to push the Yugoslav state over the brink. The heart of the Yugoslav national question has always been the Serb–Croat relationship, since these two longstanding rivals together constituted about 56 percent of the country's population. Accordingly, the turning point came in the form of an uprising by Croatia's small Serbian minority (11.6 percent of Croatia's total population). This uprising was adumbrated in summer 1989, when Dr. Jovo Opačić, a forty-five-year old Serbian economist, attempted to establish a cultural society for Croatia's Serbs (to build up special the-

aters, newspapers, radio stations, and other cultural and media infrastructure in the Serbian variant of the language). Croatia's then-Communist authorities balked and put Opačić in prison. Developments took a dangerous
turn in July 1990, when Croatian Serbs set up a Serbian National Council.
Since this council was organized in defiance of the Croatian authorities and
since its chief purpose was to work for Serbian autonomy within, or secession from Croatia, it was, in fact, a potentially revolutionary body.
During August and September 1990, the Council conducted an illegal referendum among Croatia's 567,317 Serbs; some 567,127 Serbs voted for
Serbian autonomy.[9] Serbs living outside Croatia were also invited to vote in
the referendum, and Tanjug admitted that the number of "yes" votes
(189,422) cast by this group was larger than the number of voters (183,464)
from outside the republic—which tells something of the care with which
the referendum was conducted. But the Serbian uprising only turned violent in October, when local Serbs raided gun shops and police stations,
arming themselves, set up barricades, and mined sections of railway lines
leading into the districts of greatest Serbian concentration. Soon, arms shipments, supposedly earmarked for the Yugoslav National Army, were "inex-
plicably" routed through the Croatian town of Knin (center of the Serbian
rebellion), where local Serbs unloaded the arms.[10]

About the same time, the army halted shipments of arms to Slovenia and
Croatia and started confiscating those already consigned to the territorial
defense militias in those republics.[11] The army also became involved in the
formation of the Chetnik militias in Croatia, dispatching JNA officers to train
the new militias for combat.[12] Meanwhile, the JNA retired Slovenian and
Croatian officers, promoting Serbs to take their places.[13] The Serb-controlled
JNA made similar preparations in Bosnia. In an operation code-named
RAM, Serbian authorities began arming newly established Bosnian Serb
militias in eastern Herzegovina, the Bosnian "Krajina," and the mountain-
ous Romanija region near Sarajevo as early as 1990.[14] "On April 9, 1991"—
according to Donia and Fine—"Bosnian police stopped three trucks containing over 1,000 [automatic] rifles near Mostar. . . . A similar incident in
May 1991 involved trucks bringing arms into Bosnia from Montenegro."[15]

With Slovenia already threatening secession, Croatia promised to secede
if Slovenia did so, and Bosnian President Alija Izetbegović underlined, on
several occasions, that Bosnia would not remain associated with a trun-
cated Yugoslavia ruled by Milošević and that if Croatia seceded so, too,
would Bosnia.[16] Serbian president Milošević, in turn, declared that if the
federation broke up, Serbia would seek to annex Serbian-inhabited portions of Croatia and Bosnia—which was geopolitical nonsense, since the
populations, especially in Bosnia, were dispersed in such a way that it was
utterly impossible to draw a clear border dividing ethnic groups, unless
population exchanges, voluntary or involuntary, were employed. In March

1991, Serbia organized Serbian defense units, not under federal command,[17] following similar moves by Slovenia and Croatia. Meanwhile, angry Serbs, spurred on by Milošević, formed "citizens' militias" in Croatia and Herzegovina; these militias were, of course, beholden to Milošević, not to the local governments of the republics in which they have operated.

The Serbian-dominated army, meanwhile, grew apprehensive of Slovenian and Croatian moves to slash their contributions to the military budget and in November formed a revived Communist Party, with Slobodan's wife, Mirjana, among the leading figures of the party. In December, General Veljko Kadijević, federal minister of defense, told a *Danas* reporter that the army would not permit Yugoslavia to become another "Lebanon,"[18] and the following month the army came close to invading Croatia. An eleventh-hour interrepublic agreement averted immediate danger, but the threat prompted Slovenia and Croatia to conclude an agreement to coordinate in the spheres of security and defense. A subsequent "assurance" from the army (in March) that it would not interfere in the political negotiations that continued among the heads of the six republics was not particularly assuring, in that the generals' communique clearly left open the possibility of military intervention to suppress Slovenian self-determination and quash the conflict between Serbs and Croats[19]—moves that would self-evidently be directed at Slovenia's and Croatia's expense and that many, including the present writer, suspected could only contribute to intensifying interethnic hatreds and igniting civil war. Rumors circulated in early 1991 to the effect that Admiral Branko Mamula, a former defense minister, supposedly intended to launch a coup, declare military rule, and set himself up as dictator.[20] But neither Kadijević nor Mamula was in a position, in this multiethnic country, to play Jaruzelski. And even Jaruzelski, it will be recalled, ultimately failed and was forced to scuttle his own regime.

THE DISINTEGRATION OF THE ECONOMY

The Yugoslav economy had, by 1990 for all practical purposes, disintegrated. With unemployment standing at more than 15 percent, an annual inflation rate of 127 percent (as of March 1991), a foreign debt of $22 billion, and a 1990 trade deficit of $2.7 billion, the economic infrastructure itself was becoming unraveled, holding the promise of continued deterioration. All six republics experienced economic decline in 1990. Worst off was Montenegro, where industrial production fell 15.8 percent in the first nine months of 1990. During the same period, industrial production declined 13.5 percent in Serbia, 10.8 percent in Croatia, 10.6 percent in Slovenia and Macedonia, and 6.2 percent in Bosnia-Herzegovina.[21] Marković's widely touted program of economic reform, which was introduced in the beginning of 1990, froze wages and prices and brought inflation down from a rate of 2,000 percent annually to about 4 percent, virtually overnight. But soon inflation once again crept upward. Marković's reform itself included pegging the dinar to the German mark, thus making the Yugoslav currency convertible. Unfortunately, the fixed exchange rate gave the dinar artificial strength, and the immediate result was a surge in imports and the bankruptcy of many once wealthy exporters.[22] Foreign currency reserves plunged from $6.5 billion to $3.6 billion within a year,[23] forcing the Marković government to abandon convertibility and devalue the dinar.

Reprivatization came too late to avert economic catastrophe. Although the private sector had been measurably more efficient than the social sector,[24] Yugoslavia's 16,490 private firms (as of February 1991) accounted for only 2.4 percent of the overall income of the Yugoslav economy—too little to make a difference. Meanwhile, foreign investors were once again scared off. Political instability and the talk of civil war and military coup were bad enough. But add to that the severe difficulties in doing business across republic lines and the fact that local courts no longer recognized the validity of other republican laws, and potential investors could only view Yugoslavia as an especially undesirable investment prospect. Nationalism played a role in this, too, as the republics took actions injurious to the economic interests of companies based in other republics. In Serbia, for example, the Croatian-based INA petrochemical company was forced to pay a 150 percent surcharge on all gasoline sales, even though Serbian petrochemical companies paid no such tax; as a result, INA decided, early in 1991, to curtail its operations in Serbia.

The Yugoslav government approached the West, hat in hand, with a request for yet another economic bailout, this time to the tune of $4 billion. Meanwhile, the Swiss newspaper, *Neue Zürcher Zeitung,* questioned whether it was realistic to pin any hopes on yet another infusion of money into this economically inefficient country, underlining that for all practical purposes the productive sector in Yugoslavia had collapsed.[25] Even in relatively more prosperous Slovenia, before the JNA wreaked severe damage on the republic's economic infrastructure in June 1991, local authorities expected the economy to decline for at least another two years before any revival could begin.

THE FEDERAL BUDGET

All of this provided the backdrop for serious damage to the federal budget. Already in November 1990, Slovenia, Serbia, and Vojvodina announced that they would make no further tax payments to the federation.[26] After the Milošević government stole some $1.8 billion from the federal treasury in December—essentially distributed among Serbs in the form of wage increases, in order to "buy" the election for Milošević—the Slovenian and

Croatian governments announced that they would recognize no further debts incurred by the federal government. As a result of these pressures, in December, the federal government was operating at a level 15 percent below its basic budgetary needs and had had to lay off some 2,700 federal officials, thus reducing the ability of the central government to function.[27] The federal government was unable, in turn, to meet its commitments to the republics (in the form of subsidies to the three less developed republics, funds for stimulating exports, war veterans' pension supplements, and other funds), and in March the government of Bosnia announced that unless the federal government settled its debts with Bosnia "within a week" Bosnia would cease all payments to the federal budget.[28] The governments of Montenegro and Macedonia also complained about the federal government's failure to honor financial commitments.[29] The republics, most especially Serbia, Croatia, and Slovenia, also slowed their contributions to the military budget. More particularly, the Slovenian government declared that it would not pay off its obligations to the army so long as there was a threat of the introduction of emergency measure, and that it was unilaterally reducing its contribution to the 1991 military budget from 15 billion dinars to about 3 billion dinars.[30] As a result, the army was not able to pay its bills, and some food suppliers refused to send any more provisions to the army because they had not been paid in two months. To address this situation, the Federal Executive Council redirected some funds earmarked for other purposed to the army and in February took out a loan with the National Bank of Yugoslavia in order to permit the army to continue to function.[31]

THE REPUBLICS AWAKEN

Enough has been said already to make it clear that the will to remain in union had, already by 1989, seriously atrophied. As of late 1990, some 88 percent of Slovenes considered secession their best option. In May 1991, 94.3 percent of Croats likewise voted for independence. A sizable majority of Albanians (in Kosovo) and a growing number of Macedonians were also coming to favor this solution for their own regions.[32] The figures for Slovenes and Croats were close to 100 percent by mid-1991. The governments of Slovenia and Croatia became openly secessionist. Prosecessionist movements emerged among the Muslims of Novi Pazar, the Albanians of Kosovo, and the Macedonians, alongside Serbian secessionist groups operating in parts of Croatia, Montenegro, and Bosnia, seeking annexation of all or parts of those republics to Serbia.[33] By the beginning of 1991, thus, Milošević's earlier disavowal of any aspiration to redraw any interrepublican borders[34] was starting to seem cruelly prophetic of the Serbian leader's real intentions.

Kosovo occupied the top of the agenda for almost a decade after the spring 1981 riots.[35] Since February 1989 (if not before) Kosovo has been in a state of siege. The provincial assembly was shut down by Milošević in July 1990, the major Albanian-language daily newspaper was suppressed on orders from Milošević, even the local youth organization "no longer exists."[36] At the same time, while the Serbian government continued to fire Albanian employees in Kosovo indiscriminately, local Albanians and Serbs organized antagonistic "self-defense units," arming themselves for a showdown.[37] Authorities subsequently confiscated arms held by Albanians on several occasions, taking even those for which the Albanians in question had proper licenses, leaving only the Serbs in possession of firearms.[38]

The army, far from playing a tranquilizing role, itself contributed to the tensions when reports surfaced that Serbian conscripts had murdered Albanian recruits.[39] A survey conducted in early 1991 by the popular Albanian-language newspaper, *Zeri i Rinise,* found that more than half of Kosovar Albanians surveyed hoped for annexation by Albania, while 31 percent were in favor of an armed struggle against Serbia, and only 7 percent saw any point in attempting to enter into dialogue with the Serbs.[40]

Croatia and Bosnia likewise became dangerous flashpoints. The proclamation of secession from Croatia, by Serbs of the so-called Krajina, was one of the more dangerous developments of early 1991, the gravity of which was amply demonstrated in the armed incursion by Serbs, on 31 March, into the Plitvice National Park, which some Serbs evidently wanted to annex. In Bosnia, Alija Izetbegović, now president of Bosnia, declared in late October that "if the republics of Slovenia and Croatia secede from Yugoslavia, the Republic of Bosnia-Herzegovina will immediately proclaim its independence."[41] Two weeks later, Radovan Karadžić, leader of the Serbian Democratic Party of Bosnia-Herzegovina, promised that if Bosnia seceded from Yugoslavia, the Serbs of Bosnia—who did not, it will be recalled, inhabit a compact area—would secede from Bosnia, in effect plunging Bosnia into serious chaos.[42]

In Montenegro—long divided between pro-Serbian and anti-Serbian Montenegrins—the biggest change in the months between September 1990 and June 1991 was an increase in pressure on Montenegro by Milošević's supporters to submit to annexation by Serbia. A Movement for the Unification of Serbia and Montenegro was organized and on 6 November submitted an appeal, signed by 10,000 citizens of Montenegro and Serbia, to the Serbian and Montenegrin assemblies for a referendum on the unification of the two republics. The Montenegrin government resisted such pressures, even as pro-Serbian and anti-Serbian groups proliferated in the republic.

Even Macedonia saw a sudden rise in national consciousness among all the nationality groups living there: Macedonians, Albanians, Serbs, Gypsies, and others. There were at least two active nationalist organizations in Macedonia, both of which demanded immediate secession from Yugoslavia: the Movement for All-Macedonian Action, and the Internal

Macedonian Revolutionary Organization–Democratic Party for Macedonian National Unity.[43] The latter urged that the Yugoslav National Army be withdrawn from Macedonia. In that organization's view, "only the Territorial Defense of Macedonia can stand as the legitimate defender of Macedonia."[44] Not surprisingly, the Bulgarian government expressed its opinion about Macedonian statehood, but in a complete reversal of the irredentist policy of the Zhivkov era, the Bulgarian Foreign Ministry declared its full support for an independent Macedonian state and affirmed that it no longer nurtured any territorial pretensions vis-à-vis Macedonia.[45] This Bulgarian declaration was probably designed to further weaken Milošević's position in the south.

There was even new wind filling the sails of regional autonomist movements. Aside from the aforementioned movements of Muslims in the Sandžak of Novi Pazar and of Serbs in Croatia and Bosnia-Herzegovina, there were also signs in 1990–1991 of waxing autonomism in Istria,[46] Dalmatia,[47] and Vojvodina, as well as a sharp anti-Hungarian backlash among some of Vojvodina's Serbs.[48]

In October 1990, Slovenia and Croatia had issued a joint proposal for transforming the Yugoslav state into a confederation.[49] This proposal was immediately rejected by Serbia and Montenegro. During the early months of 1991, Slovenia, Croatia, and Macedonia argued for confederalization, Bosnia was willing to go along with confederalization, and Serbia and Montenegro remained opposed. Of the six republics, four of them viewed their borders as state borders not subject to administrative change by Belgrade; only Serbia and Montenegro held to the view that the borders separating the republics were administrative in character and subject to revision. Slovenia, Croatia, and Bosnia wanted to depoliticize the army——a move opposed by Serbia and Montenegro—while Macedonia had not yet worked out a clear policy in this area.[50]

Throughout the early months of 1991, the six republics conducted a series of summit talks to avert civil war and find a path to interrepublican agreement, but none of these meetings produced any progress. And it was unclear, as long as Milošević remained in power in Serbia, how any progress might be made. In this context, the massive anti-Milošević demonstrations in Belgrade for several days in March seemed a hopeful sign; they certainly indicated a new confidence among his local opposition. Predictably, the Milošević government responded with bans, tear gas, and arrests. Helsinki Watch commented,

> The actions of the Serbian government, and particularly the Serbian police force, violated Principle VII of the Helsinki Final Act which calls on participating states to "respect human rights and fundamental freedoms." Also, the use of excessive force by the Serbian police. . . . violates Article 6 of the International Covenant on Civil and Political Rights (ICCPR). . . . The Serbian government's actions on March 9 and 10 also violated Article 2 (1) of the ICCPR, which states that parties

to the Covenant will undertake "to respect and ensure" the rights recognized in the Covenant. The Serbian government's interference with the demonstrations on March 9 and 10 also infringed the right of peaceful assembly and association, as guaranteed in Articles 21 and 22 of the ICCPR. Moreover, the arrests of some demonstrators on March 9 violated Article 9 of the ICCPR, which claims that: "No one shall be subjected to arbitrary arrest or detention."[51]

Ultimately, the demonstrations won a few concessions in the media and compelled the resignation of Serbian Interior Minister Radmilo Bogdanović the following month.[52] But Milošević remained in power, and his policy remained unchanged.

In the absence of an interrepublic agreement, the republics increasingly simply bypassed the federal government. Milan Kučan, the president of Slovenia, put the issue very succinctly, in an address to the Slovenian Assembly on 20 February:

> We [have] proceeded from the fact that Yugoslavia, as a joint federal state, has politically and economically disintegrated. The federal state and its entities have been functioning with an increasing number of difficulties, and now are doing so under the conditions of a financial blockade on the part of the republics. The republics have built up or are building up their autonomous, constitutional-political, legal, and economic systems and, on that basis—despite the fact that they do not admit it—they behave very much as independent subjects from a constitutional and legal aspect.[53]

ON THE BRINK

By April 1991, Bosnia and Macedonia had converted to the confederalist cause being advocated by Slovenia and Croatia.[54] Slovenia, Croatia, and Bosnia had already declared their sovereignty, and Slovenia and Croatia were, by then, making preparations for independence. On 7 April, the Internal Macedonian Revolutionary Organization–Democratic Party for Macedonian National Unity followed in their footsteps and approved a statute advocating the "comprehensive political, economic, and spiritual independence of the Macedonian state."[55]

The interrepublican summit meetings remained deadlocked, with Serbia and Montenegro unwilling to turn back from their hegemonist course. Meanwhile, the country continued to unravel. Slavonian Serbs—including many who had come to the region from Serbia and other parts in the 1970s in search of jobs[56]—declared their intention to secede from Croatia and join Vojvodina, thus coming under Milošević's rule.[57] The self-proclaimed Krajina, declared by Croatia's Serbs, announced its plan to seek annexation to Serbia. Meanwhile, Croats living in the Krajina region took steps to register their opposition to this move and to proclaim their intention to remain part of Croatia.[58] After the seizure of Croatia's Plitvice National Park by Serbian armed militias in late March, the JNA sent its tanks to occupy the park.[59] In fact, the JNA repeatedly intervened in Serb–Croat conflicts during the early months of 1991 without authorization from either the collective presidency or the Republic of Croatia.

In mid-May, Borislav Jović (a Serb) was supposed to step down as president of the collective presidency. He was supposed to be succeeded in office by Stipe Mesić, the noncommunist representative from Croatia. But Mesić naively commented, in advance, that upon his succession he intended to fire the army chief of staff and his deputies because they had been acting without the constitutionally required authorization of the collective presidency.[60] When it came time for Mesić to assume office, Milošević used the four votes he controlled in that body (Serbia, Montenegro, Kosovo, and Vojvodina) to block Mesić's succession, thus disrupting the work of that body. The Croatian Republic appeared unprepared for this development, but, all the same, Croatian President Franjo Tudjman agreed to meet Serbian President Slobodan Milošević, and they concluded what he (Tudjman) thought of as a "special agreement" between the two.

As this was going on, acting JNA commander General Adžić declared himself in favor of a prophylactic "extermination of tens of thousands of Croats [which] would provoke some grumbling around the world but [which] would be soon forgotten."[61] The army clashed with Croatian workers in Slavonski Brod, when the latter tried to prevent the army from removing 100 new tanks from an arms factory.[62] Army tanks and troops were also deployed against Croats in Listica (a Croatian town in Bosnia). In several instances, there were reports that Serbian forces were making use of former members of Romania's secret police, the Securitate, who had fled Romania after the ouster of Romanian President Nicolae Ceausescu in December 1989. Croatian police, in fact, intercepted some radio transmissions among Serbian forces; they were in Romanian.[63] In Borovo Selo, a Croatian town whose largely Serbian population were among those who had entered Slavonia in the 1970s in search of work, shooting erupted in early May, resulting in sixteen deaths and an unspecified number of wounded. When Croatian authorities dispatched police to the region, the Serbs agreed to give the police safe passage under a white flag. But when the Croatian police entered the village, white flags in hand, the Serbs opened fire on them, killing thirteen police and wounding twenty-one. Some Croatian police were mutilated by Serbs: their eyes were gouged out, their throats slit, and their genitals cut off.[64] Once again, the army sent in troops, as it had done in previous weeks in Plitvice National Park, as well as in Kijevo, Šibenik, and other towns in Croatia.

In mid-May, the procommunist chiefs of staff of the Yugoslav army, navy, and air force met in Belgrade, behind closed doors, to plan the disposition of forces in the coming action. "Duties were determined for the army commands, units and institutions of the Yugoslav People's Army," said a Defense Ministry statement after the meeting.[65] The army amassed large concentrations of forces in the northern part of Bosnia-Herzegovina,[66] sent troops to Maribor the night of 26 May to arrest Colonel Vladimir Milošević (no relation to Slobodan), the commander of Slovenia's eastern territorial defense district,[67] and drew up plans for seizing control of Slovenia's borders and the airport at Ljubljana.[68] Meanwhile, the JNA continued to demand the complete disarmament and disbanding of the Slovenian and Croatian defense militias—moves that would have left those republics defenseless and that were accordingly resisted. Slovenia and Croatia turned to private arms merchants in Western Europe and the United States, in search of heavy artillery and other weaponry.[69]

But Slovenia and Croatia faced a serious obstacle. In spite of early expressions of sympathy from the German, Austrian, and Italian governments, the states of Western Europe held back from offering diplomatic recognition or support to these two republics. On the contrary, the United States, Soviet Union, China, France, and other states issued statements supportive of Yugoslav unity and hostile to Slovenian and Croatian secession. Where the United States was concerned, this policy was the fruit of the Bush administration's concern not to do anything to aggravate or to send the "wrong message" to the Soviet Union. In fact, the Bush administration applied pressure on the European Community to ostracize Slovenia and Croatia, made IMF loans contingent upon the preservation of Yugoslav unity, and sent Secretary of State James Baker to Yugoslavia in June 1991 to declare publicly that the republics should "negotiate." The only form of "negotiation" compatible with the preservation of Yugoslav unity, as Bush and Baker should have known, would have been the complete surrender of the Slovenian and Croatian governments to Serbian *diktat,* resulting in the removal of local democratic forces, whether by Milošević or by local discontents.

The Slovenian government had previously announced that it would secede from Yugoslavia by 26 June if no progress had been made by then toward resolving the crisis. When Slovenia followed through on this threat, JNA units stationed in Croatia crossed into Slovenia and seized control of the border and the airport, according to plan. Slovenian forces put up strong resistance and inflicted losses on the JNA. The loss of life and infrastructure damage caused by the JNA were already noted at the outset of this chapter. The United States responded to this assault by urging the Slovenian government to withdraw its declaration of independence and to "negotiate" with Serbia.

As of June 1991, the JNA had 138,000 troops on active duty and 400,000 troops in the reserves. It had 1,850 battle tanks (mostly old Soviet T-54 and T-55 tanks, but also some Yugoslav T-72s). It had some 2,000 towed artillery pieces, 500 armored personnel carriers, and other Soviet-made weaponry. The navy commanded 10,000 troops, with 4 frigates, 59 patrol and coastal craft, and 5 small submarines at its disposal. The 32,000-strong air force had 455 combat aircraft, including MiG-29s, and 198 helicopters.[70]

Slovenia had a small militia comprising about 20,000 troops as of June 1991, but both Slovenia and Croatia claimed to be able to mobilize about 200,000 troops on short order.[71] Slovenia and Croatia also possessed an unspecified number of tanks, antitank weapons, and other weaponry, most of it allegedly imported from Germany and Hungary.

Slovenia had, to some extent, relied on a defense agreement, which it had concluded with Croatia, to present a solid front against Serbia. But in May 1991 Croatian President Tudjman had allowed himself to be persuaded to abandon his Slovenian ally in exchange for Serbian promises of goodwill. Hence, when JNA tanks were sent rolling out of Croatia into Slovenia, Tudjman made no move to hinder their advance. Tudjman did not believe that these same tanks might be used against Croatia once the battle in Slovenia had ended.

The chances of reviving Yugoslav had died long before the JNA's brutal assault on Slovenia in late June 1991. But the assault, undertaken in the name of "unity," was a logical capstone to the program pursued by Milošević since 1987 and a fulfillment of longstanding fears among Yugoslavs that this multiethnic country was heading toward civil war.[72] The delayed confirmation of Stipe Mesić as president of the collective presidency on 30 June could not dispel the tensions created by the resort to military force and came too late to constitute a very hopeful sign.

WAR

On 27 May, Stipe Mesić, whose accession to the Yugoslav presidency was still in limbo, delivered a confident speech in Krasic, at a ceremony to mark Croatian statehood. Debunking pessimistic forecasts, Mesić reviewed the failed efforts to topple the Marković government[73] and said that any recourse to the army had "no chance." He concluded that it was "quite unlikely" that the army would take any steps to block the secession of either Slovenia or Croatia.[74] Two days later, the Serbian parliament refused to take up Croatian Serbs' appeal for annexation to Serbia—thus giving some encouragement to Croatia.[75]

However, scarcely a month later the army moved, first against Slovenia, turning later against Croatia. By the beginning of July, mediation by the European Community had obtained JNA agreement to pull its troops out of Slovenia,[76] though the process was only completed in October.

But no sooner did things calm down in Slovenia than tensions flared in Croatia, where the local secessionist Serbian council was said to enjoy the confidence and support of all Serbs living in the "Krajina."[77]

From July to October, Serbian militias in Croatia seized large chunks of Croatian territory, destroying villages and towns and setting the local population to flight. By the end of October, Serbian insurgents controlled about a third of Croatia and continued to press forward. About that time, a Serbian spokesperson from Croatia declared, "The Serbs in Croatia [11.6 percent of the republic's population according to the April 1991 census] are not a minority and the [European Conference] on Yugoslavia has understood that."[78] Of course, if 11.6 percent of the population is not to be understood as a "minority," then it follows that it construes itself as a "majority"—meaning, at the same time, that the remaining 88.4 percent is the "real minority". One is reminded that Lenin's Bolsheviks acquired their name in a claim to represent the majority of the Social Democratic Party, although, in fact, they were, at the time the claim was made, in a distinct minority.

Aside from Vukovar (prewar population of about 50,000), which by October 1991 had been reduced to rubble, Serbian militias, backed by the JNA, also laid siege to Osijek (population 200,000, including 30,000 Serbs),[79] Dubrovnik (population 60,000, including fewer than 6,000 Serbs), Petrinja (which fell to Serbs after a struggle), Glina (which *Danas* reporter Jasmina Kuzmanovič dubbed the "Croatian Alamo,"[80] Okučani (14 km. from the Bosnian border), Vinkovci (a city near Vukovar in eastern Slavonia), Borovo, and other Croatian towns and villages. Zagreb, Karlovac, Osijek, Vukovar, Borovo, and other towns were subjected to aerial bombardment,[81] and in early October, air strikes were carried out against the presidential palace in Zagreb, nearly killing Croatian President Tudjman. In the midst of the fighting, Serbian President Milošević accused Croatia of trying to pursue a "policy of genocide."[82]

By the end of December 1991, more than half a million persons had been driven from their homes, many of them fleeing abroad (chiefly to Germany and Hungary). At least 3,000 persons had been killed in the war, and thousands more wounded. Up to 40 percent of Croatia's factories had been destroyed, and the cost of rebuilding was estimated at some $18.7 billion.[83]

Between July and mid-November, some twelve cease-fires collapsed. Peace plans by the European Community proved unacceptable to Serbia, and peace plans proposes by Serbia proved unacceptable to other republics.[84]

In early August, Milošević called for a meeting of the representatives of three of the four republics that, as of then, had not seceded from Yugoslavia, namely, Serbia, Montenegro, and Bosnia. The purpose of the meeting was to discuss the restructuring of the Yugoslav state.[85] The meeting took place on 12 August and was attended by: Milošević, the president of Serbia, Aleksandar Bakočević, president of the National Assembly of Serbia, Momir Bulatović, the president of Montenegro, Risto Bukčević, the

president of the Assembly of Montenegro, and Momčilo Krajišnik, the president of the Assembly of Bosnia-Herzegovina. Alija Izetbegović, president
of Bosnia, had of course been invited to attend, but he had refused.
Krajišnik's participation, thus, reflected intra-elite discord at the highest
level within Bosnia-Herzegovina.[86] The meeting issued a call for a new constitution, enumerating a number of bland principles.[87] Krajišnik, hailed in
Belgrade, faced severe criticism back in Bosnia for having attended the
Belgrade meeting at all.[88]

Macedonia and Bosnia at first held back from issuing any declarations,
but under the pressure of events first Macedonia, then Bosnia, declared
their intention to secede. And in October, the Albanian opposition in
Kosovo conducted a referendum among that province's Albanian population: an overwhelming majority of those taking part voted for secession and
annexation to Albania. For them, the Yugoslav option was likewise dead.

At the same time, demands were heard in Serbia that historic Dubrovnik
be taken away from Croatia. The Belgrade magazine *Intervju* published an
interview with academician Miroslav Pantič, who demanded that the
Dubrovnik area be set up as an "independent" republic, separate from
Croatia. Pantič blamed Austria and the Catholic Church for Croatizing
Dubrovnik and claimed that a group of Dubrovnik citizens—how many he
did not say—had framed a demand in 1945 that the city be set up as an autonomous province, if not as a republic.[89] Despite international protests, the
Serbian-dominated army kept a stranglehold on historic Dubrovnik, reinforcing its siege force in late October. The army informed the city's defenders that "only surrender can save Dubrovnik."[90]

In July 1991, the federal government issued a statement that it was slash-
ing the military budget from $34 billion to just $15 billion.[91] This decision
was quickly countermanded and Belgrade began printing money, without
backing, to pay the army.[92] As a result, instead of shrinking, the military
budget increased as a proportion of the total federal budget from 40 percent to 65 percent by October.[93] A Western diplomat assigned to Belgrade
commented, "Only 25 percent of the budget is covered [by reserves]. They
are printing the rest."[94] At the same time, Serbia was losing hard currency
income on sales of electric power to Italy and Austria because the grid that
ran through Croatia was closed down by the war. Croatia also shut down
the oil pipeline to Serbia.[95] Industrial production slumped everywhere as a
result of the war, including in Serbia, and Western credits dried up.[96]

By late September, there were confirmed reports that the JNA was ex-
periencing growing problems recruiting soldiers.[97] But on 7 November
1991, the Serbian government renamed the army and abandoned any pre-
tense that that force represented any republics other than Serbia and
Montenegro.[98] Meanwhile, within Serbia itself, critical voices could still be
heard.[99] Some domestic critics expressed the conviction that Milošević

would ultimately fall. "Milošević is not a man of vision," said Miloš Vasić, editor of the privately owned Belgrade magazine, *Vreme,* and one of Milošević's more deadly critics. "The Greater Serbia that he is trying to create will be undefendable and unsustainable."[100] Dragan Veselinov, head of the opposition Serbian Peasant Party, linked Milošević's fortunes to the war: "The moment Milošević stops his territorial campaign, he will face social unrest in Serbia."[101] And Zoran Djindjić, leader of the opposition Democratic Party in Serbia, seconding this point of view, told an American correspondent, "It's impossible to defeat Milošević in Serbia. All our internal problems have been dissolved in the war. Milošević, like Napoleon, will be defeated on the battlefield. The army in Croatia will come back to Serbia and they will overthrow Milošević. . . . The only question is how long it will take to defeat him."[102]

Such views were commonly expressed in 1991 and even in the early months of 1992. But Milošević has confounded his opposition and as of December 1994 appeared more firmly in control than ever. Moreover, with steady economic and materiel support from Russia, Greece, Romania, and China, and de facto diplomatic support from Britain and France, Milošević appeared to have a chance even to ride out his economic woes.

NOTES

1. *Financial Times* (London) (26 June 1991), p. 1. See also editorial, p. 16.

2. For further discussions of Milošević's role, see Sabrina P. Ramet, "Serbia's Slobodan Milošević: A Profile," *Orbis,* Vol. 35, No. 1 (winter 1991); and Aleksa Djilas, "A Profile of Slobodan Milošević," *Foreign Affairs,* Vol. 72, No. 3 (summer 1993).

3. For details, see Ivo Banac, *The National Question in Yugoslavia: Origins, History, Politics* (Ithaca, N.Y.: Cornell University Press, 1984).

4. Ibid., pp. 298–299.

5. *Borba* (Belgrade) (6 March 1991), p. 3.

6. Franjo Tudjman, *Bespuča povijesne zbiljnosti: Rasprava o povijesti i filozofiji zlosilja* (Zagreb: Nakladni zavod Matice Hrvatske, 1989).

7. Noel Malcolm, *Bosnia: A Short History* (New York: New York University Press, 1994), p. 205.

8. Interview with the author, Zagreb, 8 September 1989. The full text of the interview is published in *South Slav Journal,* Vol. 12, No. 3–4 (autumn–winter 1989), pp. 87–93.

9. Tanjug (1 October 1990), trans. in *Foreign Broadcast Information Service (FBIS), Daily Report* (Eastern Europe), 1 October 1990, p. 63.

10. For details, see Sabrina P. Ramet, "The Breakup of Yugoslavia," *Global Affairs,* Vol. 6, No. 2 (spring 1991).

11. Branka Magaš, *The Destruction of Yugoslavia: Tracking Yugoslavia's Breakup 1980–92* (London: Verso, 1993), p. 267.

12. Ibid., p. 311.

13. Ibid., p. 333.

14. Robert J. Donia and John V. A. Fine, Jr., *Bosnia and Hercegovina: A Tradition Betrayed* (New York: Columbia University Press, 1994), p. 216.

15. Ibid., pp. 215–216.

16. See, for instance, *Oslobodjenje* (Sarajevo) (25 February 1991), p. 3, trans. in *FBIS, Daily Report* (Eastern Europe), 1 March 1991, p. 38.

17. *Daily Telegraph* (London) (18 March 1991), p. 1.

18. *Danas* (Zagreb), No. 459 (4 December 1990), pp. 10–12.

19. *Daily Telegraph* (20 March 1991), p. 15.

20. *Frankfurter Allgemeine* (2 February 1991), p. 2. See also Croatian Democracy Project, news release, 7 February 1991.

21. *Danas*, No. 459 (4 December 1990), p. 18.

22. *Wall Street Journal* (18 March 1991).

23. *Neue Zürcher Zeitung* (Zurich), 29/30 March 1991, p. 18.

24. Tanjug (28 February 1991), in *FBIS, Daily Report* (Eastern Europe), 1 March 1991, p. 39.

25. See *Neue Zürcher Zeitung* (8 February 1991), p. 16, and (29–30 March 1991), p. 18.

26. *Oslobodjenje* (12 November 1990), p. 1, trans. in *FBIS, Daily Report* (Eastern Europe), 29 November 1991, p. 74.

27. Regarding the 15 percent shortfall, see *Borba* (26 December 1990), p. 3. Regarding the layoff of 2,700 employees, see Tanjug (3 March 1991), trans. in *FBIS, Daily Report* (Eastern Europe), 4 March 1991, p. 41.

28. Tanjug (4 March 1991), trans. in *FBIS, Daily Report* (Eastern Europe), 5 March 1991, p. 56.

29. Tanjug (5 February 1991), in *FBIS, Daily Report* (Eastern Europe), 6 February 1991, p. 57. Also *Borba* (7 September 1990), p. 3.

30. Tanjug (11 January 1991), trans. in *FBIS, Daily Report* (Eastern Europe), p. 57; and Tanjug (15 March 1991), in *FBIS, Daily Report* (Eastern Europe), 18 March 1991, p. 56.

31. Tanjug (21 February 1991), trans. in *FBIS, Daily Report* (Eastern Europe), 25 February 1991, p. 52.

32. Regarding the Slovenes, see *Frankfurter Allgemeine* (27 December 1990), p. 2; on the Croats, see *Neue Zürcher Zeitung* (22 May 1991), p. 1; on the Albanians, see Belgrade Domestic Service (10 February 1991), trans. in *FBIS, Daily Report* (Eastern Europe), 12 February 1991, p. 59; on the Macedonians, see *Vjesnik* (Zagreb) (13 September 1990), p. 3; and Tanjug (23 February 1991), in *FBIS, Daily Report* (Eastern Europe), 25 February 1991, p. 55.

33. Regarding Serbs in Bosnia, see Radovan Karadžič's interview in *Borba* (12 November 1990), p. 4.

34. See Slobodan Milošević, *Godine raspleta*, 5th ed. (Belgrade: Beogradski izdavačko-grafički zavod, 1989), pp. 264–271 (reprinting Milošević's speech to the seventeenth Session of the CC LCY, Belgrade, October 1988).

35. For a full account of these riots and an analysis of the ethnic problems in Kosovo, see Sabrina Petra Ramet, *Social Currents in Eastern Europe: The Sources and Consequences of the Great Transformation*, 2d ed. (Durham, N.C.: Duke University Press, 1995), Chapter 8.

36. *Borba* (17 August 1990), p. 3.

37. Regarding the Serbs, see Tanjug (10 August 1990), trans. in *FBIS, Daily Report* (Eastern Europe), 13 August 1990, p. 56.

38. *Flaka e Vellazerimit* (Skopje) (27 January 1991), p. 4, trans. in *FBIS, Daily Report* (Eastern Europe), 31 January 1991, p. 57.

39. Tanjug (8 January 1991), in *FBIS, Daily Report* (Eastern Europe), 9 January 1991, p. 43.

40. *Zeri i Rinise*, as summarized in Belgrade Domestic Service (10 February 1991), trans. in *FBIS, Daily Report* (Eastern Europe), 12 February 1991, p. 59.

41. Tanjug (30 October 1990), in *FBIS, Daily Report* (Eastern Europe), 31 October 1990, p. 73.

42. *Borba* (12 November 1990), p. 4.

43. *Borba* (3 August 1990), p. 3; and Tanjug (23 February 1991), in *FBIS, Daily Report* (Eastern Europe), 25 February 1991, p. 55. See also *Vjesnik* (13 September 1990), p. 3.

44. *Borba* (6 March 1991), p. 3, trans. in *FBIS, Daily Report* (Eastern Europe), 8 March 1991, p. 56.

45. *Borba* (1 March 1991), p. 9.

46. In a poll conducted by *Mladina* among 265 people in summer 1990, 5.3 percent favored an independent Istrian state, 22.2 percent wanted to join Italy, 38.6 percent preferred to be transferred to Slovenia, and 18.4 percent preferred to remain in Croatia, but on condition that the region be granted local autonomy. This poll is reported in Milan Andrejevich, "Relations Between Croatia and Slovenia," in RFE/RL Research Institute, *Report on Eastern Europe*, Vol. 2, No. 12 (22 March 1991), p. 35.

47. Tanjug (11 March 1991), trans. in *FBIS, Daily Report* (Eastern Europe), 13 March 1991, p. 71.

48. *Nepszava* (Budapest) (26 February 1991), pp. 1, 2, trans. in *FBIS, Daily Report* (Eastern Europe), 1 March 1991, p. 39.

49. Full text in *Vjesnik* (12 October 1990), p. 5.

50. The republics' stands on these and other issues are compactly summarized in *Vjesnik* (2 February 1991), p. 4, trans. in *FBIS, Daily Report* (Eastern Europe), 12 February 1991, p. 47.

51. "Yugoslavia: The March 1991 Demonstrations in Belgrade," *Helsinki Watch: A Committee of Human Rights Watch* (1 May 1991), pp. 1–2.

52. *The Globe and Mail* (Toronto) (11 April 1991), p. A7; and *Neue Zürcher Zeitung* (12 April 1991), p. 4.

53. *Delo* (Ljubljana) (21 February 1991), p. 3, trans. in *FBIS, Daily Report* (Eastern Europe), 7 March 1991, p. 33.

54. *Neue Zürcher Zeitung* (7–8 April 1991), p. 6.

55. Tanjug (7 April 1991), trans. in *FBIS, Daily Report* (Eastern Europe), 8 April 1991, p. 56.

56. *The Times* (London) (4 May 1991), p. 10.

57. Belgrade Domestic Service (31 March 1991), trans. in *FBIS, Daily Report* (Eastern Europe), 1 April 1991, pp. 49–50; and *Politika* (19 March 1991), p. 9.

58. Tanjug (3 April 1991), in *FBIS, Daily Report* (Eastern Europe), 4 April 1991, p. 25.

59. *Neue Zürcher Zeitung* (3 April 1991), p. 3.

60. Croatian Democracy Project, news release, 13 May 1991.

61. Quoted in ibid.

62. *The Independent* (London) (8 May 1991), p. 1.

63. Croatian Democracy Project, news release, 13 May 1991.

64. *Neue Zürcher Zeitung* (4 May 1991), p. 2, and (5–6 May 1991), p. 1; *The Times* (4 May 1991), p. 6; and *The Independent* (8 May 1991), p. 1.

65. Quoted in *New York Times* (19 May 1991), p. 8.

66. *Vjesnik* (17 April 1991), p. 4.

67. *Süddeutsche Zeitung* (Munich) (25–26 May 1991), p. 5.

68. Reported in *Neue Zürcher Zeitung* (29 May 1991), p. 5.

69. *Neue Zürcher Zeitung* (15 June 1991), p. 2.

70. *Daily Telegraph* (8 May 1991), p. 8.

71. *Neue Zürcher Zeitung* (4 June 1991), p. 2; and *Daily Telegraph* (8 April 1991), p. 11.

72. It also confirmed the accuracy of both early warnings of the risk of gravitation toward civil war (as in Pedro Ramet, "Yugoslavia and the Threat of Internal and External Discontents," *Orbis*, Vol. 28, No. 1 [spring 1984], p. 114) and forecasts on the eve of the war itself (as in Sabrina P. Ramet, "The Breakup of Yugoslavia," *Global Affairs*, Vol. 6, No. 2 [spring 1991], p. 97).

73. Regarding one such attempt, see *Politika—International Weekly* (Belgrade) (3–16 August 1991), p. 2.

74. Tanjug (27 May 1991), trans. in *FBIS, Daily Report* (Eastern Europe), 29 May 1991, p. 41.

75. Tanjug (29 May 1991), in *FBIS, Daily Report* (Eastern Europe), 30 May 1991, p. 25.

76. *Neue Zürcher Zeitung* (2 July 1991), p. 1.

77. *Neue Zürcher Zeitung* (5 July 1991), p. 5.

78. Miša Milošević, official representative of Serbs in Slavonia, Baranja, and western Srem, as quoted in *Politika* (Belgrade) (9 October 1991), p. 1.

79. *Neue Zürcher Zeitung* (10–11 August 1991), p. 7, and (22 August 1991), p. 2.

80. *Danas* (16 July 1991), p. 9.

81. *New York Times* (18 October 1991), p. A4.

82. Quoted in *New York Times* (8 September 1991), p. 6.

83. *New York Times* (16 January 1992), p. 1.

84. Regarding Serbian proposals, see *Neue Zürcher Zeitung* (27 July 1991), p. 3, and (14 August 1991), p. 2.

85. *Politika* (10 August 1991), p. 1.

86. *Politika* (14 August 1991), p. 1.

87. *Politika* (13 August 1991), p. 1.

88. *Politika* (14 August 1991), p. 1.

89. Reprinted in *Politika* (17 August 1991), p. 10.

90. *Süddeutsche Zeitung* (26–27 October 1991), p. 6.

91. Radio Slovenia Network (Ljubljana), 15 July 1991, trans. in *FBIS, Daily Report* (Eastern Europe), 15 July 1991, p. 35.

92. *Financial Times* (13 September 1991), p. 2; confirmed in *New York Times* (13 October 1991), p. 6.

93. *New York Times* (13 October 1991), p. 6.

94. Quoted in ibid.

95. *New York Times* (12 September 1991), p. A3.

96. See *Neue Zürcher Zeitung* (7 August 1991), p. 17.

97. *Neue Zürcher Zeitung* (27 September 1991), p. A3.

98. *Financial Times* (8 November 1991), p. 2.

99. For details, see Sabrina P. Ramet, *Nationalism and Federalism in Yugoslavia, 1962–1991*, 2d ed. (Bloomington: Indiana University Press, 1992), pp. 262–265.

100. Quoted in Michael Dobbs, "Serbian Leader Looks Vulnerable in the Long Term," *Washington Post*, reprinted in *Manchester Guardian Weekly* (29 September 1991), p. 18.

101. Quoted in ibid.

102. Ibid.

PART TWO

---- ◆ ----

Culture and Society

CHAPTER FOUR

◆

The Press

IN THE YEARS AFTER TITO died (that is, after May 1980), the Yugoslav press figured as a fairly precise barometer of the broader institutional and political context. Like Yugoslavia itself, the press was dramatically decentralized, and all efforts to achieve a "unified information system" proved unavailing. Like Yugoslavia itself, the press experienced a period of "release" after the death of Tito; during this period, in the absence of the helmsman, the press shared in the new, general exploration of new paths, in particular in launching the general discussion of the Goli Otok prison camp.[1] As in the case of the Yugoslav system more broadly, subsequent attempts (1983–1985) to rein in the press by and large failed[2]—and, indeed, throughout much of the 1980s the press continued to repeat the dissatisfaction of responsible agencies with its work. Like Yugoslavia itself, the press reflected the more general chaos that afflicted Yugoslavia on both the interrepublican and intrarepublican level and that resulted in a measure of at first unintended liberalization. As journalists repeatedly discovered in Communist Yugoslavia, if it proved impossible to publish something in one periodical outlet, regardless of the reason, it might be a simple matter to get it published in a different periodical: the youth press has often provided this kind of service as an "alternative" outlet; other times it was a matter of crossing interrepublican borders and taking one's story to a periodical based in another federal unit.

In 1962, there were some 1,949 newspapers and magazines being published in Yugoslavia. This figure rose to 2,080 in 1975 and reached 3,020 in 1981. In 1987, there were 3,063 newspapers and magazines being published in Yugoslavia of which 27 were daily newspapers. Their total circulation came to about 2.7 million copies.[3] The Yugoslav National Army accounted for 22 of these periodicals,[4] while religious organizations published some 200 newspapers and other periodicals of a religious nature.[5] In 1962, there were some 3,300 professional journalists working in Yugoslavia. This figure rose to 4,700 in 1975 and 11,000 in 1981. As of 1987, there were some 202 radio stations in Yugoslavia and television centers in all the republics and provinces.

THE PURPOSE OF THE PRESS
AND THE APPLICATION OF CENSORSHIP

The Titoists, like Communists elsewhere, conceived of the press explicitly in terms of underpinning the system. "The purpose of the social system of information," said a 1987 source, "is to supply data and information indispensable for self-management and delegate decision-making at all levels."[6] Objectivity was explicitly scorned as a "bourgeois" notion. Journalists, rather, were instructed to serve as "a meaningful subject force in society" and to be "decisive" in the struggle "against exploitative consciousness and counterrevolutionary ideology."[7] The Titoist system of controlling editorial appointments and weeding out journalists who became too independent in their thinking reflected this assigned purpose.

It has often been said that Yugoslavia, unlike the other Communist countries of Eastern Europe, did not have a censorship *office*. Strictly speaking, this was true—at least formally. But there were various levels and ways in which censorship *activity* was carried on and in which political authorities attempted to assure that the general contents of publications accorded with what they considered acceptable. To an outside observer this may seem incomprehensible in view of the intense polemics that frequently raged in the Yugoslav press, in view of the repeatedly demonstrated ability of the Catholic weekly, *Glas koncila,* to defend itself against mudslinging throughout the Communist era, and in view of the "alternative outlet" syndrome. The explanation of this complexity is to be sought in three sources. First, as previously mentioned, the press lay within the jurisdiction of republican authorities, hence the evolution of Yugoslavia after 1963 into a set of eight often warring republican/provincial power centers was accompanied, necessarily, by a republicanization of the press. Second, even within a single republic, the authorities always appreciated that the press had to be diverse if it was to operate effectively and hence that the youth press, the women's press, even the pornographic press had to have sphere-specific areas of leeway if they were to reach their audiences and function effectively. Third, the Communist authorities simply did not have the resources or the will to assert bloc-style control (and indeed, the supervisors of the youth press were often sympathetic to the coverage of that press).

During the era of communism (roughly speaking, to the end of 1989), every publisher was required by law to send copies of the galley proofs to the Office of the State Prosecutor before a given issue of a periodical was actually published. This requirement applied to every periodical published in Yugoslavia regardless of its sponsorship, content or intended audience.[8]

The Prosecutor's Office was understaffed, however, and read comparatively little of the voluminous material that crossed its desk: amateur radio magazines, fashion magazines, sports magazines, and so forth were apt to be ignored, for instance, with greater attention paid to the mainline secular press (*Borba, Politika, Vjesnik,* etc.) and secondarily to the religious press. Partly for that reason there were few stories of prepublication censorship in late-Titoist Yugoslavia.[9] More typically, if the authorities found something amiss, the issue in question had not only been printed but also distributed—and the article in question would no doubt have been read by many. The authorities then had to reckon with the fact that suppression of the issue would inevitably heighten public interest in the issue. The editor of the Serbian Orthodox Church newspaper, *Pravoslavlje,* recounted his experiences with the authorities:

> Our newspaper has been banned three times in all, three times over a span of twenty years. But the bad thing when they ban an issue is that they come to your office and they demand the addresses of all the subscribers and you must give all the addresses, and then they go to the churches and confiscate the unsold issues. And then, if they want to do so, they go to the subscribers and demand to have the issue surrendered. It's dreadful. The previous editor told me they received letters from old people saying please don't send the newspaper to us any more because the police came late in the night and said, "You received an 'enemy' newspaper. Give it to us." So in a way it is better if an issue is banned before distribution.[10]

A ban could be issued by either federal or republican authorities, the latter exercising this prerogative more rarely than the former. A republican ban applied only within the borders of the republic, so that, for instance, if Croatian authorities were to ban an issue of *Mladost,* the very same issue could be freely and openly sold in Serbia, Bosnia, and elsewhere in Yugoslavia. Both the federal and republican bans could be challenged in court, and from time to time this resulted in a ban being overturned.

The State Prosecutor's Office was concerned with the day-to-day routine and had its eyes fixed, as it were, on the trees rather than on the forest. Other review agencies were responsible for monitoring the overall performance of the press, namely, the Commission for Ideological Work and the Commission for Political-Propaganda Activity in Information, both attached to the Central Committee of the League of Communists of Yugoslavia (LCY), the Section for Information and Public Opinion of the Socialist Alliance of Working People of Yugoslavia (SAWPY), the Committee for Press, Radio and Television of the CC SAWPY, and republican branches of these bodies. These bodies were required to issue annual reports on the functioning of the press.[11] These reports, judging from reports in the press itself, tended to dwell on perceived shortcomings and problems.[12] In addition, the Association of Journalists of each given federal unit periodically reviewed the performance of its members.[13]

The State Secretariat for Information was the body authorized to announce news bans, but in practice news bans in socialist Yugoslavia were announced by others as well. In February 1986, for instance, the president of the Federal Assembly told the sixty Yugoslav journalists accredited to cover the Assembly's deliberations that they were not to write about what irate Serbs from Kosovo were saying that day in the Assembly. But since this ban was illegal and since it affected one of the most burning issues of the day, namely, Serb–Albanian tensions in the province of Kosovo, journalists protested, some wrote sharp commentaries about the news "embargo," and within a few days several publications printed the substance of the meeting, the embargo notwithstanding.[14] Journalist Mihailo Rasić voiced the sentiment of many in the media in describing that ban as a "semi-private action" imposed without proper authority.[15]

Authorities repeatedly resorted to news bans in the late 1980s. Perhaps the most controversial was the abortive attempt to limit news coverage of the April 1981 riots in Kosovo to official communiques prepared by the government.[16] In another instance of an unsuccessful ban, authorities at first tried to prevent reportage of the 10 March 1986 session of the CC of the Croatian party, at which Milka Planinc and Jure Bilić failed to be nominated to represent Croatia in the Presidium of the CC LCY. Similarly, in October 1985, Yugoslav newspapers were not allowed to report that Palestinian terrorist Abu Abbas was in Belgrade,[17] while the Yugoslav press became much more reticent in the late 1980s than it had been earlier in discussing Yugoslavia's foreign debt. Writing in the pages of the party weekly, *Komunist,* Zdravko Leković complained in June 1987 that one could legitimately speak of "a censorship of information in a broad sense," adding that information about events in Kosovo was still being blocked and that the press had been unable to obtain basic statistics about many investments even though they were *not* secret.[18] There were other sundry specific proscriptions, as well as limits in the spheres of foreign policy, national mythology, religious policy, and nationalities policy,[19] though these limits changed somewhat over time and were, in any case, periodically tested by daring editors.

In addition to the political authorities themselves, the army also occasionally expressed its opinion about coverage of its activities in the press. In March 1985, for instance, the Ljubljana Army District Command prepared an analysis of the public information media in Slovenia and, while generally satisfied with the treatment it had been accorded in the press, found several articles in the Slovenian youth press "unacceptable and extremely harmful . . . because they present a distorted picture of life and work in the

Yugoslav National Army. The publishing of such texts," the statement continued, "cannot be permitted any longer."[20]

In general, when one abstracts the situation to a "global" level, authorities tended to believe that the press's basic assignment was to strengthen the values of socialist self-management and to support the policies of the LCY, assisting the politicians in finding and implementing "necessary solutions."[21] In September 1985, *Komunist,* the organ of the LCY, described itself as aspiring "to be the class weapon of the League of Communists [and] to contribute . . . to the strengthening of the unity in action and thought of the League of Communists."[22] Accordingly, in the Communist era, Yugoslav newspapers were apt to be criticized for failing to support (or even for being at variance with) party policy, for confronting the public with differing analyses, for "confusing" the public, for overemphasis of negative phenomena in society, for loss of "seriousness," even for "neutrality" in the treatment of burning social issues.[23] Yugoslavia's 11,000 journalists—90 percent of whom were party members as of 1987[24]—were expected, during the Communist era, to take their cues from the party. When they displayed too much independence, they were apt to be criticized for setting themselves up as independent judges of society or as "some kind of arbiter or conscience of society."[25] This, however, led to some strange dilemmas with circumspection and uncertainty leading to a situation where, as one Yugoslav journalist put it, "many journalists, and the younger ones in particular, find it difficult to decide what their position is due to the fact that the LC is often late in taking necessary actions."[26]

NATIONALISM AND THE REPUBLICANIZATION OF THE PRESS

The federalization of the Yugoslav political system was intended to defuse nationalism by granting nationality-based federal units wide-ranging autonomy. Instead of defusing nationalism, however, federalization transformed the nationalities factor by shifting the center of gravity from the federal government to the republican governments and by arming those governments with the powers to seek "national" objectives (e.g., Serbian and Montenegrin interest in the construction of the now-completed Belgrade–Bar railway).

In the years since Tito died, it became increasingly evident that the nationalities factor was far from being solved. In the initial months after the April 1981 riots, the Albanian-language press in Kosovo was subjected to stiff criticism, and some editors were replaced. Already in mid-June 1981, an extraordinary session of the Association of Kosovo Journalists was convened in order to identify shortcomings that needed to be corrected. Yet, two years later, the Provincial Committee for Information found that reportage in the province's Albanian-language daily, *Rilindja,* differed rather substantially from what was offered in the local Serbo-Croatian daily, *Jedinstvo.* Subsequently, a session of the Information Commission of the LCY noted, in November 1987, that while *Jedinstvo* reported evidence of discrimination against Serbo-Croatian, reported that the emigration of Slavs from the province was rising, and adhered to the official line, *Rilindja* discounted any discrimination, reported that outmigration was declining, and talked of "unacceptable" demands from Serbs and Montenegrins.[27] In late 1985, Kosovo's journalists were still being told to counter "counterrevolutionary ideologies and action" and to find ways to discourage the emigration of Serbs and Montenegrins from the province.[28] Later, in August 1986, *Rilindja* was said to be marred by "superficiality, one-sidedness, lack of commitment, and . . . an excessive insistence on national elements that very often leads to the very brink of nationalism."[29] *Jedinstvo* was simultaneously charged with having engaged in "masquerades" designed to obscure the position of the journalist and the paper.[30]

The sector for public information of the Republic Committee for Information of SR Serbia carried out an analysis of the provincial press of Kosovo and Vojvodina, covering the period 14 September 1987 to 20 January 1988, and examining the following papers: *Dnevnik, Magyar Szó,* and *Stav* from Vojvodina, and *Jedinstvo* and *Rilindja* from Kosovo. The study found that the Hungarian-language *Magyar Szó* devoted more space than did the Serbo-Croatian language *Dnevnik* to commentary on the proposed constitutional changes, especially where measures affecting the position of the Hungarian minority were concerned. Of the three Vojvodinan papers, *Stav,* the organ of the provincial youth organization, was the most openly and explicitly critical of the proposed changes. In Kosovo, there were more fundamental differences in coverage: the Albanian-language daily, *Rilindja,* fiercely criticized the proposed changes, whereas the Serbo-Croatian daily, *Jedinstvo,* assumed a noncommittal posture.[31] Moreover, *Rilindja's* staff criticized the press from other republics for "one-sidedness" in their treatment of Kosovo.[32]

The chief culprit among these "other republics" was surely Serbia, whose press was criticized for "petit-bourgeois liberalism and nationalism" during a session of the Presidium of the CC LC Serbia in February 1983. Momčilo Baljak, who presented the opening report at that session, seemed particularly upset that "no editorial office is willing to criticize the texts to be found in the book, *Stvarno i moguće* [The Real and the Possible], by Dobrica Ćosić, which has just been published by Otokar Keršovani, the Rijeka publishing house. These texts are permeated with anxiety for the Serbian people, and in essence they reflect the socio-socialist and unitarist concept of our society."[33] Two months later, Dragoljub Trailović resigned his post as chief editor of the influential Belgrade daily, *Politika,* amid charges of

Serbian nationalism and complaints that he had failed to respond appropriately to the staging of a play inspired by Greater Serbian nationalist con-
cepts.[34]

This did not settle matters, however, and the same issue came up for discussion in September 1987, when Ivan Stojanović, director of the Politika
publishing house, and Živana Olbina, a member of *Politika's* editorial staff,
created a stir by accusing the newspaper of indulging in a nationalist obsession with Kosovo and of sensationalizing nationalist causes.[35] At the end
of a stormy session at which the staff by and large rejected her charge that
Politika was sliding into "anticommunism," Olbina resigned from the council. The following month Stojanović was himself forced to resign amid
charges that he had failed to exercise proper control over the periodicals
being published by Politika publishers. The result, as his critics pointed out,
was that the periodicals being published by Politika frequently disagreed
among themselves about facts or the interpretations of facts, even at times
to the point of conducting polemics with each other.[36]

In late 1987, after seizing power in Serbia, Milošević moved to assert his
control of the Serbian press. He replaced the editors of publications at
Belgrade's Politika publishing house, and a number of good writers were
sent off to glorious exile as foreign correspondents. In this way, Milošević
assured himself of subservience and unanimity of viewpoint on the part of
the Serbian press. Interestingly enough, the editor-in-chief of *Politika* had
never been a political appointee until Milošević's arrival.[37] Belgrade's Borba
publishing house, by contrast, which publishes the daily papers *Borba* and
Večernje novosti, remained independent because all the Yugoslav republics
enjoyed influence in its operation.

Slovenia similarly produced controversy in this area. In February 1987
the cultural monthly, *Nova revija,* brought out its issue no. 57, devoted entirely to the Slovenian national question. The contributors to this issue, who
included some of the leading Slovenian intellectuals, suggested that
Slovenia had suffered by its incorporation into Yugoslavia, described the
so-called National Liberation Struggle as a civil war punctuated by a struggle for power, and argued that the Communist-controlled Anti-Fascist
Council of 1943 had no legitimate basis for behaving as a government.[38]
One of the contributors—Tine Hribar, in his article, "Slovenian
Statehood"—called the Socialist Republic of Slovenia an inadequate reflec-
tion of Slovenian sovereignty, while another writer—Alenka Goljevšček—
outlined a program of virtual independence for Slovenia in which the
Slovenian government would dispose of its own armed forces.[39]

Jože Smole, president of the Republic Conference of SAWP Slovenia,
called the views expressed in that issue "unacceptable."[40] The editor of
Nova revija was quickly fired. And various party bodies throughout
Slovenia issued sharp condemnations of the journal.[41] The original 3,500

copies of the issue quickly sold out, but *Književne novine* in Belgrade soon put out a special issue, setting forth all the essentials of the controversial issue, only now in Serbo-Croatian translation. The issue became a *cause célèbre*. Politicians and other public figures throughout Yugoslavia spoke out against *Nova revija,* and there was talk of banning the issue. In March 1987, the executive council of the journal met and lent its full support to the editorial board of *Nova revija,* while the journal's new editor underlined that he endorsed the controversial issue and intended to assert continuity in editorial policy. Ultimately, the Slovenian public prosecutor engaged in polemics with the federal prosecutor over the issue, and the journal found enough backers within the Slovenian leadership to ride out the storm.[42]

Slovenia, Serbia, and Kosovo were the areas where nationalism in the press became the most controversial, but they were not the only ones. In October 1986, for instance, the Macedonian party CC expressed discontent with its local press, finding that certain papers were giving undue attention to local troubles. CC member Metodi Petrovski mentioned, in particular, excessive coverage by Macedonian media of a brawl between Albanian and Macedonian youth. He urged more even reporting of news from other Yugoslav republics.[43]

Despite the old Titoist formula, according to which party spokespersons should restrict themselves to criticizing nationalist phenomena in their own republics, the very opposite became the case and the various newspapers preferred to criticize nationalist excesses of *other* nationality groups.[44]

Explicit nationalism was not the only symptom of the republicanization of the press, however. There was a kind of implicit nationalism, better described as *localism,* which some papers had been trying hard to steer clear of. *Borba* had long taken particular pains to assure the "all-Yugoslav" character of its coverage,[45] and it may well have been the only genuine *Yugoslav* newspaper among the major dailies. In the late 1980s, *Vjesnik* started looking beyond its Croatian horizons and, for a time, aspired to a countrywide audience.[46] This phase was short-lived, however, and even before 1990, *Vjesnik* gave up this aspiration. *Politika,* of course, looked back with pride to its long tradition as an independent paper and, at least until Milošević's seizure of power and subjugation of the Politika Publishing House, liked to think of itself as a paper for all Yugoslavia; realistically speaking, its readership has always been limited to Serbs and Montenegrins, however, since most Croats do not bother to learn the Cyrillic alphabet.[47]

A NEW LAW ON THE PRESS

Yugoslavs began talking about a new law concerning the press and public information in early 1979,[48] but due to the amount of controversy generated, it was not until May 1985 that the law was finally adopted. The chief purpose of the new legislation, as tirelessly pointed out in the press itself, was to produce greater uniformity in the press across republican boundaries. Beyond that, the law was also intended to strengthen the founding agencies' control over their organs, whether the agency concerned was one of SAWPY's branches, the LCY, or a sociocultural organization.[49] Shortly after the passage of the new law, *Komunist* spoke optimistically of "the fact that with this law a unified regime for public information for all of Yugoslavia has been introduced."[50] This optimism proved illusory. Even where *Komunist* itself was concerned, there was not much unity among its various local editions. Indeed, *Mladost,* the magazine published by the Socialist Youth Federation, pointed out that nothing had changed almost a year and a half later. On the contrary, as *Mladost* observed, "In the eight editions of *Komunist,* whose mastheads differ only in reflecting the republic or provincial names, the Yugoslav portion has been melting away more and more, and has almost disappeared, because republic and provincial editorial boards have been carrying more and more articles in accordance with their republic and provincial top leaders' attitudes."[51] And again, if the law had really succeeded in creating a "unified information system," it should have been possible to avoid the dispute of December 1986. On that occasion, the Slovenian SAWP organization criticized the Croatian SAWP organization for allowing *Vjesnik* to publish a commentary that was alleged to be injurious to the interests of the Slovene minority community in Italy as well as to wider Slovenian interests.[52]

Despite the shortcomings of the new law, its passage gave rise to talk of "the importance of coordinating the republican and provincial information media laws with the federal ones."[53] Going one step further, and in harmony with more general aspirations in S. R. Serbia to erode some of the autonomy enjoyed by the autonomous provinces of Kosovo and Vojvodina (both administratively parts of S. R. Serbia), the Serbian Assembly proposed in 1987 that the two provinces agree to the passage of a unified republican law on public information. In effect, the proposal asked the provinces to decline to pass their own information laws and merely to accept the extension of the Serbian law into the areas of their jurisdiction. A few months later the Serbian League of Journalists proposed to revise the statute of the Yugoslav League of Journalists to give the provincial associations lesser representation in the presiding council of the Yugoslav organization. Not surprisingly, both provinces rejected these initiatives, and polemics ensued.[54]

By 1988–1989, there was growing consensus among Yugoslav journalists that the 1985 Law on Press and Information was already obsolete. For one thing, Yugoslav appeals courts were repeatedly overturning the temporary ban of specific papers. In March 1988, for example, a court ruled that there was no cause to ban an issue of *Mladina,* the youth paper of Slovenia. The

issue in question had included an article to the effect that Yugoslavia's leaders were responsible for leading the country into "hopeless crisis." The
court, however, ruled that the article in question "contained no untrue information which could disturb the public."[55] Later, in August 1988, a decision by the Split public prosecutor to ban an issue of *Omladinska Iskra,* for
having published the text of a speech by Milovan Djilas at a meeting in
Maribor, was overturned by the Supreme Court of Croatia.[56] And that same
month the Split District Court overturned a ban of the August 28 issue of
Nedjeljna Dalmacija, which the public prosecutor had claimed had "hostile" content.[57]

Yugoslav journalists were bridling at the rein. Already in October 1988,
at its annual conference, the Union of Yugoslav Journalists "called for an
end to the 'informal marriage' of political structures and mass media and
demanded a greater measure of independence for their profession."[58] "The
existing press law is obsolete and needs to be revised completely," a prominent Slovenian journalist told me in 1989. "According to the letter of the
law, we could be charged with infringements every day. But we just go
ahead and publish what we want, and take our chances."[59] In particular,
federal law included an article (No. 139), relating to high treason, formulated so vaguely that people could be—and in the past had been—prose-
cuted for bad intentions. Another grievance had to do with the appointment of editors. Many prominent Yugoslav papers were, until the late
1980s, the organs of the Socialist Alliance of Working People—including
Borba, Vjesnik, and *Delo*—which meant that the editor-in-chief, the managing editor, and the director were all appointed by the Alliance rather than
being selected by the journalists themselves (as the journalists preferred).

THE YOUTH PRESS

Various bits of evidence suggest that in certain concrete ways (e.g., coverage of the rock group Laibach) the party gave the youth press more latitude than was enjoyed by the mainline daily press. At the same time, the
recurrent testing of the limits by the youth press and the recurrent impulses,
on the part of the authorities, to ban specific issues suggest that part of this
relatively greater latitude should be attributed to the greater daring and
even recklessness of some journalists and editors in publications intended
for young people.[60]

The most visible youth periodicals in Yugoslavia in the late 1980s were
Mladina and *Katedra* from Slovenia, *Mladost* and *Studentski list* from
Croatia, *NON, Student,* and *Vidik* from Serbia, and *Naši dani* and *Valter*
from Bosnia. Of these, *Mladina* was probably the most controversial. I
propose to throw some light on the youth press by examining the case of
Mladina in some detail.

Mladina was long officially the organ of the Socialist Youth Organization of Slovenia, which, in theory, picked the editor. In practice, the editorial board had chosen the editor for quite some time, subject (until about 1990) to the approval of the now defunct youth organization. The editorial staff clashed with the authorities over editorial policy throughout the 1970s, but even when the authorities intervened more directly in the selection of the editor, *Mladina* remained defiantly independent. In fact, *Mladina* and Ljubljana's Radio Student played an important role in opening up the discussion of previously taboo subjects (such as political prisoners) in the early 1980s.[61] A staff member of *Mladina* recalls that period: "The first reaction of the authorities was to ban specific issues of *Mladina*. Then they would call the people of Radio Student to party headquarters and they told us that what we were doing was not right. They threatened to kick us out of the party. But the party organization in Radio Student stood up for its people and defended us."[62] Democratic centralism, thus, had proven fictitious.

In late 1984 the Yugoslav authorities decided to put half a dozen Serbian intellectuals on trial for "dissent." *Mladina*[63] defended them, resulting in a boom for *Mladina's* circulation, which rose from 10,000 when the trial began to 18,000 by the time the trial was over, climbing subsequently to 28,000 by mid-1987. In October 1985, *Mladina* published a long interview with Vladimir Šeks, a lawyer from Osijek. Before taking up duties as a lawyer, Šeks had been a public prosecutor, and in this capacity he had found out (in 1981) that the security police were routinely opening all foreign correspondence coming into Osijek. He decided to take the police to court but as a result immediately lost his job and was himself taken to court on charges of Croatian nationalism. Šeks did not serve any time then, but after serving as the defense lawyer for the six Serbian intellectuals in 1984 the earlier sentence was revived and Šeks went to prison for six months.[64] His interview with *Mladina* was conducted shortly after his release from prison.

Slovenian authorities were dismayed and banned the issue. But the *Mladina* staff took the case to the Supreme Court of Slovenia, which overturned the ban, allowed *Mladina* to re-release the issue, certain that the abortive ban could only have excited wide interest in the issue. This stimulated a certain self-confidence among the staff of *Mladina,* who took to describing the incident as the "last" time the magazine was banned. In late July 1987, however, the public prosecutor in Ljubljana imposed a temporary ban on a double issue scheduled for release by *Mladina*.[65]

Mladina started to play tricks on the authorities. Well aware that the galley proofs would be checked "higher up," the staff on one occasion prepared a dirty poem about Tito without intending to publish it. When the magazine came out, the police were ready with an order to ban it, but the poem was not in the magazine.

The year 1986 brought new confrontations. In February, *Mladina* was preparing to publish an article criticizing Prime Minister Branko Mikulić for political trials in his native Bosnia. The article suggested that his record disqualified him as prime minister. The editorial staff was abruptly summoned before the Central Committee of the Slovenian party and threatened with imprisonment unless the article was withdrawn. The staff caved in, but the page on which the article had been scheduled to appear was left blank. Later, the article was published in the youth newspaper from Maribor, *Katedra*.[66]

The following month, *Mladina* featured an article about the elections, speculating that the Communist Party would "probably" win and describing them as "elections of the delegates of delegates of delegates of delegates." Other satirical articles followed. By late summer, Pavel Car, the Slovenian public prosecutor, was openly complaining of

> a mass sowing of bitterness, pessimism, carping, and political insinuations, that has been perpetrated by the press, radio and television, publishing houses, various tribunes, and round-table conferences . . . that "craftily walk on the brink of the criminal zones." . . . In Car's words, the specific culprits include three Slovenian newspapers, *Mladina, Nova revija,* and *Katedra,* and in addition to them the Commission for the Protection of Thought and Writing of the Writers Association of Slovenia.[67]

The editors of *Mladina, Katedra,* and *Nova revija* joined the chairman of the Slovenian Commission for the Protection of Thought and Writing and the president of the Slovenian Writers' Association in signing a letter protesting Car's statements.[68] But Car refused to retract anything.[69]

Katedra, the organ of the students of the University of Maribor, has been increasingly visible since the mid-1980s and showed itself repeatedly ready to take risks. In January 1987, for instance, the newspaper published an interview with Serbian intellectual Kosta Čavoški, coauthor of an important study of the Yugoslav Communist Party's consolidation of its power monopoly in the late 1940s.[70] In March the paper published an interview with Yugoslav dissident Milovan Djilas: the interview had originally been scheduled to appear in *Mladina,* but when authorities prevented *Mladina* from publishing it, the text was passed on to *Katedra*. It was the first time Djilas had been heard in his own country since his disgrace in 1954.[71] When *Katedra* returned less than three months later with an open letter from Serbian nationalist Vojislav Šešelj, said to "insult the representatives of the socio-political life of our country," authorities banned the issue.[72] Yet when *Mladina* criticized Defense Minister Branko Mamula in February 1988 for his involvement in an arms sale to Ethiopia and for assigning a group of soldiers (among them Slovenes) to help build a villa for his use in Opatija, the federal prosecutor instructed the Slovenian prosecutor to initiate legal proceedings against *Mladina's* editor, Franci Zavrl. Among other things, *Mladina* had called Mamula a "merchant of death." But the Slovenian prosecutor decided to arraign Zavrl not on the charge suggested by Belgrade—of "offending the honor of Yugoslavia and of its army"—but on the minor charge of personal defamation, which carried a maximum penalty of three months in prison or a fine.[73]

Two months later, *Mladina* published materials showing that the army was preparing a plan to arrest politically "undesirable" figures (including journalists) in Slovenia and quash the movement for democratization. A Slovenian human rights publication records, "At the meeting of the [Yugoslav] Military Council, the Commander of Ljubljana Army Region is given the duty to come to an agreement with the Slovene Ministry for Internal Affairs, concerning security measures in Slovenia on the basis of the opinions of the Military Council, [to] begin criminal prosecution of the writers of some of the army about the army, and [to] order imprisonments . . . if, as a result, there was public unrest."[74] Orders were sent to stop publication of the offending issue, and three journalists and one enlisted man were put on trial. The trial electrified the Slovenian public and directly contributed to the proliferation of independent committees and parties in Slovenia.[75]

Mladina remained in the forefront of the movement for democratization, publishing the results of a poll in December 1988 showing that 64 percent of Slovenes considered it necessary to introduce a multiparty system and that in free elections the Communists would obtain only 7.3 percent of the vote (as compared with 26.9 percent for the social democrats, 18.7 percent for the Christian Democrats, and 14.2 percent for the Greens).[76]

Among other youth publications, the Serbian youth-oriented publications *Student* and *Vidik* likewise repeatedly came under critical scrutiny, were sometimes chastened for lapsing into "anti-Marxist" views,[77] and from time to time had their wrists slapped—for example, in late September 1987, when the deputy editor and five members of the editorial staff of *Student* were forced to resign.[78] There were also complaints in 1986 about "bourgeois" orientations in Croatia's youth press,[79] while the Albanian-language organ of the Kosovo Socialist Youth Federation, *Zeri i Rinise,* was criticized that same year for failing to take a forceful line against Albanian nationalism and irredentism.[80]

Finally, a brief mention of the Sarajevo weekly magazine, *Naši dani,* is warranted. Already by 1988 *Naši dani* was being praised as the vanguard of a movement to liberalize the Bosnian press.[81] This magazine made a decisive contribution to the history of Yugoslav journalism with its 3 March 1989 issue, in which it ran an article headlined "Journalism Is a Dangerous Profession." In particular, the article outlined the persecutions suffered by courageous journalists, such as Belgrade journalist Milovan Brkić (arrested and charged some 200 times) and Sisak journalist Ratko Dmitrović (jailed for three months because he dared to write an article critical of a local party baron).[82] Needless to say, this issue of *Naši dani,* like others before and after, was quickly banned.

LIFE OF A JOURNALIST

A journalist's life, in Yugoslavia, was difficult—or as Austrians are supposed to be fond of saying, "hopeless but not serious." The "average" Yugoslav journalist was male, forty years old (as of 1989) and had less than twenty years to live—(54 percent of Yugoslav journalists died before reaching retirement age). He had one child but was either divorced or about to be divorced. He smoked forty cheap cigarettes a day, drank brandy, suffered from recurrent stomachaches, rented his apartment, and did not own his own car. Eighty-one percent of journalists surveyed in 1989 were members of the League of Communists, and 65 percent had a university degree.[83] The average journalist's monthly salary was about $150–200. In Montenegro, 60 percent of journalists in Radio-Television Titograd and 50 percent of the journalists writing for *Pobjeda* did not own their own apartments in 1983.[84] In Slovenia, journalists were complaining that their incomes were low and their living standards in decline.[85] Stress was a constant occupational hazard[86]

Journalists were cautioned to write "responsibly." If they were thought to have failed in this task, they could be subject to prosecution. But when journalists were fired not through their own fault they were assured financial sustenance from the official "solidarity fund" of the journalists' association. In the course of 1986, a group of Serbian journalists took the initiative in setting up an independent solidarity fund—the implication being that they could not rely on the official fund. Authorities quickly declared that the independent fund was "unnecessary" and that its real purpose was to organize a forum for political opposition. At least two journalists were expelled from the (Vojvodina) Journalists' Federation because of their affiliation with the independent solidarity fund.[87] But before the end of the year, a similar solidarity fund was set up in Slovenia.

About the same time, Slovenian journalists took an initiative that betrayed their desire for ideological latitude. Specifically, in October 1986, the Slovenian Journalists' Association unanimously adopted a resolution to drop from its statutes a clause requiring members to be "consciously loyal to the ideas of Marxism-Leninism" and promised to seek "even more extensive changes to the Yugoslav journalists' charter."[88] *Delo,* the Slovenian daily, carried an article defending the proposal that the affirmation of loyalty to Marxism-Leninism be dropped from the Yugoslav Journalists' Charter, while the Bosnian daily, *Oslobodjenje,* criticized the proposal. The latter in its unattributed commentary, was certainly hostile to the Slovene proposal and argued that "what is obviously offered and wished [for] is that our press should de jure open itself to all possible ideological and political orientations and in fact legalize the breakthrough of authors of largely rightist or falsely leftist positions, a breakthrough that has been virtually realized in some newspapers."[89] The subject was also taken up in *Politika*. But eventually, with the disintegration of Yugoslavia, the entire question became moot.

A CRITICAL PRESS

The Yugoslav press was famous for being critical. But, of course, it was critical in different ways. One may perhaps, distinguish between criticism that was directed "inward" and criticism that was directed "outward." By the former, I mean criticism of the government (in the Communist era) or the party, or of Communist Party policies, or of persons in the political establishment, or investigative reporting that probes issues of the day. By the latter, I shall mean criticism directed specifically against nonparty sectors of society, such as rock musicians, dissidents, and religious institutions.

Inward criticism has always been, of course, the more problematical from the authorities' point of view. The Communists, in particular, were well aware that a critical/investigative approach contributed to making a publication interesting and that in the absence of such an approach a publication could adhere to party formulae and end up being boring and ineffective. The party organ *Komunist,* as was repeatedly admitted, suffered from this problem, and its influence as of 1987 was correspondingly described as "minimal."[90] In 1989, publication of *Komunist* was terminated. Still, it is understandable that those being criticized took umbrage at the fact: Tomislav Bardin, a delegate to the Serbian Assembly, objected when *Duga* published an article critical of that body's discussion of language equality in Kosovo[91]; the veterans' organization in Zagreb raised a small clamor about how it was being portrayed in *Danas, Polet, NIN,* and *Politika;*[92] even where the 1987 Agrokomerc scandal is concerned, there were polemics about press coverage.[93]

NIN was in the forefront of investigative journalism in the early 1980s. Later, the biweekly Belgrade feature magazine, *Duga,* with its feisty interviews, became a magazine to watch. Illustrative of *Duga's* bold journalism was an interview with Miso Pavičević, a member of the Council of the Federation, published in October 1985. In this interview, Pavičević spoke of the older (partisan) generation "losing its way" and noted that the present crisis in Yugoslavia could only be described as the result of "a process which has been going on for over a decade and a half." By this he meant above all the process of decentralization, which had contributed to satisfying the autonomist aspirations among Yugoslavia's diverse nationality groups. The result, for Pavičević, was that Yugoslav policymaking was frequently deadlocked or strangled, and in his view little time remained for Yugoslavia to find a solution before it would be threatened with serious disintegration.[94] *Duga* was also prepared to probe scandals and to allow public figures to vent their frustrations. At times, *Duga* allowed itself to get carried away by its enthusiasm for "exposing" the "truth." The pages of *Duga* started to recall the muckraking tradition of turn-of-the-century America. And eventually, *Duga*, along with *Reporter* (a now-defunct semipornographic magazine), and *Ilustrovana politika,* would find itself accused of sensationalistic and tendentious reporting.[95] After 1987, *Duga* became simply another mouthpiece for Milošević.

In September 1986, the Republican Conference of SAWP Serbia reviewed *Duga*'s performance and concluded that the magazine had "published a number of articles whose content and message [are], from an ideological and political standpoint, unacceptable. This relates, in particular, to certain interviews, letters, and features that, in a sensationalist way, sow distrust, stimulate nationalist sentiment, and provoke disputes." The conference also complained of "articles containing historical lies and that wrote in an unacceptable way about LCY cadres."[96] The following year *Duga*'s editor (along with the editors of *NIN, Intervju,* and *Svet*) was replaced, but even so, Serbian party chairman Slobodan Milošević declared, "The situation in *Duga* will not change until there are broader changes in the editorial staff of *Duga*."[97]

Then there is the case of Ranka Čicak, an enterprising journalist who, after uncovering a scam operation involving pig farmers and local politicians, was charged with having insulted Tito in a private conversation and with having justified both Croatian separatism and Albanian irredentism, imprisoned for six months, and later injured in a mysterious traffic accident.[98]

Again, when party authorities banned a professional meeting of the Philosophical Society of Serbia, which was to have discussed "the possibilities of reform in socialist countries," *Književne novine* provided a forum in which the society's president could register his protest.[99]

The Communist authorities said they wanted criticism but such criticism had to be "progressive," "in line with self-management," and not contrary to LCY policy.[100] In a micro-example of this kind of thinking, the traditionally conservative *Borba,* upon canceling publication of a preannounced interview with drama director Ljubiša Ristič in 1984, wrote, "The editors of this paper are not in agreement with some of Ristič's views and he did not consent to having them excluded. So, as a result, we are publishing another . . . discussion [instead]."[101]

And finally, there is *outward* criticism, in the sense in which I have defined it. Outward criticism was not a feature in the entire secular press. The youth press contained very little, if any, outward criticism, at least not at the party's bid. Magazines like *Duga, Start,* and *Reporter* likewise engaged in little outward criticism, and for that matter *Danas* and *NIN* also did not make much space for criticizing persons outside the party. The daily press, on the other hand, was, in Communist times—and in Milošević's Serbia, still is—a routine vehicle for outward criticism.

The churches were (until the late 1980s) one target of *outward criticism.* Where the Catholic Church is concerned, such criticism ranged from complaints about Cardinal Kuharić's annual defense of Cardinal Stepinac (d. 1960), who was convicted, in a rather dubious trial in 1946, of collaboration with the fascists during World War II,[102] to charges that unnamed church circles were calling on believers "to settle accounts with the Communists, emphasizing that the Communists [were] on the top of the list for liquidation, if another government [took] over,"[103] to insinuations that Pope John Paul II went to Chile to endorse the Pinochet regime when in fact the very opposite was the case,[104] to claims that the Church organ *Glas koncila* called communism one of the "most reactionary ideologies of the century."[105] In September 1986, the Novi Sad daily, *Dnevnik,* published an article adorned with a caricature of a man in an Ustasha uniform, standing in front of a barbed wire fence and waving a copy of *Glas koncila.*[106] The clear implication was that the paper—the official organ of the Zagreb archdiocese—was advocating fascistic ideas. Usually *Glas koncila* contented itself with expostulations on its editorial page. On this occasion, however, the editor took *Dnevnik* to court. The district court refused to consider the case; so *Glas koncila* took the case to the Higher Court in Novi Sad.[107] The court ultimately handed down a judgment in *Dnevnik's* favor. The decision, signed by President of the Court Mirjana Carić, explained that "the connection of part of the Catholic clergy in Croatia . . . with the Ustasha movement and its activity during the National Liberation War, *as well as later,* is not new or unknown, but falls into [the category of] historically established fact.[108] Hence *Glas koncila,* which was established only in the mid–1960s, could be "legitimately" portrayed as pro-Ustasha. But *Dnevnik* and Belgrade's *Večernje novosti* were, for some time, the most hostile toward the Catholic Church, while other papers increasingly adopted a more balanced approach.

The Serbian Orthodox Church likewise found that its treatment at the hands of the secular media was uneven (until the end of 1987). Misleading and disparaging reports surfaced most frequently in *Oslobodjenje,* the Bosnian daily, although these reports were sometimes reprinted in other newspapers.[109]

Outward criticism—whether of religious leaders or dissident intellectuals or rock stars or other persons—would sometimes portray the persons concerned as engaged in illegal activity (though usually no one would be arrested or brought to trial) or as morally degenerate or politically disloyal or as disseminating disinformation (which typically would be challenged only in a polemical or sarcastic way) Outward criticism, thus, unlike inward criticism, has had more to do with trying to cast a pall over the reputations of certain people and with signaling to the readership that these people were, at least for party members, "off limits," than with any serious effort to raise and discuss issues. Outward criticism was a political tool of sectors of the political establishment; inward criticism was more usually a vehicle for persons (whether inside or outside the establishment) who were critical of the regime.

THE STRUGGLE FOR THE PRESS

After March 1988 and the entire *Mladina* affair, there was a subtle change in the attitudes and confidence of journalists vis-à-vis the authorities. Specific issues of prominent publications such as *Književne novine, Start,* and *Nedjeljna Dalmacija* were banned—the first-named for publishing material "that could cause public concern"[110]—and in summer 1988, the influential weekly magazine, *NIN,* was subjected to a "housecleaning," as various members of the editorial staff were fired and punished.[111] Meanwhile, Belgrade's Politika Publishing House (of which *NIN* was, for that matter, a part) became the craven instrument of Slobodan Milošević, and its newspapers started publishing a string of mendacious stories—falsely alleging that Albanian locals in Kosovo had fired mortars and bazookas at Serbian police,[112] falsely alleging that Croatian President Tudjman was receiving "instructions" from the Vatican and West Germany, and so forth.

By 1989, there were clear signs of revolt among journalists. As early as September 1989, the Society of Journalists of Croatia registered a strong protest against the policy of using the press as a "transmission belt" for the party line.[113] In Montenegro, when local party authorities sought to replace the editor of *Pobjeda* for political reasons, six of the paper's journalists called foul.[114] In Vojvodina, journalists protested editorial appointments and demanded the right to select their own editors.[115] And in Serbia, journalists of *Politika,* together with staff writers of Belgrade Television, joined in criticizing the political control of editorial policy and in demanding a relaxation of control.[116]

Pluralist-minded journalists scored an early victory in September 1989, with the disbanding of the *Komunist* party organization and the cessation of its work. *Komunist* had been one of the least credible and least read papers, despite its enormous print run (500,000 copies weekly in 1983). In

Slovenia and Croatia, pluralization was achieved incrementally, so that one can scarcely find a date on which to pin the label "watershed." In Serbia, by contrast, Milošević suffered a temporary setback in March 1991, when he was forced to surrender his absolute control of the press. In Novi Sad, political appointee Svetozar Gavrić was forced to step down as editor only four hours after his appointment because journalists of *Dnevnik* were no longer willing to accept the old practice of political appointments.[117] In Belgrade, more than 100 journalists of the Politika Publishing House demanded the resignation of the editors of *Politika, Politika ekspres, NIN, Intervju,* and *TV Politika* and their replacement by professionals respected by the journalists. These developments were closely followed, on 18 March, by *Politika* journalists' call for journalistic independence.[118]

In essence, the journalists themselves abolished the old party monopoly of the press. The Federal Assembly adopted a new press law in November 1990, legalizing the free press, abolishing the censorship (which *Borba* explicitly referred to as such), and allowing foreign investors to own up to 49 percent of the stock in any periodical.[119] The Serbian Assembly followed on 28 March 1991—within two weeks of the aforementioned protests—and likewise proclaimed an end to censorship and political control of the press. On the following day, *NIN* proclaimed its independence, with a commentary headlined "Fall of the Bastille."[120] In the same issue, *NIN* called on the Milošević government to step down.

Meanwhile, a string of new, privately owned periodicals began appearing, including *Vreme* (Belgrade), *Bastina* (Belgrade), *RI Telefax* (Rijeka), and *Novi tjednik* (Rijeka).

THE MEDIA AND THE DISSOLUTION OF THE SFRY

The republicanization of the press was a basic fact of Yugoslav public life and was one of a number of factors that pushed the country toward disintegration. People in Bosnia commonly said that local Muslims read the Bosnian republic press (*Oslobodjenje, AS*), local Croats read the Croatian republic press (chiefly *Vjesnik* and *Večernji list*), and Bosnian Serbs read the Serbian republic press (chiefly *Politika* but also *Politika ekspres*). In October 1989, the Belgrade daily, *Borba,* published the results of a public opinion poll in which 120 persons (20 per republic) were asked which papers they considered the most influential in the country, which they most respected, which they least respected, and which they read most frequently. While the results for Slovenia and Macedonia were clearly affected by the fact that the peoples of these republics speak different languages, it is clear that for all republics there was a close correlation between republic of residence and orientations toward the press (see Tables 4.1 and 4.2).

TABLE 4.1   Which Periodical Do You Respect the Most? (120 people, 1989) (percentage)

	Bosnia	Croatia	Macedonia	Montenegro	Serbia	Slovenia
Serbian Papers						
Politika	25	–	27	27	31	–
NIN	–	–	13	7	5	–
Duga	–	–	–	–	9	–
TV Revija	–	–	–	7	–	–
Croatian Papers						
Vjesnik	4	10	–	–	–	–
Start	–	14	–	–	14	–
Slobodna Dalmacija	–	19	–	–	–	–
Večernji list	7	5	–	–	–	–
Slovenian Papers						
Delo	–	–	–	–	–	23
Večer	–	–	–	–	–	14
Mladina	–	–	–	–	–	9
Other Papers						
Borba	–	–	10	–	–	–
Večernje novosti	–	–	–	10	–	–
Nova Makedonija	–	–	6	–	–	–
Oslobodjenje	11	–	–	–	–	–
Pobjeda	–	–	–	10	–	–
Women's magazines	–	–	–	–	–	23
None	–	–	19	–	–	9

SOURCE: *Borba*, 2 October 1989, p. 7, translated in *Foreign Broadcast Information Service, Daily Report* (Eastern Europe), 23 October 1989, pp. 58–59.

Only Macedonians (8 percent), for example, cited the Skopje daily, *Nova Makedonija*, as one of the most influential papers in the country, and only Slovenes cited Slovenian periodicals (*Delo*, 18 percent; *Mladina*, 11 percent; and *Večer*, 7 percent) among the most influential. Fifty-four percent of Serbs mentioned *Politika*, but only 8 percent of Croats did so. Only residents of Croatia and Bosnia cited the Croatian press.[121]

Asked which periodicals they most respected, 54 percent of Serbs cited a Serbian periodical, 58 percent of Croats cited a Croatian periodical, and 58 percent of Montenegrins cited either a Montenegrin or a Serbian publication. The results in the other republics were more mixed.

In terms of readership, 56 percent of Macedonians relied chiefly on Macedonian periodicals, 42 percent of Serbs relied chiefly on Serbian or Vojvodinan (*Dnevnik*) periodicals, 79 percent of Croats relied chiefly on Croatian periodicals, 72 percent of Slovenes on Slovenian periodicals, 68 percent of Montenegrins on Montenegrin or Serbian periodicals, but only

TABLE 4.2   Which Periodical Do You Read Most Frequently? (120 people, 1989) (percentage)

	Bosnia	Croatia	Macedonia	Montenegro	Serbia	Slovenia
Serbian Papers						
Politika	9	–	12	18	30	–
NIN	–	–	8	7	6	–
Croatian Papers						
Vjesnik	–	15	–	–	–	–
Start	–	7	–	–	6	–
Slobodna Dalmacija	–	26	–	–	–	–
Večernji list	9	19	–	–	6	–
Danas	–	–	–	–	–	–
Slovenian Papers						
Delo	–	–	–	–	–	24
Večer	–	–	–	–	–	10
Mladina	–	–	–	–	–	5
Ljubljanski Dnevnik	–	–	–	–	–	10
Revija	–	–	–	–	–	20
Macedonian Papers						
Nova Makedonija	–	–	33	–	–	–
Politikin zabavnik	–	–	17	–	–	–
Večer	–	–	6	–	–	–
Other						
Večernje novosti	11	12	6	10	6	–
Oslobodjenje	20	–	–	–	–	–
Pobjeda	–	–	–	35	–	–
Women's magazines	17	–	–	–	–	–

SOURCE: *Borba,* 2 October 1989, p. 7, translated in *Foreign Broadcast Information Service, Daily Report* (Eastern Europe), 23 October 1989, pp. 59–60.

26 percent of residents of Bosnia relied chiefly on Bosnian publications for their information. Only in Bosnia did a large number of respondents (17 percent) cite women's magazines as their major source of news and information.

Naturally, the influence any newspaper enjoyed fluctuated over time. *Borba* and *Slobodna Dalmacija* were marginal papers in the 1970s; by 1989, they were, together with *Delo*, arguably the most widely respected papers in the country. But neither *Slobodna Dalmacija* nor *Delo* could claim a wide readership outside their respective republics. Leaving aside ethnically mixed Bosnia, only the Serbian periodicals *Politika* and *NIN*, the Croatian weekly magazine *Danas* and fortnightly *Start*, and the Belgrade publications *Borba* and *Večernje novosti* could claim a wide readership that extended beyond the boundaries of the republic in which they were published.[122]

TABLE 4.3   Yugoslav Newspapers with Circulations Larger than 10,000
in Rank Order (1990)

	1990 Sales (no. of copies)	1983 Sales (no. of copies)
Večernje novosti (Belgrade)	222,282	339,859
Večernji list (Zagreb)	221,942	309,839
Politika ekspres (Belgrade)	198,790	249,758
Politika (Belgrade)	184,551	243,826
Slobodna Dalmacija (Split)	107,483	71,571
Družina (Ljubljana, Catholic)	100,000[a]	n/a
Glas koncila (Zagreb, Catholic)	100,000[a]	n/a
Delo (Ljubljana)	94,280	99,840
Ognjišče (Koper, Catholic)	n/a	80,000[b]
Vjesnik (Zagreb)	74,563	73,030
Sportske novosti (Zagreb)	70,597	141,247
Večernje novine (Sarajevo)	66,911	35,049
Novi list—Glas Istre (Rijeka)	56,586	71,274
Večer (Maribor)	54,561	55,476
Mali koncil (Zagreb, Catholic)	n/a	50,000[d]
Oslobodjenje (Sarajevo)	47,690	71,557
Sport (Belgrade)	45,670	106,781
Sportski žurnal	42,142	n/a
Dnevnik (Novi Sad)	39,677	34,158
Borba (Belgrade)	31,408	30,976
Preporod (Sarajevo, Islamic)	n/a	30,000[d]
Nova Makedonija (Skopje)	23,404	25,089
Večer (Skopje)	22,948	31,959
Pravoslavlje (Belgrade, Orthodox)	n/a	22,000[c]
Magyar Szö (Novi Sad)	20,708	26,485
Pobjeda (Titograd)	19,570	20,073
Glas Slavonije	12,349	26,485

[a] 1987.

[b] 1973.

[c] 1982.

[d] Number printed.

SOURCES: Naša štampa (July-August 1983), pp. 9–10; Naša štampa (February 1984), p. 9; AKSA (May 20, 1983); NIN (May 22,1983), trans. in Foreign Broadcast Information Service, Daily Report (Eastern Europe), June 1, 1983; interviews, Belgrade and Zagreb, July 1982; and interviews, Zagreb and Ljubljana, June-July 1987; and Slobodna Dalmacija (Split), March 21, 1991, p. 23, trans. in FBIS, Daily Report (Eastern Europe), April 9, 1991, p. 42.

The highest circulations were enjoyed by the evening tabloids (*Večernje novosti, Večernji list,* and *Politika ekspres*), although *Politika* and *Slobodna Dalmacija* also had circulations over 100,000 (see Table 4.3). Among Church publications, only the Catholic papers, *Družina* and *Glas koncila,* had circulations in excess of 100,000.

I began this chapter by noting that the SFRY press reflected the more general chaos that characterized the country. But this chaos—both at the systemic level and within the sphere of journalism specifically—was in part the deliberate design of the Tito era and served certain functions, in part the product of the partially successful struggle of certain editorial staffs (especially of *Start, Duga, NIN,* and the youth press) to broaden their latitude, in part the by-product of federalization, republicanization and devolution, and in part a by-product of the gathering crisis and weakening of authority at the center. Ultimately, the republicanization of the press played a role in propelling the country toward interethnic war.

As Joseph Klapper noted in 1960, the media, and perhaps especially the print media, have an enormous power to create opinion, to conjure issues into the public arena, to change public opinion, and to suggest appropriate remedies for conjured inequities and problems, whether real or imaginary.[123] Moreover, the prestige and respect attached to the given source gives the message being communicated far more power than it would bear if conveyed by some less prestigious source.[124] Thus, the role played by the Serbian media, and most especially by the magazines *Duga* and *Intervju,* and by the newspapers *Politika* and *Politika ekspres,* in creating resentments against Croatia and Slovenia for an alleged "theft" of Serbian factories, in stirring up anger against Kosovo's Albanians for alleged acts of rape and arson against local Serbs, and in debunking Tito and Titoism, including even Tito's dream of "brotherhood and unity," cannot be underestimated. Without the active participation of the press, the Serbian national movement could never have created the angers and resentments that, in time, would drive the Serbs into battle against their erstwhile fellow Yugoslavs—angers and resentments that were muted or, in certain cases, even nonexistent prior to the period 1986–1987.

The media thus contributed to both the breakup of the SFRY and the outbreak of interethnic warfare. And yet, the media was adversely affected by these developments, at least in Serbia and Croatia. For while the dissolution of the SFRY permitted Slovenia and Macedonia to loosen the reins (especially where the print media has been concerned) and to move beyond the strictures of censorship and self-censorship,[125] in Serbia and Croatia alike, the new political authorities have taken steps to tighten government control of the media, even to the extent of assuming effective ownership of some of the leading newspapers and magazines.[126] These developments are taken up briefly in Chapter 10.

NOTES

This is an updated and revised version of a paper originally published in John B. Allcock, John J. Horton, and Marko Milivojević, *Yugoslavia in Transition: Choices and Constraints—Essays in Honour of Fred Singleton* (Oxford and Hamburg: Berg; New York: St. Martin's Press, 1991). Reproduced here by kind permission of the editors and publishers. (c) J.B. Allcock, J.J. Horton, M. Milivojević, 1991. All rights reserved.

1. Interview with magazine editor, Belgrade, July 1982; and interview with newspaper editor, Ljubljana, July 1982.

2. See Pedro Ramet, "The Yugoslav Press in Flux," in Pedro Ramet, ed., *Yugoslavia in the 1980s* (Boulder, Colo.: Westview Press, 1985).

3. Report by Vitomir Sudarski, in *Dvanaesti kongres Saveza komunista Jugoslavije, Beograd, 26–29 juni 1982,* Magnetofonske beleške, vol. 3 (Belgrade: Izdavački Centar Komunist, 1983), p. 226; and *Handbook on Yugoslavia* (Belgrade: Exportpress, 1987), p. 214.

4. Report by Ivan Hocevar, in 6. *Sednica CKSKJ. Sto godina od smrti Karla Marksa. Obrazloženje uz Predlog poslovnika o organizaciji i načinu rada CKSKJ. Idejna kretanja, problemi i pojave u oblasti informisanja i propaganda i zadaci SKJ* (Belgrade: Izdavački Centar Komunist, 1983), p. 58.

5. Tanjug (30 March 1984), trans. in *FBIS, Daily Report* (Eastern Europe), 3 April 1984, p. 113.

6. *Handbook,* p. 219.

7. Marko Lolić, "Savez komunista i savremena uloga javnih glasila," *Socijalizam,* Vol. 30, Nos. 10–11 (October–November 1988), p. 95.

8. Interview with former editor of a religious periodical, Belgrade, July 1987; confirmed in interview with former editor of a youth periodical, Ljubljana, July 1987.

9. One exception concerns the front page of an issue of the Croatian weekly, *Hrvatski tjednik,* in late 1971, which its editors defiantly published with a blank page and a brief notice that the material intended for that page had been administratively suppressed.

10. Interview, Belgrade, July 1987.

11. Interview with staff members of *Vjesnik,* Zagreb, July 1982.

12. See *Oslobodjenje* (Sarajevo) (21 January 1982), p. 6; *Politika* (Belgrade) (16 January 1985), p. 6, and (25 December 1985), p. 6; *Komunist* (Belgrade edition) (20 December 1985), p. 17; *Borba* (Zagreb edition) (22–23 February 1986), p. 8, and (11 September 1987), p. 3; and *Vjesnik* (Zagreb) (9 July 1987), p. 3.

13. See, for example, *Politika* (19 December 1985), p. 6.

14. *NIN* (Belgrade), No. 1836 (9 March 1986), p. 9.

15. *Večernje novosti* (Belgrade) (14 March 1986).

16. Discussed in Stevan Nikšić, *Oslobodjenje Štampe* (Belgrade: Mladost, 1982).

17. Tanjug's director, Mihajlo Saranović, later complained about this in a speech reported in *Vjesnik* (14 March 1986).

18. *Komunist* (26 June 1987), p. 12.

19. Detailed in Ramet, "The Yugoslav Press in Flux," pp. 104–106.

20. *Politika* (30 March 1985), p. 6.

21. Tanjug (24 September 1986), trans. in *Foreign Broadcast Information Service (FBIS), Daily Report* (Eastern Europe), 25 September 1986, p. 17; and *Večernji list* (Zagreb) (9 July 1987), p. 5.

22. *Komunist* (13 September 1985), p. 8.

23. See, for example, *Politika* (12 July 1984), p. 6; Tanjug (9 December 1985), trans. in Joint Publications Research Service (JPRS), *East Europe Report* No. EER–86–008 (21 January 1986), p. 101; *Politika* (25 December 1985), p. 6; and *Borba* (Zagreb edition) (16 September 1987), p. 4.

24. Dennison I. Rusinow, "Yugoslavia 1983: Between 'Continuity' and 'Crisis,'" *University Field Staff International Reports,* No. 3 (1983), p. 10; and *Vjesnik* (7 February 1987), p. 3.

25. *Vjesnik* (3 November 1982), p. 5.

26. Tanjug (9 December 1985), p. 102.

27. Tanjug (12 June 1981), and (6 June 1983), trans. respectively in *FBIS, Daily Report* (Eastern Europe), 16 June 1981, pp. 113–114, and 9 June 1983, p. 1; and Louis Zanga, "News Media Coverage of Events in Kosovo," *Radio Free Europe Research* (20 November 1987), p. 2.

28. Tanjug (7 October 1985), trans. in *FBIS, Daily Report* (Eastern Europe), 17 October 1985, p. 13.

29. *Borba* (Belgrade edition) (22 August 1986), p. 3.

30. *Borba* (26 August 1986), p. 3.

31. Dragana Roter-Crkvenjakov, "Pokrajinska štampa o promenama ustava SR Srbije," *Novinarstvo,* Vol. 24, Nos. 1–2 (1988), pp. 59–60.

32. *Vjesnik* (15 June 1987), p. 3.

33. Quoted in Tanjug (7 February 1983), trans. in *FBIS, Daily Report* (Eastern Europe), 8 February 1983, p. 116. The term "socio-socialist" was not explained but, taken in context, it is clear that the expression is equivalent to *pseudo-socialist.*

34. *Le Monde* (Paris) (11 May 1983), p. 6, trans. in *FBIS, Daily Report* (Eastern Europe), 11 May 1983, p. 19.

35. *Vjesnik* (16 September 1987), p. 5.

36. Stojanović had only been on the job nine months. See *Politika* (13 October 1987), pp. 1, 5–7; and *Borba* (Zagreb edition (13 October 1987), pp. 1, 3.

37. Interview with staff members of *Delo,* Ljubljana, 1 September 1989.

38. As summarized in *Vjesnik* (21 February 1987), p. 3.

39. As summarized in *Politika* (23 February 1987), p. 6.

40. *Vjesnik* (21 February 1987), p. 3.

41. *Politika* (15 March 1987), p. 6.

42. Interviews, Ljubljana, July 1987. See also Tanjug (11 March 1987), trans. in *FBIS, Daily Report* (Eastern Europe), 6 April 1987, p. 18; *The Economist* (London), 11 April 1987, p. 50; and *Borba* (Zagreb edition) (11 September 1987), p. 3.

43. Tanjug (30 October 1986), trans. in *FBIS, Daily Report* (Eastern Europe), 6 November 1986, p. 15.

44. See the report of the session of the CC Presidium's Commission for Information and Propaganda Activity in *Večernje novosti* (9 December 1986).

45. Discussed in *Večernji list* (29 May 1987), p. 5.

46. See discussion in *Vjesnik* (9 July 1987), p. 3.

47. *Borba* was, for a time, published in both Cyrillic and Latin-alphabet editions.

48. Tanjug (15 March 1979), trans. in *FBIS, Daily Report* (Eastern Europe), March 16, 1979, p. 110.

49. See, for instance, *Borba* (Zagreb edition) (17 January 1986), p. 3; also *Komunist* (19 June 1987), p. 6.

50. *Komunist* (26 July 1985), p. 4.

51. *Mladina* (1986), as quoted in *Borba* (Belgrade edition) (3 October 1986), p. 11.

52. Tanjug (9 December 1986), trans. in *FBIS, Daily Report* (Eastern Europe), 10 December 1986, p. 14, referring to a commentary published in *Vjesnik* on 3 December 1986.

53. Tanjug (9 December 1985), trans. in JPRS, *East Europe Report,* No. EER–86–008 (21 January 1986), p. 103.

54. See *Borba* (Zagreb edition) (4 September 1987), p. 4, and (13 October 1987), p. 3.

55. Quoted in *Christian Science Monitor* (23 March 1988), p. 2.

56. Tanjug Domestic Service (15 August 1988), trans. in *FBIS, Daily Report* (Eastern Europe), 16 August 1988, p. 24.

57. *Politika* (31 August 1988), p. 11.

58. Tanjug (28 October 1988), in *FBIS, Daily Report* (Eastern Europe), 31 October 1988, p. 71.

59. Interview, Ljubljana, 1 September 1989.

60. The examples I provided in "The Yugoslav Press in Flux" (pp. 111–112) in 1985 should be quite sufficient to justify this portrayal.

61. Interview with a staff member of *Mladina,* Ljubljana, July 1987.

62. Ibid.

63. And Radio Student.

64. Interview with a staff member of *Mladina,* Ljubljana, July 1987.

65. *Borba* (Zagreb edition) (1–2 August 1987), p. 6.

66. Interview, Ljubljana, July 1987.

67. *Delo* (Ljubljana) (19 September 1986), p. 6, trans. in *FBIS, Daily Report* (Eastern Europe), 1 October 1986, p. 19.

68. *Delo* (19 September 1986), p. 6, trans. in *FBIS, Daily Report* (Eastern Europe), 1 October 1986, pp. 19–20.

69. *Delo* (20 September 1986), p. 4, trans. in *FBIS, Daily Report* (Eastern Europe), 1 October 1986, pp. 110–111.

70. The *Katedra* article was translated in *South Slav Journal,* Vol. 10, No. 1 (spring 1987), pp. 38–45.

71. *The Economist* (11 April 1987), p. 50.

72. *Večernji list* (2 July 1987), p. 4.

73. *Christian Science Monitor* (9 March 1988), p. 2; *The Economist* (19 March 1988), p. 48; and *New York Times* (19 March 1988), p. 15.

74. "Slovenian Spring—Centralism or Democracy?," *Independent Voices from Slovenia,* Vol. 4, Special edition (October 1988), p. 6.

75. For a more detailed discussion of the effects of this trial, see Chapter 2, above.

76. *Mladina* (Ljubljana) (9 December 1988), pp. 18–19, trans. in *FBIS, Daily Report* (Eastern Europe), 16 December 1988, pp. 57–58.

77. *Die Presse* (Vienna) (22 January 1982), p. 2.

78. *Borba* (Zagreb edition) (1 October 1987), p. 3.

79. Zagreb Domestic Service (8 December 1986), trans. in *FBIS, Daily Report* (Eastern Europe), 10 December 1986, p. 11; and *Politika* (December 11, 1985), p. 6.

80. Tanjug (9 October 1986), trans. in *FBIS, Daily Report* (Eastern Europe), 15 October 1986, p. 17.

81. *Danas* (Zagreb), No. 333 (5 July 1988), p. 76.

82. *Naši dani* (Sarajevo), No. 962 (3 March 1989), p. 25.

83. *Münchner Merkur* (Munich) (15–16 March 1986), p. 4; *Večernji list* (14 September 1989), p. 5; and *Večernje novosti* (14 September 1989), p. 19. See also *NIN,* No. 1840 (6 April 1986), pp. 22–23.

84. *Christian Science Monitor* (9 June 1988), p. 13; and report by Marinko Bulatović, in 6. *Sednica,* p. 53.

85. *Borba* (Zagreb edition) (6 February 1986), p. 3; and *Borba* (Belgrade edition), 28 October 1986, p. 3.

86. *Politika* (15 March 1986), p. 6.

87. Tanjug (24 July 1986), and (2 April 1987), trans., respectively, in *FBIS, Daily Report* (Eastern Europe), 25 July 1986, p. 110, and 3 April 1987, p. 19; and *Politika* (21 February 1987), p. 6, and (19 March 1987), p. 6.

88. Tanjug (10 October 1986), trans. in *FBIS, Daily Report* (Eastern Europe), 22 October 1986, p. 113.

89. *Oslobodjenje,* as reprinted in *Borba* (Belgrade edition) (17 October 1986), p. 11, as summarized in *FBIS, Daily Report* (Eastern Europe), 13 November 1986, p. 16.

90. *Politika ekspres* (Belgrade) (25 June 1987), p. 2.

91. See *Duga* (Belgrade) (13–26 June 1987), p. 11.

92. *Večernji list* (23 June 1987), p. 4.

93. *Borba* (Zagreb edition) (6 October 1987), p. 5.

94. *Duga* (5–18 October 1987), as trans. in *South Slav Journal,* Vol. 8, No. 3–4 (autumn–winter 1985), pp. 81–88.

95. Report by Sanije Hiseni, in 6. *Sednica,* p. 101.

96. Tanjug (19 September 1986), trans. in *FBIS, Daily Report* (Eastern Europe), 22 September 1986, p. 14.

97. Quoted in *Danas,* No. 278 (16 June 1987), p. 8.

98. *Vjesnik* (24 December 1982), p. 14, trans. in *FBIS, Daily Report* (Eastern Europe), 3 January 1983, p. 17; *Los Angeles Times* (3 April 1983), Pt. I-A, pp. 8–9; and *Neue Zürcher Zeitung* (Zürich) (9 May 1984), p. 4.

99. *Književne novine* (Belgrade) (1 September 1987), p. 3.

100. Tanjug (7 November 1985), trans. in *FBIS, Daily Report* (Eastern Europe), 8 November 1985, p. 17.

101. *Borba* (Belgrade edition) (15–16 September 1984), p. 9, trans. in JPRS, *East Europe Report,* No. EPS–84–127 (12 October 1984), p. 109 (punctuation altered slightly).

102. *Politika* (18 February 1987), p. 6; and *Vjesnik* (26 February 1987), p. 4.

103. *Novi list* (Rijeka) (17 April 1987), as quoted in *Glas koncila* (26 April 1987), p. 2.

104. *Vjesnik* (5 April 1987), as cited in *Glas koncila* (12 April 1987), p. 2.

105. *Danas,* No. 279 (23 June 1987), p. 25.

106. *Dnevnik* (Novi Sad) (8 September 1986), p. 5.

107. Interview, Zagreb, June 1987.

108. A copy of the decision (No. 132/87, dated 18 March 1987) is in the author's file.

109. Interview, Belgrade, July 1987.

110. Tanjug (5 July 1988), trans. in *FBIS, Daily Report* (Eastern Europe), 13 July 1988, p. 68.

111. *Vjesnik* (1 July 1988), p. 4.

112. Cited in *Los Angeles Times* (24 July 1990), p. H2.

113. *Večernji list* (18 September 1989), p. 4.

114. *Vjesnik* (13 September 1990), p. 3.

115. Ibid. (6 October 1990), trans. in *FBIS, Daily Report* (Eastern Europe), 26 October 1990, p. 51; and Tanjug (26 November 1990), trans. in *FBIS, Daily Report* (Eastern Europe), 30 November 1990, p. 70.

116. Tanjug (25 October 1990), in *FBIS, Daily Report* (Eastern Europe), 26 October 1990, p. 51; and Tanjug (26 November 1990), trans. in *FBIS, Daily Report* (Eastern Europe), 30 November 1990, p. 70.

117. Tanjug (14 March 1991), trans. in *FBIS, Daily Report* (Eastern Europe), 15 March 1991, p. 58.

118. Tanjug (13 March 1991) and (18 March 1991), trans., respectively, in *FBIS, Daily Report* (Eastern Europe), 14 March 1991, p. 49, and 19 March 1991, p. 59.

119. *Borba* (2 November 1990), p. 1.

120. Tanjug (28 March 1991), trans. in *FBIS, Daily Report* (Eastern Europe), 29 March 1991, p. 45; and Tanjug (29 March 1991), in *FBIS, Daily Report* (Eastern Europe), 12 April 1991, p. 28.

121. *Borba* (2 October 1989), p. 7.

122. According to the data reported in ibid.

123. Joseph T. Klapper, *The Effects of Mass Communication* (New York: Free Press, 1960), pp. 53–57, 62–97.

124. Ibid., p. 99.

125. Regarding censorship and self-censorship in Yugoslav journalism in the 1980s, see Slaven Letica, *Intelektualac i kriza* (Zagreb: August Cesarec, 1989), pp. 192–201.

126. For further discussion, see Sabrina Petra Ramet, *Social Currents in Eastern Europe: The Sources and Consequences of the Great Transformation,* 2d ed. (Durham, N.C.: Duke University Press, 1995), pp. 418–420, 427–428.

CHAPTER FIVE

◆

Rock Music

Yugoslavia, on your feet and sing!
Whoever doesn't listen to this song,
Will hear a storm!

—Goran Bregović and Bijelo dugme,
in "Pljuni i zapjevaj, moja Jugoslavijo" (1987)

WHEN GORAN BREGOVIĆ AND his group White Button (Bijelo dugme) began singing their song. "Spit and Sign, My Yugoslavia," their fans would rise to their feet, tens of thousands of them, and sing along. The mood of the song was defiant. It was, Bregović maintains, "a song that can frighten the politicians."[1] Later, in spring and summer 1988, when supporters of Serbian leader Slobodan Milošević took to the streets in tens of thousands to protest against the governments of Vojvodina and Montenegro and to show support in Serbia for Milošević, they sang this song. It was, it turned out, a song of insurrection. The governments of Vojvodina and Montenegro fell and were replaced with supporters of Milošević.

This story is unusual only in degree, not in essence. Yugoslav rock music was long deeply colored by political messages and political allusions. In this respect, Yugoslav rock music was more typical of the East than of the West, where rock had reverted, by the 1970s, to its original cast as entertainment and is less likely to engage in political communication. In the Communist world, by contrast, including Yugoslavia, rock was very much attuned to political messages.

Many Yugoslav rock musicians were quite conscious of their role as bards or social critics, and many of their songs were topical, reflecting broader public moods and concerns. As Goran Bregović put it, "We can't have any alternative parties or any alternative political programs. So there are not too many places where you can gather large groups of people and communicate ideas that are not official. Rock 'n' roll is one of the most important vehicles for helping people in Communist countries to think in a different way."[2]

Rock music in a culturally diverse, politically decentralized environment such as Yugoslavia inevitably develops differently from the way it develops in an ethnically homogeneous, politically centralized system—let alone in a pluralist Western system. To begin with, the composite nationality groups of Yugoslavia have diverse musical cultures and psychological frameworks, so that musical devices that strike a resonant chord in, let us say, Macedonia, may seem arcane and very foreign in Slovenia or Croatia. Second, in conditions of republic "etatism" (as the Yugoslavs call their version of federalized state ownership), the market is fragmented and divided, with clear barriers. For rock musicians, the absence of a unified market means that there have long been in essence five independent rock networks in Yugoslavia—in Slovenia, Croatia, Bosnia, Vojvodina, and Serbia—and a star may hit it big in one republic and be ignored elsewhere.[3] There is an "intermittent" rock scene in Macedonia, centered in Skopje, but both because of tighter financial constraints in that republic and because of the language (which restricts the market), there is no record company in Macedonia. As a result, many Macedonian rock groups are unable to make albums and therefore, in the absence of publicity, wither away.[4]

THE EARLY YEARS

The prehistory of rock music in Yugoslavia was not propitious for the free development of the new genre. World War II was scarcely over when Milovan Djilas, then head of propaganda of the CPY, set the tone for the regime's cultural policy in the early years. "America," said Djilas in 1947, "is our sworn enemy, and jazz, likewise, as the product of [the American system]."[5] Tito himself told his biographer, Vladimir Dedijer, at that time, "I like our folk music, but not stylized, as people start to do nowadays. . . . Jazz, in my opinion, is not music. It is racket!"[6] Shortly after the war, therefore, Marshal Tito summoned some of Yugoslavia's top composers to his palace and told them that pop music and jazz cheated people of their money and spoiled young people.

With Tito's expulsion from the Cominform on 28 June 1948, music became potentially dangerous, as many unfortunate Yugoslavs discovered. Singing the wrong song could mean prison or penal labor. Russian songs—in political vogue for the three years immediately prior—were now definitely *out*. American tunes were just as risky, however, as rival groups struggled to prove their Communist "purity." Even Yugoslav folk songs risked accusations of bourgeois nationalism (even if Tito did like that genre). Some music had served several masters—a traditional Croatian football song from earlier in the century had later been adapted, with new words, to serve as a patriotic song for the fascist regime. In the postwar period, the Communists wrote new words. Other songs, innocent in their incarnation, might have become pernicious through later association, and unless the singer was certain, it was better not to sing indigenous music. These factors contributed, thus, to the sudden popularity of Mexican folk songs among the public, above all because they were ideologically and politically safe.

But 1948 ultimately set Yugoslavia on a different course from the Soviet bloc states. Tito's decision, after his break with Stalin in 1948, to open Yugoslavia to contacts with the West was fateful for the development of rock 'n' roll, because it meant that Western rock would penetrate Yugoslavia more quickly and more easily than it could other countries in Eastern Europe. It meant, in consequence, that Yugoslav rock music would develop much more rapidly than rock music in, let us say, Hungary or Czechoslovakia, let alone Romania or Bulgaria.

As early as 1953, thus, Yugoslav jazz musicians were able—despite the authorities' dislike of the genre—to establish a musicians' association. By 1957, Predrag Ivanović and his Orchestra were at the height of their popularity; their fare—American pop music of the day. By the latter 1950s, rock 'n' roll was making its first inroads in the Balkans.

The early years of rock music in Yugoslavia were very much under the shadow of the West. Indeed, at its inception, the only interesting rock music came from either the United States or Great Britain. Bill Haley and the Comets, Chuck Berry, Buddy Holly, Jerry Lee Lewis, and Little Richard were among the artists whose music was heard in Yugoslavia before the end of the 1950s. Interest among Yugoslav young people in rock music took a leap at the beginning of the 1960s, when they started listening to the British groups Johnny and the Hurricanes and the Shadows. Then the Zagreb record company Jugoton signed a deal with RCA to release some of Elvis Presley's records in Yugoslavia and later brought out a domestic pressing of Chubby Checker's "Let's Twist Again." The Belgrade record company PGP RTB (a spin-off company from Radio-Television Belgrade) released a pressing of Johnny Hallyday's "Twist" also at this time.[7]

One of Yugoslavia's earliest rock stars was Karlo Metikoš, who in 1964 launched his recording career with a PGP RTB record, *Matt Collins Sings R&R.* Singing under a pseudonym, Metikos was the first Yugoslav artist to record covers of some of the original rock classics.[8]

In the years 1960–1961, it was still relatively difficult for Yugoslavs to travel. But local rock musicians, who at that time were largely copying British and American songs, were determined to keep up with the latest releases. They would listen to Radio Luxemburg every night, and at 2 AM, Radio Luxemburg would play the top ten songs of the day. At that time, the Shadows were the most influential group for Yugoslav rockers; hence, because the Shadows had three guitars and one percussionist, every Yugoslav group at that time had three guitars and one percussionist.[9]

In 1961, Josip Kovač, a composer from Subotica (Vojvodina), came up with the idea of organizing a festival of popular music by young talent. The first festival was so successful that it was repeated a year later; the result was an annual pop festival in which, over time, the rock component became ever more important. Some of Yugoslavia's biggest rock stars have performed at the Subotica Festival at one time or another. The thirtieth annual festival in Subotica was held 24–27 May 1990.[10]

The Beatles were scarcely noticed in Yugoslavia until 1964 or 1965, but then they arrived in force. The Rolling Stones briefly eclipsed the Beatles in popularity in Yugoslavia, after the release of their album, *Satisfaction*. But the Beatles soon recaptured the limelight. The 25 June 1967 satellite emission of "All You Need Is Love" was seen by an estimated 150 million people around the world, including many young people in Yugoslavia. By October of that year, Jugoton released a domestic pressing of *Sgt. Pepper's Lonely Hearts Club Band*. And by then there were also Yugoslav pressings of *A Collection of Beatles Oldies,* the Beach Boys' *Greatest Hits,* Jimi Hendrix's *Are You Experienced?,* and singles by various other artists, including the Walker Brothers, the Spencer Davies Group, and Arthur Brown.[11]

At that time, Yugoslav groups were exclusively oriented toward the American and British repertoire. Groups such as White Arrows (Bijele strijele), Red Corals (Crveni koralji), the Golden Boys (Zlatni dečaci), Indexes (Indeksi), Chameleons (Kameleoni), Silhouettes (Siluete), Robots (Roboti), Elipse, the Boyfriends (Rdečki dečki), the Five Flames (Plamenih pet), and Dreamers (Sanjalice) were characteristic of this trend. Some of these groups, in particular Elipse (from Belgrade), Hurricanes (Uragani, from Rijeka), Robots (from Zagreb), and We (Mi, from Šibenik), became interested in black music, especially the music of Aretha Franklin, Wilson Pickett, and Otis Redding. Later, some of these groups started to write their own soul music, in Croatian, though on the whole without success.[12]

About this time, Drago Mlinarec put together a band he called Group 220. The group played original music, modeled on American rock of the time, but showed some versatility, e.g., by doing a rock version of a traditional *Schlager* hit, "Večer na Robleku."

The most important rock groups in Sarajevo in the late 1960s were Čičak and Codex (Kodeksi). While groups in Belgrade and Zagreb were playing soul music, these Sarajevo bands tuned in to progressive rock currents. Codex, in particular—led by Željko Bebek—showed an affinity for the musical styles of Cream and Jimi Hendrix.

One of the most often mentioned groups from the 1960s is Korni Group, named for its leader, Kornell Kovač, a classically trained pianist who would later devote himself to composing and producing records. Korni Group was formed in 1968 in Belgrade and played for six years. The group constantly tested the limits of the market, composing rock "symphonies" and showing a clear preference for longer pieces rather than short commercially oriented songs. Korni Group created a small scandal at a Zagreb concert in 1969 by playing a twenty-minute song; audiences at that time were not accustomed to such things. Korni Group was also the first Yugoslav band to put out an LP on the international market, with an album produced by Carlo Alberto Rossi in Milan.[13]

REBELLION OR CONFORMITY

Deliberations about rock 'n' roll took place at the highest level, and Tito and Kardelj are said to have personally decided against the repressive approach favored in Moscow, Prague, Bucharest, and Tirana, for example. They believed that a policy of toleration within carefully controlled limits could produce better results. The result, according to journalist Dušan Vesić, was that "from the middle of the 1960s until only a few years ago, [Yugoslav] rockers were the greatest servants of the Tito regime!"[14]

Hence, although almost from the beginning the party's cultural commissars were sensitive to rock's potential for stirring rebellious sentiments, they opted for cooptation rather than repression. Astutely, they made it worthwhile for rock musicians to cooperate. The result was a pronounced sycophantic streak in Yugoslav rock, beginning at an early stage.

The group Indeksi, for example—prominent in the mid-1960s—penned a song, "Yugoslavia," which included the lines,

We knew that the sun was smiling on us,
because we have Tito for our marshal!

Much later, Indeksi veteran Davorin Popović produced an album, *Mostar Rain: Our Name Is Tito,* which was released shortly after Tito's death in May 1980. It included a song titled, "After Tito, Tito" (lyrics by J. Sliska, based on a text by Miša Marić):

While he lived, he was
with us and with the world
While he lived, he was
the sun above the planet.
While he lived, he was
a wild hero in a tale
While he lived, he was
such, that we were proud of him.

And what now, southern land?
If anyone should ask us,
we shall say, again Tito:
After Tito, Tito.
We shall say, again Tito.
Tito lives with us
Tito was just one man,
but we are also Tito![15]

Kornell Kovačh, who retired from performing in 1974 in order to devote himself to composing, has been described, unflatteringly, by *Pop Rock* magazine as having been "the greatest patriot of Yugoslav rock 'n' roll."[16] His early song, "People's Government," celebrated Tito's smashing of "the traitorous clique."

Even Bora Djordjević, who donned the mantle of rock rebel in the 1980s, was circumspect in the Tito era. In 1977, for example, he sang a panegyric song, "The World of Tito," in duet with Gorica Popović, on the album, *Brigadier Songs*. Željko Bebek (at one time, a close associate of Goran Bregović's) and pop singer Djordje Balašević are other performers who were willing to "carry the torch" for Tito. Not all rock musicians played "panegyric rock," but many did. Their presence and subsequent success provide clues as to the nature of the Tito and post-Tito regimes.

YUGOSLAV ROCK COMES OF AGE

As Ljuba Trifunović points out, 1974, the year in which Korni Group folded, was also the year in which Goran Bregović created White Button. Bregović's new group drew unabashedly on ethnic melodies and succeeded, in the process, in giving a "Yugoslav" stamp to rock music. White Button quickly established itself as one of the most popular groups in the country—a position it never lost until the war drove Bregović into exile in Paris in 1992. Already in the late 1970s, White Button concerts were rousing young fans (especially of the opposite sex) to paroxysms of "Buttonmania."[17]

By 1976, members of the establishment began to notice that the rock scene was growing. University of Belgrade Professor Sergij Lukač wrote a series of hard-hitting articles for *NIN*, which blasted White Button. Similarly, Sladjana Aleksandra Milošević, a soft rock vocalist from Belgrade, was subjected to regular press attacks at this time; the articles typically criticized her Western-style attire and attacked her for "erotic aggressiveness."[18] Other rock performers were also given rude, even vicious treatment in the press, but for the most part these had no practical significance for the rock scene and no party forum ever undertook to campaign against rock or to obstruct the holding of large rock concerts.[19]

The 1970s were, in fact, the years of the big "Boom" rock festivals in Yugoslavia, drawing thousands of fans to Woodstock-style events in Ljubljana, Novi Sad, and eventually Belgrade. The "Boom" festivals were eventually stopped—for commercial reasons[20]—but smaller festivals continued in Skopje, Zemun, Novi Sad, Avala, and elsewhere.

By the 1970s, Yugoslav rock groups, which at first had felt (like rock groups throughout the world) that rock could only be sung in English, were composing and singing in their own languages—Serbo-Croatian, Slovenian, and, in much smaller numbers, Macedonian.

The major rock groups of the late 1970s were White Button, Azra (now defunct), Index (the first Yugoslav group to play its own material), Bora Djordjević's Fish Soup (Riblja Čorba) from Belgrade, and the Macedonian group, Bread and Salt (Leb i sol). The last two bands were established only in 1978.[21]

Belgrade and Sarajevo were the clear centers for rock 'n' roll in the 1970s, with Zagreb and Ljubljana close behind, and for commercial reasons Serbo-Croatian was the language of rock. Bread and Salt aspired to a national audience and therefore sang most of its songs in Serbo-Croatian, not Macedonian. Similarly, the Slovenian group Bulldozer (Buldožer), seeking a national audience, sang in Serbo-Croatian rather than in Slovenian.

Bulldozer became, in fact, one of the legends of the 1970s. A kind of Yugoslav equivalent of the Mothers of Invention, Bulldozer took up political themes at a time when most Yugoslav rock groups still avoided politics. In their song, "Good Morning Madame Jovanović," for example, they seemed to satirize both Jovanka Tito and the Yugoslav National Army at the same time—daring in any era.[22]

Yugoslavia has shared in *all* the major American and world trends in rock music. When punk developed in Britain, for instance, it quickly spread to Yugoslavia, where groups like the Bastards (Pankrti, from Ljubljana), Electric Orgasm (Električni orgazam, from Belgrade), and Dirty Theater (Prljavo kazalište, from Zagreb) got their start playing punk. Ljubljana became a center for punk and even punk-Nazi music, with groups such as Epidemic and the Trash of Civilization. Now, in the post-punk era, Ljubljana is still a haven for underground music, as served up, for example, by the bands Demolition Group and Del Masochistas. Some of these groups—Bastards, Dirty Theater, and Electric Orgasm, in particular—later evolved away from punk.

New wave (*novi talas*) came to Yugoslavia at the end of the 1970s. Rockabilly, heavy metal, trash metal, speed metal, death metal, and assorted other currents have also won adherents in the country. By 1986, heavy metal had built up sufficient presence to make it possible to hold what proved to be only the first in a series of annual heavy metal concerts in Sarajevo. Groups such as Storm Cloud (Storm klaud), Bombarder, Earthquake (Zemljotres), Formula 4, Dr. Steel (from Rijeka), and Legion (Legija, from Zagreb) took part in the first such festival, attended by some 2,000 fans. By 1988, the festival had become a two-day event, and the list of participating bands had grown to include Atomic Shelter (Atomsko sklonište), Kerber, the Eighth Traveler (Osmi putnik, from Split), Heavy Company, and Fiery Kiss (Vatreni poljubac, from Sarajevo).[23]

The most important rock groups in Yugoslavia in 1990 were: the Belgrade groups Fish Soup, Bajaga and the Instructors (formed in 1984), and Yu-Group; Sarajevo's White Button; Ljubljana's Laibach (formed in 1980) and Falcons (formed in summer 1989); and Skopje's Bread and Salt. Other groups that have attracted attention since 1988 include three Zagreb bands—Dee Dee Mellow (formed in 1988 and discussed below), Witches (formed in 1989), and Modesty (formed from the wreckage of two demo bands)—and the Belgrade band, Department Store (Robna kuća), formed at the medical faculty of the University of Belgrade in April 1988 and enjoying considerable popularity in Belgrade by 1990. Zagreb's Dirty Theater slowly built its reputation as a solid band and was widely considered Croatia's most popular rock band in 1990 and 1991. Also strong are the band Electric Orgasm from Belgrade, though it has not performed in public since about 1988, and the riotous and ever-popular Party Breakers (Partibrejkers), also from Belgrade. These latter two groups probably do not, however, enjoy quite the influence that most of the aforementioned bands do. Some all-female acts also deserve mention, specifically Cacadou Look (established in the mid-1980s in Opatija and singing largely in English) and Boja (a Vojvodina band). The Rijeka group Flight 3 (Let 3) features females on guitar and bass guitar, while their male lead singer has performed in lingerie.[24]

Yugoslavia's top female solo vocalist since the mid-1980s was Snežana Mišković Viktorija, voted top female vocalist by *Pop Rock* readers in a 1988 survey.[25] Other women to make their mark in the late 1980s or early 1990s include Marina Perezić (a member of a duo, Denis and Denis, which made two records before she left the duo and went solo), Neda Ukraden (a pop singer from Sarajevo), Josipa Lisac (who got her start in the early 1970s in Zagreb), Kasandra (a Croatian singer whose album *Ice Cream* was released in 1995), and Baby Doll (alias Dragana Šarić, from Belgrade, who recorded one album and a few singles, spinning exotic songs built on Arabic themes, after spending six months in Cairo).[26] A special mention should also be made of YU-Madonna (alias, Andrea Makoter of Maribor), who performed at a number of festivals in summer 1988, mimicking *the* Madonna in singing style, attire, mannerisms, etc.[27] Among the top male vocalists one may mention Oliver Mandić (a Belgrade singer who created a small storm in the mid-1980s by performing in drag), Rambo Amadeus (whom I like to think of as the PDQ Bach of rock music, because of a piece he once staged for twelve vacuum cleaners),[28] and Tonny Montano (an ever-changing, ever-present entertainer who has evolved from punk to rockabilly to parody with a "beat" look). Aside from these, one may make a special mention of Djordje Balašević, a bard singer with wide influence, performing message-songs. In Russia, Balašević would be counted as a "rock" performer because of his lyrics; in Yugoslavia he is considered a pop singer, as he would be in the West, because of his music.

THE ETHNIC IMPULSE

When rock first came to Yugoslavia, musical adepts approached it in much the way that one would learn a new language. They studied the existing patterns and techniques and worked to master and replicate them. There was little thought given, at first, to innovation. But as young Yugoslav musicians mastered the new "language" and matured musically, they became increasingly willing to innovate and to look to autochthonous sources of musical inspiration. Inevitably, some of them turned to the folk heritage of Yugoslavia.

The first group to do so was White Button, and the Sarajevo group repeatedly drew upon folk idioms for inspiration. Bregović himself argues that ethnic and folk music is the richest source for material and that it is the most promising future for rock music (not just in the Balkans).

But White Button was not alone in this. Fiery Kiss, for example, during the ten years of its existence (1977–1987), incorporated many folk elements into their melodies, and some of their songs used a syncopation that is native to Balkan folk music, not to rock. The group adapted Bosnian folk music, with its blend of Turkish and Arabian elements, and played it on traditional rock instruments. The symbiosis of folk and rock in the performance art of Fiery Kiss was reflected in the fact that a lot of their songs were picked up by the popular folk singer Hanka Paldum and marketed as "folk" songs. In a fitting close to this story, the group's leader, Milić Vukasinović, eventually became dissatisifed with the modest earnings as a rock musician and made the switch to folk.[29]

Another Sarajevo band, Blue Orchestra (Plavi Orkestar), which enjoyed considerable popularity among teenagers, did something similar in its record, *Death to Fascism!* (Smrt fasizmu!—the old partisan greeting from World War II). Released in 1987, the album blended folk musical motifs with partisan themes, singing about the war, the liberation of Belgrade, and Jovanka Tito, the late president's widow. In one song, the group sang the refrain, "Fa-fa-fascist! Don't be a fascist!" The album was celebrated as a species of "new patriotism" and inevitably provoked controversy. Some people suggested (ludicrously) that their lyrics had been written by the Central Committee; others attacked them as "state enemy no. 1."[30] They found themselves cast as the "new partisans" of Yugoslav rock music. Saša Losić, the leader of Blue Orchestra, went into deep depression, and when he emerged out of this depression in 1989, with the release of a new album, he was preaching a new musical philosophy: "Rock 'n' roll has reached its limit, the end of its possibilities. We keep going back to the 1950s, the 1960s, the 1970s. Punk was, in reality, a primal energy for rock 'n' roll. Then there were the new romantics of sympho-rock in the 1970s. Now we are returning to the trends of the 1970s."[31]

Ethnic music figures in an entirely different way in the music of the Zagreb group Dee Dee Mellow. Instead of drawing on indigenous sources, the group has looked beyond European frontiers for inspiration, and their first album included a rendition of a Peruvian Indian song ("Adios Pueblo de Ayacucho") and an adaptation of an American Indian song, sung in the Sioux language ("Sitting Bull Song").[32] Put together largely by former members of the then dormant group Haustor—specifically, Jura Nolosević, Srdjan 'Gul' Gulić, and Igor Pavlitza—Dee Dee Mellow continues Haustor's tradition of social commentary, but with a new twist. Instead of brooding about the gravity of the situation, the new group responds with silliness (the next stage after despair). Hence, in one song, written at a time when newspapers already cost 3,000 dinars and literally everybody had become a "millionaire" in inflated dinars, they sing,

What am I going to do
with all of this money?
Wine, yoghurt,
and a half a loaf of bread.

Other bands have also drawn upon ethnic music. For example, YU-Group, at the end of the 1970s, did a song ("Kosovo Flower") using traditional Albanian rhythms.

Finally, there are regionally specific trends in Vojvodina and Macedonia that reflect the synthesis of folk elements and rock music. The Hungarian inhabitants of Vojvodina share in a musical phenomenon common also to Hungary and the Hungarian population of Transylvania. Known as *Šogor* rock (brother-in-law rock), the genre uses the rythms of Hungarian folk music and even some of the traditional folk instruments but plays them in a rock format. The performers themselves are generally attired rather more in the tradition of folk performers than like rock musicians, and their music has no resonance beyond the Hungarian population. *Šogor* rock started in hotels and bars in the late 1970s, but the first *Šogor* records were released only in 1987.

Macedonia is far more interesting in this regard, having given birth to a new tendency that, for lack of a better term, one may call "Byzantine rock." To a considerable extent, this is the brainchild of Goran Trajkovski, later the leading musical figure in the independent multimedia cultural group Aporea (*Apo*krifna *rea*lnost, Apocryphal Reality). Trajkovski explained his thinking in these terms: "Everything in Macedonia is connected with Orthodoxy, and Orthodoxy is very much the legacy of Byzantium. The Church was the chief civilizing force here for hundreds of years. So our religion always connects us with our past. As a result, the sense of history is very different here from what it is in Slovenia, for example. Our ideas in Aporea, our work, our music, are all derived from Orthodoxy."[33]

In 1984, Trajkovski created the Fall of Byzantium (Padat na Vizantija) and began to work with Orthodox liturgical music in a rock format. The effect was to preserve the spirit of the traditional music but to transform it into patterns that are intelligible to the modern listener. The Fall of Byzantium folded in 1985, but its work was continued, in a multimedia format, by Aporea (although it would be hard to call Aporea's music "rock").

Another neo-Byzantine group in the 1980s was the rock group Mizar, which was created in 1981 as a kind of post-punk band. At first it seemed oriented toward something akin to Pink Floyd,[34] but even so, from the very beginning, Mizar drew upon traditional Macedonian music and culture for inspiration.[35] Later Mizar likewise began to look to Orthodox music for material, but with a difference. Whereas Aporea glorifies Byzantine culture, Mizar, according to Trajkovski, "rejected Byzantium and Byzantine culture." For almost two years (1985–1987), Mizar was cooperating closely with Aporea, but in 1987 there was a rift and Mizar went its own way. Like the Fall of Byzantium, Mizar sang largely in Macedonian (a point that distinguished it from the better known band, Bread and Salt), although Mizar also sang some songs in Old Church Slavonic (the language preferred by Aporea).

Mizar has since disappeared from the Macedonian rock scene, but new groups, such as the rather conventional hard rock group, Area, have taken its place.

POLITICIANS AND ROCK

There is something intrinsically "oppositionist" about rock music: that is completely obvious to everyone. Rock is, in its very soul, about freedom, about individual self-determination, about self-expression. That is why any effort to harness rock music to a role supportive of official policy—as was made in the USSR in the case of the official group Happy Guys in the pre-Gorbachev era—is bound to end up looking ridiculous. That is also one reason, though not the only reason, why the first generation of rockers invariably confronted distrust, fear, and even hostility from political authorities—not just in Yugoslavia but throughout the world, including in the United States, even, to some extent, if they were willing to serve the authorities.[36]

The Sarajevo band Smoking Forbidden (Zabranjeno pušenje) had an experience that may illustrate the point. During a concert in Rijeka in November 1984, one of the loudspeakers (brand name "Marshal") suddenly stopped functioning. Disgusted with this unforeseen inconvenience, band leader Nele Karajlić exclaimed, "The marshal has broken down." Everyone at the concert knew that he was talking about the amplifier. But a month later unknown persons hostile to the group decided to create trouble, and a series of sharp attacks appeared in *Vjesnik, Politika, Borba,* and elsewhere, asking why Karajlić had not said, instead, "The Marshal *is dead.*" The papers then insinuated that Karajlić had deliberately shown disrespect.[37] The band suffered. Previously scheduled concerts were abruptly canceled, and new bookings could not be obtained. Finally, in early 1985, Karajlić wrote an open letter to *Politika* explaining the situation and making it clear that no disrespect to Marshal Tito had been intended. The letter was published, and in February 1985 the group staged a "comeback" concert in Belgrade, attended by some 10,000 fans. The atmosphere was nervous, and the first two rows were taken by police.[38]

Fish Soup's Bora Djordjević was taken to court twice—in 1987[39] and in 1989—but was acquitted both times. In both cases, his lyrics got him into trouble. But that did not prevent him from publishing four books of poetry and being elected to the Serbian Association of Writers.

White Button's Goran Bregović was *threatened* with court action after the group performed a song in which the traditional national hymns of the Serbs and Croats were played back to back, but nothing came of it.

On the whole, however, it is rare that the political authorities take the trouble to discuss the political merits or demerits of a particular ensemble. The Republic of Slovenia provided a rare exception when the Faculty of Political Science of the University of Ljubljana organized a roundtable discussion about "punk-Naziism," attended by the Slovenian republic secretary for internal affairs and representatives from the Ljubljana City Secretariat for Internal Affairs and the Supreme Court of Slovenia.

The most problematic rock group, from the standpoint of the political authorities in the early 1980s, was the art rock group, Laibach, which has, from its beginning, performed in Nazi-style regalia and adopted a proto-fascist demeanor in both its visual presentation and its musical format. Laibach introduced itself as the Musical Division of a totalitarian movement calling itself Neue Slowenische Kunst (New Slovenian Art). German was the preferred language for this movement because it is historically identified with Naziism. A member of Neue Slowenische Kunst told me in 1987, "The very fact that Naziism is always tarred as the blackest evil is a way of not dealing with its social content and meaning." Another NSK member told me in 1989, "We want a great totalitarian leader. God is a totalitarian being. Totalitarianism, for us, is a positive phenomenon. We admire leaders like Alexander the Great, Caesar, Napoleon. As for Hitler, his mistake was to confuse the general with the particular." And yet, Laibach is clearly fixated on Hitler: he is the central inspiration for their artistry, in both form and substance. Their record covers feature swastikas, they sing militant, Nazi-sounding "rock" in German; and when the group decided to do a cover of the Beatles' album *Let It Be* in 1988, they pointedly left out the title song and replaced it with a militant rendition of "Auf der Lüneburger Heide." The effect is right out of a Nazi propaganda film.

Earlier, in 1987, the group released an album significantly titled *Opus Dei*—the Work of God. Taking a song, "Life Is life," that had originally been performed by a German group, Opus, as an innocent, soft rock number, Laibach recast it as a militant, eerily totalitarian march. They sing,

When we all give the power
We give our best,
All that we can, our fullest efforts,
With no thought to rest.
And we all get the power
We all get the best
When everyone gives everything
Then everyone will get everything.
Life is life!
Life is life.
When we all feel the power,
Life is life.
When we all feel the pain,
Life is life.
It's the feeling of the people,
Life is life.
It's the feeling of the land.

Laibach clearly benefited from the relatively more liberal atmosphere prevailing in Slovenia. In other parts of Yugoslavia, the group might have been banned altogether. But even in Slovenia, authorities would not allow anything to be published in the republic about Laibach until 1983 or 1984, except in the youth magazine, *Mladina*.[40] Elsewhere, Laibach experienced at first hand the significance of decentralization in a federalized system. Laibach was prevented from performing in many cities in Yugoslavia.[41] For example, until 1986, Laibach was banned from appearing in Bosnia-Herzegovina altogether, and the group did not actually play in that republic until 7 April 1989, when it performed at Sarajevo's Center for the Social Activities of Youth. When the manager of that center first scheduled them to perform, there was tremendous pressure on him from the authorities to cancel the concert, including threatening phone calls to his unlisted home phone. He did not sleep for two nights before the concert, but he refused to cave in, and the concert went ahead as planned. Predictably, after the concert, the authorities bragged about what good democrats they were to have authorized the concert.

Created in September 1980, Laibach has released about a dozen albums overseas, although the albums can be purchased, as imports, in Slovenia. They have succeeded, unlike any other Yugoslav rock group, in building a worldwide following, and in 1989, for example, the group did an American concert tour, performing in New York, Washington, D.C., Boston, and Los Angeles, and they performed in Seattle in 1993.

CENSORSHIP—NOW YOU SEE IT, NOW YOU DON'T

Tito did not establish a separate Office of Censorship per se, and there certainly has not been any government office entrusted with the task of listening to rock demos and determining what may and may not be pressed. All the same, the Communist system was set up in such a way that censorship resulted. In any recording company, the responsible editor was always a party member and was required to review all rock songs before a disc would be pressed. Even though they might be sympathetic to the rock musicians, record producers, studio directors, and concert managers frequently feared what *might* happen to them if they allowed certain things to be performed. Hence, rather than take a chance, they tended to play it safe. The result was that rock musicians had to change their costumes, change their record jackets, delete certain songs from certain albums, adjust their repertoire at certain concerts, and even rewrite their lyrics. Talking to rock musicians in Yugoslavia, I heard numerous stories of intervention by nervous record producers and so forth. The intention was sometimes not primarily to suppress anything but simply to save their own skins. The result was a form of censorship.

For example, Smoking Forbidden made a rock video, "Maniac," about a politician, a family man, who has an illicit romantic adventure, literally going mad in the process. In the video, the mad politician uses "Tops" crackers as bait to lure the girl of his dreams. The video was made in March 1987, a few months before the Agrokomerc corruption scandal broke. But as it turned out, "Tops" crackers were made by Agrokomerc. Nobody would believe that the video had been made *before* Agrokomerc made the headlines. That was a contributing factor to keeping the video off TV.

Goran Bregović's White Button likewise had its share of problems. In 1976, for example, Bregović wanted to title his album *Hey! I Want to Be Stupid*. He had to be happy with the bland *Hey! I Want*. Nor were the authorities happy when Bregović took on religion, and in 1979 he had trouble with the line, "and Christ was a bastard and a worry [to his mother]," intended for a song for the album, *Batanga and the Princess*. Even in 1986, Bregović ran into trouble when he wanted to engage Vice Vukov to sing a song on his album, *Spit and Sing, My Yugoslavia!* Vukov had been viewed as a kind of bard of Croatian nationalism back in 1970–1971 and now, fifteen years later, the chief of police of the Republic of Bosnia took part in discussions about Bregović's desire to involve Vukov in one song.[42] Vukov finally made his comeback in 1989 with a record of Neapolitan songs.

Bora Djordjević has had similar problems with his songs and poems. In 1970, for example, he was prevented from singing the line, "Yet another scabby day"—lest this pessimism be taken as directed against the system.[43] In 1982, after the release of the latest Fish Soup album, the Veterans Association of Macedonia became upset because some of the old partisans felt that one of the songs included lines insulting to veterans of the national liberation struggle. Some hotheads in the Veterans Association said the album should be banned; others wanted to ban Fish Soup altogether. A few even talked about getting rock music banned altogether in Yugoslavia—as it was, at the time, in Albania. But Bora had contacts in high places, including a close relative, and eventually an unnamed high official contacted Kosta Nadj (the head of the Veterans Association of Yugoslavia) and told him to call off the hounds.[44]

Again, in 1984, Bora was preparing his album, *Tonight, Drunk Musicians Play for You,* for release by Jugoton, when the recording company's chief editor, Dubravko Majnarić, rejected Bora's song, "Sudba, Udba, Ozna,"[45] with the rhetorical question, "Young man, what do you know about UDBa and OZNA?"[46] The song "Power of the Opposition" could not be included on his 1987 album *The Truth* (Istina) for political reasons but was released on videocassette a year or two later.[47] Various texts originally intended for his second book (published in spring 1987, while Ivan Stambolić was still the party boss in Serbia)[48] were prohibited at that time, only to be passed for publication in his subsequent book,[49] by which time Slobodan Milošević had replaced Stambolić as the party boss in Serbia. Among the poems originally banned are several nationalist poems about Kosovo, for example:

Eenie meenie minie mo,
I'm a little rabbit
I eat little chickens
I have a big stomach
I eat little Serbs.

No one could mistake the fact that the poem was about Kosovo's Albanians. Or again:

I don't buy that pure shit
that they come to šumadija,
but if they come to šumadija,
I prefer to kick the bucket.
I don't need that Balkan city,
I need the Patriachate of Peć.
I need a little change
in surnames in Prizren.
And never will there be any peace
between me and the "Illyrian."
Is it possible that some Shiptar
will seize the Serbian crown and scepter?

These poems, out of favor in Stambolić's day, came very much into favor with the political authorities once Milošević took charge in Serbia. Similarly, Bora Djordjević's original criticisms of Tito were courageous when Stambolić was in charge. Now Milošević himself criticizes the man he prefers to call "Josip Broz."

But there is more to Bora than just nationalism; he is, above all, quintessentially anti-establishment. In another once banned poem, he writes,

Oh God, give me a black Mercedes,
with a little registration,
so that I can finally view myself
as an official fool.
Oh God, give me a black Mercedes
with at least six doors
so that I can tap my Havana
into a gold ashtray.
Oh God, give me a black Mercedes
because it is a miracle above all miracles.
It is beautiful to drive unpenalized
over flowers and people.[50]

Sometimes, record producers have approved an album but pressured the group to make alterations. The Bastards, for example, were compelled to change an album cover in 1982 because the producer was nervous about the original design.[51] Or again, Goran Bregović's White Button had to put up with having sections of their songs literally spliced out, after being recorded, because the words were considered "potentially offensive." Needless to say, this left some telltale signs in their early albums.

It is symptomatic of the nature of a watched society that people fear to get involved in others' troubles. The result, as Vesić dolefully noted in 1990, was a lack of solidarity among Yugoslav rock musicians. When White Button was under fire in 1976, not a single band came to its defense. When the Veterans Association of Macedonia attacked Bora's Fish Soup in 1982, again not a single rock musician or rock band raised a voice in protest, and Bora had to rely on his own resources.[52] Rock musicians who tried to play the gadfly found it impossible, thus, to ignite anything like a protest movement. Or, to put it analogically, in Tito's Yugoslavia the system did not allow enough freedom for anyone to be able to play a role anything like Joan Baez or Bob Dylan did in the late 1960s in the United States.

Editorial interventions of a political nature were thus commonplace, but one should not exaggerate their frequency either. There are many groups who have never had any problems with "intervention," especially commercial bands with no social awareness. The problems began when a band became socially aware.

To be socially aware is not necessarily to be politically controversial or critical, however. Rock groups have addressed issues of social isolation, growing up, ethnic feuding, and other issues that are not necessarily troubling to the authorities. The late President Tito (elected "without termination of mandate") likewise was long a favorite theme for Yugoslav rock groups. For example, the Elvis J. Kurtović Band of Sarajevo released an album in 1988 with the tongue-in-cheek title, *The Wonderful World of Private Business*. It includes a song nominally about Emperor Haile Selassie of Ethiopia:

When I was young
the teacher took us to the main street
to see his Majesty Haile Selassie
drive past in a black limousine.
We were all so happy,
and the street was packed with people
all to see our friend from nonaligned Ethiopia.
He was an amazing man,
loved by the masses,
wise like Gandhi,
and as handsome as Nasser.
Of all our friends,
he was the best.
He led his people
to wealth and happiness.

Set to rock rhythms, it was perfectly clear that the lyrics were not intended to be taken solemnly. Thus, even though the song appeared on the album, the group was not allowed to perform it on television.[53]

Another Sarajevo group, Smoking Forbidden (Zabranjeno pušenje), tried to capture people's mood when Tito died—the sense of loss, the sense of greatness past. The song works allegorically, talking about the great soccer player Hase's last match:

> *The people go into the stadium*
> *and it was hushed.*
> *People said,*
> *Today is Hase's last game . . .*
> *They spoke of his past glories,*
> *Of what a great player he had been.*
> *They talked of how he beat the Germans*
> *and the Russians*
> *and the British.*
> *And then the referee blew the whistle,*
> *With the game tied at 1-to-1.*
> *The people leave in silence,*
> *nobody is talking.*
> *Sunday stops in its tracks,*
> *but May goes on.*
> *Some fans chant,*
> *"Go team, charge.*
> *There is only one Hase."*[54]

NEW PRIMITIVISM

When Elvis J. Kurtović, "Dr." Nele Karajlić, and a few other rock musicians in Sarajevo decided to satirize the cultural and political backwardness of some of their fellow citizens, they gave their "movement" a name—"new primitivism." The idea took shape at a cafe in the Bašćaršija district of Sarajevo, over a copy of the local newspaper, *Oslobodjenje*. It was 1981, and *Oslobodjenje* was reflecting on a new film, *Quadrophenia,* which dealt with teddy boys and mods in Great Britain. *Oslobodjenje* launched into a long jeremiad about "long-haired punks and hippies" whom "local good youths" would "devour." Kurtović, Karajlić, and friends knew, of course, that punks don't have long hair like hippies. But the text inspired them. They decided to satirize these "local good youth" by dressing and acting like them and singing about them; they adopted the name "new primitives." "We started to dress without any taste, quite deliberately," Kurtović recalls. "We looked like those *Gastarbeiter* in the film, *Montenegro.* Our music combined American rock ideologies, Japanese technology, and local domestic primitivism."[55] Their satire was not appreciated by the "old primitives," however, who understood that they were the butt of "new primitive" humor. But the "new primitives" made a serious point. In Karajlić's words, "The basic problem in Yugoslavia is not politics, but culture. There is no great culture here—no great classical composers, only a few important writers, a handful of great sculptors. If you don't have great culture, you can't have great ideas. And if you are behind in ideas, everything else follows."[56] Or in Kurtović's words, "The problem of this country is primitivism. We can change the whole system and adopt capitalism, but we won't be like West Germany, we'll be like Turkey—primitive."

A classic product of "new primitivism" was the song, "Anarchy All Over Bascarsija," which dealt with the reflections of a typical "old primitive." He feels good about having beaten up a young hippie, gets nervous when he sees the letter "A" scrawled on a wall in the Bašćaršija district, and broods about the West, because it is changing the way young people dress.[57]

New primitivism was, of course, never a movement as such. But this satirical treatment won the Elvis J. Kurtović Band and Karajlić's Smoking Forbidden a loyal following among Yugoslav young people and won them the respect of intellectuals in the country.

THE SUPPORT SYSTEM

Rock music is a product that must be managed, promoted, advertised, and sold. The "support system" was, thus, a critical factor in the Yugoslav rock scene.

There were eleven record and cassette companies in Yugoslavia that produced at least some rock (as of 1987). The major companies were Jugoton of Zagreb, which issued about thirty new rock albums each year, and PGP RTB of Belgrade, which issued forty-five to fifty new rock albums each year. Together these two companies thus accounted for 75–80 percent of all new albums marketed in Yugoslavia.[58] The chief recording outlets for Slovenian groups were the Ljubljana companies Helidon and RTV Ljubljana. Relatively few records were reissued after the initial pressings were sold out, and many groups that were popular in their own republics (e.g., the Bastards in Slovenia, and the Niš group Galija in Serbia) received little or no organized promotion outside their own republics. A hundred thousand in sales was widely viewed as the barrier to be broken, but experimental bands generally had to be happy with sales of 2,000–5,000. Several people told me that while the companies put a lot of money into promoting folk music, they made no serious efforts to promote rock music and that there were, for example, practically no commercials for rock records at all. Even so, some rock records have sold 500,000 copies or more.

The key person in the life of a rock 'n' roll band is its manager. Some managers work exclusively with one band (e.g., Bajaga's Saša Dragić); others work with two or more groups at once (e.g., Goran "Fox" Lisica, who worked as manager for the Slovenian group Videosex and the Macedonian group Mizar, and more recently has been managing and promoting rock groups in Rijeka and Opatija); still others work within an agency or as the musical director of a Student Cultural Center or House of Youth (such as Skopje's Pande Dimovski); and still others operate as "free-lance managers," working as intermediaries between student cultural centers and the individual groups (such as Belgrade's Ilija Stanković). Managers face various problems in their trade, including the low motivation of directors in subsidized clubs (some clubs, such as Sarajevo's Center for the Social Activities of Youth, are *not* subsidized) and the low prices charged for tickets in economically strapped Kosovo and Macedonia—making it difficult to cover expenses in those regions and hence to schedule concerts by visiting groups there, except as large gala events. In Kosovo, the most successful rock concerts have been produced in Priština's Bora i Ramiz Hall— the largest hall in town—which has a capacity of 10,000.[59] Because the support system is relatively underdeveloped the group manager sometimes finds himself having to engage in relatively mundane tasks such as chauffeuring, delivering mail, and distributing posters.[60]

The media are also a crucial part of the support system. The "super" channel on television carries a lot of rock videos, from both Yugoslavia and abroad, and this is an important medium for promotion. There are also various television and radio programs that feature individual artists and groups, such as the weekly interview show *U sred srede* (In the Middle of Wednesday), featured on Belgrade Television, and a weekly radio rock interview show carried on Belgrade's Radio Studio B. *U sred srede*, directed by Tanja Petrović, has the distinction of being the only long program on Belgrade television (three hours weekly) to play strictly Yugoslav rock.[61]

Finally, the printed media play an important role. In 1989, there were at least five magazines oriented exclusively toward the rock scene. These were Pero Lovšin's now-defunct *Gram* (Ljubljana, in Slovenian), *Heroina* (Zagreb, in Croatian), *Ritam* (Belgrade, in Serbo-Croatian), *Disko selektor* (Skopje, in Macedonian), and *Ćao* (Belgrade, Serbo-Croatian, focusing on foreign rock). *Petar Popović's Rock* magazine (later *Pop Rock*) was the most influential rock magazine in the late 1980s, but it folded abruptly in 1990. In its heyday, *Pop Rock* had come under fire, from time to time, for favoring Belgrade groups in its coverage, but *Pop Rock* in fact carried articles about all the major groups, including those based in other cities and republics. Aside from these, there are a large number of newspapers and magazines that have regular or semi-regular columns devoted to rock, including *Mladina* (Ljubljana), *Polet* (Zagreb), *Valter* (Sarajevo), *Iskra* (Split), *Mlad Borec* (Skopje), and *Politika ekspres* (Belgrade).

THE END OF YUGO-ROCK

Yugoslav rock made international news in May 1989 when Boardwalk (Riva), a hitherto little-known soft-rock band from Zadar, took first prize at the Thirty-Fourth Eurovision Music Festival at Lausanne, with its song, "Rock Me."[62] The fact that the group came from the small coastal town of Zadar was significant in that it showed that rock 'n' roll in Yugoslavia was by no means the monopoly of the big cities. Later that same year—in September—Novi Sad was host to the Seventh Festival of the European Radio Diffusion Union, a mammoth international event that drew entertainers from such countries as Britain, Ireland, the Soviet Union, Finland, the Netherlands, Hungary, and Sweden.[63] At one time or another, the SFRY hosted many world-class rock performers, including Alice Cooper,[64] Tina Turner,[65] Black Sabbath,[66] David Bowie,[67] Jerry Lee Lewis,[68] and Sisters of Mercy.[69]

The rock scene in Yugoslavia was highly diverse, replicating most, if not all, trends worldwide, including rap music, techno-pop, and—as the Slovenian group Borghesia epitomized—industrial rock containing sado-masochistic overtones.[70] Improvisational rock also had its practitioners, for example, the Zagreb underground band, Voodoobuddah. In 1988, Yugoslavia produced its first rock operetta, Vladimir Milačić's *Creators and Creatures* (Kreatori i kreature),[71] and in 1989 its first rock movie, *The Fall of Rock 'n' Roll*, featuring original compositions by Vlada Divljan, Srdjan 'Gele' Gojković, and Dušan 'Koja' Kojić. In the film, Kojić—otherwise the leader of the Belgrade group, Discipline of the Spine (Disciplina kičme)— played the role of a mini-superhero who wanted to ride on public transport without a ticket and whose big enemy was, thus, the ticket inspector.

Rock music is seen by many of its purveyors as transnational, as a force that can bring people together and create ties of mutual acceptance. Symptomatically, some of the leading figures in the Yugo-rock scene emphasized that they were "Yugoslavs," rather than Serbs or Croats. But as the general political situation in Yugoslavia worsened, bands were increasingly identified with their respective republics. Bands that at one time were able to play in Slovenia, for example (such as White Button and Electric Orgasm), found it impossible, by 1989, to book concerts there. Other bands, like the Serbian group Fish Soup, found that attendance at their concerts in other parts of the country (specifically Croatia, in the case of Fish Soup) dropped in the years after 1987, when nationalism started to rise. Jasenko Houra, lead singer of Dirty Theater (a Zagreb group), told the Croatian weekly *Danas* in 1989 that among Zagreb rock groups only Psychomodo Pop (Psihomodo pop) was still welcome in Belgrade.[72] Like everything else in the SFRY, rock music too was affected by the "national question." This was not hard and fast, of course. At the Avala Rock Festival in Belgrade (in mid-August 1990)—to take an example of interrepublican exchange—groups came from many parts of the country, including Sarajevo (Blue Orchestra), Rijeka (Fit), Split (Devils), and Zagreb (a revived Haustor). Members of the Niš rock group, Galija, talked of wanting to play all over the country and to serve as a cultural bridge.[73] But already by the

end of the 1980s many groups had no ambitions to reach audiences beyond their own republics. Zagreb's Dirty Theater, for example, disclaimed
any interest in playing outside Croatia,[74] while the Skopje group, Memory,
which produced the first Macedonian-language rock LP in Yugoslavia in
1990 (Mizar having produced only cassettes), expressly geared itself to
Macedonian national identity and culture.[75]

The partial pluralization of 1988–1991 inevitably had effects on the rock
scene. In most republics, rock groups started to enjoy greater freedom (although Slobodan Milošević kept a tight reign on culture in Serbia in those
years), but as the economy plummeted in the period 1990–1991, the purchasing power of rock fans declined, contributing to declines in concert attendance throughout the country.[76] The proliferating sense of hopelessness,
which made people more vulnerable to nationalist manipulation and chauvinist appeals, could also be detected in the rock scene at that time. For example, the east Slavonian band, Satan Panonski (from a village near
Vinkovci), played with an equation of *nation* and *punk* in its 1990 album,
Nuclear Olympic Games, capturing some of this sense of hopelessness in
the song, "Hard Blood Shock" (sung in English):

> *auto-destruction is eruption*
> *it will destroy all my enemies*
> *my victory is toxicant peace*
> *this is not punk*
> *this is not rock*
> *this is this is*
> *hard blood shock.*[77]

As the country slid toward war, as we shall see in more detail in Chapter
13, rock groups took up diverse positions, either identifying themselves
with one national cause or another, or associating themselves with the
weak antiwar movement, or fleeing into romantic escapism.

NOTES

1. Interview with Goran Bregović, leader of Bijelo dugme, Sarajevo, 14
September 1989.

2. Ibid.

3. Conversation with Dražen Vrdoljak, Radio Zagreb music department, Zagreb,
10 September 1989.

4. Interview with Goće Dimovski (director of the House of Youth) and Pande
Dimovski (music manager of the House of Youth), Skopje, 26 September 1989.

5. Quoted in Dušan Vesić, "Novi prilozi za istoriju Jugoslovenskog rock'n rolla,"
Part 1, "Josip Broz i rock'n roll," *Pop Rock* (10 May 1990), p. 2.

6. Quoted in Ibid., p. 4.

7. Ljuba Trifunović, *Vibracije* (Belgrade: Kultura, 1986), pp. 99–100.

8. Ibid., p. 100.

9. Interview with Zoran Simjanović, former leader of Elipse, Belgrade (telephone), 28 September 1989.

10. *Pop Rock* (21 February 1990), p. 35.

11. Trifunović, *Vibracije,* p. 102.

12. Interview with Dražen Vrdoljak, Zagreb, 22 June 1987; and interview with Simjanović, 28 September 1989.

13. Interview with Kornell Kovačh, former leader of Korni Group, and Bora Djordjević, leader of Riblja Čorba, Belgrade, 18 July 1988.

14. Vesić, "Novi prilozi," Part 1, "Josip Broz i rock'n'roll," p. 4.

15. Quoted in Ibid., p. 13.

16. Ibid., p. 12.

17. See Darko Glavan and Dražen Vrdoljak, *Ništa mudro—Bijelo dugme: Autorizirana biografija* (Zagreb: Polet Rock, 1981), pp. 13–18. For a recent interview with Goran Bregović, see *Globus* (Zagreb), 9 June 1995, pp. 28–29.

18. See, for instance, *Sarajevske novine* (22 March 1979). Sladjana Milošević later moved to Los Angeles. See *Vreme International* (Belgrade), 5 June 1995, p. 45, and 7 August 1995, p. 43.

19. This was emphasized and confirmed in interviews with several knowledgeable people, including Vrdoljak, 10 September 1989; Simjanović, 28 September 1989; and Darko Glavan, freelance writer, Zagreb, 28 August 1989.

20. Interview with Vrdoljak, 10 September 1989.

21. Regarding Leb i sol, see *Oko* (7–21 September 1989), p. 27. Regarding a recent concert that this group gave in Belgrade, see *Naša borba* (Belgrade) (22 March 1995), p. 14.

22. Interview with Igor Vidmar, musical coordinator of Radio Student, Ljubljana, 30 June 1987; and interview with Glavan, 28 August 1989. For articles on Buldožer, see *Vjesnik* (16 February 1985), p. 11; and *Pop Rock* (12 July 1989), p. 22.

23. *Pop Rock* (Belgrade) (October 1988), p. 37.

24. *Pop Rock* (21 February 1990), pp. 16–17; and *Vjesnik* (6 October 1990), p. 18. For a recent article about Electric Orgasm, see *NIN* (Belgrade), no. 2307 (17 March 1995), p. 35. For a recent article about Flight 3, see *Arkzin* (Zagreb) (23 December 1994), p. 28. Regarding Witches, see *Narodni list* (Zadar) (3 February 1995), p. 22.

25. *Pop Rock* (3 May 1989), p. 20 (reporting the results of a survey conducted in 1988).

26. Interview with Dragan Todorović, editor of *NON* and staff writer for *Rock* magazine, Belgrade, 10 July 1987; and *Globus* (Zagreb), 30 June 1995, p. 27.

27. See *Vjesnik* (19 July 1988), p. 7, (21 July 1988), p. 7, and (24 August 1988), p. 13.

28. See his interview in *Pop Rock* (24 January 1990), pp. 20–21.

29. Interview with Mimo Hajrić, former member of Vatreni poljubac, Sarajevo, 15 September 1989.

30. Interview with Saša Losić, in *Pop Rock* (March 1989), pp. 16–17.

31. Interview with Saša Losić, in *Pop Rock* (28 June 1989), p. 16.

32. Interview with Jura Nolosević and Srdjan 'Gul' Gulić, members of Dee Dee Mellow, Zagreb, 28 August 1989.

33. Interview with the author, Skopje, 25 September 1989. Regarding Trajkovski's latest ensemble, Anastasia, see The European Magazine (London), 16–22 June 1995, p. 19.

34. Interview with Valentino Skenderovski, former member (1985–1986) of Mizar, Sarajevo, 15 September 1989.

35. *Pop Rock* (17 May 1989), p. 22.

36. Regarding the hostility confronted by early rockers in the United States, see John Orman, *The Politics of Rock Music* (Chicago: Nelson-Hall, 1984).

37. See, for instance, Tanjug (26 February 1985), trans. in *Foreign Broadcast Information Service (FBIS), Daily Report* (Eastern Europe), 27 February 1985, p. 18.

38. Interview with Nele Karajlić, leader of Zabranjeno pušenje, Sarajevo, 16 September 1989.

39. See *Večernje novosti* (Belgrade) (30 December 1987), p. 4.

40. Interview with Miha Kovač, former editor-in-chief of *Mladina*, Ljubljana, 3 July 1987.

41. *Pop Rock* (17 May 1989), p. 20. For a recent article about Laibach, see *Permission,* no. 6 (spring 1995), pp. 27–31.

42. *Pop Rock* (13 June 1990), p. 15.

43. Ibid.

44. Ibid.

45. *Sudba* means fate. OZNA and UDBa were successive incarnations of the Yugoslav secret police.

46. Quoted in *Pop Rock* (13 June 1990), p. 15.

47. The song lyrics were also subsequently published in Bora Djordjević's second book, *Hej Sloveni* (Belgrade: Glas, 1987).

48. Ibid.

49. Bora Djordjević, *Necu* (Belgrade: Književna zadruga, 1989).

50. Ibid., p. 123.

51. The story is recounted in Pedro Ramet, "Apocalypse Culture and Social Change in Yugoslavia," in Pedro Ramet, ed., *Yugoslavia in the 1980s* (Boulder, Colo.: Westview Press, 1985), p. 14.

52. Vesić, "Novi prilozi," Part 1, "Josip Broz i rock'n'roll," p. 5.

53. Interview with Elvis J. Kurtović, Sarajevo, 15 September 1989.

54. Interview with Nele Karajlić, Sarajevo, 14 September 1989.

55. Interview with Kurtović, 15 September 1989.

56. Interview with Karajlić, 14 September 1989.

57. There was, in fact, a gang of "old primitives" in Sarajevo who terrorized young people who dressed in Western fashions. After the war reached Bosnia-Herzegovina in 1992, Karajlić left Sarajevo and took up residence in Belgrade. Kurtović, on the other hand, remained in Sarajevo and has continued to play to local audiences. For a recent article about Elvis J. Kurtović, see *Nedjeljna Dalmacija* (Split) (30 December 1994), p. 13.

58. These figures all date from 1987. Interview with Siniša Škarica, program director of Jugoton, Zagreb, 24 June 1987; and interview with Aleksandar Pilipenko, editor for Rock and Pop Records, PGP RTB, 20 September 1989.

59. Interview with Ilija Stanković, free-lance manager, Belgrade, 18 September 1989.

60. Interview with Saša Dragić, in *Rock* magazine [original title of *Pop Rock*] (January 1988), p. 50.

61. Interview with Tanja Petrović, director of *U sred srede* show, Belgrade, 23 September 1989.

62. *Borba* (8 May 1989), pp. 1, 14; *NIN,* No. 2002 (14 May 1989), pp. 30–31; and *Danas,* No. 378 (16 May 1989), pp. 71–72.

63. *Oslobodjenje* (Sarajevo), 14 September 1989, p. 6; *Nedjeljna Dalmacija* (Split), 24 September 1989, p. 19; and *Pop Rock* (4 October 1989), p. 30.

64. *Danas,* No. 437 (3 July 1990), pp. 76–77; and *Pop Rock* (8 August 1990), pp. 1–5.

65. *Pop Rock* (11 July 199), p. 12.

66. *Rock* (December 1987), p. 39.

67. *Vjesnik* (6 September 1990), p. 12, and (9 September 1990), p. 14.

68. *Vjesnik* (9 October 1990), p. 8.

69. *Vjesnik* (2 November 1990), insert.

70. For a brief article on Borghesia, see *Danas,* No. 347 (11 October 1988).

71. Vladimir Milačić, *Kreatori i kreature,* RTB 210404 (1988).

72. *Danas,* No. 405 (21 November 1989), p. 75. For a recent article about Jasenko Houra, see *Globus* (Zagreb, 26 May 1995, pp. 20–22. Regarding Srdjan Gojković, see *Vreme International* (7 August 1995), pp. 40–41.

73. *Pop Rock* (11 July 1990), p. 14. The group Galija was included in a cultural delegation sent by Belgrade to Moscow in March 1995 and played to Russian audiences. See *Naša borba* (21 March 1995), p. 13. Regarding Nenad Milosavljević, leader of Galija, see also *Vreme International* (24 July 1995), p. 39.

74. *Pop Rock* (20 September 1989), p. 20.

75. *Pop Rock* (16 May 1990), pp. 20–21.

76. Telephone interview with Pero Lovšin, leader of the Falcons and chief editor of *Gram,* Seattle–Ljubljana, 21 June 1991.

77. Quoted in *Pop Rock* (11 July 1990), p. 20.

CHAPTER SIX

◆

Women and Men

CULTURE MAY BE VIEWED as a web of values, norms, and social mores, which predetermine modal attitudes and affect behaviors. Culture, in that sense, is reducible to a complex of constituent parts, which will include ethnic culture (of a specific group, including recollection and an interpretation of the group's history), religious culture (based in one or another religious organization), aesthetic culture (determining the dominant modes of entertainment and artistic expression, and the comparative values attached to different genres), and gender culture, among others. All of these cultures tend to perpetrate an illusion of continuity, presenting themselves, at any given time, as the rock of tradition, inherited unchanged over the ages—regardless of the recency of the "tradition" or how many changes have in fact occurred. Sexual conservatives of the late twentieth century, for example, imagine that they are trying to preserve and maintain a way of life that has been unchanged and unchallenged until the generation of the 1960s. They forget the ancient world, the Renaissance, the ribald fifteenth and sixteenth centuries, and other eras, when the pendulum swung toward liberality, promiscuity, diversity, and tolerance.

Gender culture, specifically, defines how women and men must behave in order to be viewed as socially integrated or "normal" (conforming to a set of norms imposed from outside). It provides the basis for claims of precedence, dictates how the relationship between love and sex is viewed (markedly differently in past cultures of Japan, the Middle East, Italy, and America, for example), and even prescribes norms for relations between the parents of each sex and their offspring.

Aside from a general gender culture, we may also speak of specific cultures for women and men. Women are raised to know and understand female culture, and men to know and understand male culture. And except in unusual cases (e.g., transsexuals), the boundary is rarely crossed: men, thus, tend to find it impossible to understand female culture (although women are often quite adept at understanding male culture). The existence of this cultural boundary and consequent male difficulty in understanding female culture constitute important sources of communications break-downs between the sexes generally and of the persistence—despite all logic—of male chauvinism more specifically.

Gender cultures are themselves linked with and affected by their associated cultures. In particular, the Muslim and Orthodox religious cultures in Yugoslavia bolster values and attitudes less tolerant of women than, by contrast, the Protestant and Catholic cultures in this same country. These religious cultures have regional concentrations (Muslims in Bosnia and Kosovo, Orthodox in Serbia, Macedonia, and Montenegro, Catholics in Slovenia and Croatia, and pockets of Protestants in Vojvodina, as well as in the larger cities of Slovenia and Croatia). As a consequence, gender cultures in Yugoslavia differ quite considerably from republic to republic, north to south.

Gender culture is also affected by the presence or absence of institutional alternatives to the dominant Church. This is at least one reason why there are such strong differences, in all countries, between urban culture and rural culture. And again, because traditional culture in Yugoslavia is patriarchal (differing in degree from region to region), urban culture, insofar as it provides some attenuation of traditional culture, is more conducive to the advancement of women than is rural culture.

Finally, to complete the picture, social class must be calculated as a factor in gender relations. Generally, families in which both partners are educated and hold more prestigious jobs tend to be more egalitarian than families in which the marital partners are less well educated and working in unskilled jobs or in agriculture. Or to put it simply, a female lawyer has a better chance of being treated with genuine respect and as an equal by men, than a peasant woman or a florist.

Certainly, other factors influence gender relations in the family, such as alcoholism, insanity, loss of one's job, sickness, and personality quirks, to mention only a few. But these factors cannot be determinative of larger social patterns and can at most mediate those larger culturally determined patterns at the level of the specific family.

This interwoven cultural bedrock makes it difficult for feminists to change behaviors because, in order to do so, they must modify attitudes at a number of levels and challenge the target audience to rethink norms that have tended to be taken for granted. If, among rural Albanians of Kosovo, women have tended, for as long as they can remember, to feed the men, letting them eat by themselves, before sitting down only after the men have finished, to eat the leftovers, how do you go about convincing Kosovo's women and men that they should eat together and treat each other as equals? Bette Denich recorded, in 1974, that similar customs were characteristic also of traditional rural Serbs as well as other South Slav peoples:

> In Serbia ceremonial seating arrangements are by ranks, with males from elders through adolescents seated at the head of the table, with all women—beginning with the eldest—lined up below the lowest-ranking males. Within the household stylized behaviors also reiterate the theme of female subordination. In some South Slavic pastoral regions custom requires that a new daughter-in-law show respect by kissing the hands of all males in the household—including the children. In Serbia, women's subsidiary status is reenacted whenever there are guests: men serve as hosts, sitting and drinking with the guests, while the women prepare food and carry it to the table but do not sit with the guests. Sarakatsani men and women always eat separately, the men first eating their fill, [and] the women taking the leftovers. Albanian men are served by women, who then eat separately in the kitchen with the children. In many Yugoslav regions, women's degradation ceremonies include washing the feet of their husbands and fathers-in-law.[1]

Such behaviors are reinforced by normative structures shared by both the female and male cultures in the society.

There are distinct female and male cultures. They must necessarily complement each other. When one of them—whether the female or male culture—changes, the result is change in the compatibility of the cultures, producing stress. This stress can be relieved only by changing the partner culture in some compatible direction or by repressing the change in the original culture. For example, a culture of female subservience is compatible with a culture of male domination. Feminism changes the former, producing tension. This, in a word, is the dynamic of feminism, and it encapsulates an important aspect of gender relations in Ljubljana, Zagreb, Belgrade, and other urban environments in Yugoslavia.

Viewed in this way, patriarchal society is not just discriminatory against women as individuals with specific genitalia and reproductive functions; on the contrary, it is the systematic effort to assert the primacy (rather than equality) of male culture over female culture. It discriminates against a culture. Male culture is declared, under patriarchy, to be the norm, and female culture is ghettoized.[2]

SERBIAN PASTORALISM AND THE MALE COMPLEX

Slovenia, on the one hand, and Serbia and Kosovo, on the other, figure as extremes along a continuum defining female status in multicultural ex-Yugoslavia. In Slovenia, women enjoy a status equivalent to Austrian or Czech women, and their essential equality and participation in public life are taken for granted, even if some social inequality prevails here, too. Slovenian women enjoy much greater independence and status than the women of Serbia and Kosovo. In the latter regions, by contrast, women are pointedly made to feel inferior. In Serbia, this is aptly symbolized by the common male practice of frequent expectoration on public streets and sidewalks—a practice that affirms the spitter's claim to some ill-defined "superiority" over his environment. Serbian women, by contrast, do not spit in public places.

Differences in religious faith, I suggested above, may have something to do with the regional differences in the status of women in Yugoslavia, but other factors are also involved. Bette Denich has drawn attention to the importance of socioeconomic organization for gender relations in the Yugoslav context: in her view, pastoral societies, specifically Serbia, Macedonia, Montenegro, and Kosovo, tend to be more patriarchal and more sexually stratified than agricultural communities, such as Slovenia and Croatia. Without exaggerating the relative advantage enjoyed by Slovenian and Croatian females, one may at least concede that the definite transition from traditional extended families to nuclear families in these parts has worked to the advantage of females (both adults and children). "In Montenegro"—by contrast—"daughters were not even reckoned by fathers enumerating their children."[3]

What accounts for this difference between pastoral and agricultural societies in Yugoslavia and elsewhere? Anthropologist Andrei Simić highlights the association of the institution of the extended family with enhanced status for older women. He notes that as Serbian women age, they come to enjoy status, authority, and freedoms that would have been unthinkable for them at an earlier age. Related to this is a magnified status for mothers. Simić relates, for example, that adult Serbian males frequently consult their mothers before making important decisions, while ignoring their wives' views on the issues at hand.[4] In pastoralist Serbia, in fact, the mother exerts an authority over her children that the father cannot rival. The Serbs themselves say, "Even God has a mother" (*Majku i Bog ima*)—an aphorism that emphasizes the centrality of the mother. Ironically, however, the pivotal role of the mother in the family fuels patriarchy and machismo. In Serbia, for example, sentimental songs about mothers are highly popular with men—even moving them to tears—even though those same men repeatedly feel the need to "prove" their masculinity by engaging in rowdy, macho behavior in which the following elements typically figure:

> open-handed hospitality and the seemingly heedless expenditure of money . . . ; heavy drinking, usually in the company of a small group of male friends but sometimes including prostitutes, bar girls, or female singers; the destruction of

property, most often glasses, tableware, and bottles, but occasionally tables, chairs, and other barroom fixtures as well; trancelike ecstatic behavior induced by a combination of alcohol and the performance of erotic love songs; and not infrequently, brawling and more serious forms of physical violence.[5]

As sociologist Nancy Chodorow has noted, women's role as the primary socializers of men results in a pervasive "dread of women" among adult males.[6] Margaret Mead claims that girls gain a sense of female identity more easily than boys acquire their sense of male identity because for girls the closeness with the mother facilitates the acquisition of the relevant identity, while for boys it obstructs such identification.[7] Femininity is assimilated through attachment to the mother, while masculinity is defined through separation. Harvard Professor Carol Gilligan says that this dynamic leads to a situation in which "males tend to have difficulty with relationships, while females tend to have problems with individuation."[8] Moreover, the combination of maternal authority and lower female status makes female roles and behaviors deeply threatening, even disturbing, to boys, who unlike girls feel the need to "prove" their masculinity by making "correct" choices, as prescribed by the hierarchy. One consequence of this—well known—is that females in such societies tend to enjoy greater sex-role freedom than do males: the "tom boy" is smilingly acknowledged, while the "pansy" is ridiculed. It is easy to understand how societies in which the maternal role is enhanced (as in Serbia and Montenegro) tend to be characterized by greater fear of women and hence a stronger assertion of the patriarchy and a more powerful tendency toward male chauvinism. In this regard, Serbia is a classic case. As Chodorow notes, "Like violent behavior, male narcissism, pride, and phobia toward mature women—[all] indications of compulsive assertion of masculinity—seem to be prevalent in societies in which boys spend their earlier years exclusively or predominantly with women, and in which the degree of physical or emotional distance between mother and father as compared with that between mother and child" is great.[9]

Machismo, then, should be seen as a violent backlash against maternal authority, inspired by fear of women, and seeking "revenge" in the denigration and subordination of women. Machismo is a specifically *male* complex, for which no female equivalent exists.

Among the pastoralists (Serbs, Montenegrins, Macedonians, Albanians), women were traditionally expected to walk several paces behind their husbands and to carry whatever burdens there were. If the couple had a donkey, the man would ride on it, and the woman walked behind. Among Albanians, female subordination extended even to the suppression of women's names: specifically, after marriage, an Albanian woman would be known only by the possessive form of her husband's first name.[10]

Against this backdrop, it should come as no surprise that it is precisely in "macho" Serbia that patriarchal backlash was strongest (among Yugoslav republics) in the late 1980s and early 1990s. The entire Milošević phenomenon is, in fact, rooted in *fear*: fear of Albanians, Croats, and even, eventually, Slovenes; fear of new political movements; fear of randomness, freedom, chaos; and fear of women. The primordial linkage of these fears is the explanation as to why Slobodan Milošević's support comes overwhelmingly from males—middle-aged peasant males being the core and largest part of his support—while his opposition draws women as well as men to its ranks and to its rallies.

Fear, of course, readily translates into hatred, prejudice, chauvinism, and violence—all hallmarks of Milošević's rule and following. Since his advent on the scene in 1987, feminist activity in Belgrade has been thrown on the defensive, men have been told that they deserve preferential hiring in times of economic duress, and women have been advised to return to their "traditional duties"—kitchen, children, Church.

I have even heard the demented Otto Weininger's *Sex and Character* (originally published in Vienna in 1903) cited with favor in Serbia. Weininger, it was, who told the world,

> Women have no existence and no essence; they are not, they are nothing. Mankind occurs as male or female, as something or nothing. Woman has no share in ontological reality, no relation to the thing-in-itself, which, in the deepest interpretation, is the absolute, is God. Man, in his highest form, the genius, has such a relation. . . . [But] woman has no relation to the idea, she neither affirms nor denies it; she is neither moral nor anti-moral; mathematically speaking she has no sign; she is purposeless, neither good nor bad, neither angel nor devil, never egotistical (and therefore has often been said to be altruistic); she is as non-moral as she is non-logical. But all existence is moral and logical existence. So woman has no existence.[11]

PROSTITUTION

If there is a direct line from maternal authority to male complex to machismo, it is worth adding that the ready availability of prostitutes is a natural concomitant of macho culture. Belgrade, the capital of Serbia, is said to have had some 600 prostitutes even in 1901, when the total population of the city came to only 60,000; by 1928, Belgrade had some eighty brothels—all illegal.[12] Obviously a high percentage of young females was engaged in prostitution—itself a sure clue to the presence of macho culture in turn-of-the-century Belgrade. Nor were the Communists able to eradicate prostitution, and there continued to be arrests of prostitutes over the years. Table 6.1 shows the number of prostitutes arrested and charged in Serbia, 1968–1975.

TABLE 6.1   Number of Prostitutes Arrested and Charged in Serbia Proper, 1968–1975

Year	Number
1968	300
1969	180
1970	154
1971	n/a
1972	102
1973	78
1974	n/a
1975	99

SOURCE: Dragan Radulović, *Prostitucija u Jugoslaviji* (Belgrade: Filip Višnjić, 1986), p. 41.

Prostitution was, of course, found in many parts of Yugoslavia. In 1964, for example, there were 431 registered prostitutes in Belgrade, 360 in Ljubljana, 169 in Rijeka, and additional numbers in Zagreb, Split, Skopje, and elsewhere.[13] Yugoslav prostitutes were typically of rural origin. A 1985 study found that 70 percent of prostitutes in Belgrade had been born outside the city, most often coming from poorer parts of Bosnia or southern Serbia.[14] Prostitutes may come from nationality groups that are in the minority locally: for example, in Skopje in 1974, 70.2 percent of prostitutes were non-Macedonians—more than half of them Serbs.[15]

AGRICULTURIST SOCIETY: SLOVENIA AND CROATIA

In discussing pastoralist society, I have focused largely on Serbia, chiefly because most of the available data pertain to Serbia, but also with the awareness that Serbs are by far the largest nationality group in Yugoslavia. Much of what was said about Serbian patriarchy would apply equally to the Montenegrins, the Macedonians, and the Kosovar Albanians.

By contrast, Slovenes and Croats (together with the diverse peoples of Vojvodina) are agriculturists. (The Slovenes and Croats are also Catholics—another contrast with the largely Orthodox and Muslim affiliation of the pastoralists—and were ruled for centuries by the Habsburgs, while the pastoralists were ruled by the Ottomans.) Although the agriculturists are likewise organized on patrilineal and patricentric lines, they exclude "extreme forms of actual and ritual subordination of women to men."[16] Traditionally, wives in Slovenia and Croatia have participated in family decisionmaking, in marked contrast to the situation outlined for pastoralist Serbia. Again, unlike Serbia, where the male asserts supreme authority even in the kitchen, in Slovenia and Croatia the female is clearly in charge of her own kitchen. Slovenia and Dalmatia (regions earlier attached to the Austrian half of the Austro-Hungarian empire) have long been characterized by a toleration of

TABLE 6.2   Women in Leadership Organs of the LCY (1984) (percentages)

	Women in Party Membership	Women in Central Committee (CC)	Women in CC Presidency
LCY	27.0	14.1	0.0
Bosnia	29.2	19.5	7.7
Montenegro	26.1	13.2	11.1
Croatia	27.5	21.6	15.4
Macedonia	23.0	21.9	13.3
Slovenia	32.1	20.5	7.7
Serbia	27.5	17.8	4.8
Kosovo	13.5	14.7	7.7
Vojvodina	31.6	23.5	15.4

SOURCE: Jasna A. Petrović, "Žene u SK danas," *Žena*, Vol. 44, No. 4 (1986), p. 7.

female engagement in premarital sexual relations and even, in Slovenian villages, of illegitimate births. The traditional pastoralist custom of automatic execution of a woman suspected of marital infidelity is unknown among the agriculturists. Nor is infidelity escalated into an affair of the entire extended family. As Denich notes, "[female] adultery diminishes the honor of the cuckolded husband, but not the collective status of an entire kin group."[17] Consistent with patriarchy, however, the betrayed wife in this rectangle does not suffer diminution of honor, because male unfaithfulness is either tolerated or even considered (by males) to be "manly."

In the agriculturist republics, larger proportions of public officials and of workers in the social sector are women, though, of course, here too women's share in public and economic life is less than men's. In 1986, for example, women accounted for 51.6 percent of the Croatian population but only 42 percent of the labor force in the socialized sector and 29.7 percent of delegates to the Seventh Congress of the League of Communists of Croatia.[18] Figures (for 1984) on the proportion of women in the central committees of the party organizations of the respective federal units largely confirm the expected pattern: Slovenia, Croatia, and Vojvodina were among the four units with the highest representation of women at this level, while Serbia, Montenegro, and Kosovo were decisively lower. Interestingly enough, where CC presidencies were concerned, only in Croatia and Vojvodina did women account for more than 15 percent of the local presidency (see Table 6.2).

THE BROADER PICTURE

According to the 1981 census, there were, at the time, 11,340,933 women and 11,083,778 men living in Yugoslavia. The average age of Yugoslav females (in 1987) was 35.2 and of males 32.8. Female life expectancy (as of

1987) was 68.6 years—several years longer than men's.[19] As of 1982, women constituted only 36 percent of the Yugoslav labor force, but accounted for a strikingly high 45 percent of the Slovenian labor force. At that time, following a pattern established a long time ago, women were concentrated in very specific (less prestigious) occupations: in health and social services, 75 percent of the labor force was female; in hotels and tourism, 60 percent. At the same time, 55 percent of all persons registered as unemployed were female.[20] The latter figure was unchanged at the end of 1988.[21]

The education of women has long been a problem, as patriarchy has tried to enforce conditions in which women would accept household work as their "natural lot." An extreme reflection of this tendency is the fact that, at the end of World War II, 93 percent of all illiterates in Kosovo were women.[22] Even in 1981—across Yugoslavia as a whole—15.0 percent of women remained illiterate, as compared with only 6.7 percent of men.[23] The education of women is marked by steady attrition, so that the proportion of females declines the higher up the educational scale one goes. Of pupils in elementary schools, thus, 48 percent were females in 1982. But females constituted only 45 percent of middle school students and 43 percent of high school students.[24] The figures for universities and graduate schools were even smaller. In some communities, especially in Kosovo, there were continued difficulties even in the 1980s in assuring that village girls (in this case, Albanian village girls) attended primary school regularly.[25]

One consequence of the lower education of women is the disproportionate acquisition of skills necessary to obtain nonagricultural jobs. This translates into the steady, incremental femininization of the agricultural labor force in the postwar period.[26]

The lower valuation, lower education, and lower skills of women all contribute to their greater difficulty in making gains in the job sector. Indeed, Yugoslav sources repeatedly conceded that even where women's skills are equal to or better than men's skills, men are frequently given preference in hiring. This results in a situation not unknown in the West: namely, when economic trends take a downturn, women are laid off first. This has occurred several times in Yugoslavia's postwar development. In the years 1949–1951, for example, after several years of steady growth marked by the expanded hiring of women, the number of women employed in the social sector declined in absolute terms, dropping precipitously from 465,166 in 1949 to 375,166 by 1951.[27] Slow economic recovery after 1952 was associated with a revived expansion in the employment of women. By the early 1960s, the economy was becoming bottlenecked and stagnant. The economic reforms of the years 1963–1965 assured temporary economic recovery, but at the expense of layoffs. As could have been predicted, women were the hardest hit by the rise in unemployment in the mid-1960s.[28] The cultural dimension of this was a resurgence of traditional values, which meant that economic liberalization was associated with a revival of cultural traditionalism.

The short-lived economic boom of the 1970s had ended by 1978, as high inflation, creeping unemployment, soaring foreign debts, and general economic inefficiency combined to drive the economy downward. The result was a steady rise in the proportion of women unemployed, reaching 55 percent throughout the 1980s. Alongside this was another problem: the systematic underpayment of the female labor force. In fact, Yugoslav women in the industrial sector earn about 80 percent of what men earn.[29]

Turning now to the representation of women in positions of managerial responsibility, the figures are discouraging. Of the 445,539 delegates elected to serve on communal, political, and economic assemblies, only about a quarter (107,322) were women (as of 1986).[30] Of the 441,816 members of workers' councils that same year, about a third (142,375) were women.[31] Among presidents of workers' councils, only 6 percent were women (in 1982).[32] Women occupied 8.4 percent of leadership positions in middle schools and only 3.5 percent of such positions in high schools, even though some 52.9 percent of total faculty in these two branches were women. Women comprised 41.9 percent of the employed sector in scientific institutes, but only 5.5 percent of the managerial positions in these institutes were occupied by women.[33] As of 1987, only 28.8 percent of the Yugoslav diplomatic service was female, and only two women had risen to the rank of ambassador.[34] The authorities themselves saw the problem, and from time to time one could read public admissions that the representation of women in the political system was disproportionately low,[35] and so forth.

And yet, Yugoslav officials insisted that the "woman question," as they called it, was in some sense "solved." Thus Veljko Vlahović already in 1961: "The basic problems of the legal and political position of women in our country have been solved."[36] With this self-congratulation as a basis, Yugoslavia's Communists could proceed to declare themselves opposed to feminism, "because it is a movement which is always expressive of partial interests and demands, because it is in favor of dividing women from men in a formal-legal way, and because it devalues the class question."[37] Some observers went so far as to claim that Yugoslav society had already reached a "postfeminist" stage, on the argument that the right to obtain an abortion, improved access to professional careers, and other gains constituted a total solution of the problem of equality.[38] Would males show equal equanimity if only 6 percent of the presidents of workers' councils were *men,* if males held only 14 percent of the seats in the nation's top decisionmaking body, if only two Yugoslav ambassadors were males, and if male illiteracy were three times as high as female illiteracy?

YUGOSLAV WOMEN IN TROUBLED TIMES

As Yugoslavia faltered in the 1980s, politicians increasingly found them-selves confronted with the trying issues of pressure for political freedom, economic instability, gender equality, ethnic toleration, environmentalism, etc. In Slovenia, whose relative prosperity reduced social pressure, Communist politicians dealt with the issues on their own terms. Elsewhere, the situation was more complicated. In Serbia, Slobodan Milošević owed his success to his ability to manipulate ethnic chauvinism and swept other issues to the side. Concomitantly, male chauvinism acquired new strength in Milošević's Serbia. From time to time, women protested the shift from a policy of promoting gender equality to one of upholding so-called tradi-tional values.[39] But they have had increasing difficulty even being heard. The typical reply of the unconscious: "There are more important things to worry about right now than women's equality." Translated: "There are more important things to worry about now than human dignity."

In this context, lesbianism clearly figures—as it often does elsewhere as well—not merely as a matter of sexual preference but also as a political al-ternative. To be a lesbian is to opt out of patriarchal society, to refuse to play the game. In Ljubljana, a lesbian working group was organized in 1987—linked to the feminist organization, Lilith.[40]

Political organization was another alternative to which Yugoslav women had recourse. This took two chief forms: feminist groups and political par-ties. The former dated essentially from 1976 and functioned in three cities—Ljubljana, Zagreb, and Belgrade—although there was some interest in fem-inism in other cities as well. The SFRY's feminists tended to be professionals, intellectuals, and middle-class. They concentrated on organizing open dis-cussions of sensitive issues and on publishing articles and books advocat-ing the feminist alternative.[41] It would be easy enough to dismiss the SFRY's feminists as having been ineffective and unsuccessful. Yet, as Barbara Jancar points out, they succeeded in generating an "interest in feminist ideas [that went] beyond a small collection of feminist intellectuals."[42]

Feminists also took advantage of the partial opening of the political sys-tem in 1990 to create their own political parties: a Croatian League of Women (founded in Zagreb in March 1990), a Democratic Movement of Women (founded in Kragujevac and registered in November 1990), and the Women's Party of Belgrade (also registered in November 1990).[43] Although seeming to offer some promise, all these organizations proved unable to withstand the onslaught of rabid nationalism in the media and in public life and largely withered away.

Indeed, just as economic crisis hit women hardest, so too the alternative responses to crisis—whether chauvinist authoritarianism (as in Serbia) or nationalist presidential rule (as in Croatia)—have also posed new threats to women's interests; even in Slovenia, women have been pushed onto the defensive, forced to defend rights and prerogatives that, in Communist times, could be taken for granted. In Milošević's Serbia, women find their voices stifled and their organizations marginalized and increasingly constrained to concentrate on assistance to battered wives[44] while married couples without children have been threatened with a punitive tax. In Tudjman's Croatia, the Catholic Church took advantage of the new political situation to try to push women more firmly into their "traditional" role of housekeeper, targeting abortion as the arena for struggle. Belgrade feminist Sonja Licht commented in 1990, "Conservative attitudes toward women are resurfacing throughout Eastern Europe, usually with strong ties to nationalism. I often call the newly emerging democracies *male democracies*."[45] Others have suggested the term *phallocracies*.

PHALLOCRACY AND WAR

In the new postcommunist systems that have emerged not only in the Yugoslav successor states but across all of Eastern Europe, as I have written elsewhere,

> Women's representation in the political and administrative spheres plunged immediately. An ideological climate is being created that is hostile to women's education and advancement, as female employment is being repeatedly portrayed as a "danger" to the family. Even the rhetoric about the dignity and equality of women has vanished. It has been replaced by rhetoric about the dignity and importance of the *mother*, and not just the mother in general, but the *Croatian* mother, the *Slovak* mother, the *Hungarian* mother, and so on. In nationalist democracies [and nationalist dictatorships alike], women are reduced to instrumentalities for the reproduction of the nation.[46]

As unequal as women were in the Communist systems of Eastern Europe, they are, in fact, becoming even more unequal in the postcommunist systems of the region.

Thus, feminism in the Yugoslav successor states, as elsewhere, faces a challenge: how to defend or retrieve such small gains as had been made under communism, while continuing to struggle to replace a system based on the subordination of women and the use of force to defend interests, with one based on genuine equality and consensus. The linkage of patriarchy, nationalism, and war has been explored rather insightfully by George Mosse,[47] and his work reminds one yet again that processes of social change do not exist in isolation but are parts of a much larger, interconnected web of interactions.

But feminism cannot, in fact, win its struggle at the political level. To achieve its political goals, it must carry its struggle to the cultural level, so that new ideas, new attitudes, new behaviors can percolate upward, affecting politics in their wake. Collective action and organization are essential, as feminists realize, but they must ultimately transform not just laws and regulations but the family, the community, and eventually, the nation. Such a change can only occur over generations, as each new generation assimilates new ideas. It is for this reason that Yugoslavia's feminists concentrated much of their efforts on analyzing, critiquing, and revising schoolbooks in order to present children with a new image of human society.

The war has had devastating effects on the struggle for women's equality. In Serbia, feminists have been atomized and driven from politics, and "traditional" values have been pressed upon them. In Croatia, feminists have been demonized and, in some cases, even driven from the country.[48] And in Bosnia-Herzegovina, the longer the war has continued, the more prominent the role of all three religious communities has become, and they, in turn, have asserted "traditional" values and pushed women to assume subservient roles, obedient to their husbands.

The war has also seen the organization of systematic rape of large numbers of Muslim women by Bosnian Serb men, transmuting ethnic conflict to the sexual plane. This subject and other issues relating to gender relations since 1991 are taken up in Chapters 12 and 13.

NOTES

1. Bette S. Denich, "Sex and Power in the Balkans," in Michelle Zimbalist Rosaldo and Louise Lamphere, eds., *Woman, Culture, and Society* (Stanford, Calif.: Stanford University Press, 1974), p. 253.

2. See the discussion in Sherry B. Ortner, "Is Female to Male as Nature Is to Culture?," in Rosaldo and Lamphere, *Woman, Culture, and Society;* and Casey Miller and Kate Swift, *Words and Women* (Garden City, N.Y.: Anchor Press/Doubleday, 1977). Regarding the concept of gender cultures, see Sabrina P. Ramet (ed.), *Gender Reversals and Gender Cultures: Anthropological and Historical Perspectives* (London: Routledge) forthcoming in 1996.

3. Denich, "Sex and Power," p. 250.

4. Andrei Simić, "Machismo and Cryptomatriarchy: Power, Affect, and Authority in the Contemporary Yugoslav Family," *Ethos,* Vol. 11, Nos. 1–2 (spring–summer 1983), p. 67.

5. Ibid., pp. 79–80.

6. Nancy Chodorow, "Being and Doing: A Cross-Cultural Examination of the Socialization of Males and Females," in Vivian Gornick and Barbara K. Moran, eds., *Woman in Sexist Society: Studies in Power and Powerlessness* (New York: Basic Books, 1971), p. 274, citing Karen Horney.

7. As cited in ibid., p. 271.

8. Carol Gilligan, *In a Different Voice: Psychological Theory and Women's Development* (Cambridge, Mass.: Harvard University Press, 1982), p. 8.

9. Chodorow, "Being and Doing," p. 280.

10. Denich, "Sex and Power," pp. 252–253.

11. As quoted in Bram Dijkstra, *Idols of Perversity: Fantasies of Feminine Evil in Fin-de-Siecle Culture* (New York: Oxford University Press, 1986), p. 220.

12. Dragan Radulović, *Prostitucija u Jugoslaviji* (Belgrade: Filip Visnjić, 1986), pp. 21, 25.

13. Ibid., p. 40.

14. B. Djukanović, "Prostitucija," in *Socijalni problemi jugoslovenskog druš*tva *(1985), as cited in ibid., p. 48.*

15. Radulović, *Prostitucija u Jugoslaviji,* p. 47.

16. Denich, "Sex and Power," p. 256.

17. Ibid., pp. 257–258.

18. Jasna A. Petrović, "Žene na Kongresu sindikata Hrvatske," *Žena,* Vol. 44, Nos. 2–3 (1986), pp. 6–8.

19. *Statistički godišnjak Jugoslavije 1989* (Belgrade: Savezni zavod za statistiku, 1989), p. 129.

20. Report by Branka Lazić, in *Dvanaesti kongres Saveza Komunista Jugoslavije, Beograd, 26–29 juni 1982,* Magnetofonske beleške, Vol. 3. (Belgrade: Izdavački centar Komunist, 1983), p. 213.

21. *Statistički godišnjak,* p. 158.

22. Report by Bahtije Abrasi, in *Dvanaesti kongres,* Vol. 3, p. 247.

23. *Statistički godišnjak,* p. 131.

24. Report by Branka Lazić, p. 213.

25. Report by Bahtije Abrasi, p. 248.

26. Raža First-Dilić, "Žena u socijalističkom razvoju poljoprivrede," *Socijalizam,* Vol. 20, Nos. 7–8 (July–August 1977), p. 1398; and Eva Berković and Mirosinka Dinkić, "Ekonomski položaj žene i ostvarivanje društvene jednakosti polova," *Sociološki pregled,* Vol. 14, Nos. 3–4, (1980), p. 9.

27. Dušan Bilandžić, "The League of Communists of Yugoslavia on the Social Position of Women," *Socialist Thought and Practice,* Vol. 21, No. 9 (September 1981), p. 44.

28. Berković and Dinkić, "Ekonomski položaj žene," p. 9. See also Olivera Burić, "Položaj žene u sistemu društvene moći u Jugoslaviji," *Sociologija,* Vol. 14, No. 1, (1972), pp. 61–76.

29. See Vesna Pusić, "Žene i zaposlenost," *Sociologija,* Vol. 23, Nos. 3–4, (1981), pp. 337–344.

30. *Statistički godišnjak,* p. 123.

31. Ibid., p. 124.

32. Report by Branka Lazić, p. 213.

33. These figures date from 1972. See Olivera Burić, "Izmena strukture društvene moći: uslov za društvenu ravnopravnost žene," *Sociologija,* Vol. 17, No. 2 (1975), p. 208.

34. *Mladost* (Zagreb) (30 March–12 April 1987), p. 20.

35. *Borba* (Belgrade) (18 July 1977), p. 5.

36. Veljko Vlahović, *Sabrani radovi,* Vol. 2 (Titograd: Pobjeda, 1981), p. 72.

37. Marko Bezer, in interview with *Vjesnik: Sedam dana* (Zagreb) (5 January 1980), p. 7.

38. *Vjesnik: Sedam dana* (11 April 1987), p. 8.

39. See, for example, *Borba* (28–30 November 1990), p. 20.

40. *Danas,* No. 308 (12 January 1988), p. 72.

41. The most important books in this vein from the 1980s are Blaženka Despot, *Žensko pitanje i socijalističko samoupravljanje* (Zagreb: Cekade, 1987); Slavenka Drakulić-Ilić, *Smrtni griješi feminizma* (Zagreb: Znanje, 1984); Vjeran Katunarić, *Ženski eros i civilizacija smrti* (Zagreb: Naprijed, 1984); Nada Ler-Sofronić, *Neofeminizam i socijalistička alternativa* (Belgrade: Radnička štampa, 1986); Snežana Pejanović, *Društvena jednakost i emancipacija zene* (Belgrade: Prosvetni pregled, 1984); Lydia Sklevicky et al., *Žena i društvo: Kultiviranje dijaloga* (Zagreb: Socijalističko društvo Hrvatske, 1987); and Slavka Veljković, *Feminizam i oslobod-jenje Žene* (Pirot: Grafika, 1982).

42. Barbara Jancar, "Neofeminism in Yugoslavia: A Closer Look," *Women and Politics,* Vol. 8, No. 1 (1988), p. 26.

43. Tanjug (22 March 1990), trans. in *Foreign Broadcast Information Service (FBIS), Daily Report* (Eastern Europe), 23 March 1990, p. 89; and Tanjug (1 November 1990), trans. in *FBIS, Daily Report* (Eastern Europe), 2 November 1990, p. 71.

44. Interview with a feminist intellectual, Belgrade, September 1989.

45. Quoted in *New York Times* (25 November 1990), Section 4, p. 2.

46. Sabrina Petra Ramet, *Social Currents in Eastern Europe: The Sources and Consequences of the Great Transformation,* 2d ed. (Durham, N.C.: Duke University Press, 1995), p. 444.

47. George L. Mosse, *Nationalism and Sexuality: Middle-Class Morality and Sexual Norms in Modern Europe* (Milwaukee: University of Wisconsin Press, 1985).

48. See the rabid attack on five Croatian feminist "witches" in *Globus* (Zagreb) (11 December 1992), p. 33.

◆

PART THREE

Religion, Up to 1991

CHAPTER SEVEN

◆

The Catholic Church

IN AUGUST 1990, FRANJO TUDJMAN, the newly elected noncommunist president of Croatia, gave a television interview in which he addressed the subject of Catholicism. The Catholic Church, Tudjman argued, had been the only organized force that had provided consistent resistance to Communist rule and that had nurtured Croatian national consciousness.[1] In Communist times, the Catholic Church was kept on the defensive, subject to harassment and the target of endless small "stings" from Titoist officialdom. Now, in postcommunist Slovenia and Croatia, the newly installed governments look on Catholic interests with favor, and the Catholic Church has revealed an ambition to return to conditions of the precommunist era. This, in turn, prompted Zdenko Roter, a distinguished Slovenian sociologist of religion with demonstrated sympathies for the Catholic Church, to express concern that some Church leaders might try to turn the new postcommunist political order into "a servant of the Catholic Church."[2]

THE SYMBOLOGY OF THE CHURCH IN YUGOSLAVIA

Relations between the Catholic Church in Yugoslavia and the Communist regime were colored by three central symbols: Strossmayer, Stepinac, and the Vatican II Council. For the regime, Bishop Josip Juraj Strossmayer of Djakovo (1815–1905) represented the spirit of "Yugoslavism" (promoting the cultural and political unity of Serbs, Croats, Slovenes, and Macedonians) and of cooperation between Church and state, while Alojzije Cardinal Stepinac (1898–1960) symbolized exclusivist Croatian nationalism and the spirit of defiance. For the Church, on the other hand, Strossmayer is remembered also as an active missionary, as an ecclesiastical "liberal" who opposed introduction of the principle of papal infallibility, and as a champion of Slavic (vernacular) liturgy in Catholic churches in Croatia; Stepinac is associated, in Church eyes, with heroic efforts to protect Serbs and Gypsies from slaughter by the Ustasha fascists during World War II, with

defiant outspoken criticism of both the Ustasha and the Communists, and
with unflinching loyalty to the Church. In certain ways, thus—for both
regime and Church—twentieth-century Stepinac symbolized the Church's
traditional pastoral care for the nation, while nineteenth-century
Strossmayer symbolized adaptability, liberality, and hence modernity. It is
worth noting, however, that through his progressive social programs and
his use of Church funds for charitable programs, Stepinac may be said to
have anticipated the "Church of the poor" of the Vatican II period.

The Vatican II Council (1962–1965) was a watershed for the Church and,
more particularly, the point at which modernizing currents within the
Church received strong encouragement, in certain aspects, from the Holy
See. The results were a new impetus to self-assertion in the Church, a new
direction for the Church in its social presence, and a deepening of the division within the Church between traditionalists and modernizers.
Interestingly enough, while the Belgrade regime expressed enthusiasm for
the "modernizing" Strossmayer, it felt threatened, according to Zlatko
Markus, by the reformist wing of the Church, which it viewed as "danger-
ously" active.[3] Far more to the liking of at least some elements in the regime
was the opinion once expressed by Archbishop Frane Franić of Split (retired in 1988), to the effect that the Church is called upon "to administer
the sacraments and to conduct Church services, but political and social revolution should be left to others. That is not our calling."[4] The result is that
theological conservatives in the Church (including the mixed conservative,
Franić, and the generally conservative one-time archbishop of Sarajevo,
Smiljan Čekada) enjoyed better relations, than did some of their theologically more liberal colleagues, with those elements in the Communist regime
who sought to constrict Church activity.

In Yugoslavia, as elsewhere, the traditional–modern dichotomy mani-
fests itself against the backdrop of another—partly reinforcing, partly cross-
cutting—dichotomy between hierarchy and lower clergy. In the early postwar years, tensions between hierarchy and lower clergy centered on the
establishment of priests' associations—a move encouraged and supported
by the regime. More recently, tensions developed between the episcopal
conference and the Christianity Today Theological Society, over the latter's
unilateral decision, in 1977, to reorganize itself as a self-managing enterprise and thereby obtain certain tax exemptions. The society is responsible
for running a formidable publishing house and for issuing the *AKSA* news
bulletin.

THE DAWN OF COMMUNIST RULE

Although the Communist regime would later try to portray the Catholic
Church's role during World War II monochromatically as the advocacy of

Croatian independence and Ustasha rule, a rather substantial number of Catholic clergymen actually cooperated with or fought on the side of the partisans, including Archbishop Kuzma Jedretić, Fr. Franjo Poš from Prezid, Franciscans Bosiljko Ljevar and Viktor Sakić, and the pastor of St. Mark's Church in Zagreb, Msgr. Svetozar Rittig, lauded by one Yugoslav author as "the most important figure in the people's liberation struggle, among Catholic priests."[5] Rittig, who joined the partisans in 1943 and later became first president of the Croatian Commission for Religious Affairs, remaining active on the political scene until his death in July 1961, is said to have been devoted, in particular, to the ideas of Bishop Strossmayer. By contrast, according to Ćiril Petešić, "only a part of the clergy, and a small part at that," actually endorsed the Ustasha program, mostly young priests, while most of the older clergy are said to have been pro-Yugoslav.[6]

From the beginning of partisan warfare, the partisans had need of priests to cater to the religious needs of their combatants, and this led to the establishment of a Religious Department of the AVNOJ[7] Executive Committee in December 1942. Behind partisan lines, where religious schools were concerned, the partisans were eager for religious instructors to teach about Cyril and Methodius (who created the Glagolitic alphabet), Sava Nemanjic (founder of the autocephalous Serbian Orthodox archdiocese), and Bishop Strossmayer.[8]

After the trying experiences under the Kingdom of Yugoslavia,[9] the Croatian Catholic hierarchy initially welcomed the establishment of a separate Croatian state.[10] Some clergy, such as Archbishop Ivan Šarić of Sarajevo, remained sympathetic to the Ustasha until the very end. Other hierarchs were more critical, on the other hand. Bishop Alojzije Misić of Mostar, for instance, began condemning Ustasha oppression of Serbs as early as 1941.[11] Similarly, Zagreb Archbishop Stepinac repeatedly contacted Minister of the Interior Andrija Artuković (e.g., in letters dated 22 May 1941, and 30 May 1941) to register his objection to the new legislation affecting Catholics of Jewish descent, declared membership in Catholic Action and the Ustasha movement to be incompatible (in December 1941), worked quietly to obtain the release of Orthodox believers from prison, and spoke out in his sermons against racism, genocide, and Ustasha policies (for example, in his sermon of 25 October 1943).[12]

But if the local clergy were divided in their attitudes toward the Ustasha, and some frankly ambivalent about the Croatian state, the Vatican had a clear line where *communism* was concerned. The difficulties experienced by the Church in the USSR provided a troubling precedent, and Pope Pius XII adopted a forcefully anticommunist stance. *Katolički list* (24 April 1937) had put it this way: "Communism is in its very essence evil. Therefore, the person who values Christian culture will not cooperate with [communists] in a single thing. If some are seduced into error and on their part help communism to grow stronger, they will be the first to be punished for that error."[13] Thus, there was no basis, at that time, for a relationship of trust between the Vatican and the emerging Communist parties in Eastern Europe.

Meanwhile, as the partisans captured districts of Croatia, they massacred both civilians and priests, including more than two dozen unarmed Franciscans at the monastery of Široki Brijeg.[14] The Independent State of Croatia collapsed in May 1945, and the Communist Party now set up its administration in the remaining parts of the country.

On 2 June 1945, Communist Party General Secretary Josip Broz Tito, Croatian President Vladimir Bakarić, and Msgr. Rittig held a meeting with Catholic bishops Franjo Sališ-Seewis and Josip Lach. Tito's statement on that occasion has given rise to so much subsequent controversy that it is worth quoting at length. Replying to a statement presented by Bishop Sališ, Tito said:

> As I have already explained to Msgr. Rittig, I would like to see a proposal worked out, as you see fit, as to how to solve the question of the Church in Croatia, the Catholic Church, because we shall be discussing the same thing also with the Orthodox Church. On my own part, I would say that our Church needs to be national [*nacionalna*], that it be more responsive to the [Croatian] nation. Perhaps that will seem a bit strange to you when I so strongly support nationality. . . . I must say openly that I do not want to undertake the right to condemn Rome, your supreme Roman jurisdiction, and I will not. But I must say that I look at it critically, because [Church policy] has always been attuned more to Italy than to our people. I would like to see that the Catholic Church in Croatia now, when we have all the preconditions there, would have more independence. I would like that. That is the basic question. That is the question which we want to see resolved, and all other questions are secondary questions which will be easy to work out.[15]

Given the consistency with which Communists in other East European countries were pressing Catholic hierarchs to break with the Vatican,[16] it seems reasonable to interpret this statement along the same lines (though Tito later denied that this was his intention). After all, the so-called Old Catholic Church in Croatia had already provided a precedent. Indeed, this Church, which had formed in reaction to the proclamation of the doctrine of papal infallibility in 1870, was even able to set up additional independent organizations after World War II in Slovenia, Serbia, and Vojvodina.[17]

The following day, Tito and Bakarić received the papal delegate, Abbot Ramiro Marcone, together with his secretary, Don Giuseppe Masucci, who complained that the Communist media were relentlessly attacking the clergy and the Vatican, even claiming that the Vatican had wanted a Nazi victory, and that the children were being taught in the schools that there is no God and trained to sing, "We will fight against God! There is no God!"[18]

On 4 June, Tito and Bakarić received Stepinac and, on this occasion, Tito praised Pope Leo XIII for having backed Strossmayer in a dispute with the Court of Vienna about Russia and asked Stepinac to support Belgrade in its dispute with Italy in Istria. Stepinac, in turn, urged Tito to meet with representatives of the Croatian Peasant Party and even those of the Ustasha movement and to try to heal the emotional wounds of war.[19] In spite of this meeting, the Communist government continued to arrest Catholic priests and believers, including the bishops of Križevci, Split, and Krk.

Archbishop Stepinac was receiving hundreds of appeals from Croats asking him to intercede with the new authorities on behalf of imprisoned relatives. On 28 June 1945, he took up the matter with the president of the Croatian government and urged the authorities to drop the campaign against "collaborators" because, as Stepinac noted, it would be necessary then to imprison ordinary workers, peasants, and so forth. But part of the reason for the campaign was sheer opportunism on the part of particular individuals in the party, including their desire to seize the opportunity to settle old scores.[20] Stepinac also criticized the secret trials being conducted at the time, calling it inconsistent with the regime's claim to be a "people's" government.

Meanwhile, the regime decided to abolish all private high schools, following completion of the 1945–1946 school year, and moved to eliminate religious instruction from the curriculum of state elementary schools. In late summer 1945, the authorities began bulldozing the cemeteries in which combatants from other sides were buried, stirring protests from believers in the areas affected. Within a month of the war's end, the Communist authorities also began forcible confiscations of Church property in Križevci, Zagreb, Remete, and elsewhere, seized Caritas property and property of the Zagreb archbishopric, and outlined a more extensive program of agrarian land reform, which promised to produce further confiscations. When Stepinac complained about these developments in a letter to Tito, the latter replied by alluding to his interest in receiving a reply from the Catholic bishops with respect to "the possibility of coming to an agreement about certain matters between Church and state."[21]

In these circumstances, the first episcopal conference in Yugoslavia in six years was convened by Stepinac on 17–22 September to discuss the new situation in which the Church found itself. Immediately upon convening, the episcopal conference sent a letter to Tito asking for withdrawal of the law on agrarian reform, respect for Christian marriage, respect for continuation of religious instruction in elementary schools, and respect for Catholic cemeteries and offering to consult with the state on a new law on agrarian reform. The following day, after further discussions, the conference sent a second letter to Tito asking for the release from detention of Bishop Janko Simrak, freedom of the press, continuance of the private schools, and the return of confiscated property to the Church.[22] And at the close of the conference the assembled bishops issued a joint pastoral letter recounting the hardships suffered by the Church at the hands of the Communists (243 priests and 4 nuns killed over four years, 169 priests still in prison, and 89 unaccounted for) and demanding complete freedom for Church activities, institutions, and press. This pastoral letter was read in the churches, with copies sent to the Commission for Religious Affairs in each of the federal units.[23]

The letter convinced the Communist authorities that Archbishop Stepinac would be as much a thorn to them as he had been to Ustasha leader Ante Pavelić. They therefore reached a decision, shortly after the letter was issued, that a case would be prepared against him and that he would be put away in prison.[24]

THE TRIAL OF ARCHBISHOP STEPINAC

The authorities continued to try to persuade Archbishop Stepinac to break relations with Rome; instead, Stepinac denounced the proposal in yet another pastoral letter.[25] The authorities then tried to persuade the Vatican to remove Stepinac from his seat in Zagreb; the Vatican refused.[26] The archbishop was therefore arrested on 18 September and put on trial together with fifteen other persons who were being tried on criminal charges connected with the excesses of the NDH. On 30 September, the charges against Stepinac were read in court. Specifically, he was accused of collaborating with the Ustasha in the calculated hope of enriching the Church and the upper clergy, of allowing the Križari (Crusaders) and Catholic Action to work for fascism, of using traditional religious celebrations as political manifestations in support of the Ustasha, of encouraging the coercive conversion of Orthodox Serbs to Catholicism, of serving as a rallying point for enemies of the Communist state after the war, and of concealing Ustasha archives and materials of the Croatian Foreign Ministry, under an agreement concluded with Ante Pavelić.[27]

The *official* (edited) record of the trial shows Stepinac refusing to cooperate with his interrogators:

> *Presiding judge: Nedjelja* No. 15 of 27 April 1941 carries a report with the following content: "Archbishop Dr. Alojzije Stepinac, as representative of the Catholic Church and Croatian metropolitan, visited General Slavko Kvaternik as deputy of the Poglavnik in the homeland and conducted a lengthy conversation with him. In that way, as Radio Zagreb reports, the most cordial relations were established between the Catholic Church and the Independent State of Croatia."

Why did you consider it necessary, only two days after the establishment of the Independent State of Croatia and the occupation of our country by the enemy, to hurry to visit the Ustasha commander, Slavko Kvaternik?

The accused: I have nothing to say.

Presiding judge: Did you visit Pavelić on 16, April 1941, four days after the occupation of our country but two days before the capitulation of the Yugoslav army, which was at war with the enemy?

The accused: I decline to answer. . . .

Presiding judge: . . . Did you, immediately in the first days of the occupation, i.e., in mid-April or early May, take part in a meeting to which you invited Ustasha emigrants, returnees?

The accused: I have nothing to say. If necessary, the defense lawyers appointed for me can answer that.[28]

The prosecution made use of a string of citations from Catholic and Ustasha press to try to incriminate the archbishop. But most of the Catholic periodicals cited by the prosecution in substantiation of its charges were published in dioceses lying outside Stepinac's jurisdiction: in particular, the Franciscan publication *Andjeo Čuvar,* the Jesuit publication *Glasnik Srca Isusova,* the Sarajevo weekly *Katolički tjednik,* and the Sarajevo publication *Glasnik sv. Antuna.*[29] The prosecution claimed that Stepinac and other clergy had received decorations from the Croatian government in gratitude for their political support and produced pictures showing the archbishop together with Ustasha ministers on official occasions and at official receptions.[30]

Chief prosecutor Jakov Blažević dwelled at length on the Church's cooperation with the Ustasha in carrying out forced conversions of Orthodox believers. The archbishop defended himself by insisting that the Church had exerted no pressure on the Orthodox and could not be held responsible for coercion applied by others and by pointing out that a large number of Catholics had converted to Orthodoxy, under pressure, during the period of the Yugoslav kingdom.[31] Against the archbishop's denials, Blažević insisted that between 1943 and 1944 Archbishop Stepinac became involved in vaguely defined "conspiratorial work" with Pavelić and Croatian Peasant Party leader Vlatko Maček, and—in a bizarre turn—"charged" the archbishop with having sent Christmas wishes to Croatian prison laborers in Germany.[32]

L'Osservatore Romano, the Vatican newspaper, scoffed at the charges and held that the real reason for the trial was the pastoral letter of 22 September 1945.[33] By continually returning to the subject of this letter, the authorities seemed to confirm this interpretation:

Presiding judge: In the pastoral letter of last year, 1945, one finds, among other things, the claim that the Franciscans at Široki Brijeg were well-known antifascists. Here is a photograph, taken at Široki Brijeg, showing Ustasha colonel Jure Frančetić with Fr. Bonaventura Jelačić, an "'antifascist' from Široki Brijeg." Also in the photograph are [other] Franciscans of Široki Brijeg together with Ustasha and Italian officers. Is this the famous antifascist stance of the Franciscans from Široki Brijeg?

The accused: I have nothing to say.

Presiding judge: You could correct your declaration in the pastoral letter—were they not, maybe, fascists?

The accused: I think that we have nothing to correct.[34]

Blažević later returned to this subject in order to assail the idea of freedom of the press:

> *J. Blažević*: . . . Defendant Stepinac, in connection with the facts which have been revealed and established in this trial, I ask you please, for what purpose did you convene the episcopal conference in September 1945 and for what purpose did you write the pastoral letter?
>
> *The accused*: I have nothing to say.
>
> *J. Blažević*: I will cite some passages from the pastoral letter to you and then I will ask you some questions about it. Speaking of the persecutions of priests etc. . . . you say this: "And when we explain all this to you dearest believers, we do not do so in the hope of provoking a battle with the state authorities. We neither desire such battles nor do we seek them." Defendant, you say that you have always sought peace and stable political life and you say, "That peace is so necessary to everyone today, but we are deeply convinced that that peace can only be founded on the pacification of relations between Church and state." What do you say to that, defendant Stepinac?
>
> *The accused*: I have nothing to say.
>
> *J. Blažević*: You have nothing to say, because you are ashamed. In the pastoral letter, in order to realize the principles that you stress, you seek complete freedom for the Catholic press. Is that freedom for the press we have been reading? . . .
>
> *The accused*: I have nothing to say.
>
> *J. Blažević*: You have nothing to say. In the pastoral letter you write, "Only under those conditions can circumstances be put in order in our state and can lasting internal peace be achieved." So, you demand freedom for your press, that is, the Catholic press which you commanded and which you converted completely into an instrument of fascism. That press could only return if fascism would return, if the Ustasha were to return. . . . It's clear that you seek to introduce fascism in our country anew, that you seek [foreign] intervention in the country.[35]

The court rejected most of the witnesses proposed by the defense; on the other hand, most of the fifty-eight witnesses summoned by the prosecution to testify against Stepinac were not from his archdiocese. The trial ended on 11 October, when the court found all but three of the defendants guilty[36] and sentenced Archbishop Stepinac to sixteen years at hard labor, followed by five years' deprivation of civil and political rights. *L'Osservatore Romano* condemned the proceedings as a complete sham whose outcome had been determined in advance and whose script had been drafted to serve political ends and challenged the authenticity of some of the documents produced by the prosecution.[37] (Stepinac was offered his freedom if he agreed to leave the country, but he declined. Despite the sentence, Stepinac did not in fact have to perform hard labor, and the authorities constructed a special double cell for him; a chapel was built into half of this double cell. In 1951, when Tito was trying to improve relations with the Vatican, Stepinac was released from prison but confined to his native village. Elevated to the College of Cardinals shortly thereafter, Stepinac died in 1960.)

Some time after the trial, Milovan Djilas—then still a prominent member of the political establishment—admitted in private conversation that the real problem with Stepinac was not his politics vis-à-vis the Ustasha, but his politics vis-à-vis the Communists themselves, and in particular his fidelity to Rome. "If he had only proclaimed [the creation of] a Croatian Church, separate from Rome," said Djilas, "we would have raised him to the clouds!"[38] More recently—in February 1985—Blažević himself admitted this in an interview with the Croatian youth weekly, *Polet*. Admitting that Tito had wanted Stepinac to cut the Croatian Church's ties with Rome, Blažević commented, "That trial of Stepinac was forced on us. If Stepinac had only been more flexible, there would have been no need of a trial."[39]

THE PRIESTS' ASSOCIATIONS

Since it had proved impossible to coopt the Church hierarchy, the authorities quickly pursued an alternative policy of trying to sow divisions and discord within the Church and to win over *portions* of the clergy into a cooperative relationship. One token of this was the regime's response to the pastoral letter of 22 September 1945. *Borba,* for example, reported that many Catholic priests in Bosnia-Herzegovina refused to read the letter in their churches,[40] while other papers carried a story claiming that Archbishop Nikola Dobrečić of Bar had criticized those bishops who had signed the pastoral letter.[41]

A more tangible symptom of this strategy was the promotion of priests' associations, which would lie outside the authority of the bishops. However, after the controversial trial and imprisonment of Archbishop Stepinac, the clergy, especially in Croatia, were ill disposed to cooperate with the regime. All the same, the first Catholic priests' association was created in Istria in 1948, under the presidency of Dr. Božo Milanović, and most Istrian priests joined. That same year an attempt was made to set up an association in Slovenia. The first attempt failed, however, and the matter had to be taken up again the following year. These first two associations were

more or less spontaneous on the part of the priests, though actively encouraged by the government.

A third priests' association was set up in January 1950 in Bosnia-
Herzegovina. The government set up health insurance for members and
pressured priests to join, for example, by making permission to give religious instruction contingent on membership (a policy adopted in 1952 but
eventually abandoned). By the end of 1952, nearly all the priests in Istria
were association members, along with 80 percent of priests in Bosnia-
Herzegovina and 60 percent of priests in Slovenia.[42]

The bishops were opposed to these associations and, in a statement
dated 26 April 1950, declared them "inexpedient." Two and a half years
later, after consulting the Vatican, the bishops issued a decision forbidding
the clergy altogether to join the associations. This move provoked a crisis
in Church–state relations when the Yugoslav government sent a note of
protest to the Holy See on 1 November 1952. The Holy See replied on 15
December, detailing the troubles being experienced by the Church, but this
note was returned unopened. On 17 December the Yugoslav government
terminated diplomatic relations with the Vatican.[43]

By the end of 1953, three more priests' associations for Catholic clergy
were created—in Croatia, Serbia, and Montenegro. The associations thus
paralleled the federal structure of the political system, with one association
per republic. These associations served as conduits for state subsidies—
which were welcome given the destruction caused by the war. The Bosnian
Franciscan Province, for example, began receiving state subsidies through
this source in 1952, and in the period 1952–1964, received a total of 63 million old dinars in subsidies (estimated as equivalent to 315,000 West
German marks).[44] Nor were the Franciscans the only ones to receive state
aid: other institutions of the Catholic Church also received aid, such as the
Theological Faculty in Ljubljana (which received several state subventions),
the diocese of Djakovo (where Strossmayer once presided, which received
a subsidy to restore the cathedral), and the diocese of Senj (which received
a state subsidy to restore the episcopal palace).

In addition to health insurance, subsidies, and better relations with the
bureaucracy, the priests' associations also enjoyed preferential treatment
where publications were concerned. Thus, Dobri pastir, the Bosnian association, was able to publish a religious periodical and a calendar beginning
in 1950, i.e., even at a time when almost all of the rest of the Church press
was suppressed.[45]

The priests' associations were integrated into the structure of the Socialist
Alliance of Working People of Yugoslavia (SAWPY) and were officially
viewed as a means for clergymen to protect and realize their "professional
interests." Despite claims by various observers[46] that the associations benefited the Church, the hierarchy remained deeply suspicious. In 1970, for ex-

ample, Archbishop Frane Franić of Split wrote that the Franciscans, insofar as they constitute three quarters of Dobri pastir's membership, were "true collaborators with the people's authorities."[47] A meeting of representatives of clergymen's associations in 1978 showed that the antagonism felt by the hierarchy toward the associations was working against the latter. Vinko Weber, secretary of the Society of Catholic Priests of Croatia, told that meeting that his once vibrant organization was "now in its last gasp," that it had not been allowed to distribute its publications on Church premises, and that it had subsequently even lost its printing facilities. Weber continued,

> Unfortunately, the days of "non licet non exedi" are still with us. This ban has remained in force right up to the present day. And let me tell you why this is so! Our society has its own statutes, and these statutes include the famous article 3, which, inter alia, states that members of the Society of Catholic Priests shall promote the brotherhood and unity of our peoples, defend the achievements of the national liberation struggle, promote ecumenism, and so on. And this is the crux of the matter, that is, they cannot forgive us for incorporating this article into our statutes, and this is why they keep trying to foil us in everything we do. Things have finally reached the point where even certain Catholic societies in other republics are starting to refuse to have anything to do with us, thinking that we are some kind of black sheep, and this is only because they have been misinformed. But the upshot of all this is that nowadays our society is barely managing to keep itself together.[48]

Similarly, the Association of Catholic Priests of Montenegro, which attracted more than twenty of the thirty Catholic priests serving in that republic in 1954, could count only six members as of 1978—and all of them retired priests. Thus, far from being able to serve as an effective mediary between Church and state, the priests' associations turned out to be at the most a useful mechanism for health insurance and other material benefits, or, on the other hand, irrelevant vestiges of a failed strategy. In Slovenia, by contrast, the Catholic priests' association was always weak and served, in the 1980s, chiefly as the publication outlet for a quarterly newsletter and for a series of religious books for children.

PHASES IN CHURCH-STATE RELATIONS

The years 1945–1953 were the most difficult period for the Church. The Catholic press shriveled, and where there had been about a hundred periodical publications prior to the war, the Church could count only three publications now: *Blagovest* (in Belgrade and Skopje), *Dobri pastir* in Bosnia, and *Oznanilo* in Slovenia, which appeared as a two-page (front and back) bulletin from 1945 to 1946, and as a four-page bulletin, in the years 1946–1952. (As of 1987, by contrast, the Catholic Church was publishing 134 periodicals in Croatia alone.[49]) Catholic hospitals, orphanages, and homes for the aged were seized and closed, and Catholic secondary schools were nationalized. Seminaries were likewise confiscated, for example, in Zagreb, Split, Travnik, Sent Vid, Ljubljana, Maribor, and Sinj.[50] Some 600 Slovenian priests were imprisoned. The faculties of theology of the universities of Ljubljana and Zagreb were separated from the universities by governmental decree in 1952.

The passage of a special Law on the Legal Status of Religious Communities (27 April 1953) stirred hope for change, insofar as it guaranteed freedom of conscience and religious belief. Perhaps as important was Tito's call, in a speech at Ruma that same year, for a "halt to physical assaults on the clergy"[51]—partly in concession to Western public opinion, now that Tito's Yugoslavia had broken with the Soviet bloc. The years 1953–1964 saw some reduction in the pressures against believers, though as Paul Mojzes notes, "excesses—such as torture, imprisonment on false charges, and even murder by the secret police—were still practiced from time to time, more in some parts of the country than in others."[52] Both Church and state were clearly groping toward a *modus vivendi* during this period. Hence, when Yugoslavia's bishops submitted a memorandum in September 1960 detailing their complaints and demands (including the unhindered prerogative to build and repair churches), they also included a calculated invitation to dialogue, noting that "the Constitution guarantees freedom of faith and conscience to all citizens, while the Law on the Legal Status of Religious Communities [gives form to] and defines this constitutional provision more closely. These legal provisions contain the nucleus of all that is necessary for relations between the Church and the State to develop in line with the principle of a free Church in a free State."[53]

By early 1964, there were unmistakable signs of a new atmosphere in Church–state relations. By 1965 Belgrade and the Holy See were engaged in negotiations, and on 25 June 1966, Belgrade and the Vatican signed a protocol and exchanged governmental representatives. In the protocol, Belgrade guaranteed the Roman Catholic Church "free conduct of religious affairs and rites," confirmed the Vatican's authority over Catholic clergy in Yugoslavia in religious matters, and guaranteed the bishops the right to maintain contact with the Vatican. On the other side, the Vatican undertook that priests in the country would respect Yugoslavia's laws and that the clergy "cannot misuse their religious and Church functions for aims which would have a political character."[54]

The hierarchy in Yugoslavia welcomed the protocol. Archbishop Franić saw in it the promise of "a new era for our Church,"[55] while Franjo Cardinal Šeper, then archbishop of Zagreb, commented in 1967, "The Catholic community cannot escape being engaged. But that presumes a greater amount of freedom. We hope that that freedom will steadily increase for the Catholic Church as well as for other social communities. . . . In the Belgrade

Protocol, the Catholic Church accepted the existing legislation of Yugoslavia as a starting point. That at least presumes the possibility of legislative development in religious questions, so that [religious policy] would not lag behind the development of reality and become an anachronism."[56] Four years later, Yugoslavia reestablished full diplomatic relations with the Vatican, and in March 1971 Tito paid an official visit to the Vatican.

The general liberalization in Yugoslavia in the late 1960s permitted the launching of a series of Church periodicals, including the fortnightly newspaper (now weekly), *Glas koncila,* which has become an important organ for Church opinion. The Church also began to revive its social programs for youth, not only in Croatia and Slovenia but also in Bosnia, where the authorities showed especial misgivings at the Church's new self-confidence.[57] Catholic clergy in Rijeka, Split, Zadar, and Zagreb responded enthusiastically to the Croatian liberal-nationalist groundswell of the years 1967–1971, and in Bosnia-Herzegovina Franciscan priests gathered data on the number of Croats occupying administrative posts in that republic.[58]

It was this renewed self-assertion of the Church, combined with the purge of the liberal faction in the party, in the period 1971–1973, rather than the protocol and exchange of emissaries, that colored Church-state relations at the outset of their fourth postwar phase, 1970–1989. On the Church's part, the tenth anniversary (in 1970) of the death of Cardinal Stepinac was commemorated as demands emerged for his canonization.[59] For the regime, however, the rehabilitation of Stepinac seemed fraught with danger, since his trial had converted him into something of a Croatian mythological hero. Accordingly, Croatian sociologist Srdjan Vrcan warned a seminar at Krapinske Toplice, in January 1973, that "viewpoints, completely political and totally nonreligious in spirit, have again been revived as the widest ideological base, viz., viewpoints that the Croats and Serbs are two completely separate worlds between which no kind of stable and positive form of unity can be established."[60] Stepinac became the focal point for the self-defense of the Croatian Catholic Church (as witnessed in Franjo Cardinal Kuharić's annual sermons in defense of Stepinac) and the foundation of the attempted self-legitimation of the regime.

In the period 1970–1989, there were at least six issue areas that complicated the Church–state relationship.

First, the Church never reconciled itself to the inclusion of courses in atheism and Marxism in the school curricula and repeatedly asked for equal time or, alternatively, the removal of these courses from the schools. The point of view of the League of Communists of Yugoslavia (LCY) was summarized by *Nedjeljna Dalmacija* in 1972: "The LC cannot accept the concept of an ideologically neutral school nor a school pluralism based on the individual right of each parent, because the educational system is the social obligation and affair of a social institution."[61]

The Church, however, complained that it was dissatisfied "with the method [of teaching], with the content, with the textbooks, with the sundry provocations through which believing children . . . are indoctrinated and atheized."[62] And in late 1987 the Episcopal Conference of Yugoslavia issued a statement calling on the government to respect the right of parents to obtain a religious education for their children.[63]

In autumn 1987, the Episcopal Office set up a theological institute in Mostar, Herzegovina, in cooperation with the Franciscan Province in Mostar. The institute planned to offer a three-year theological program to lay persons and quickly registered forty-five students for the 1987–88 academic year. Despite the fact that there were precedents for such an institute (in Zagreb, Split, Ljubljana, and Maribor), republic authorities closed it down already in November 1987. The Yugoslav news agency Tanjug explained that the establishment of the institute was "directly opposed to the law on the legal position of religious communities in the Socialist Republic of Bosnia-Herzegovina, which, in article 20, states emphatically that religious communities can form religious schools only for the training of religious officials. Scientific and educational treatment of believers outside the church itself is, therefore, not in conformity with the law."[64] The Catholic paper, *Glas koncila,* issued a strong protest of this action.[65]

Second, the Church from time to time questioned the legitimacy of excluding believers from the ranks of the LCY. In 1971, for instance, the Slovenian Catholic weekly, *Družina,* published an article urging that the opportunities provided by SAWPY to Christians were inadequate and that their exclusion from the party was a token of political inequality.[66] Again, in 1987, Cardinal Kuharić raised this issue in an interview with the Catholic journal, *Veritas,* adding that believers were excluded from high posts in various sectors of public life.[67] The party repeatedly repudiated this interpretation, however, and even urged party members to eschew marriage with believers and to stay away from Church ceremonies.[68] On the other hand, a 1988 article about religious life in Serbia found that only a third of party members in Serbia called themselves atheists, with most giving a positive description of religion.[69]

Third, the Church repeatedly challenged the regime over human rights—whether civil, national, or even the human rights of believers qua believers. In a public statement, Kuharić used his 1987 Easter sermon to plead on behalf of twenty-six-year-old Croatian dissident Dobroslav Paraga. Paraga had been charged with "slandering the state" after he gave an interview to the Slovenian youth magazine, *Mladina,* in which he discussed the treatment he had received during a three-year prison sentence for antistate activity.[70] The defenselessness of believers in the face of slander by the secular press also preoccupied the Church, which deplored the lack of objectivity and fairness in the mass media and the inability of those calumniated to reply in the same media.[71] *Glas koncila* figured as probably the Church's single most important vehicle for self-defense against insinuations and distortions in the Communist press.

Fourth, the Church continued to complain that believers were, in other ways, treated as second-class citizens by the Communists, who, the Church claimed, treated religious belief as an *alienable* right. In particular, the Church complained of the fact that military personnel were not allowed to attend Church services in uniform or to receive Church newspapers or religious books in the barracks. The Church also long sought to obtain access to incarcerated believers, regardless of the issue for which they were in prison.[72] The Church also expressed concern about continued discrimination against believers in hiring practices in the public sector: this issue was raised by the Split archdiocesan journal, *Crkva u svijetu,* in late 1987 and by a special commission of the Provincial Episcopal Conference of Slovenia in 1988.[73]

Fifth, some elements in the Communist political establishment periodically tried to foster and aggravate internal divisions within the Church. For a while, the Christianity Today Publishing House seemed to some to be the ideal beneficiary of official favor in its "liberal defiance" of the hierarchs. Earlier, *Glas koncila* expressed concern that *Nedjeljna Dalmacija* was seeking to drive a wedge between the archbishop of Zagreb and the archbishop of Split and to set them at odds, manipulating the latter's statements to suggest opposition to or divergence from the policy of the Zagreb archbishopric.[74] This strategy was epitomized by the rival formula that recurrently praised the "vast majority" of the clergy, while condemning the "political extremism" of a "reactionary minority."

And sixth, the legislation governing religious practice was itself an important bone of contention between Church and state, both in the preparatory stage and in discussions about the execution of policy. With the passage of the 1974 Constitution, the Religious Law of 1953 was suspended and the republics were entrusted with the task of passing their own legislation in this domain. The new religious laws took effect in Slovenia on 26 May 1976 and in Bosnia-Herzegovina on 4 January 1977. After a vocal debate, Croatia was the last of the eight federal units to pass a new law, which took effect on 17 April 1978. Among the issues in contention were the ban on Church sponsorship of recreational activities, the absence of legal sanction for Church access to radio and television, and an article requiring the consent of the minor before parents could enroll her or him in religious instruction. *Glas koncila* objected, "Many citizens who are believers quite properly observe that neither they nor their minor children are asked for consent to be introduced in the course of their schooling to Marxism in its emphatically atheistic form."[75] The authorities compromised on the last point mentioned, and the final version of the Croatian law required the child's consent from age fourteen on, rather than from age seven, as specified in the draft.

INTERNAL DIVISIONS

In an earlier study, I described the presence of three opinion groupings within the Communist establishment where religious questions were concerned, namely, orthodox Marxists (who had no interest in genuine dialogue with the Churches and believed that they should disappear under communism), passive contract Marxists (who were willing to adopt a passive attitude toward religion provided that the Churches adopted a passive posture toward society and politics), and liberals (who were interested in dialogue and believed the Churches could make a positive contribution to society).[76] These divisions inevitably had consequences for Church-state relations.

In this section, I propose to focus on three sources of internal discord within the Catholic Church in Yugoslavia: the heterogeneity of responses to the Vatican II Council, the controversy surrounding Christianity Today, and the rivalry in Herzegovina between the secular bishop and the Franciscan Order.

Some twenty-five of Yugoslavia's twenty-nine Catholic bishops (at the time) participated in the Vatican II Council. Four Yugoslav bishops also participated in the work of the commissions, namely Archbishop Franjo Šeper of Zagreb and Archbishop Frane Franić of Split in the Theological Commission, Archbishop Gabrijel Bukatko of Belgrade in the Commission for Eastern Churches, and Bishop Alfred Pichler of Banja Luka in the Liturgical Commission.

Two things quickly became clear: first, that the more general division between theological traditionalists and theological progressives was replicated within the ranks of Yugoslavia's bishops; and second, that certain bishops espoused a mix of "traditional" and "progressive" views. On the whole, Šeper figured as a "progressive," Archbishop Smiljan Čekada of Sarajevo as a "traditionalist," and Franić as a mixture. In fact, Franić himself conceded that while he took a "traditional" stance on some issues, on others he was innovative and prepared to try new approaches.[77]

Šeper and Franić favored introduction of the vernacular for Holy Mass, for example, with Franić favoring use of the vernacular for all Church rituals; Čekada preferred to retain Latin as the universal language of liturgy. Again Šeper and Franić both supported ecumenism and efforts to patch up old conflicts with particular Churches. But when a specific application of the ecumenical spirit came up—namely, a proposal to build a cathedral in Skopje for joint use by Catholics and Orthodox—Čekada resisted, calling this "an infantile and romantic ecumenism." Šeper and Franić split on the proposed introduction of married deacons, on the other hand, with Šeper favoring it but Franić and fifteen other Yugoslav bishops opposed; Franić argued that people had more respect for a celibate minister than for one who married. Franić also found himself among the traditionalists in defending the notion of the personal primacy of the Pope and proposed that the vow of poverty, hitherto taken only by orders, also be extended to secular clergy. Much of the discussion during the Council centered on proposals to expand the role of the laity in the Church generally and in the liturgy in particular. Predictably, Čekada spoke out against laicization.[78]

The Vatican II Council ended in a compromise between the traditionalist and progressive wings, but not without strengthening the latter current and reinforcing the self-awareness of the former tendency. The result was a reinforcement, within Yugoslavia, of a polarization of opinion among clergy that goes back well over a hundred years.[79]

In some ways, the Theological Society Christianity Today is a product of the Vatican II Council.[80] Founded in 1968 as a research and publishing center, Christianity Today soon became a haven for theologically progressive clergymen. In May 1977, the society reorganized itself as a self-managing association in order to free itself from the rather overwhelming tax burden to which it had been liable previously. Several of the bishops condemned this move, arguing that it had not been cleared by an episcopal authority and that it opened the prospect for the society to come under Communist Party supervision and thus figure as a "Trojan horse."[81] Archbishop Franić became one of the most vocal critics of Christianity Today, banned priests in his archdiocese from having any contacts with the association, and told *Glas koncila*, in an interview in 1981,

> Some of our theologians tell us that the Church has in its history adapted to all social systems, and that it can and must adapt today, say, to self-managing socialism. . . . It is also said that this is in fact the doctrine of the Vatican II Council.
>
> I hold that this is an altogether mistaken interpretation of the council and of Church history. The Church has, to be sure, adapted to all social systems, for example, even to slave-owning society and feudal society, and today to capitalist and socialist society. . . . However, the Church did not introduce into its structures either the slave-owning system or the feudal system or the capitalist system. So, accordingly, it cannot introduce the system of self-managing socialism into its structures either. In this sense, neither the Church nor its theology nor its pastoral work can be based on the principles of self-managing socialism, nor can they enter into self-managing socialism as a part or branch, since this socialism of ours, although it is a more humanist form of Marxism and of the dictatorship of the proletariat, is still essentially aimed at creating a new civilization that is supposed to be atheist.[82]

Priests in Croatia and Bosnia-Herzegovina have been divided over this decision by Christianity Today, with the Jesuits tending to be among the most critical. Moreover, with the issuance of the encyclical "Quidam Episcopi" on 8 March 1982, directed against the Czechoslovak priests association, Pacem in Terris, the Episcopal Conference wielded yet another weapon in its battle with the progressive theologians of Christianity Today.[83] The danger, as the bishops saw it, was that the publishing house would carry out its tasks "outside Church structures" and foster clerical independence of episcopal authority.[84] The danger, as the Christianity Today theologians saw it, was that a traditionalist view of episcopal authority would result in the strangulation of a perfectly pragmatic adjustment to fiscal realities. Thus the controversy surrounding Christianity Today was simultaneously a controversy between traditionalist and theologically progressive points of view, a controversy between hierarchy and theologians, and a controversy about possible channels of regime penetration of Church institutions.

The third and final focus of internal Church discord to be treated here is the longstanding rivalry between the diocesan clergy in Bosnia-Herzegovina (most particularly the bishop of Mostar) and the Franciscan Order. The Franciscans are (with 1,094 members in 1978) the largest order in Yugoslavia, far ahead of the next largest order—the Salesians (103 members in 1978).[85]

A delicate balance prevailed in Franciscan–diocesan relations. Hence, in the period 1945–1978, of the seventeen new parishes established within Bosnia-Herzegovina, eight were entrusted to the Franciscans, seven to the diocesan clergy, and two were split between them.[86] Beginning in the mid-1960s, there were repeated clashes between pro-Franciscan parishioners and diocesan clergy over efforts to place Franciscan parishes in the hands of diocesan clergy, or to redraw parish boundaries.[87]

Starting in 1976, the then bishop of Mostar, Pavao Žanić, pressed hard to roll back Franciscan jurisdiction. In early 1981, two young Franciscans—Ivica Vego and Ivan Prušina—refused to relinquish their posts in Mostar and became the center of considerable strife and controversy. Bishop Žanić declared them "suspended" and initiated action to obtain their expulsion from the order. Shortly thereafter, six youngsters whom these two Franciscans had been counseling began to report apparitions of the Madonna, who, they said, was endorsing the Franciscans and blaming the bishop of Mostar for his "severity."[88] The apparitions continued on a daily basis, with Franciscans taking the lead in ministering to the thousands upon thousands of pilgrims who have been flocking to the site of the apparitions in the Herzegovinan village of Medjugorje. In these circumstances, it became inopportune for the bishop to take any further steps against the Franciscans. Žanić, thus frustrated by the Franciscans, referred to the apparition as the "Franciscan miracle" and was said to have stacked the initial investigative commission with skeptics in order to defuse the miracle as fast as possible.

Even this brief elaboration of three important sources of internal discord should make it clear that the Catholic Church in Yugoslavia cannot be considered a monolith and that Church-state relations must accordingly be diffracted by this political complexity.

TABLE 7.1   Proportions of Believers and Nonbelievers in Yugoslavia, 1953–1984 (percentage)

	1953	1964	1969[a]	1984[a]	1984[b]
Believers	87	70.3	53.1	45	51.9
Indifferent or undecided	–	0.5	32.1	37	27.4
Atheists	13	29.2	14.2	18	18.6
No answer	–	–	0.6	–	2.1

[a] Zagreb region.
[b] Secondary school children in Split.
SOURCES: Zlatko Frid, *Religija u samoupravnom socijalizmu* (Zagreb: Centar za društvena djelatnosti omladine RK SOH, 1971), p. 33; Branko Bosnjak and Stefica Bahtijarevic, *Socijalističko društvo, crkva i religija* (Zagreb: Institut za društvena istraživanja Sveučilišta u Zagrebu, 1969), p. 29; *Nedeljni vjesnik* (1 April 1984); and *Slobodna Dalmacija* (Split) (2 March 1987).

BELIEF AND UNBELIEF

In the years since the Communist takeover of Yugoslavia, religiosity has declined overall. This decline has been sharpest among the traditionally Orthodox[89] and least noticeable among the Muslims, while the smaller neo-Protestant sects such as Seventh Day Adventists and Jehovah's Witnesses have probably grown in membership, if anything. In varying degrees, as the figures in Table 7.1 make clear, the trend has been unmistakably toward the secularization of society, especially of the urban areas.

A 1960 survey, conducted among youth, found that Croats recorded the greatest proportion of believers, followed by Slovenes and Muslims (both ten percentage points behind the Croats), Macedonians, Serbs, and Montenegrins.[90] A 1985–86 survey among more than 6,500 Yugoslav young people found similar results. Of those from Catholic families, 62.3 percent said they were religious, as compared with 43.8 percent of those from Muslim families and only 26.2 percent of those from Orthodox families.[91] Among the traditionally Catholic republics of Croatia and Slovenia, moreover, while the 1970s and 1980s have seen a continued decline in religiosity in Slovenia, the same period (1968–1985) recorded an increase in religious observance in Dalmatia: where 32 percent of Dalmatian youth declared themselves religious in 1968, 52 percent did so in 1985.[92] A 1985 survey of obituary notices in the press confirmed these results, showing 46 percent religiosity and 54 percent indifference or atheism.[93]

Following a pattern typical of transitional societies, urban residents and young people are less likely to be religious. The difference between city and village, when it comes to religiosity, is reflected, for example, in the 1986 report that while 95 percent of young Catholics in Yugoslav villages

TABLE 7.2   Responses to the Question, "Do You Accept Marxism?"
(1969, percentage)

	Yes	No	Partly	Not Acquainted
Believers	18.5	2.3	10.7	66.0
Undecided	32.8	0.0	23.8	41.9
Nonbelievers	61.1	0.0	15.0	23.9
Atheists	82.7	0.0	4.7	12.6

SOURCE: Bošnjak and Bahtijarevic, *Socialističko društvo, crkva i religija* (Zagreb: Institut za društvena istraživanja Sveučilišta u Zagrebu, 1969), p. 122.

obtained religious instruction, only 10 percent of those in cities did so, averaging 60 percent for the country as a whole.[94] And for reasons unclear, a 1986 survey in Belgrade showed that the proportions of *both* atheists and believers were shrinking, with an increasing number of people reporting themselves "agnostics."[95] Already in 1975 a group of Zagreb sociologists found that 40 percent of respondents had no definite or clear worldview.[96] The persistence and even increase of agnosticism was probably related to the more general failures of Yugoslav ideology and socialization.

For all that, party members tended, at least until the late 1980s, to see religion as an unwelcome social phenomenon. Branko Bošnjak and Stefica Bahtijarević conducted an extremely comprehensive survey of attitudes toward religion among residents of Zagreb and its immediate vicinity in 1969. Their results showed that 28.7 percent of LCY members viewed religion as actually "damaging," as compared with 18.7 percent of government functionaries, 15.8 percent of World War II veterans, 10.3 percent of members of administrative organs, and 8.5 percent of SAWPY members.[97]

Other results showed a clear relationship between atheization and socialization to accept Marxism and to respond positively to the Communist system, thus confirming LCY suspicions of religion, though perhaps only with circular logic. In Table 7.2, for example, three times as many nonbelievers as believers accepted Marxism, while believers were the most likely to report nonacquaintance with the Marxist creed. Table 7.3 shows a clear inverse correlation between religious belief and participation in public meetings. And asked whether Church teachings influenced their participation in public life, 33.2 percent answered in the affirmative.[98]

Other questions touched on the practice of religion in Yugoslavia. Of the sample polled, 46.8 percent said they felt that they could practice their faith freely in Yugoslavia, versus 6 percent who felt they could not (7.8 percent answered with a qualified "yes," adding that they avoided conversations about religion, while 37.8 percent were not believers, and 1.6 percent declined to answer).[99] Asked if they considered it easy to safeguard their faith in an atheist environment, 25.1 percent of the sample replied in the nega-

TABLE 7.3   Responses to the Question, "How Often Do You Participate in Public Meetings?" (1969, percentage)

	Regularly, or Very Often	Sometimes	Never
Believers	17.5	40.0	40.9
Undecided	30.6	48.6	19.5
Nonbelievers	39.5	47.2	13.3
Atheists	51.7	37.4	10.9

SOURCES: Bosnjak and Bahtijarevic, *Socijalističko društvo, crkva i religija* (Zagreb: Institut za društvena istraživanja Sveučilišta u Zagrebu, 1969), p. 101.

tive, with an additional 16.4 percent replying merely that they did not reveal their religious belief to others: this makes for a composite negative reply of 41.5 percent.[100]

Finally, when asked whether believers are more moral than nonbelievers, 1.6 percent of party members answered in the affirmative—indicating that not all LCY members were convinced "atheists."[101] A subsequent poll, conducted anonymously in 1987, found that 7.7 percent of Communist Party members surveyed (in the Zagreb region) were believers and that 12.5 percent admitted that they were sending their children to religious instruction.[102] Table 7.4 shows the proportion of Yugoslavs reporting religious beliefs in 1985.

Yugoslav society was a partly secularized and partly secularizing society—and not merely because of LCY rule. In this context, the Catholic Church has had to adapt to changed circumstances and to discover new strategies for maintaining and propagating the faith. Many clergymen have called for coexistence, such as Croatian theologian Tomislav Šagi-Bunić, who, in his *Ali drugog puta nema* (1969), wrote: "The political community

TABLE 7.4   Proportion of Population Reporting Religious Belief (November 1985), by Federal Unit

Federal Unit	Percent
Kosovo	44
Croatia	33
Slovenia	26
Macedonia	19
Bosnia-Herzegovina	17
Serbia	11
Vojvodina	10
Montenegro	10

SOURCE: *Intervju* (March 28, 1986), as reported in AKSA (April 4, 1986), in *AKSA Bulletin* (August 5, 1986), p. 8.

and the Church are independent and autonomous of each other, each in its own sphere. Both stand in service, although for different reasons, at the personal and social summons of the very same people. Thus, . . . appropriate cooperation between them is necessary so that they can better carry out their service toward people."[103]

THE MIRACLE AT MEDJUGORJE

On 24 June 1981, six Catholic youngsters saw what they believed was the Madonna on a hill on the outskirts of Medjugorje, a village of 3,000 inhabitants near Čitluk, in Herzegovina. Word spread quickly, and within a short time at least 6,000 people were making a pilgrimage to Medjugorje each day. In time, the alledged miracle became known to believers around the world, who likewise started to flock to this village in droves. The youngsters continued to experience daily visions (as noted earlier in this chapter), at the same time each evening. By 1988, 10 million pilgrims had visited Medjugorje.[104]

On a less ethereal plane, the "miracle" was, in fact, the work of local Franciscans, who needed a miracle to save their parishes from takeover by the diocesan Church. Back in 1923, the Franciscans controlled sixty-three of the seventy-nine existing Catholic parishes in Bosnia-Herzegovina and also operated twenty-nine monasteries, five seminaries, and a few hospitals in the region.[105] But in the early 1960s, with the warming of relations between the Catholic Church and the Yugoslav state, the bishop of Mostar took advantage of the new atmosphere to press for an extension of diocesan jurisdiction. The bishop signed a secret agreement with the state authorities of Bosnia in 1966 and also courted the Vatican, eventually securing a revision of the 1923 apportionment of parochial jurisdictions. By 1967, thanks to the bishop's energetic expansionism, the Franciscans' jurisdiction in Bosnia-Herzegovina had been reduced to just thirty parishes. Then, in 1975, Rome took under consideration the question of transferring yet another five parishes to the bishop of Mostar. The Franciscan father superior sent a letter of protest to Rome and, for the letter, he was suspended. The bishop of Mostar interpreted this as an authorization for him to take over *all* remaining Franciscan parishes and began to attempt to do so, only to find local parishioners barricading their churches and forcibly barring the entry of diocesan priests. The alleged appearance of the Madonna, who was even kind enough to tell the children that the Franciscans were "right" and that Bishop Žanić should apologize, was profoundly empowering for the Franciscans, whose number in the diocese of Mostar quickly rose from 80 to more than 120.[106] The Franciscans, in fact, used the devotional movement to build international recognition and support for the order's presence in the area; and in the United States, the Franciscan Center in Steubenville, Ohio, took charge of worldwide publicity about Medjugorje. Žanić remained bitterly opposed to the apparitions, which he characterized as a "collective hallucination," provoked by Franciscan machinations.[107] Entrusted by the Vatican with the task of appointing a commission to investigate the apparitions and to offer a recommendation as to whether it was genuine or not, Žanić stacked the commission with known skeptics.[108] After more than a decade, the invalidation of the first commission and the appointment of a second, and even the retirement of Žanić from the episcopacy, the Vatican has still not come to a final judgment about the "miracle" and probably considers it inexpedient to do so. Meanwhile, Ratko Perić, Žanić's successor as bishop of Mostar, told the Synod of Bishops in October 1994 that he expected the Vatican to declare the apparitions at Medjugorje inauthentic[109] and, in this way, to enable Perić to restore ecclesiastical "unity" in Herzegovina on *his* terms.

Commenting on similar apparitions in nineteenth-century Germany, David Blackbourn said recently, "There is no doubt that modern apparitions [of the Virgin] were commonly triggered by larger events: periods of wartime or post-war stress, political conflict, socio-economic crisis. It is also plain that many apparitions had an impact in turn on contemporary political conflicts, above all in helping to foster Catholic identity against the claims of the state or the challenge of anticlericals."[110] Indeed, the miracle in Herzegovina has helped to rally Catholic Croats and give them hope and even a sense of peace in a time of profound chaos and conflict. According to several witnesses who have recently traveled to Medjugorje, the village remains an oasis of repose in a bitter war zone and seems to have been immune to all efforts on the part of Serbs to bomb the region. Witnesses claim that Serbian missiles fired at Medjugorje simply disappear into thin air, leaving the village and its surrounding area uniquely unharmed.

THE END OF YUGOSLAVIA

As Serb–Croat polemics heated up in the course of the period 1989–1990, the Catholic Church was ineluctably drawn into the fire. Serbian politicians revived the old Communist canard that the Catholic Church had been pro-Ustasha in World War II and stirred up fears of partition by talking of the supposedly Orthodox origins of Dalmatia.[111] The Church rebuffed these attacks and replied with a sharp article that suggested that Serbian revanchists might still nurture dreams of including as much as 70 percent of the territory of Yugoslavia within the borders of an enlarged Serbia.[112]

Not surprisingly, it was Slovenia—where both Strossmayer and Stepinac have always been largely irrelevant—that Church–state relations first acquired a somewhat friendlier tone. This was signaled in December 1986, when Ljubljana's Archbishop Šuštar became the first Yugoslav hierarch in the postwar period to be allowed to wish his flock a Merry Christmas over public radio.[113] The decision sparked a lively national debate, but privately,

Slovenian clergy expressed confidence that Christmas would soon be declared a public holiday—if not in 1987, then by 1988—at least in the Republic of Slovenia.[114] Šuštar's Christmas greetings were once again broadcast in December 1987, but only amid massive controversy and discussion in the press. Meanwhile, Mitja Ribičič, a prominent Slovenian politician, suggested that rather than engaging in endless debate about the rectitude of broadcasting the prelate's Christmas greetings, it would be better to discuss how to improve the access of believers to jobs in both local and federal governmental agencies.[115] This was followed by the announcement in 1988 that the Catholic Faculty of Theology in Ljubljana, which had been forced to separate from the university shortly after the war, would shortly be reincorporated into the University of Ljubljana.[116]

Slovenes started to talk openly of the liquidation of priests by Tito in early postwar Slovenia.[117] Slovenian society began opening up. In February 1989, it was announced that Catholic journalists would be allowed to join the Society of Journalists of Slovenia.[118] Four months later, a Society of Catholic Journalists in Yugoslavia was established in Zagreb.[119]

As the Communist monopoly broke down, Catholic prelates joined in the general debate about the country's future. In November 1989, for example, the Iustitia et Pax Commission of the Episcopal Conference of Yugoslavia published a statement urging progress in repluralization, stressing, in particular, the central importance of the establishment of an independent judiciary.[120]

When the first free elections were conducted in Slovenia and Croatia in spring 1990, the Catholic bishops of Ljubljana and Zagreb issued a statement supportive of democracy but declining to endorse any particular party. On the contrary, Church elders warned clergy not to become involved in partisan politics.[121] But in other ways the Catholic Church took advantage of the new liberalism to stretch its wings. In July 1990, already, Franciscans in Herzegovina asked for a lifting of the ban on associations based on religious and ethnic affiliation. In Croatia and Slovenia, Catholic prelates began to press for a restoration of (Catholic) religious instruction as a mandatory subject in public schools—succeeding in this endeavor in Croatia but failing in Slovenia (as will be explained in more detail in Chapter 11). And in both republics, the Catholic Church began to demand that abortion be delegalized. Nor has the Church held aloof from the most burning questions of the day. Cardinal Kuharić, in particular, took up the subject of confederalization in an article for *Vjesnik* and argued that "the question of confederation does not pass by the religious communities."[122]

The breakup of Yugoslavia and the outbreak of war have confronted the Catholic Church in Slovenia, Croatia, and Bosnia with both new challenges and new opportunities. These subjects will be taken up in Chapter 13, in the context of a broader examination of the responses of the religious communities to the war in Bosnia.

NOTES

This chapter is a revised and updated version of my earlier chapter, "The Catholic Church in Yugoslavia, 1945–1989," originally published in Pedro Ramet, ed., *Catholicism and Politics in Communist Societies* (Durham, N.C.: Duke University Press, 1990). The author wishes to thank Duke University Press for granting permission to reproduce the chapter here. I am grateful to Stella Alexander, Ivo Banac, and Christine Hassenstab for their helpful comments on earlier drafts of this study.

1. *Keston News Service,* No. 357 (30 August 1990), p. 11.
2. *Keston News Service,* No. 359 (27 September 1990), p. 8.
3. Zlatko Markus, "Sadašnji trenutak crkve u Hrvatskoj," *Hrvatska revija* (Buenos Aires), Vol. 25, No. 2 (June 1975), pp. 223–224.
4. Frane Franić, *Putovi dijaloga* (Split: Crkva u svijetu, 1973), quoted in Markus, "Sadašnji trenutak," p. 219.
5. Ćiril Petešić, *Katoličko svećenstvo u NOB-u 1941–1945* (Zagreb: VPA, 1982), p. 130.
6. Ibid., p. 55.
7. AVNOJ = Antifascist Council of the People's Liberation of Yugoslavia.
8. Petešić, *Katoličko svećenstvo,* pp. 32, 36.
9. See Ivo Banac, *The National Question in Yugoslavia: Origins, History, Politics* (Ithaca, N.Y.: Cornell University Press, 1984).
10. Fikreta Jelić-Butić, *Ustaše i NDH* (Zagreb: S. N. Liber and Školska Knjiga, 1977), p. 214.
11. Petešić, *Katoličko svećenstvo,* p. 95.
12. Richard Pattee, *The Case of Cardinal Aloysius Stepinac* (Milwaukee: Bruce, 1953), pp. 114, 276–281, 300–305. Stepinac's efforts on behalf of the Orthodox are noted in Ivan Cvitković's generally unsympathetic biography, *Ko je bio Alojzije Stepinac,* 2nd ed. (Sarajevo: Oslobodjenje, 1986), p. 209.
13. Quoted in Branko Bošnjak and Stefica Bahtijarević, *Socijalističko društvo, crkva and religija* (Zagreb: Institut za društvena istraživanja Sveučilišta u Zagrebu, 1969), p. 159.
14. O. Aleksa Benigar, *Alojzije Stepinac, Hrvatski Kardinal* (Rome: Ziral, 1974), p. 492.
15. Quoted in ibid., pp. 502–503.
16. See Pedro Ramet, *Cross and Commissar: the Politics of Religion in Eastern Europe and the USSR* (Bloomington: Indiana University Press, 1987), p. 29.
17. Rastko Vidić, *The Position of the Church in Yugoslavia* (Belgrade: Jugoslavija, 1962), pp. 69–70.
18. Giuseppe Masucci, *Misija u Hrvatskoj 1941–1946* [Diary] (Madrid: Drina, 1967), pp. 204–205.
19. Benigar, *Alojzije Stepinac,* p. 508.
20. See article by Dragoljub Petrović, in *Književne novine* (15 October 1985).
21. Quoted in Benigar, *Alojzije Stepinac,* p. 536.

22. Ibid., pp. 540–541.

23. Ibid., pp. 519, 542–543.

24. Ibid., p. 555; confirmed in *New York Times* (20 September 1946), p. 9.

25. *New York Times* (24 September 1946), p. 11.

26. *New York Times* (28 September 1946), p. 5.

27. Benigar, *Alojzije Stepinac,* p. 578; and *New York Times* (26 September 1946), p. 7.

28. Jakov Blažević, *Mać a ne mir. Za pravnu sigurnost gradjana* [Vol. 3 of Memoirs, 4 vols.] (Zagreb/Belgrade/Sarajevo: Mladost/Prosveta/Svjetlost, 1980), pp. 208–209.

29. Benigar, *Alojzije Stepinac,* p. 601.

30. Blažević, *Mać a ne mire,* pp. 211, 234–236.

31. Ibid., pp. 237–238. Pattee (*The Case,* p. 129) estimates that some 200,000 former Catholics who had been pressured into Orthodoxy were among those converting to Catholicism during the war.

32. Blažević, *Mać a ne mir,* pp. 360, 284–285.

33. *L'Osservatore Romano* (30 September 1946), summarized in *New York Times* (1 October 1946), p. 15.

34. Blažević, *Mać a ne mir,* pp. 210–211.

35. Ibid., p. 374.

36. Stella Alexander, *The Triple Myth: A Life of Archbishop Alojzije Stepinac* (Boulder, Colo.: East European Monographs, 1987), p. 178.

37. *L'Osservatore Romano* (12 October 1946), trans. into Croatian in Benigar, *Alojzije Stepinac,* pp. 635–638; and *L'Osservatore Romano* (31 October 1946), excerpted in *New York Times* (1 November 1946), p. 17.

38. Quoted in Benigar, *Alojzije Stepinac,* p. 639.

39. *Polet* (8 and 15 February 1985), as quoted in *Glas koncila* (24 February 1985), p. 3.

40. *Borba* (24 October 1945), p. 3.

41. This latter story seems to have been a complete fabrication, however, since on 10 December 1945 twenty priests from the Bar archdiocese sent a letter to Stepinac objecting that Archbishop Dobrečić had made no such statements to the press as had been claimed. See Benigar, *Alojzije Stepinac,* p. 546.

42. Stella Alexander, *Church and State in Yugoslavia Since 1945* (Cambridge: Cambridge University Press, 1979), p. 126.

43. Report in *Borba* (18 December 1952), reprinted in Vladimir Dedijer, ed., *Dokumenti 1948,* Vol. 3 (Belgrade: Rad, 1979), pp. 466–468.

44. Fra Ignacije Gavran, *Lucerna Lucens? Odnos vrhbosanskog ordinarijata prema bosanskim Franjevcima (1881–1975)* (Visoko: N.p., 1978), p. 155.

45. Rudolf Grulich, *Kreuz, Halbmond und Roter Stern: Zur Situation der katholischen Kirche in Jugoslawien* (Munich: Aktion West-Ost, 1979), p. 62.

46. E.g., Gavran, *Lucerna Lucens,* pp. 158–159; and Grulich, *Kreuz, Halbmond,* p. 62.

47. Quoted in Gavran, *Lucerna Lucens,* p. 158n.

48. *Vjesnik* (15 July 1978), trans. in Joint Publications Research Service (JPRS), *East Europe Report,* No. 72058 (17 October 1978).

49. *NIN,* No. 1900 (22 March 1987), p. 32.

50. Interview, Ljubljana, July 1982.

51. Quoted in Alexander, *Church and State,* p. 229.

52. Paul Mojzes, "Religious Liberty in Yugoslavia: A Study in Ambiguity," in Leonard Swidler, ed., *Religious Liberty and Human Rights in Nations and in Religions* (Philadelphia: Ecumenical Press, 1986), pp. 25–26.

53. Quoted in Zdenko Roter, "Relations Between the State and the Catholic Church in Yugoslavia," *Socialist Thought and Practice,* Vol. 18, No. 11 (November 1974), p. 69.

54. *New York Times* (26 June 1966), p. 4.

55. Quoted in Zdenko Roter, *Katoliška cerkev in drzava v Jugoslaviji 1945–1973* (Ljubljana: Cankarjeva založba, 1976), p. 203.

56. Ibid., p. 206.

57. For details, see Pedro Ramet, "Catholicism and Politics in Socialist Yugoslavia," *Religion in Communist Lands,* Vol. 10, No. 3 (winter 1982), pp. 261–262.

58. *Borba* (9 October 1970), p. 6. For further discussion of the Catholic Church's association with Croatian nationalism, see Pedro Ramet, "Religion and Nationalism in Yugoslavia," in Pedro Ramet, ed., *Religion and Nationalism in Soviet and East European Politics,* revised and expanded ed. (Durham, N.C.: Duke University Press, 1989).

59. "Vjernost Alojziju Stepincu—za reviziju sudskog procesa i kanonizaciju!," *Hrvatska revija,* Vol. 20, No. 1 (March 1970), pp. 85–87.

60. *Borba* (14 January 1973), p. 7, trans. in JPRS, *Translations on Eastern Europe,* No. 58221 (13 February 1973).

61. *Nedjeljna Dalmacija* (Varaždin) (9 December 1972), quoted in *Glas koncila* (7 January 1973), p. 12, trans. in JPRS, *Translations on Eastern Europe,* No. 58479 (14 March 1973).

62. *Glas koncila* (25 December 1980).

63. *Frankfurter Allgemeine* (2 November 1987), p. 4.

64. Tanjug (15 November 1987), quoted in *Keston News Service,* No. 290 (17 December 1987), p. 14.

65. *Glas koncila* (6 December 1987), p. 2, and (13 December 1987), p. 2; and *AKSA Bulletin,* Catholic news summary translation service edited by Stella Alexander with Muriel Heppell and Kresimir Sidor (26 January 1988), pp. 5–6.

66. *Družina* (1 August 1971), cited in *Borba* (1 August 1971), p. 5.

67. Interview with Franjo Cardinal Kuharić, in *Veritas* (March 1987), excerpted in *Glas koncila* (8 March 1987), p. 3.

68. Dionisie Ghermani, "Die katholische Kirche in Kroatien/Slowenien," *Kirche in Not,* Vol. 27 (1979), p. 93; *Glas koncila* (19 February 1984), p. 4, and (16 June 1985), p. 3.

69. *Delo* (Ljubljana) (20 February 1988), as reported in *AKSA* (26 February 1988), in *AKSA Bulletin* (14 April 1988), p. 4.

70. *Keston News Service,* No. 274 (30 April 1987), pp. 16–17.

71. *Glas koncila* (25 October 1981), p. 3.

72. Interview with Archbishop of Belgrade Dr. Franc Perko, in *Danas,* No. 260 (10 February 1987), p. 26; and *Keston News Service,* No. 290 (17 December 1987).

73. Drago Simundža, "Ustavni i stvarni položaj vjernika u društvu," *Crkva u svijetu,* No. 4 (1987), reprinted in *Glas koncila* (25 December 1987), p. 5; *Frankfurter Allgemeine* (17 March 1988), p. 1; and *Glas koncila* (3 April 1988), p. 5.

74. *Glas koncila* (7 January 1973), p. 12.

75. *Glas koncila* (22 January 1978), p. 3, trans. in JPRS, *East Europe Report,* No. 70836 (24 March 1978).

76. See Pedro Ramet, "Factionalism in Church–State Interaction: The Croatian Catholic Church in the 1980s, *Slavic Review,* Vol. 44, No. 2 (summer 1985), reprinted as Chapter 6 of Ramet, *Cross and Commissar.*

77. Zlatko Frid, *Religija u samoupravnom socijalizmu* (Zagreb: Centar za društvene djelatnosti omladine RK SOH, 1971), p. 118.

78. Ibid., pp. 109–113. Yet there were churches in the diocese of Kotor that even in the 1980s continued to be used by both Catholics and Orthodox.

79. Viktor Novak, *Velika optužba,* 3 Vols., (Sarajevo: Svjetlost, 1960), I: 20–34; and *Glas koncila* (27 March 1983), p. 8.

80. *Glas koncila* (15 December 1985), p. 6.

81. *Frankfurter Allgemeine* (23 July 1980), p. 5; and *Vjesnik: Sedam dana* (24 April 1982), p. 17.

82. *Glas koncila* (19 April 1981), pp. 7, 9.

83. *Vjesnik: Sedam dana* (30 April 1982), p. 10; and *Frankfurter Allgemeine* (8 February 1983), p. 10, (5 July 1983), p. 8, and (21 February 1985), p. 12.

84. *Vjesnik: Sedam dana* (31 July 1982), p. 14.

85. Rudolf Grulich, *Die Katholische Kirche in der Sozialistischen Föderativen Republik Jugoslawien* (Zollikon: Glaube in der 2. Welt, 1980), p. 11.

86. Gavran, *Lucerna Lucens,* p. 146.

87. See Ibid., pp. 146–151.

88. Rene Laurentin and Ljudevit Rupčić, *Is the Virgin Mary Appearing at Medjugorje?* (Washington, D.C.: Word Among Us Press, 1984), pp. 113–114.

89. *Duga* (25 August 1984), as reported in *AKSA* (31 August 1984), in *AKSA Bulletin* (28 November 1984), p. 5.

90. Manojlo Bročić, "The Position and Activities of the Religious Communities in Yugoslavia with Special Attention to the Serbian Orthodox Church," in Bohdan R. Bociurkiw and John W. Strong, eds., *Religion and Atheism in the USSR and Eastern Europe* (London: Macmillan, 1975), pp. 364–365.

91. Srdjan Vrcan, "Omladma osamdesetih godina, religija i crkva," in S. Vrcan et al., *Polozaj, svest i ponašanje mlade generacije Jugoslavije: Preliminarna analiza rezultata istiazivanja* (Zagreb: IDIS, 1986), p. 159.

92. *AKSA* (22 February 1985), as extracted in *AKSA Bulletin* (17 April 1985), p. 5.

93. *Nedjeljna Dalmacija* (21 April 1985), reported in *AKSA* (26 April 1985), as extracted in *AKSA Bulletin* (25 July 1985), p. 5.

94. *AKSA* (6 June 1986), in *AKSA Bulletin* (5 August 1986), p. 4; and *Keston News Service,* No. 257 (21 August 1986), p. 12.

95. *Borba* (Zagreb ed.) (6 February 1986), p. 3.

96. Grulich, *Kreuz, Halbmond,* pp. 58–59.

97. Bošnjak and Bahtijarević, *Socijalisticko društvo,* p. 33.

98. Ibid., p. 134.

99. Ibid., p. 83.

100. Ibid., pp. 83–84.

101. Ibid., p. 63.

102. *Nedjeljna borba* (Zagreb) (14–15 February 1987), summarized in *AKSA* (20 February 1987), in *AKSA Bulletin* (26 May 1987), p. 2.

103. Quoted in Bošnjak and Bahtijarević, *Socijalisticko društvo,* p. 133.

104. Mart Bax, "The Madonna of Medjugorje: Religious Rivalry and the Formation of a Devotional Movement in Yugoslavia," *Anthropological Quarterly,* Vol. 63, No. 2 (April 1990), p. 63.

105. Ibid., p. 64.

106. Ibid., p. 68.

107. Quoted in *The Economist* (London) (26 January 1985), p. 46.

108. Details in Pedro Ramet, "The Miracle at Medjugorje—A Functional Perspective," *South Slav Journal,* Vol. 8, Nos. 1–2 (spring–summer 1985), p. 16.

109. *National Catholic Reporter* (21 October 1994), p. 7. See also *Slobodna Dalmacija* (Split) (19 October 1994), p. 6.

110. David Blackbourn, *Marpingen: Apparitions of the Virgin Mary in Nineteenth-Century Germany* (New York: Knopf, 1994), p. xxvii.

111. Bishop Nikodim Milaš, *Pravoslavna Dalmacija* (Belgrade: Sfairos, 1989).

112. This suggestion was made indirectly, by publishing an old Chetnik map of Yugoslavia in the pages of *Glas koncila.* See *Glas koncila* (24 September 1989), p. 3; also ibid. (30 July 1989), p. 5, and (8 October 1989), p. 2.

113. *NIN,* No. 1879 (4 January 1987), pp. 15–16; and *Frankfurter Allgemeine* (2 January 1987), p. 4.

114. Interview, Ljubljana, July 1987.

115. *Borba* (Zagreb ed.) (31 October–1 November 1987), p. 3; *Dnevnik* (Novi Sad) (13 November 1987), summarized in *AKSA* (13 November 1987), as reported in *AKSA Bulletin* (26 January 1988), p. 7; and *Glas koncila* (3 January 1988), p. 3.

116. *Delo* (6 January 1988), reported in *AKSA* (8 January 1988), in *AKSA Bulletin* (9 March 1988), p. 10; and *Ilustrovana politika* (Belgrade) (2 February 1988), reported in *AKSA* (19 February 1988), in *AKSA Bulletin* (14 April 1988), p. 8.

117. *Glas koncila* (8 January 1989), p. 6.

118. *Glas koncila* (26 February 1989), p. 3.

119. *Glas koncila* (18 June 1989), p. 6.

120. *Keston News Service,* No. 342 (25 January 1990), p. 23.

121. *Keston News Service,* No. 348 (20 April 1990), p. 11, and No. 360 (11 October 1990), p. 11.

122. *Vjesnik: Panorama subotom* (6 October 1990), p. 6.

CHAPTER EIGHT

◆

The Serbian Orthodox Church

BETWEEN 1984 AND 1987, there was a dramatic transformation of the status of the Serbian Orthodox Church. Long treated as a despised pariah whose gospel was the dispensation of depraved reactionaries, the Serbian Orthodox Church regained some of its earlier stature and prestige and has more recently been treated—as in the interwar kingdom—as the most constant defender of the Serbian people and their culture.

THE SOUL OF THE CHURCH

Prior to 1984, however, the Serbian Orthodox Church became accustomed to vilification. Over time, this affected the psychological state of Orthodox clergy, who came to see themselves as embattled warriors for their Christ, profoundly threatened by a dangerous world. For much of the postwar period, it was more or less routine for the Communist press in Yugoslavia periodically to assail the Serbian Orthodox Church for chauvinism, Greater Serbian nationalism, and reactionary attitudes. The sensitivity with which that Church often reacted to such attacks betrayed a psychological vulnerability fostered by the vicissitudes in the Church's fortunes during the twentieth century and by the erosion of its power on several fronts and expressed in the hierarchy's self-image as a *suffering* Church, even of a Church marked out for *special* suffering. Having lost a fourth of its clergy and many of its churches during World War II, the Serbian Church had to endure the postwar harassment of its priests and the continued obstruction of church construction. Having lived to see the extinction of the artificially created Croatian Orthodox Church, the Belgrade patriarchate had to deal with two further schisms, resulting in the loss of effective jurisdiction over part of the American and Australian congregations as well as the Macedonian dioceses. And while most of the Serbian clergy resisted the Nazis and their allies tenaciously, they found themselves strangely isolated, derided, chastened—until quite recently. The Serbian Church remained de-

fiant, but there was a sense of pessimism or perhaps of impotence to that
defiance. Accordingly, in the new arcadia of Church-state rapprochement
created by Slobodan Milošević, the Serbian priests behave as if they are unsure whether these "freedoms" are here to stay and privately express concern that everything could be rescinded and retracted overnight. The
Church, thus, retains a sense of insecurity and has not forgotten that, in the
greater scheme, it remains impotent.

It was not always this way. In the early part of the century, the Serbian
Church took its numerous privileges for granted and identified the purposes of the Serbian kingdom so totally with its own purposes as to be incapable of comprehending differences of interest, except as misinterpreta-
tions of their common interest. Yet it should be stressed that the
comparatively weak position of the Serbian Church since the war is not the
result merely of the decimation of World War II, let alone of Communist
rule, but has its roots deep in the past.

The second suppression of the Serbian patriarchate of Peć in 1766 no
doubt undermined the institutional power of the Church. Thus, at the opening of the twentieth century, the Serbian Orthodox Church was organized
differently in the different political systems in which it had dioceses and
lacked a centralized authoritative head. In the Kingdom of Serbia, for instance, the leading Church figure was the metropolitan of Belgrade, assisted
by a synod, and the clergy received state salaries. In Montenegro, the
Montenegrin government set up a synod, in 1903, as the highest Church authority in that principality, including in its membership all Montenegrin
bishops, two archimandrites, three protopriests, and a secretary. In
Hungary, Orthodox Church affairs were regulated autonomously by a national Church council over which the metropolitan of Karlovci presided.
And in Bosnia-Herzegovina, the Orthodox clergy again regulated the internal life of the Church independently, although the Austrian emperor appointed its bishops.[1]

More significant for the vitiation that began in the late nineteenth cen-
tury were the ideas of materialism, positivism, and progressive secularism,
which infected even some of the clergy (e.g., Jovan Jovanović, rector of the
Orthodox Theological Seminary in Belgrade), and the persistent encroach-
ments by the state on ecclesiastical turf. Repeated intellectual attacks on the
Serbian Church, combined with the increasingly poorer training given to
Serbian clergy, eventually resulted in a sapping of religiosity among the
Serbs. Meanwhile, infused with notions of social activism, many of the
clergy became involved in Serbian political parties, which encouraged the
state to interfere more and more in ecclesiastical affairs. By 1881, with the
dismissal of Belgrade Metropolitan Mihailo and the passage of a new law,
whereby the government was able to pack the Church synod with its own
lay delegates, the state had effectively taken over the Church, reducing it

to something akin to a state agency; even the reinstatement of Mihailo in 1889 did not reinvigorate the Church's power.[2] The very organization of the Serbian Orthodox Church was eventually regulated by a law on Church districts passed by the state with the consent of the Church.

Yet there were benefits for the Church in the old Kingdom of Serbia, too. For one thing, under the Serbian Constitution of 1903, Orthodoxy was recognized as the official state religion and all state and national holidays were celebrated with Church ritual. Orthodox religious instruction was mandatory throughout Serbia. And all bishops, Serbian Church officials, religious instructors, and army chaplains received state salaries. Moreover, after the establishment of a unified Yugoslavia at the end of 1918 and the revival of the patriarchate, the Serbian patriarch would sit on the Royal Council, while several orthodox clergymen had seats in the National Assembly as deputies of various political parties.

Given the disunity in Church organizations that existed in the first two decades of this century, it was inevitable that the Serbian Church viewed the unification of the South Slavs as *also* a unification of the Serbian Orthodox Church and thus perhaps even as a great turning point. Within six months of the establishment of the interwar Kingdom of Serbs, Croats, and Slovenes (as Yugoslavia was initially called), the Serbian bishops convened in Belgrade and proclaimed the unification of all the Serbian Orthodox provincial churches into a single unified ecclesiastical structure. The following year, on 12 September 1920, the bishops completed the process by solemnly proclaiming the reestablishment of the Serbian patriarchate, in the presence of the highest dignitaries of both Church and state. These moves were fully canonical, undertaken with the concurrence and blessing of the Ecumenical Patriarchate.

The state's interest in this was clear from the outset. Even before the unification conference a governmental delegate, Dr. Vojislav Janic—later to become the minister of faiths—revealed that it was "the wish of the government that the reestablishment of the patriarchate be accomplished as soon as the Church is unified."[3] Furthermore, once the patriarch had been elected, the government lost little time in drafting a law that would have imposed greater legislative and judicial unity on the Church and thus made it simpler to regulate and control. Because this draft bill provoked immediate protests from all sides, but especially in the metropolitanate of Karlovac and in Bosnia-Herzegovina, where the local clergy dreaded the diminution of their autonomy, it was withdrawn and a different bill was submitted to the assembly at the end of 1923. This draft also failed to be passed, and two further drafts were likewise defeated before the government finally succeeded, in 1929, in passing a law drafted by the minister of justice, Milan Srškić. The prolonged controversy over this law revealed the existence of considerable differences of opinion between Church and state regarding state jurisdiction over the Church and also considerable division within the Serbian Church itself.

In the meantime, the Serbian Church and the government signed an agreement in 1926 (between the Episcopal Synod and the Ministry of Faiths) that was the equivalent of a concordat, arranging many questions pertaining to their mutual relations. The state now discovered that instead of simplifying its control over the Church, the reestablishment of the patriarchate gave the Church new resources; and in the course of the 1920s, as a result both of the passage of a new Church constitution (in 1924) and of the fluidity produced by the drawn-out controversy over the Church law— as well as the financial strength derived in part from state subventions to the Church—the Serbian Orthodox Church improved its position vis-à-vis the state and showed itself willing to confront the state over matters of importance. The Church became, at the same time, a unified structure, as differences between provincial Churches disappeared.

Under Yugoslavia's King Alexander (1921–1934), "not only was the dynasty Serbian, but all the important ministries were monopolized by Serbs, the bureaucracy was predominantly Serbian, the police were controlled by Serbs, [and] the high ranks of the military were occupied by Serbs."[4] The monarchy gave the Serbian Orthodox Church generous subsidies. As a result of these, the Serbian Church was able to establish a metropolitanate in Zagreb and to construct three churches in Catholic Slovenia.[5] There was even talk, in the early 1920s, that the Serbian Orthodox Church might open a theological faculty in Zagreb.[6] During the 1920s, non-Orthodox believers repeatedly complained that the Serbian Church was manipulating the state to serve its own confessional objectives, and reports that the Royal Dictatorship (established in 1929) was persecuting Catholic schools only deepened the alienation of the Catholic sector of the population.[7]

Although it enjoyed, in some ways, a privileged position in the interwar kingdom, or perhaps precisely *because* it did, the Serbian Church was deeply troubled by the Roman Catholic Church's quest for a concordat, which, it feared, would greatly strengthen the position of the Catholic Church throughout Yugoslavia. Catholic Archbishops Bauer and Stepinac were very much in favor of the concordat, and Vlatko Maček, chair of the Croatian Peasant Party, lent his endorsement to the Holy See's efforts to secure it. The concordat was finally signed on 25 July 1935, shortly after Milan Stojadinović became prime minister, though the state did not publish its contents. The Serbian Orthodox Church, however, published what was purported to be a complete draft of the concordat, together with a point-by-point critique.[8]

The Serbian patriarchate claimed that the concordat was designed to give the Catholic Church exclusive privileges in Yugoslavia. These privileges were said to include: the guarantee that Catholic bishops, clergy, and believers would enjoy complete freedom of direct contact with the Vatican, whereas in the case of the Serbian Church, only the patriarch was guaranteed such access to fellow Orthodox clergy abroad; an extension to Catholic clergy of the same state protection enjoyed by state employees and the protection of the privacy of the confessional; the right to retain buildings and property even in hypothetical cases in which the local congregation should convert en masse to another faith; privileged exemption from the payment of telegraph tax; the assurance that Catholic bishops would enjoy unlimited rights to inspect religious instruction, whereas the Serbian Church could conduct such inspections only once a year, and the Islamic community only twice a year; the guarantee that Catholic school children not be obliged or even invited to attend religious instruction of any non-Catholic denomination and that the school program be arranged so as not to obstruct Catholic students from carrying out their religious obligations; and the exemption of Catholic priests and monks, but not Orthodox clergy, from military conscription, except in case of general mobilization.[9] The Serbian Church also objected to Article 8 of the proposed concordat, because it would have banned *all* clergymen in *all* Churches from participation in political parties, even though the Serbian Orthodox Church had not been consulted in this regard.[10] Finally, the patriarchate claimed that in the broad sense, the guarantee in Article 1, that the Catholic Church might carry out its "mission," could embrace a right of proselytization, "which is contrary to Article 16 of the state constitution and which can disturb the interconfessional balance."[11]

The Serbian Orthodox Church created a huge uproar over the bill. The Serbian Church even allied itself with opposition Serbian parties in efforts to bring down the proconcordat administration. The government offered to guarantee the Serbian Church the same privileges, but the uproar did not die down. On 23 July 1937, despite violent confrontations between Orthodox believers and police, Stojadinović pushed the bill through the Assembly (the lower house in the bicameral legislature), by a vote of 166 to 128. The same night the patriarch died, and rumors spread that the government had had him poisoned. The Orthodox Synod refused the state funeral that would have been customary for a deceased patriarch and punished the Orthodox parliamentary deputies who had supported the concordat by suspending their rights in the Church.[12] These additional pressures broke the government's will to continue, and Stojadinović decided not to present the document to the senate for approval. On 27 October 1937, Stojadinović informed the Catholic episcopate that the concordat was decidedly dead. The concordat was formally withdrawn on 1 February 1938. This constituted a major victory for the Serbian Orthodox Church, which had been fighting the concordat for more than twelve years.[13] Thus, on the eve of World War II, the Serbian Church could congratulate itself on two major victories—in the controversy over the Church law and in the struggle over the concordat.

THE GREAT CATASTROPHE

The systematic destruction of hundreds of monasteries and church buildings, the liquidation of hundreds of Serbian Orthodox clergy, and the wartime deaths of at least six of the Church's top hierarchs[14] (three murdered by the Ustasha) had a traumatic effect on the Serbian clergy, and even today they live with a complex of bitterness rooted in the wartime debilitation. The Serbian Church had shared in the Serbian nationalist enthusiasm to see Croatia as a zone for Serbian political, economic, cultural, and confessional expansion and viewed Catholicism as a degenerate form of the true faith; this orientation made it all the more painful for the Serbian Church to bear the fruit of wartime Croatia's program of eliminating all traces of Serbdom and Orthodoxy from Croatia. The fact that the program of forced exile and liquidation was supplemented by the coercive conversion to Catholicism of part of the Orthodox population in the fascist Independent State of Croatia (Nezavisna Država Hrvatska, or NDH), in order to "Croatize" them, deepened both the identification of Serbdom and Orthodoxy in the consciousness of the Serbian Church and the sense of threat from the Ustasha party of the NDH. Moreover, the Catholic Church by and large seemed to welcome the conversions, even if it sometimes distanced itself from the coercion employed. Mile Budak, NDH *doglavnik* (second-in-command to Ante Pavelić) told an assemblage of representatives of the Catholic Action organization on 8 June 1941: "The Orthodox came to these districts as guests. And they should now leave these parts once and for all. Of course, many will not be able to leave, but in that case they will want to convert to our faith."[15]

In April 1941, there had been 577 Serbian Orthodox clergymen in the territory of the NDH. By the end of 1941, all of them had been removed from the scene: 3 were in prison, 5 had died of natural causes, 217 had been killed by the Ustasha, 334 had been deported to Serbia, and 18 had fled to Serbia earlier.[16] Serbian Clergy were treated in a similar fashion in parts occupied by other powers. In Vojvodina there was pressure on Orthodox believers. In Bulgarian-occupied Macedonia the Bulgarian Orthodox Church asserted its jurisdiction (in the conviction that Macedonians are Bulgarians rather than Serbs, as the Serbian Church has always insisted), expelled or arrested those clergy who considered themselves Serbs, and sent in about 280 of its own clergy to administer the faith in Macedonia.[17] In the Italian-occupied littoral, Orthodox clergy were imprisoned and executed, and numerous church edifices were destroyed.[18]

The losses suffered by the Serbian Church during the war were colossal both in real terms and in psychological terms. Of the more than 4,200 churches and chapels and 200 monasteries owned by the Serbian Church in Europe prior to the war,[19] almost 25 percent had been completely destroyed and 50 percent of those in Yugoslavia were seriously damaged. As much as a fifth of the clergy in Yugoslavia as a whole had been killed (perhaps as many as 700), and another 300 had died of natural causes during the war. Of a total of 8.5 million believers before the war, Slijepčević claims that 1.2 million had lost their lives.[20] The Communist government later claimed that 1.7 million Yugoslavs had lost their lives in the war. At war's end, without any assured income and with an estimated wartime damage of 2.4 billion dinars, the Serbian Church still had 2,100 parish priests, 537 lay employees, and about 1,000 retired priests (on pension).[21] Under these circumstances, the Serbian Church was faced with a difficult challenge. The Church wanted to rebuild its world as it had been before, but the preconditions for that world no longer existed.

THE COMMUNIST ASSAULT AND THE EFFORT TO REBUILD

Understandably, the Serbian clergy had taken an active part in the resistance against the occupation, and some of its clergy, including Patriarch Gavrilo and Bishop Nikolaj Velimirović, had been incarcerated in German concentration camps. But the Serbian Church had naturally viewed the resistance in quite different terms from the Communist Party. For the Church, the resistance was a nationalist cause of the Serbian people against traitorous Croats and imperialist Nazis. For the Communists, on the other hand, the war—which Yugoslav Communists referred to as the national liberation struggle (*narodnooslobodilačka borba*)—was at the same time a social revolution whereby the different peoples of Yugoslavia would subordinate their divisive ethnic interests to joint class interests and through which exploitative "vestiges of the past," such as the Serbian Orthodox Church, would be pushed into an inferior position, in which they could subsequently be snuffed out. Serbian nationalism, which has always been close to the heart of the Serbian Church, was seen by the Communists not merely as an archenemy of the new Yugoslavia but even as an enemy of the Serbian people itself.

The aims of the Communist Party of Yugoslavia (CPY) diverged from those of the patriarchate in a number of ways. The CPY wanted, first of all, to legitimize its federation and most especially its reconquest of Macedonia in every possible way. Hence, if there were Orthodox clergy in Macedonia eager to set up an autonomous or autocephalous Church, so much the better, as this would reinforce the image of a distinctive Macedonian ethnicity.

The patriarchate, which was an expression of union achieved only with some difficulty in 1920, was hostile to any assault on its unity.

Second, the CPY wanted a tame and cooperative Church that would eschew anything smacking of opposition but be available to support CPY policies when such support was desired. To this end, the government revived the priests' associations (which actually traced a tradition back to 1889), hoping, with some cause, to use these associations to control the Church. The patriarchate was prepared to cooperate with the new regime but not to be its tame and obedient tool. Thus, while there were those on each side who desired to reach an accommodation, there was much less agreement as to the form that accommodation should take.

Third, the CPY, then still in its Stalinist phase, wanted to uproot religion and to resocialize the population according to the precepts of atheistic dialectical materialism. That is, it was willing to tolerate Churches as institutions, but not as teachers and leaders of the people. The regime therefore initiated a policy of obstructing religious education, confiscating Church buildings, and fining the clergy on various pretexts. Orthodox clergy were, in the early postwar years, harassed, beaten up, and imprisoned on trumped-up charges. In the hope of compromising the prestige of the Church elders, the regime began a practice—which continued until Slobodan Milošević seized the reins of power in Serbia in late 1987—of accusing various Serbian hierarchs of wartime collaboration with the Nazis, such as Bishops Irinej Djordjević and Nikolaj Velimirović, though in fact both of these bishops had been interned by the Axis and were as antifascist as they were anticommunist.[22] But therein lay another problem, for the Communist regime was strongly opposed to an anticommunist clergy. Velimirović was, moreover, an outspoken Serbian nationalist.

There were, at the same time, two respects in which the Serbian Church could be useful to the Communist regime. First, insofar as the patriarch of the Serbs would be seen to be on decent terms with the regime, this would tend to give the lie to accusations that the regime was anti-Serb; this was especially important in the early period, when the regime was preparing to put Chetnik leader Draža Mihailović on trial. Second, the Serbian Church could be useful as a vehicle for maintaining contacts with other Communist countries in which there were prominent Orthodox Churches, i.e., the Soviet Union, Romania, and Bulgaria.

There was thus an ambivalence in the Communist attitude toward the Serbian Church—an ambivalence not shared by the patriarchate, though it must be emphasized that many lower clergy felt disposed to strive for accommodation with the regime, and at least a part of the membership of the priests' associations seems to have felt this way. Reformist lower clergy met as early as November 1942 to revive the Orthodox priests' association, and at war's end priests' associations were set up with government backing along federated lines, corresponding to the federal units erected by the regime. According to Stella Alexander, these Orthodox priests' associations were, in the beginning, "completely under government control."[23] By mid–1952, *Borba* would claim that some 80 percent of the remaining active clergy (approximately 1,700) were members of priests' associations.[24] It was these associations that were now authorized to publish the newspaper *Vesnik,* which began publication on 1 March 1949. *Vesnik,* supposedly a Church paper, immediately published attacks on the Serbian Church synod and on Bishops Irinej of Dalmatia and Nikolaj of Žiča (both in emigration) and in other ways showed itself to be a pliable tool for the regime. Understandably, the synod repeatedly turned down the association's application for official recognition, and the patriarchate remained formally opposed to the associations, though this opposition was, over time, tempered by some forms of accommodation. Indeed, a number of bishops were elected from the ranks of the association.[25]

In May 1953, the Communist regime passed a new Law on Religious Communities. Prior to issuing this bill, Communist authorities consulted with Orthodox and Muslim clergy, though not with either Catholics or Protestants.[26] Despite this limited consultation, the bill represented Communist interests, not Church interests. Among the more controversial stipulations in the law was one guaranteeing that no child could be forced by her or his parents to attend religious instruction. The years 1945 to 1955 were the most difficult of the entire postwar period for the Serbian Church. During these years, Belgrade gave a strict interpretation to clauses of laws curtailing the activity of Churches, imposing heavy penalties on clergymen for any infractions but light punishment, at the most, on those infringing on the rights of religious believers.[27] In a striking illustration of the mood of this period, Bishop Nektarije of Tuzla was roughed up by a mob after he pointed out that the Law on the Legal Status of Religious Communities (1953) expressly permitted the holding of religious services.[28] Under the Law on Agrarian Reform and Colonization (27 May 1945), the state seized 173,367 hectares of land belonging to the religious organizations (85 percent of their total); 70,000 hectares of what was seized had belonged to the Serbian Orthodox Church. The Serbian Church had had considerable investments in apartments, affording it a tangible rental income, but by 1958 the regime completed the nationalization of apartments, depriving the Serbian Church of 1,180 buildings, worth 8 billion dinars.[29] The Church's two printing presses were also expropriated after the war, without compensation,[30] and various difficulties were encountered in the reopening of religious seminaries and in their maintenance, due to bureaucratic pressure.

Despite all this, the Serbian Church was able to rebuild. Between 1945 and 1970, the Church built 181 churches and restored 841, built 115 chapels and restored 126, and built 8 monasteries and restored 48. Even in the

Zagreb Eparchy, 20 churches were restored and 2 new chapels built.[31] By 1949, a makeshift seminary was operating in the Rakovica monastery near Belgrade, and shortly thereafter the Church was able to reopen its seminary in Prizren. Subsequently, in 1964, Orthodox seminaries were also opened in Sremski Karlovci and at Krka, in the Dalmatian hinterland. Meanwhile, the Theological Faculty in Belgrade had, by 1966, developed a permanent staff of 8 professors and lecturers and had about 120 students.[32] As of 1982, there were 100–110 students in each of the Church's four seminaries, which was close to the capacity of 120, and there were about 70 students studying at the Theological Faculty in Belgrade. While the number of male clergy held almost steady at about 2,000 for the next two and a half decades, the number of Orthodox nuns inched upward from 468 in 1965 to 519 in 1966 to about 700 in 1980.[33]

Although the Serbian Church had had a lively and plentiful press in the interwar period, with numerous Church magazines, newspapers, and journals established in the 1920s and 1930s,[34] its publishing activity had to be rebuilt essentially from scratch after World War II. Initially this activity was limited to a single official organ. *Glasnik*, the Serbian Church's oldest journal, was being published in 2,100 copies in 1955 and, beginning in 1965, in 3,000 copies. The Church established the quarterly educational magazine *Pravoslavni misionar* in 1958, and by 1968 it was being printed in 50,000 copies. The patriarchate brought out its first popular newspaper, *Pravoslavlje*, on 15 April 1967, and as of summer 1987 it was being printed in 23,000 copies (of which 1,500 went to foreign subscribers). A monthly children's magazine, *Svetosavsko zvonce*, was added in 1968 and had a circulation of 15,000 in 1982. The wartime deaths of a number of leading theologians complicated the task of the resumption of theological publication, and *Bogoslovlje*, the scholarly journal of the Theological Faculty, which had ceased publication during the war, did not resume until 1957, although three special collections of articles (*Zbornik radova*) were issued in 1950, 1953, and 1954. A decade later, the Archbishopric of Belgrade-Karlovac created its own theological journal, *Teološki pogledi*. In addition to these theological periodicals, there is also *Pravoslavna misao,* a magazine for Church questions, which, in 1970, had a circulation of 2,000.[35] Book publication resumed slowly, after hesitation, in 1951, but by 1982 the patriarchate was literally boasting of its fine editions, scholarly tomes, ample publications, and so forth.

WHITTLING THE CHURCH DOWN

To understand the Serbian Orthodox Church is to comprehend it as an institution that has repeatedly been whittled down—sometimes unsuccessfully, sometimes successfully. The first twentieth-century challenge to the

Serbian patriarchate in this sense was the establishment of the Croatian Orthodox Church in April 1942. Although no Serbian hierarch would accept office in this artificial Church (so that two Russian emigre clergymen had to be contracted to head the dioceses of Zagreb and Sarajevo), a number of Serbian Orthodox clergy did in fact join and cooperate with that structure, in the vain hope of saving themselves and their parishioners. The attempt of the Bulgarian Orthodox Church to "annex" the faithful in Macedonia, like the shortlived Croatian Orthodox Church, likewise met ultimate defeat.

On the other hand, the Serbian patriarchate lost its jurisdiction over its Czechoslovak dioceses between 1945 and 1948, and in 1951 these became the Czechoslovak Orthodox Church. Some Serbian parishes lying within Romania's borders were similarly transferred to the Romanian Orthodox Church in 1969, though the Diocese of Timisoara is still administered by the Serbian Church. The Serbian Church suffered a formal schism in 1963, when Bishop Dionisije Milivojević of the American-Canadian diocese summoned an assembly to declare that diocese an autonomous Church. Only much later, in 1989, would there be a rapprochement between the Serbian patriarchate and the American diocese.[36] Finally, on 17 July 1967, the Macedonian clergy, in open defiance of the Serbian patriarchate to which it had taken oaths of loyalty, unilaterally declared itself an autocephalous Macedonian Orthodox Church, electing a Smederevo native, Dositej, as archbishop of Ohrid. It is natural, then, that the Serbian patriarchate was anxious whenever the Communist regime gave encouragement to ecclesiastical separatism in Montenegro, as it did in the early postwar years,[37] and in this context, Patriarch German's comment in 1970 that Montenegrins are simply Serbs by another name becomes readily intelligible.[38]

Although the Serbian Church remained apprehensive of a regime-backed Montenegrin schism at least into the early 1970s, it is the Macedonian schism that has caused the Church the most grief. Despite its inability to do anything to change the situation, the Serbian Orthodox Church has refused to recognize the schismatic Macedonian Church.

The collaboration of the Macedonian clergy with the Communists stretches back to the war. At the end of 1943, the partisan high command appointed a Macedonian, Rev. Veljo Mančevski, to take charge of religious affairs in liberated areas. Shortly after the occupation forces were driven out of Belgrade, three Macedonian clergy (Metodije Gogov, Nikola Apostolov, and Kiril Stojanov) presented themselves to the Serbian synod as representatives of the Orthodox Church in Macedonia and members of the Organizing Committee for the Founding of an Independent Church in Macedonia. A premature declaration of autocephaly at this point in time was stymied, but relations between the Serbian patriarchate and the CPY remained tense as long as the patriarchate refused to compromise. The Orthodox priests' association, often inclined to take a stance at odds with the patriarch, supported Macedonian autocephaly all along, despite the misgivings among some Serbian members. Finally, in 1958, after the Macedonian clergy declared themselves an "autonomous" Church on their own initiative, the new Serbian patriarch accepted the fait accompli, though he underlined that it should go no further than autonomy. Directly as a result of the patriarch's acceptance of Macedonian ecclesiastical autonomy, the Serbian Church's relations with the government improved markedly, and by 1961 the regime's encouragement of intraecclesiastical divisions generally seemed to have died down.[39] The interest of the government in the Macedonian Church was shown in its hints of a subvention of 60 million dinars to the Serbian Church if it came to terms with the Macedonian clergy.[40]

The Communist Party was, at this time, seriously divided between advocates of "organic Yugoslavism," led by Slovenian party ideologue Edvard Kardelj, who wanted to knit the country together by making generous allowances to the cultural and national distinctiveness of its component peoples, and advocates of "integral Yugoslavism," led by Vice President Aleksandar Ranković, who wanted to encourage the development of a Yugoslav consciousness in the ethnic sense and who tended to view non-Serbs as "less reliable" than Serbs. The former group thus favored decentralization to the federal units, while the latter favored political and administrative centralism. Ranković, whose Serbian nationalism was never much below the surface, was known for having promoted discriminatory practices against non-Serbs in Croatia, Bosnia, Vojvodina, and Kosovo.[41] The fall of Ranković in July 1966 proved instrumental in fostering a change of regime policy vis-à-vis the Serbian Church, as Ranković had wanted to prevent the erosion of the Serbian position in any sphere, including the ecclesiastical. He dealt with the Church roughly and used threats to obtain ecclesiastical compliance.[42] But as long as he was in office, the Macedonians were unable to obtain full autocephaly.

Ranković was removed from office on 1 July 1966. The Macedonian clergy immediately began preparations for declaring complete autocephaly and were ready in a matter of four months. On 18 November 1966, at a joint meeting of the Serbian and Macedonian synods, the Macedonian clergy demanded full autocephaly. When the Serbian synod demurred, the demand was renewed on 3 December, with the attendant threat of unilateral action if the Belgrade patriarchate did not concur. Since the patriarchate refused to accept this, the Macedonians declared autocephaly on their own authority at an ecclesiastical assembly in Ohrid in summer 1967. Although the Communist government repeatedly encouraged the two Churches, throughout the late 1960s, 1970s and much of the 1980s, to resolve their differences and advised the Serbian patriarchate that its failure to recognize this latest fait accompli had a negative impact on the political climate, more particularly on Serb–Macedonian relations, as well as in the party's dispute with Communist Bulgaria over the ethnicity of Macedonians, the patriarchate unbudgingly insisted (and insists today) that Macedonians are Serbs and that the Macedonian Orthodox Church has no canonical raison d'être, basing the latter position on the fact that the Macedonian Church was not established on the basis of pan-Orthodox agreement, as prescribed by ecclesiastical tradition.[43]

CHURCH-STATE RELATIONS, 1970–1986

It is a remarkable fact that Communist regimes, which always talked about wanting the complete separation of Church and state, were consistently the most eager to assert state control or influence over Church policies and appointments. In Yugoslavia, the Communists hoped that their backing of the priests' associations would lead not merely to the cooptation of those associations but to the cooptation of the Churches themselves, i.e., to the revival of the situation in old Serbia, when the Serbian Orthodox Church functioned in effect as a bureaucratic department of the state.

Instead, however, the Serbian patriarchate's relations with the associations have remained complex, and the continued activity of the latter provided yet another element of internal opposition within the Serbian Church. The Communist regime repeatedly praised the cooperation it received from the Orthodox association[44] and occasionally presented awards to its members,[45] but the patriarchate itself remained cool and distrustful toward the priests' association.[46] Indeed, this distrust occasionally provoked outbursts of frustration from convinced members of the association. In 1978, for example, Archpriest Ratko Jelić, a representative of the Croatian wing of the Orthodox Association, told members of a committee of the Socialist Alliance of Working People of Yugoslavia, which was concerned with religious matters, that the patriarchate (presumably through its organ, *Pravoslavlje*) was presenting a distorted picture of the work of the association and proposed to increase the circulation of the association's organ, *Vesnik*, as a foil to *Pravoslavlje*. He continued:

> We have been publishing our *Vesnik* for the past 30 years. True, the number of copies printed per issue is small, a mere 3,000 copies, but I believe that there is no more positive periodical among all of those published by the Church press in this country, especially among those put out by the Serbian Orthodox Church. But this periodical is, unfortunately, not accessible to the public at large. For this reason, I believe that the situation would be entirely different if we were able to inform the members of our faith as to the true nature of our association. As things now stand, it is directly and falsely suggested to them that we are some kind of communist association which wants to destroy the Church and so on and so forth. Thus, people know nothing at all about the work that is being done by our association.[47]

On the same occasion, Archpriest Milutin Petrović, president of the Central Union of Orthodox Priests of Yugoslavia, complained that some clergy had declined to join the association because they feared reprisals from the hierarchy (although 83 percent of all Orthodox priests in Yugoslavia were, in 1978, members of the association), while Veselin Cukvaš, president of the Montenegrin wing of the Orthodox association, accused the hierarchy of frustrating and ignoring the work of the associations.[48]

But even in 1889 the priests' association was conceived in the spirit of opposition to the hierarchy; over the years, the association has felt free to arrive at conclusions that have diverged from the policies of the patriarchate. Hence, it should come as no surprise that the patriarchate has viewed the Orthodox Association as an internal opposition, even as a Trojan horse.

Another species of internal opposition was highlighted by *Vesnik* in 1971. *Vesnik* charged that there was no practical ecclesiastical unity in policy matters and painted the patriarchate as a kind of bodyless head, "presiding" over a collection of eparchies that operate according to the discretion and wishes of local archpriests. According to *Vesnik*, the episcopal council was failing to reconcile these divergent views and functioned as no more than a sounding board for adamantly held positions.[49]

With only half the clergy it had before the war and a tangibly diminished income, the Serbian Church was conscious of its weakness. Despite this, it never allowed itself to be coopted by the Communist regime—at least not until 1987—and has assumed an oppositional posture from time to time. In this respect, one could speak of two realms: the assertion of Church interests and the demand for policy change, even if Church interests appear to be in opposition to the regime's; and actual opposition by the Church in matters pertaining to the Serbian nation and its culture. That is to say, the Serbian Church was an opposition force insofar as it was (and is) a nationalist institution.

Although the Catholic Church and the Islamic community experienced little difficulty in the early 1980s obtaining official approval for the construction of places of worship, and although the Macedonian Orthodox Church too did well during this time period in the area of church construction, the Serbian Orthodox Church complained of difficulties in obtaining building permits, especially in the cities.[50] Styling itself as a "patient" Church, it nonetheless spoke out in May 1977 in a petition addressed by the Holy Synod to the presidency of the Republic of Serbia and signed by Patriarch German and two other bishops. The letter asked, inter alia, for (1) routinization of permission to build new churches; (2) extension of state social insurance to the teaching staff and students at theological faculties and seminaries; (3) an end to discrimination against children enrolled in Orthodox religious education; (4) an end to state interference in Church matters; (5) an end to the practice of libeling and slandering clergymen,

both living and deceased, in the media; (6) unhindered celebration of funeral rites according to the wishes of the bereaved; and (7) the return of
confiscated Church property.[51]

Since then, the Church has chalked up some gains. In 1984, Serbian authorities granted permission for the Church to resume construction of the
monumental Church of St. Sava (started in the period 1935–1941 but left
unfinished).[52] The following year, the Republic of Croatia returned various
icons, books, manuscripts, and sacred objects from the thirteenth to the
nineteenth centuries to the Church; they had been confiscated at the end
of World War II and kept in state museums for four decades.[53] And in 1986,
permission was granted for reconstruction of the historic monastery of
Gradac in central Serbia.[54] In an even more striking move, the ideological
commission of the Serbian Socialist Youth Federation declared subsequently that young believers could enjoy full equality in the youth organization, even serving in leadership positions, and proposed to support an
initiative to create a postgraduate program in religious studies at the
University of Belgrade.[55]

Patriarch German had a reputation, both at home and abroad, for being
cautious and circumspect in his dealings with the government. That this
reputation was both deserved and open to diverse interpretation was suggested by the sending of an impassioned letter to the patriarch, on 26
February 1982, on the part of Orthodox priests from the Raška-Prizren diocese in Kosovo. Their letter touched on matters concerning Kosovo in particular, such as the harassment of Orthodox clergy and believers by local
Albanians, and issues affecting the Church's life in other parts, such as their
allegation that officials in the Šabac-Valjevo diocese were interrogating and
harassing families that attempted to send their children to Orthodox cate-
chism classes. They pointed out that the Roman Catholic Church was far-
ing tangibly better in this regard and expressed their dismay that
Pravoslavlje had ignored these problems and had limited itself to bland an-
nouncements that Church representatives and state authorities were con-
ferring about matters of "mutual interest." Their letter was not published in
the Orthodox religious press but appeared in print abroad.[56] Perhaps partly
in response to this critical latter, the patriarchate's news organ, *Pravoslavlje*,
published a long critique of the regime's policy in Kosovo in its 15 May edition, appealing for the protection of the Serbian population and Orthodox
shrines in Kosovo.[57]

The Serbian Church's clashes with the Communist regime over the
Macedonian Orthodox Church and over regime policy in Kosovo both
stemmed from the Church's self-appointed guardianship over the Serbian
people—a guardianship that the Communist regime wanted to deny but
both the Church and the state label as nationalist. The Serbian nationalism
of the Serbian Church, expressed in numerous ways over the decades, confronted the Communist regime as a challenge both to its nationality policy

and to its claim to be the *exclusive* representative of the political interests of the population. As a nationalist institution, thus, the Serbian Church was, de facto, in opposition, even if in *loyal* opposition.[58]

REHABILITATION

The seizure of power in Serbia by Slobodan Milošević in mid-December 1987 had a direct impact on the fortunes of the Orthodox Church. True, Milošević's predecessor, Ivan Stambolić, was responsible for setting in motion what was, in his day, a limited rapprochement with the Serbian Church. But Milošević extended and deepened this rapprochement. A very explicit token of this rapprochement was Milošević's meeting with a high-ranking Serbian Orthodox delegation in July 1990.[59] Where the pre-Milošević Serbian press had excoriated the Serbian Church for meddling in nationalism, under Milošević, *Politika* praised the Serbian Orthodox Church for its service to the Serbian people and even declared that Orthodoxy was "the spiritual basis for and the most essential component of the national identity [of Serbs]."[60]

The Orthodox Church has benefited from Milošević's rule in concrete ways. First of all, it has been allowed to undertake a vigorous church construction program, to include the construction of churches in areas from which it had long been barred (e.g., Novi Beograd). Again, in December 1989, permission was granted for *Pravoslavlje* to be sold at public newsstands. Third, in January 1990, Orthodox Christmas was publicly celebrated in downtown Belgrade for the first time in four decades. And again, in June 1990, the Serbian government removed Marxism classes from school curricula and replaced them with religious instruction.[61] In token of the new atmosphere, the Serbian Orthodox Church cooperated with the Milošević government in marking the six hundredth anniversary of the battle of Kosovo on 28 June 1989. In Orthodox services connected with the commemoration, pictures of Milošević could be seen among religious icons.

Not everyone was happy with this state of affairs, and some Serbian non-believers quietly registered concerns that the authorities were becoming too friendly with the hierarchy. Charges of collaboration between Serbian Orthodox Church hierarchy and the Milošević government were more volubly registered by Croatian Catholics, and in November 1990 the Serbian Orthodox Church news organ, *Pravoslavlje*, replied to these accusations by asserting that the Church's contacts with the government's Commission for Relations with Religious Communities were entirely correct and should not be interpreted as active "cooperation," let alone partnership.[62]

As noted in Chapter 7, the disintegration of Serb–Croat relations affected the religious realm as well. Where Orthodoxy is concerned, one may note that the Serbian Church repeatedly polemicized with the Catholic Church after 1989, and only, finally, in May 1991, did the new Orthodox patriarch,

Pavle, respond positively to overtures from Catholic Cardinal Kuharić and agree to a meeting.[63]

As in the case of the Catholic Church in Croatia, the Orthodox Church has played a visible role in the debate about both the federal constitution (still under discussion in spring 1990) and the proposed draft for a new constitution for Serbia. The Church has not been entirely satisfied with either draft document. In the case of the federal draft, the Church indicated that it wanted a constitutional provision to guarantee property and to provide for the return of property confiscated after World War II.[64] In the case of the Serbian draft, *Pravoslavlje* published a tough criticism by Fr. Dragan Terzić in its August 1990 issue expressing concern above all about the proposed retention of a clause barring the "misuse of religious beliefs for political purposes."[65]

CONCLUSION

What I have tried to produce here is not an exhaustive history of the Serbian Orthodox Church in recent times but rather an interpretation of the meaning of that history. To understand the Serbian Orthodox Church today is to understand its mind set, its set of working assumptions about the world, which are the product of the problems, privileges, conflicts, advantages, and setbacks experienced by the Church over the years.

The central experience of this century that colors the entire outlook of the Serbian Orthodox Church even today is the savage assault suffered in World War II. This assault, which was experienced as trauma, has both stiffened the resolve and defiance of the Church and, reinforced by the Communist takeover, deepened its pessimism. The Serbian Church views itself as identical with the Serbian nation since it considers that religion is the foundation of nationality. The hierarchs of the Serbian Church deny that Macedonians are anything but "south Serbs." For the Serbian patriarchate, then, the Macedonian Orthodox Church is, in essence, a reincarnation of the spirit of the Croatian Orthodox Church since, in the view of the patriarchate, the one, like the other, represents an endeavor to reduce the Serbian nation by transforming the religious affiliation of a part of its number. The Serbian Church might well repeat the words of the poet Tanasije Mladenović, who, in a controversial poem, asked,

Serbia, poor and wretched . . .
will you be able,
as in time past,
to renew your strength with a sudden crack?
Or will you,
discouraged and feeble,
disappear among the mountains and nations . . .
torn to pieces by apocalyptic forces?[66]

NOTES

This chapter is a revised and updated version of my earlier chapter, "The Serbian Orthodox Church," originally published in Pedro Ramet, ed., *Eastern Christianity and Politics in the Twentieth Century* (Durham, N.C.: Duke University Press, 1988). The author wishes to thank Duke University Press for granting permission to reproduce the chapter here.

1. 1. Blagota Gardašević, "Organizaciono ustrojstvo i zakonodavstvo pravoslavne crkve izmedju dva svetska rata," in *Srpska Pravoslavna Crkva* 1920–1970: *Spomenica o 50-godišnjici vaspostavljanja Srpske Patrijaršije* (hereafter SPC 1920–1970) (Belgrade: Kosmos, 1971), pp. 37–39.

2. Miodrag B. Petrovích, "A Retreat from Power: The Serbian Orthodox Church and Its Opponents, 1868–1869," *Serbian Studies,* Vol. 1, No. 2 (spring 1981), pp. 4–12.

3. Quoted in Gardašević, "Organizaciono ustrojstvo," p. 41.

4. James L. Sadkovich, "Il regime di Alessandro in Iugoslavia, 1929–1934: Un'interpretazione," *Storia Contemporanea,* Vol. 15, No. 1 (February 1984), p. 11.

5. Ibid., p. 25.

6. Bertold Spuler, *Gegenwartslage der Ostkirchen,* 2nd ed. (Frankfurt: Metopen Verlag, 1968), p. 122.

7. Viktor Pospischil, *Der Patriarch in der Serbisch-Orthodoxen Kirche* (Vienna: Verlag herder, 1966), p. 55; and Sadkovich, "Il regime," p. 25.

8. *Primedbe i prigovori na projekat Konkordata izmedju naše države i vatikana* (Sremski Karlovci: Patrijaršija štamparija, 1936).

9. Ibid., pp. 9, 22, 34, 35, 41, 43, 50, 52–53, 56.

10. Ibid., p. 36.

11. Ibid., p. 33.

12. Joseph Rothschild, *East Central Europe Between the Two World Wars* (Seattle: University of Washington Press, 1974), p. 254.

13. Ivan Lazić, "Pravni i činjenični položaj konfesionalnih zajednica u Jugoslaviji," in *Vjerske zajednice u Jugoslaviji* (Zagreb: NIP "Binoza," 1970), pp. 50–54; and Viktor Novak, *Velika optužba,* Vol. 2 (Sarajevo: Svjetlost, 1960), pp. 131–136.

14. Bosnia's Metropolitan Petar Zimonjić, Banja Luka's Bishop Platon Jovanović, Gornji Karlovac's Bishop Sava Trlajić, Zagreb's Metropolitan Dositej, Bishop Nikolaj of Herzegovina, and Vicar-Bishop Valerijan Pribičević of Sremski Karlovci.

15. *Katolički tjednik* (Sarajevo) (26 June 1941), as quoted in Dušan Lj. Kasić, "Srpska crkva u tzv. Nezavisnoj Državi Hrvatskoj," in *SPC 1920–1970,* p. 184.

16. Ibid., p. 196.

17. Marko Dimitrijević, "Srpska crkva pod bugarskom okupacijom," in *SPC 1920–1970,* p. 213.

18. See Vaso Ivošević, "Srpska crkva pod italijanskom okupacijom," in *SPC 1920–1970,* pp. 217–220.

19. Milisav D. Protić, "Izgradnja crkava u poratnom periodu," in *SPC 1920–1970,* p. 253.

20. Djoko Slijepčević, *Istorija srpske pravoslavne crkve,* Vol. 2, (Munich: Iskra, 1966), p. 687.

21. Risto Grdjić, "Opšta obnova crkvenog života i ustrojstva," in *SPC 1920–1970,* p. 243; and interview, Belgrade, July 1987.

22. Stella Alexander, *Church and State in Yugoslavia Since 1945* (Cambridge: Cambridge University Press, 1979), pp. 164–173.

23. Ibid., p. 189.

24. *Borba* (3 July 1952), cited in ibid.

25. Trevor Beeson, *Discretion and Valour*, rev. ed. (Philadelphia: Fortress Press, 1982), p. 315; and letter to the author from Stella Alexander, 17 October 1983.

26. Robert Lee Wolff, *The Balkans in Our Time* (Cambridge, Mass.: Harvard University Press, 1956), p. 551.

27. Alexander, *Church and State*, p. 224.

28. *Borba* (22 August 1953), cited in ibid., pp. 200–201.

29. Ibid., pp. 213, 219. Also *Politika* (Belgrade) (1 June 1982), trans. into German as "Die Serbisch-Orthodoxe Kirche und ihre Beziehungen zum jugoslawischen Staat," *Osteuropa*, Vol. 33, No. 1 (January 1983), pp. A53–A54.

30. Radomir Rakić, "Izdavačka delatnost crkve od 1945. do 1970. godine," in *SPC 1920–1970*, p. 291n; and interview, Belgrade, July 1982.

31. Protić, "Izgradnja crkava," pp. 254, 271–272.

32. Stevan K. Pavlowitch, "The Orthodox Church in Yugoslavia: Rebuilding the Fabric," *Eastern Churches Review*, Vol. 2, No. 2 (autumn 1968), p. 171.

33. Rastko Vidić, *The Position of the Church in Yugoslavia* (Belgrade: Jugoslavija, 1962), p. 53; Pavlowitch, "The Orthodox Church," p. 170; *Europa Year Book 1972*, Vol. 1, pp. 1435–1436, cited in Burton Paulu, *Radio and Television Broadcasting in Eastern Europe* (Minneapolis: University of Minnesota Press, 1974), p. 463; Beeson, *Discretion and Valour*, p. 291; and interview, Belgrade, July 1982.

34. For details, see Branko A. Cisarz, "Crkvena štampa izmedju dva svetska rata," in *SPC 1920–1970*, pp. 141–155.

35. Rakić, "Izdavačka delatnost," pp. 291–95; and interviews, Belgrade, July 1982 and July 1987.

36. See *NIN* (Belgrade), No. 2031 (3 December 1989), pp. 26–28.

37. Alexander, *Church and State*, p. 169.

38. Fred Singleton, *Twentieth Century Yugoslavia* (New York: Columbia University Press, 1976), p. 229. Regarding recent developments among the Orthodox of Montenegro, see Sabrina Petra Ramet, "The Serbian Church and the Serbian Nation," in Sabrina Petra Ramet and Ljubiša S. Adamovich (eds.), *Beyond Yugoslavia: Politics, Economics, and Culture in a Shattered Community* (Boulder, Colo.: Westview Press, 1995), p. 116.

39. Alexander, *Church and State*, pp. 270–271.

40. Ibid., p. 265.

41. For a fuller discussion of these political currents and of Ranković's role in the 1960s, see Sabrina P. Ramet, *Nationalism and Federalism in Yugoslavia, 1962–1991*, 2d ed. (Bloomington: Indiana University Press, 1992).

42. Interview, Belgrade, July 1987.

43. *Nova Makedonija, Sabota* supplement (10 October 1981), p. 5, trans. in Joint Publications Research Service (JPRS), *East Europe Report* (29 December 1981); and *Borba* (Belgrade) (6–7 May 1989), p. 6.

44. E.g., *Politika* (6 October 1981), p. 6.

45. E.g., Tanjug (19 June 1981), in *Foreign Broadcast Information Service (FBIS), Daily Report* (Eastern Europe), 22 June 1981.

46. Tanjug (25 February 1982), trans. in *FBIS, Daily Report* (Eastern Europe), 26 February 1982.

47. Quoted in *Vjesnik* (Zagreb) (15 July 1978), trans. in JPRS, *East Europe Report* (17 October 1978).

48. Ibid.

49. *Vesnik* (Belgrade) (1–15 January 1971), p. 1.

50. Interview with Patriarch German, *NIN*, No. 1637 (16 May 1982), p. 18; and *Keston News Service,* No. 232 (22 August 1985), p. 10.

51. "Informationsdienst," *Glaube in der 2. Welt* (February 1978), p. 5, as summarized in "News in Brief," *Religion in Communist Lands,* Vol. 6, No. 4 (winter 1978), pp. 272–273.

52. *Ilustrovana politika* (Belgrade) (20 November 1984), pp. 24–25.

53. *Keston News Service,* No. 229 (11 July 1985), pp. 8–9.

54. Ibid., No. 244 (20 February 1986), p. 11.

55. Ibid., No. 251 (29 May 1986), p. 12.

56. Stella Alexander, "The Serbian Orthodox Church Speaks out in Its Own Defence," *Religion in Communist Lands*, Vol. 10, No. 3 (winter 1982), pp. 331–332.

57. *Pravoslavlje* (Belgrade) (15 May 1982), p. 1.

58. I have examined the nationalism of the Serbian Orthodox Church in more detail in "Religion and Nationalism in Yugoslavia," in Pedro Ramet, ed., *Religion and Nationalism in Soviet and East European Politics,* revised and expanded ed. (Durham, N.C.: Duke University Press, 1989).

59. *Pravoslavlje* (1 July 1990), p. 1.

60. *Politika* (2 September 1990), p. 18.

61. *Süddeutsche Zeitung* (Munich) (23–24 June 1990), p. 8.

62. *Pravoslavlje* (1 November 1990), p. 2.

63. *Ibid* (15 May 1991), p. 1.

64. *Yugoslav Life* (April 1990), p. 3.

65. *Pravoslavlje* (1–15 August 1990), p. 1.

66. Quoted in *Los Angeles Times* (18 December 1980), Pt. I-B, p. 5.

CHAPTER NINE

◆

Islam

IN SEPTEMBER 1989 I VISITED Yugoslavia for the sixth time. As always, there was electricity in the air, and as always, the national question, as Yugoslavs fondly call it, had a great deal to do with that electricity. Serbs feared everyone (so it seemed those days), everyone feared Serbs, Macedonians and Montenegrins feared Albanians, and Montenegrins feared each other. Typical of this atmosphere was a conversation in which I found myself at a Belgrade cafe, as two local journalists drew and redrew maps of the Balkans, showing a menacingly large arrow projecting northward from Istanbul through Serbia, while they told me of their fears of a Muslim threat to European civilization. "Albanian Muslims and Bosnian Muslims are in this together," they told me, deadly earnest. "They have big families in order to swamp Serbia and Yugoslavia with Muslims and turn Yugoslavia into a Muslim republic. They want to see a Khomeini in charge here. But Belgrade is not their final goal. They will continue to advance until they have taken Vienna, Berlin, Paris, London—all the great cities of Europe. Unless they are stopped."

Psychiatrist Jovan Rašković told *Intervju* magazine in September 1989 that Muslims were fixated in the anal phase of their psychosocial development and were therefore characterized by general aggressiveness and an obsession with precision and cleanliness. (Croats, by contrast, suffer from a castration complex, according to Rašković.)[1]

Non-Muslims in Yugoslavia recalled Libyan dictator Qaddafi's generosity in providing for the Yugoslav Islamic community's mosque-building program, noted Bosnia's long-term interest in building economic and cultural contact with Syria, Iraq, and other Arab states, pointed to the Muslims' efforts to align Yugoslavia with the Arabs during the October 1973 war in the Middle East, and underlined the ongoing contacts between Islamic clerics and believers in Bosnia and their coreligionists in the Middle East, as, for example, in the case of young Yugoslav Muslims who went to the Middle East for Islamic theological training. For some non-Muslims, these were all signs that the Muslim community was in some sense a foreign implant, that Muslims were ñot fully integrated into Yugoslav society, that they should be feared.

When, after repeated delays, permission was finally granted to Muslims in 1981 to construct a new mosque in Zagreb to replace the one closed down after the war, controversy was inevitable. Like the Serbs, Croats expressed concern that their republic would be Islamicized. Three years later—in June 1984—when much of the construction on the mosque had been all but completed, a fire set by arsonists destroyed much of what had been built up to then. Finally, in September 1987, the mosque was opened, with considerable fanfare.[2]

Needless to say, this fear of the Muslims aggravated intercommunal relations within Bosnia and sharpened the recent debate about Bosnia's place in the federation. Bosnian Muslims repeatedly and unwisely talked of wanting Bosnia declared a "Muslim republic," while Serbs and Croats from time to time hinted that Bosnia might best be divided between Serbia and Croatia. Within Sarajevo, one heard people declare for a united Yugoslavia, on the argument that for inhabitants of Bosnia there was no other realistic option: any attempt at dividing it up—so they argued—would stir up intercommunal violence in this divided republic.

BASIC FACTS AND RESOURCES

Some 44 percent of Bosnia's population registered as "ethnic Muslims" in the 1991 census, as against 31 percent Serbs, 17 percent Croats, and 6 percent ethnic "Yugoslavs" (the latter usually the product of mixed marriages).[3] That made Bosnia the only federal unit in Yugoslavia in which no single nationality group constituted a local majority (see Table 9.1). More broadly, however, ethnic Muslims were always a relatively small minority in socialist Yugoslavia—tallying about 9 percent of the total population in 1981.[4] In religious terms, one could speak nominally of about 3.8 million confessional Muslims in Yugoslavia, accounting for about 16 percent of the total population of the country. Religious Muslims included not only the greater portion of ethnic Muslims but also varying numbers of Albanians, Turks, and Macedonians, as well as some Gypsies, Montenegrins, Croats, Serbs, and even small groups of Pomaks in the region surrounding Pijanac.[5]

The Islamic community in Yugoslavia was organized into four administrative regions: *Sarajevo Region* (Bosnia-Herzegovina, Croatia, and Slovenia, with its Supreme Head Office in Sarajevo); *Priština Region* (Serbia, Kosovo, and Vojvodina, with its Supreme Head Office in Priština); *Skopje Region* (Macedonia, with its Head Office in Skopje); and *Titograd Region* (Montenegro, with its Head Office in Titograd). The Reis-ul-ulema, the head of the entire Yugoslav Islamic community, had his office in Sarajevo.

TABLE 9.1   Proportion of Ethnic Muslims, Serbs, Croats, "Yugoslavs," and Other
Nationalities in Bosnia-Herzegovina, 1948–1991 (percentage)

	1948	1953	1961	1971	1981	1991
Muslims	30.7	31.3	25.7	39.6	39.5	43.8
Serbs	44.3	44.4	42.9	37.2	32.0	31.5
Croats	23.9	23.0	21.7	20.6	18.4	17.3
"Yugoslavs"	n/a	n/a	8.4	1.2	7.9	7.0
Others	1.1	1.3	1.3	1.4	2.2	1.4

SOURCES: Ante Markotic, "Demografski aspekt promjena un nacionalnoj strukturi stanovništva Bosne i Hercegovine," *Sveske,* Nos. 16–17 (1986), p. 292; and Tanjug (30 April 1991), trans. in Foreign Broadcast Information Service, *Daily Report* (Eastern Europe), 1 May 1991, p. 53.

At the dawn of the post-Tito era, the Islamic community disposed of the following institutional resources and facilities:[6]

Sarajevo Region:

- 1,092 mosques
- 569 mesdžids (smaller places of worship)
- 394 places for religious instruction
- 2 medresas (religious schools)
- 5 tekijas according to usage (cemeteries)

Priština Region:

- 445 mosques
- 125 mesdžids
- 35 places for religious instruction
- ? tekijas
- 1 medresa

Skopje Region:

- 372 mosques
- 19 mesdžids
- 10 places for religious instruction
- ? tekijas
- 1 medresa

Titograd Region:

- 76 mosques
- 2 mesdžids
- 36 other buildings

- 4 turbe (mausoleums)
- ? tekijas

In addition, every Muslim town or village had a separate graveyard for Muslims. The figures for mosques would have been much higher in 1990, having passed the 3,000 mark in 1986 and given the energetic building program that the Yugoslav Islamic community was able to maintain.

As of 1980, some 120,000 children were receiving Islamic religious instruction at the primary school level. This instruction was provided free of charge to believers. Secondary religious instruction was available at two medresas: Gazi Husrefbey's medresa in Sarajevo, and Alaudin medresa in Priština. The former is more than 450 years old. In addition, an Islamic Theological Faculty opened in Sarajevo in 1977, and a women's department was created the following year.

The Gazi Husrefbey Library in Sarajevo was an important repository for Islamic materials, and contained several thousand original manuscripts in Arabic, Turkish, and Persian. Courses in Arabic were offered in Sarajevo, Priština, and Belgrade.

Each of the four regions also had a clerical association, known as an Ilmija. These associations were integrated into the work of the Socialist Alliance of Working People of Yugoslavia and in this way acquired a legitimate role in the public arena.

The Islamic community naturally maintained a number of periodical publications. The chief ones were *Preporod,* a fortnightly newspaper published in Serbo-Croatian, in Sarajevo; *Islamska misao,* a monthly journal devoted to theological reflections and news of the community, likewise published in Sarajevo; *El-Hilal,* a Skopje journal, published in Macedonian, Turkish, and Albanian; the bimonthly journal *Glasnik,* the official bulletin of the Supreme Head Office of the Yugoslav Islamic Community, published in 15,000 copies; *Takvim,* an annual publication; *El-Islam,* which concentrated on religious information; *Edukataiislam,* an Albanian-language publication of the Priština office; and *Zemzem,* a newspaper published by the Gazi Husrefbey medresa that was said to have won credibility among young people. All four regional head offices also had extensive book-publishing programs for religious literature.[7]

Many Bosnian Muslims emigrated, some of them prior to World War I. Today there are Muslims who trace their origins to the lands of what was, until 1991, Yugoslavia living in the United States, Canada, Australia, Turkey, and in smaller numbers in several West European countries, including Austria and Germany. In 1977, Yugoslav Muslims in Canada sent a request to the Islamic Community of Yugoslavia to send a delegate to help organize their religious life. A similar request was subsequently submitted also by the Yugoslav Muslim community in Australia.

Yugoslav Muslims have also taken employment at certain times in Libya, Iraq, and Kuwait. This experience must be presumed to have strengthened the affinity of at least some Yugoslav Muslims for the Middle East.

THE SOCIAL PRESENCE OF ISLAM

Despite this formidable institutional base, the Islamic leadership adopted a much lower profile than either the Roman Catholic Church or the Serbian Orthodox Church. While the two Christian Churches were able to celebrate Christmas quite openly for several years, with Christmas Day finally declared a state holiday in Slovenia as of 1989,[8] one could not imagine the Islamic community obtaining the same access to the media in socialist Yugoslavia, let alone seeing its festivals declared state holidays in multi-confessional Bosnia.

A comparison of the leading Muslim newspaper, *Preporod,* with its Croatian Catholic and Serbian Orthodox counterparts—*Glas koncila* and *Pravoslavlje,* respectively—is telling. Whereas *Glas koncila* for years struck a defiant posture, openly polemicizing with the Communist press on a regular basis and publishing highly informative interviews, as well as articles about state atheism, Christian–Marxist dialogue, proposals to change the laws governing religious life in Yugoslavia, and other social issues, with *Pravoslavlje,* for its part, becoming ever more strident (since 1981) in its defense of Serbian interests in Kosovo and its advocacy of Serbian nationalism in general,[9] *Preporod* rarely if ever entered into the social arena, restricting itself by and large to reports on the construction of mosques and the observance of religious holidays, along with information about Islamic teachings.

This same pattern carried over into the behavior of religious leaders. Catholic prelates (such as Zagreb's archbishop Franjo Cardinal Kuharić) delivered sermons defending human rights activists (e.g., Dobroslav Paraga) or demanding an official exoneration of the late Alojzije Cardinal Stepinac, archbishop of Zagreb 1937–1960. Serbian Orthodox prelates were somewhat less bold but were found celebrating Serbian heroes such as Tsar Lazar,[10] Tsar Dušan, and Vuk Karadžić and taking part in commemorations of Serbian national holidays—most pointedly, the six hundredth anniversary (in 1989) of the famous Battle of Kosovo Polje. One could not imagine Islamic leaders being allowed to celebrate the anniversary of the Ottoman conquest of Bosnia (or considering such a celebration wise, for that matter) or feeling sufficiently confident to undertake to speak out on human rights issues—at least not in the years prior to 1990.

On the contrary, the Islamic community often found itself on the defensive. For example, in November 1987 the Republican Conference of the Socialist Alliance of Working People of Serbia discussed the activities of the

Islamic community and concluded that Islamic fundamentalism "had reached Yugoslavia and . . . threatened to spread all over Europe."[11] There were also rumors and charges from time to time, whether in Bosnia, or Macedonia, or Serbia, that Islamic religious education was inspired by nationalist and separatist orientations. (This will be taken up below.)

In fact, the Islamic community adopted a more quiescent and defensive posture—by comparison with the Catholic and Orthodox Churches—from the very beginning and from an early time was able to boast smooth relations with the authorities. In the initial years—roughly 1945 to 1966—religious policy was basically worked out in Belgrade, which meant that religious policy throughout the country was guided, within some limits, by a single vision. The decentralization of the political and administrative system that began in the late 1960s and that was designed to satisfy irresistible pressures on the ethnic level inevitably had consequences for the religious communities. The Catholic Church, with most of its believers living in Slovenia and Croatia, had to worry principally about the orientation of secular authorities in Ljubljana and Zagreb, authorities who, at least in Slovenia, generally showed themselves to be more liberal than their counterparts elsewhere in the country. The Orthodox, living predominantly in Serbia, Macedonia, and Montenegro, had an entirely different set of authorities to deal with. At times, a kind of alliance between Church and party developed at the republic level—as, for example, has occurred in Serbia under Slobodan Milošević. For the Muslims, with their largest concentrations inhabiting Bosnia and the autonomous province of Kosovo, the authorities in Sarajevo and Priština have been their principal reference points for coexistence. This has made for a more complex situation for Muslims for two reasons. First, the authorities in Bosnia tended toward the dogmatic side through much of the 1970s and 1980s. (This is not the case in postcommunist Bosnia, obviously.) This meant that Bosnian Muslims were more likely to be attacked in the press than were, for example, Slovenian Catholics or Macedonia's Orthodox and more likely to find their news organ subjected to pressure. Second, Bosnia and Kosovo were the two regions in Yugoslavia with the most delicate intercommunal relations. And while these relations were usually defined in terms of ethnic groups, there were also religious dimensions—as was patently clear in 1981 and 1982, for example, after Albanian Muslims allegedly desecrated the Orthodox shrines of Kosovar Serbs, setting fire to the monastery at Peć. An "alliance" between the Muslim community and secular authorities in either Sarajevo or Priština—on the model of Milošević's "alliance" with the Serbian patriarchate or even on the model of the friendly relationship that emerged between the Catholic Church and the Communist authorities in Ljubljana—is obviously ruled out, as Bosnia followed the lead of Slovenia and Croatia and adopted a multiparty system. The result has been liberalization and the spirit of compromise and negotiation.

Despite the tradition of dogmatic rule in Bosnia and despite the complexities arising from the republic's ethnic fragmentation, Muslims were able to maintain a vigorous mosque construction program throughout the postwar period. In Bosnia-Herzegovina alone, some 400 new mosques were built between 1945 and 1985, and some 380 mosques were renovated. By 1986, there, as already noted, were some 3,000 mosques in Yugoslavia as a whole.[12]

From time to time, the Communist press would attack the Muslim community for allegedly misusing religious training. For example, in 1973, officials of Tetovo *opština* in Macedonia estimated that some 20 percent of students were receiving religious instruction after regular school hours. The officials claimed, however, that religious instruction was not being used strictly to instruct children in matters of faith and worship. On the contrary, *Nova Makedonija* charged that "in some places, religious education is even used to orient the children in a direction entirely different from our social system, in broadening national intolerance, and in promoting other anti-socialist manifestations." But efforts to reach some understanding with local clergy proved unavailing, according to the Macedonian newspaper. "The measures that we have implemented in this respect have not brought any particular results. We have had discussions on this subject with the Islamic religious community, which has claimed the opposite."[13]

Aside from questions of the authorities, it is clear that in a multiconfessional society (e.g., Bosnia), individual religions may have to be more circumspect than would be the case in a religiously homogeneous society (such as Slovenia).

For that matter, the Islamic community in Yugoslavia was itself internally divided, insofar as the leaders of the Yugoslav Islamic community gave the cold shoulder to the dervishes (or, as they are more formally known, the Community of the Islamic Alia Dervish Monastic Order). The dervish order was introduced in Yugoslavia in 1974 and by 1986 numbered 50,000 followers, organized in seventy monasteries across southern Yugoslavia (fifty-three in Kosovo, ten in Macedonia, and seven in Bosnia).[14] At one point, the Islamic community ordered Sheikh Jemaly Haxhi-Shehu, senior leader of the dervishes, to disband the order. Shehu replied by registering his order as a "self-managing" organization, thus giving himself legal protection—a move paralleled in Croatia, if for different motivations, by the Catholic Christianity Today Publishing House.

WOMEN AND ISLAM

In the course of the 1980s, Muslim women began taking a more independent role in public life. The fact that a large group of Albanian Muslim women organized a large protest, independently, in late 1989 (to protest deteriorating conditions in Kosovo) is a sign of increased self-awareness and self-confidence. Another sign of change came earlier, in 1981, with the graduation of the first woman (Nermina Jasarević) from the Islamic Theological Faculty in Sarajevo.[15]

By 1986, the first female imams had been educated in Skopje and were delivering sermons (the first being in the Kumanovo mosque). In the course of 1986, Albanian men in Kumanovo went to the authorities to protest the appearance of women at the mosque, since, according to Islamic teaching, women and men should not mix at the mosque. It turned out that the sudden appearance of the women was the result of direct pressure from the Islamic Central Board in Skopje, whose elders were intent on upholding the equality of women and who pointed to the tradition that every mosque has a special, separate room for the women. Why had the women not come earlier? Isa Ismaili, leader of the Islamic community in Kumanovo, blamed space problems:

> For two reasons: first, until now we did not have female imams; now we have them and they are capable of delivering their sermons. Secondly, we in Kumanovo have only a single mosque, which is too small to hold even all the males; this is why we did not insist that the women come. . . . Long ago we asked the authorities for permission to build a new mosque, but we unfortunately never got an answer. . . . If our women are forbidden to go to the mosque, we will ask the men not to go either. Why should the men [be allowed to] pray and not the women? This is an attack on equality.[16]

RECENT DEVELOPMENTS

In 1989, a small publishing house in Zagreb brought out a *Bibliography of Croatian Writers of Bosnia-Herzegovina Between the Two Wars*. The publication at once stirred controversy because of its inclusion of a number of Muslim literary figures in the ranks of "Croatian writers." The Islamic community was outraged, and its organ, *Preporod*, published a lengthy commentary in which it excoriated the bibliography for the "Croatization" of some thirty-eight Muslim writers. Among this number were such Islamic-sounding names as Salih-beg Bakamović, Enver Čolaković, Abdulatif Dizdarević, Husein Dubravić Djogo, Mustafa H. Grabčanović, Kasim Gujić, Osman Nuri Hadžić, Muhamed Hadzijahić, Mehmed Handžić, and Ahmed Muradbegović. *Preporod* called this a "negation of the cultural independence of a national tradition."[17]

This controversy was symptomatic of a deeper problem that has serious implications for the Islamic community—namely the tendency of the Croatian and Serbian nations to want to claim the land on which the Muslims live for their own nations and to absorb or suppress Islamic culture. Both Croats and Serbs have claimed large parts of Bosnia in the past, and Serbs have viewed Kosovo as their ancestral heartland, depicting the

Albanian Muslims as intruders. Whereas Serbs sometimes betray a desire to suppress or eject Islamic culture from Kosovo, where Bosnia is concerned, Serbs and Croats have long registered rival claims to "annex" the Muslim community, claiming alternatively that Muslims are "really" Serbs, or Croats.[18]

It is against this background that periodic Muslim pressures to declare Bosnia a "Muslim republic" must be seen. Serb–Muslim tensions in Bosnia were becoming serious already in 1989, and instead of abating, only grew more intense over the succeeding months. Eventually, as will be explained in Chapter 12, Bosnia disintegrated into open warfare in spring 1992, when Serbs launched a genocidal policy they have called "ethnic cleansing." It is impossible to speculate as to what the long-term effects of the civil war will be for the country's Muslims. Be that as it may, it is quite clear all-the-same that there have been some sharp differences in the past in the orientation of Bosnia's Muslims, versus Kosovo's Muslims,[19] toward the question of the preservation of a Yugoslav federation/confederation. Bosnia's Muslims, at any rate, long resisted the idea that there was any reasonable alternative.

The repluralization of Yugoslavia has affected the Islamic community just as it has affected all other areas of public life. From 1946 to 1990, the Reis-ul-ulema (chair of the Islamic Council) was always a political appointee, beholden to the Communist regime. But in March 1991 Jakub Selimoški, a Macedonian Muslim, was elected to that post by a special ninety-six-member electoral body established by the Islamic community itself.[20] The Islamic community simultaneously adopted a new constitution and elected new presiding officers to head its Supreme Assembly.[21] In January 1991, in token of its new independence and new-found courage, the Islamic Supreme Assembly issued a resolution denouncing the Serbian government's policies in Kosovo and demanding the restoration of the natural rights of Kosovo's inhabitants, including a cessation of political interference in the work of the institutions of the Islamic community in Kosovo.[22]

NOTES

This chapter is a revised and updated version of an earlier article, "Islam in Yugoslavia Today," originally published in *Religion in Communist Lands* (now called *Religion, State, and Society*), Vol. 18, No. 3 (autumn 1990). The author wishes to thank the editor of *Religion in Communist Lands* and Keston Institute, the journal's publisher, for granting permission to reproduce the chapter here.

1. *Intervju* (Belgrade), No. 216 (15 September 1989), pp. 15–16.

2. *Nedjeljna Borba* (Zagreb ed.) (5–6 September 1987), p. 4; *Vjesnik* (Zagreb) (7 September 1987), p. 3; and *Danas* (Zagreb), No. 290 (8 September 1987), pp. 23–24.

3. Tanjug (30 April 1991), trans. in *Foreign Broadcast Information Service (FBIS), Daily Report* (Eastern Europe), 1 May 1991, p. 53.

4. *Statistički kalendar Jugoslavije 1982* (Belgrade: Savezni zavod za statistiku, February 1982), p. 37.

5. Ahmed Smajlović, "Muslims in Yugoslavia," *Journal Institute of Muslim Minority Affairs,* Vol. 1, No. 2, and Vol. 2, No. 1 (winter 1979–summer 1980), p. 132; and Rudolf Grulich, Der Islam in Jugoslawien," *Glaube in der 2. Welt,* Vol. 7, No. 4, (1979), p. 6. See also Sabrina P. Ramet, "Primordial Ethnicity or Modern Nationalism: The Case of Yugoslavia's Muslims, Reconsidered," *South Slav Journal,* Vol. 13, No. 1–2 (spring–summer 1990).

6. Smajlović, "Muslims in Yugoslavia," pp. 135–136.

7. Ibid., pp. 141–142.

8. *Keston News Service,* No. 336 (19 October 1989), p. 14.

9. See, for example, *Pravoslavlje* (Belgrade) (15 May 1982), p. 1.

10. Regarding Tsar Lazar, see *NIN* (Belgrade), No. 2020 (17 September 1989), pp. 42–43.

11. *Aktuelnosti kršćanski sadašnjosti (AKSA)* (13 November 1987), summarized in *AKSA Bulletin,* No. 8 (26 January 1988), p. 14. See also *Vjesnik* (12 November 1987), p. 4.

12. *Radio Free Europe Research* (30 June 1986), pp. 21–22.

13. *Nova Makedonija* (Skopje) (19 June 1973), p. 2.

14. *Start* (Zagreb) (19 April 1986), as cited in *Radio Free Europe Research* (30 June 1986), p. 21.

15. *Preporod* (Sarajevo) (15 November 1981), p. 10.

16. Quoted in *Radio Free Europe Research* (30 June 1986), p. 23.

17. *Preporod* (1 September 1989), p. 14.

18. For discussion, see Muhamed Hadzijahić, *Od tradicije do identiteta: Geneza nacionalnog pitanja bosanskih muslimana* (Sarajevo: Svjetlost, 1974); and Ramet, "Primordial Ethnicity or Modern Nationalism."

19. In February 1990, Muslim nationalist leaflets supporting Kosovo's secession and vilifying Serbian leader Slobodan Milošević appeared in Novi Pazar. See *Belgrade Domestic Service* (6 February 1990), trans. in *FBIS, Daily Report* (Eastern Europe), 8 February 1990, pp. 74–75.

20. *Tehran IRNA* (10 March 1991), in *FBIS, Daily Report* (Eastern Europe), 12 March 1991, p. 60.

21. Tanjug (16 January 1991), trans. in *FBIS, Daily Report* (Eastern Europe), 22 January 1991, pp. 38–39.

22. Tanjug (16 January 1991), trans. in *FBIS, Daily Report* (Eastern Europe), 23 January 1991, p. 43.

PART FOUR

◆

Dissolution and Ethnic War

CHAPTER TEN

◆

Serbia and Croatia at War Again

It has been said . . . that the Brankoviches of Erdely count in Tzintzar, lie in Walachian, are silent in Greek, sing hymns in Russian, are cleverest in Turkish, and speak their mother tongue—Serbian—only when they intend to kill.

—Milorad Pavić, *Dictionary of the Khazars* 1988

IT STARTED WITH THE WRITERS. At first, of course, one was struck by the sheer diversity of themes taken up by Serbian writers. But always the themes of World War II, of victim psychology, of suffering, recurred, played now one way, now another. Among the novels published in the 1960s and 1970s, most, if not all, pulled in the direction of reconciliation and of transcendence of nationalist concerns. Borislav Pekić's *The Houses of Belgrade*, for example, first published in 1970, tells the story of Arsenie Negovan, a well-to-do landowner who is consumed by an obsessive, quasi-romantic love of houses and who, after being accidentally trampled during riots on 27 March 1941, locks himself up in one of his houses for twenty-seven years, finally venturing out on the very day when, coincidentally, the student riots of summer 1968 were at their height. In Negovan's view, "*They* [the mob] always demanded the same thing. *They* wanted my houses. *They* had wanted them in March 1941 and *They* wanted them now in June of 1968!"[1] Negovan's obsession with his property even extended to impelling him to worry about his *hat* at a time when he should have been running for dear life. Negovan's solicitous concern for even his *former* houses, which took the shape of an account book in which he maintained an ongoing log of their condition and occupancy,[2] could be read as an allegorical critique of all forms of avarice, *including irredentism*. The warning went unheeded.

And there was also Danilo Kiš, perhaps the greatest Serbian writer of the late twentieth century, whose lyrical novel *Garden, Ashes* (first published in 1975), tells of the mentally unbalanced author of the *Bus, Ship, Rail, and*

Air Travel Guide, who, in preparing the third edition of his guide to schedules and transport connections, decided to expand the volume to embrace "an ingenious pantheistic and pandemoniac theory based on scientific achievements, on the principles of modern civilization and the technology of the modern era, . . . [a] *summa* of a new religion and new *Weltanschauung*"[3]—all this in the *Bus, Ship, Rail, and Air Travel Guide*. Kiš is clearly critical of the messianic pretensions of the quasi-charismatic author of the *Travel Guide* and his victim complex:

> Impotent before God, obsessed with the idea that he was destined to expiate the sins of his whole family, the sins of all of mankind, he blamed all humanity for his curse and held his sisters and other relatives responsible for all his misfortunes. He considered himself a scapegoat. . . . He wanted everyone to understand that he was a Victim, that he was the one who was sacrificing himself, the one who was fated to be sacrificed, and he wanted everyone to appreciate that and approach him as the Victim.[4]

In a collection of short stories first published in 1983, Kiš draws inspiration from the history of the anti-Semitic *Protocols of the Elders of Zion* to warn against pamphlets and manifestoes that stir up hatred and portray one's own group as the victim of conspiracies and schemes.[5] The recurrence of the theme of victim psychology and Kiš's double warning against such psychology may be taken, at a minimum, as an indication that there were traces of a victim complex in the air as early as the late 1970s and early 1980s. But it was, of course, the ill-famed Memorandum of the Serbian Academy of Sciences and Arts in 1986 that gave effulgent expression to such thinking, painting Serbia as the great "victim" of Titoist Yugoslavia and identifying the "enemies" of the Serbs, namely, the Croats, Albanians, Muslims, Slovenes, and Hungarians, in short, nearly all the non-Serbs of socialist Yugoslavia.

There was a shift in the wind after Tito's death in May 1980, and two new themes emerged: the Tito–Stalin rift of 1948 and the imprisonment of many innocent Yugoslavs in Goli Otok and other prisons; and a reassessment of World War II from the standpoint of *national* suffering. One of the first writers to test these new waters was Gojko Djogo, who, in a collection of satirical poems published in 1981, offered what were widely interpreted as scarcely veiled criticisms of the late Tito.[6] The book provoked a storm of controversy and sent the poet off to prison for a year. Ironically, an earlier collection of poetry by Radovan Karadžić, the current leader of the Bosnian Serbs, had been largely ignored until the current conflict brought its author another kind of fame.[7] Meanwhile, Dušan Jovanović's play *The Karamazovs* opened in Ljubljana in 1980 and in Zagreb in 1982, kindling a reconsideration of the Tito–Stalin split of 1948.[8] Both Jovanović's *Karamazovs* and Antonije Isaković's novel *Tren 2* dealt with the theme of the arbitrariness and injustice of the penal system in early post–1945 Yugoslavia, as did Branko Hofman's stirring novel *Noć do jutra* (Night til morning), published in 1981.

More important for our present discussion, however, are those novels and plays that took up the theme of nationalism in the early years after Tito's death.[9] Vuk Drašković, present leader of the Serbian Renaissance Party (at one time the leading opposition party in Milošević's Serbia), wrote *Nož* (Knife, a novel that drove home the theme of Serbian suffering during World War II and challenged the LCY (League of Communists of Yugoslavia) thesis that the Bosnian Muslims were a discrete ethnic group, arguing instead that they were merely Serbs whose forefathers had abandoned Orthodoxy out of opportunism.[10] Vojislav Lumbarda's novel *Anatema* was likewise inspired by Serbian nationalism, as was Milić Stanković's historical pamphlet *Sorabi*, which took up the argument that the Serbs are the oldest people in the Balkans.

Nationalism was also the theme of the highly controversial play *Golubnjača* [Pigeonhole], which opened in Novi Sad in October 1982. Written by thirty-year-old Jovan Radulović, the play was set in the Dalmatian hinterland of the 1960s and showed young Croatian and Serbian children still mired in the prejudices of the internecine struggle of World War II, in which their parents faced each other as foes. The play seemed to indict the LCY for failure to construct a society in which these prejudices could be overcome, yet at the same time complained more particularly that Serbian residents in Croatia were supposedly subjected to constant discrimination even in Tito's time.[11] The play created a sensation.

But more than any other works of fiction, two novels defined the new mood of Serbia in the 1980s, a mood that was increasingly self-absorbed, self-righteous, and self-pitying, indulging in the very kind of portrayal of self as victim against which Kiš had warned. The first of these was the mammoth, epic novel *Vreme smrti* (A time of death), which told the story of Serbia's position in World War I. Written by Dobrica Ćosić, a novelist once expelled from the LCY because of his repeated Serbian nationalist outbursts,[12] the novel shows Serbia betrayed by all her allies and left to withstand, unassisted, the combined attacks of the German, Austro-Hungarian, and Bulgarian armies, as well as, in Ćosić's reinterpretation, the Vatican itself.[13] Where Kiš had once brooded about the danger of conspiratorial thinking, Ćosić has Serbian MP Vukašin Katić tell Prime Minister Pašić, "No political idea in Europe today has as many powerful opponents as our Yugoslav cause."[14] As if the one thing on which all the powers could agree was that Serbia should be thwarted! This leads directly to the thinking captured in the following exchange: " '. . . what does our country mean to you?' 'Our country? Suffering, that's my country. People who suffer, who are tormented by pain.' "[15]

In a haunting passage in the final volume of this four-volume work, Ćosić ruminates,

> Brave men will fight for love, but, driven by hatred, all men will fight. In times of storms and tempests which pull up a nation's roots and destroy a man inside his own skin, hatred is the force which gathers and unites all energies, the force which makes survival possible. Hatred is our strongest defense in the face of great evil. . . . With hatred there's nothing a man dare not do, no limit to his endurance.[16]

This, from the pen of the principal author of the 1986 Memorandum, which did more than any other tract or pamphlet written up to then to mobilize Serbian resentment of non-Serbs and legitimate Serbian hatred of all non-Serbs, whether inside or outside Yugoslavia!

Ćosić's novel started a small blaze that gradually spread and, together with other incendiary developments, contributed to inflaming all of Serbia with a desire for a "rectification" of past "injustice." After this, the publication of Danko Popović's short novel (in 1986) about a simple Serbian peasant, Milutin, who tries, in vain, to grapple with the big questions of a nation's destiny and the impact of a nation's history on the individual, comes almost as an afterthought.[17] What Popović's novel contributed was an overt populist dimension, and the incredible popularity of this novel could have provided a clue to observers that Serbia was ready for a populist takeover.

Slobodan Milošević understood what was occurring: a shift in the wind in the cultural sector had contributed, along with other factors, to a shift in the political mood. By 1986, the Serbian public was ripe for change, for big promises, for political messianism. Milošević exploited the new mood and began championing Serbian "rights." By 1988, organized groups supposedly representing the Serbian public were on the streets, clamoring for their messiah to take charge of Kosovo, of Vojvodina, of Montenegro, as he had in Serbia, and there were rumors that Milošević envisioned himself as a "new Tito."

This shift in culture and in the political mood not only sets the context in which the Yugoslav republics became inflamed with nationalism and gravitated toward war but also provides an explanation for the fierce dialectic of nationalism that has torn even families apart and has set the agenda not only in Serbia but in a reactive way also in Croatia.

SERBIA AT WAR

On 27 March 1941, amid rioting in the streets of Belgrade, Regent Prince Paul was toppled from power and King Peter was declared of age. The coup directly brought about the Nazi invasion of Yugoslavia and the dismemberment of that country. The result was a civil war that set Ustaše,

Chetniks, Ballists, and Partisans against each other and cost Yugoslavia more than 1 million casualties. Almost exactly fifty years later, on 9 March 1991, Belgrade's streets were again the scene of riots. Overtly antigovernment (i.e., anti-Milošević in nature, the riots failed under the onslaught of police violence, which left 2 dead and 100 persons injured.[18] Their failure and the failure to remove Milošević at that time allowed the country to continue to spiral toward fragmentation and war. The result has been an ethnic war that has set Serbs, Croats, and Muslims against each other, resulting in between 150,000 and 350,000 casualties as of November 1994. In essence, 9 March was the last chance to remove Milošević and—*perhaps*—to avoid interethnic war.

Inevitably, the war contributed to a strong popular identification of the regime with Serbian nationalism itself, thus undermining the already weak position of the opposition. Political figures such as Prince Aleksandar (the heir to the Karadjordjević throne, who had returned from exile in London) and novelist Vuk Drašković, the head of the Serbian Renaissance Party—both of whom had appeared to be at least *conceivable* alternatives to Milošević as of 1990 and early 1991—were, at least temporarily, washed to the margins of Serbian politics. For two years, Milošević was absolutely secure in power, and when at last a challenger appeared, he came from the right: Vojislav Šešelj, the founder and head of the Serbian Radical Party (a party having no organic connection with Nikola Pašić's party of the same name), went so far as to set up a "shadow government" in summer 1993.[19] But when Milošević's grip on the parliament appeared to be shaken, the resourceful Serbian president dissolved parliament, called for new elections, and returned with stronger representation for his own Socialist Party of Serbia than before. Finally, in September 1994, Milošević had Šešelj imprisoned for thirty days on charges that he had physically assaulted Radoman Bozović, the speaker of the federal parliament.[20]

The Serb-Croat war, in which Serbian forces took control of at least 30 percent of the territory of the Republic of Croatia, including eastern Slavonia's oil fields, muffled the opposition, indeed made it appear impossible to be both a loyal Serb and an anti-Milošević oppositionist. Milošević, in short, had succeeded in identifying the Serbian national cause with himself. In the days around New Year's, however, the Croatian and Serbian forces signed a truce, and by February 1992 the fighting in Croatia was dramatically receding. The end of the war in Croatia once more emboldened the opposition, and on 9 March 1992, on the anniversary of the 1991 riots, some 30,000 Serbs staged an opposition rally in Belgrade, demanding Milošević's resignation, elections for a constituent assembly, political freedoms (including freedom of the press), and the formation of a transitional government in which Milošević's Socialist Party of Serbia would be permitted to hold no more than 45 percent of the posts (a proportion that accorded with its December 1990 election returns).[21] But the rally failed to generate a more general movement of political upheaval, and Milošević easily rode out the brief storm.

The launching of hostilities against Muslim and Croat communities in Bosnia (to be discussed in Chapter 12) changed perceptions within Serbia, and as of August 1992 Paul Shoup was able to report "a growing reaction in Serbia against the excesses being committed in Bosnia and Herzegovina."[22] Vuk Drašković, leader of the Serbian Renaissance Party, compared Milošević to Iraq's Saddam Hussein,[23] and in a transparent reference declared in May 1992 that "the main enemy of the Serbian people is in Belgrade."[24] Drašković's party joined other opposition parties in boycotting the 31 May elections. About half the members of the prestigious Serbian Academy of Sciences and Arts now declared themselves in favor of Milošević's resignation.[25] The tremors of discontent even reached the general staff, and that same month Milošević forced the resignation of Colonel-General Blagoje Adžić (as JNA commander), Colonel Pavlović (as army chief of staff), Lieutenant-Colonel General Živan Mirčetic (as commandant of the postsecondary military schools of the air force and air defense), Lieutenant-Colonel General Tihomir Grujić (as chief of the Serbian Republic army staff), Colonel-General Milan Ruzinovski (as director of the Center of Military Postsecondary Schools), and other high-ranking generals.[26] The extent of the purge was a sure clue to the depth of opposition to the regime's policies that had appeared in those ranks.

Serbian newspapers and magazines also started to talk openly of the possibility that civil war might break out within Serbia itself. Some imagined that such a war would take the form of a showdown between "Chetniks" and "partisans," thus replaying the struggle of fifty years earlier.[27] Almost all the political parties of Serbia now expressed themselves on the risk of internal war and outlined their ideas as to how to avert that eventuality.[28] Antiwar demonstrations on 14 June, attended by several thousand people, organized by the Citizens' Alliance of Serbia, the Belgrade Circle, Women in Black, trade unions, and the pacifist Center for Anti-War Actions,[29] and led by Serbian Orthodox Patriarch Pavle, suggested that Serbia might indeed have reached the point of crisis.

In early June, Dragoljub Mićunović's Democratic Party issued a "Platform for the Prevention of Civil War," demanding the creation of new political institutions, the establishment of a coalition government that would include representatives of the opposition, and the formation of a number of "crisis headquarters" that would act as troubleshooters to keep interethnic tensions within Serbia (between Serbs and Albanians, Serbs and Sandžak Muslims, and Serbs and Hungarians in Vojvodina) from escalating.[30] By then a number of opposition parties, including the Serbian Renaissance Party, had formed a coalition known as DEPOS. This coalition also outlined a program designed to remake the system, calling for the immediate resignation of Milošević, the formation of a coalition transitional government, the passage of new laws to regulate elections and the media, and new elections.

About that time, Crown Prince Aleksandar once again presented himself as a candidate for a restored throne, arguing that a monarchy could be a stabilizing and moderating element. But any attempt to restore the Karadjordjević dynasty, even if within a constitutional framework, might well alienate both those vestiges of the old Communist left that remain in Serbia and Montenegrins, among whom republican sentiment is strong.

In mid-July, in a move that took Serbia by surprise, Milošević brought in Milan Panić, an emigre Serb who had lived in the United States since 1955 and a self-made millionaire, to serve as prime minister of rump Yugoslavia (the Federal Republic of Yugoslavia, consisting of Serbia and Montenegro, which had been proclaimed on 27 April).[31] Panić promised to bring peace to Bosnia and to set Serbia on the road to capitalism. These were tantalizing promises.

In fact, in the course of 1992, both FRY President Dobrica Ćosić and FRY Prime Minister Panić began to criticize Milošević and to talk openly of removing him from power. Ćosić, for example, told *Politika* in October that "the existence of three republic presidents in the Federal Republic of Yugoslavia is evidence, in my opinion, that our new state is not consistently a federal state. This is some kind of 'three-storey,' 'three-phase,' composite state—bureaucratic, too expensive, inefficient. . . . I hope that the future constitutional reform will abolish at least two republic presidents and grant more rights to the assemblies and greater responsibility to one president."[32] The presidents Ćosić wanted to see removed were Serbian President Milošević and Montenegrin President Momir Bulatović.

Meanwhile, Prime Minister Panić decided to challenge Milošević for the presidency in the December 1992 elections, and foreign observers were fascinated as public opinion polls repeatedly showed Panić ahead of Milošević. However, by making use of a number of techniques, including holding up approval of Panić's candidacy until late in the race, using the media to slander Panić, and invalidating the registration of many voters who might be inclined to support the opposition, Milošević assured himself of a victory on election day.[33] In the wake of the elections, Milošević engineered the removal of Panić from the prime ministership.

Meanwhile, Ćosić was making himself all too visible. In early December he visited the command of the First Army at Topčider and addressed the assembled officers as their "supreme commander."[34] Subsequently, in May 1993, Ćosić met with army officers to discuss solutions to the "malfunctioning" of the state.[35] Milošević sensed danger and moved quickly, removing Ćosić, his supposed political superior, as FRY president on 1 June. The next day, when Vuk Drašković, his wife, Danica, and other opposition figures led a large rally protesting the unconstitutional removal of Ćosić, Milošević had the Draškovićes and several dozen other oppositionists arrested. The Draškovićes were handcuffed and then beaten by police, and Vuk Drašković had to be hospitalized. The charges lodged against the Draškovićes were only dropped after the personal intervention of Danielle Mitterrand (wife of the French president) and after an appeal from the Russian government.[36]

No sooner had Milošević disposed of Ćosić, though, than there were renewed signs of trouble within the military. Accordingly, on 26 August, Milošević executed an extensive purge of the army high command, relieving forty-two high-ranking officers of their positions. Among those sent into retirement was Života Panić (no relation to Milan Panić), the chief of the General Staff.[37]

The continued prosecution of the war in Bosnia, which has dragged on much longer than either Milošević or Karadžić had expected, has had several effects within Serbia. To begin with, the waxing nationalist temper has colored the cultural sector, giving birth to bottles of perfume called "Serb" and shaped like hand grenades,[38] revisions of school textbooks (raising Chetnik leader Draža Mihailović to hero status and dwelling at length on Croatian Archbishop Alojzije Stepinac for the purpose of demonizing him),[39] and passionate expressions of alarm on the part of Serbian Minister of Culture Nada Popović-Perišić about the alleged infiltration of Islamic and Turkish elements into Serbian folk music, producing what she has called "a hideous mixture of hip-hop, techno rhythms, antiquated disco music, Arabic yowling, and Bosnian love songs."[40]

Then there has been the economic impact. In 1993 alone, the FRY treasury spent $1.176 billion on arms, materiel, and other supplies for the Serbian militias in Bosnia and Croatia.[41] This large outlay has resulted in the general impoverishment of the citizenry[42] (a result that was to some extent reinforced by the economic sanctions). The war has also resulted in a proliferation of crime,[43] a veritable explosion of sex-related industries, and a "brain drain" that has deprived Serbia of some of its finest artistic, scientific, and political talent.[44] It has also, thanks in no small part to the unremitting chauvinist line adopted by Belgrade Television, resulted in the deepening of ethnic and religious intolerance and in a general poisoning of the political atmosphere. The violence condoned against non-Serbs has infected Serbia itself, and there has been a dramatic increase in hate crimes within that country.[45] Writing in the pages of the Belgrade newsweekly, *NIN*, Svetlana Djurdjević-Lukić reflected in sorrow:

> We are becoming accustomed to ever more terrible things. Who still remembers the kidnapping of 17 Muslims from Sjeverin, the exodus from Hrtovci, Nikinci, Priboj? . . . the machine gunning of houses, the bombs that have been thrown,

the firing on the Catholic Church in Novi Slankamen, the demolition of the 230-year-old Catholic church in Banovci, the shops of Muslims set on fire in Pljevlja, the mistreatment of schoolchildren of Slovak nationality in Kišac, the shootings at the mosque in Novi Sad and the detention of activists of the Islamic community there during Ramadan, the Hungarian houses set on fire in Irig, the murder of Omar Omerović and Jasmica Klinger in Belgrade . . . —memory is getting too short. By and large there is no information about the attackers.[46]

Research conducted in 1993 by the Social Sciences Institute in Belgrade found that about two-thirds of the citizens of the FRY displayed some form of xenophobia.[47]

Not surprisingly, this widespread xenophobia has undermined support for a democratic system, as a telephone poll taken by *NIN* in August 1993 showed. Indeed, according to that poll, a clear majority of respondents were skeptical of the reliability of a parliamentary system and told *NIN* that they did "not believe that it is possible to coordinate differing views without a strong authoritarian leader."[48]

Even so, the economic strains raised questions in many people's minds as to just how long Milošević, and Serbia for that matter, could survive.[49] By August 1993, the quickening inflation had reached an annual rate of 32 million percent ,[50] and official unemployment was pegged at 750,000, with another 1 million people holding largely nominal jobs in which they drew salaries but did little that was productive in nature (often because the lack of raw materials and machine parts had rendered many enterprises inoperative).[51] Serbia was, by then, home to 461,653 refugees, about two-thirds of them from Bosnia-Herzegovina.[52] Industrial production, exports, and labor productivity all fell, and living standards were reportedly falling at a rate of 4 percent per month.[53] By November, the monetary system was said to be near collapse and the Serbian press had published reports documenting the regime's widespread plundering of citizens' bank accounts.[54]

Meanwhile, with the virtual elimination of Ćosić, Panić, and Crown Prince Aleksandar as credible opponents, and with the demonstration of Drašković's vulnerability in the most obvious way, only Vojislav Šešelj, leader of the Serbian Radical Party (SRP), remained as a potential threat to Milošević. In September 1993, Šešelj broke with Milošević and set up a shadow government in Serbia, with Tomislav Nikolić, deputy chair of the SRP, as nominal chief of the shadow cabinet.[55] The following month, the party's Montenegrin branch set up a shadow cabinet in that republic as well, naming Drago Bakrac, an economist from Nikšić, as its head.[56] For a time, Šešelj was ranked by many as the most popular politician in Serbia, even more popular than Željko Raznjatović, better known as "Arkan." Even at this writing, despite Milošević's "disciplining" of Šešelj, Šešelj is by no means out of the game.

With the economy spinning rapidly out of control, Milošević made a bold move in December 1993, appointing Dragoslav Avramović, a hitherto little-known economist, to put together an austerity program. Avramović halted the inflationary hyperactivity of the Belgrade mint, reformed the currency, pegged the new dinar to the German mark, and overnight slashed inflation to minus 0.6 percent.[57] But the stabilization measures did not hold, and by October 1994 the dinar was slipping against the mark, prices were shooting upward once more, and electricity producers were pressing for government approval of a potentially inflationary increase of electricity prices by 50 percent.[58] The proliferation of boutiques[59] and brothels is no substitute for a healthy, productive economy.

With television controlled by the Milošević regime, the Serbian theater has offered Serbs an alternative point of view. Already in 1991, on the eve of war, Lazar Stojanović produced a revised version of Aristophanes' *The Acharnians* at a theater in Subotica, a city with a large Hungarian population. As Stojanović recalled, "In the play a man tries to draw the attention of the Athens assembly to the war with Sparta, but they will not listen. I changed the names of the cities to Belgrade and Zagreb."[60] Two years later, Belgrade audiences were treated to Aleksandar Popović's play *Dark Is the Night*, which explored a young man's reaction to being called up for military duty. Manojlo agonizes about taking flight (as more than 200,000 of his compatriots have, under similar circumstances, in order to avoid military service) but finally decides to go to the front, where he shoots himself in the leg, however. The play became an overnight success.[61]

A 1994 film, *Tito: For the Second Time Among the Serbs*, touched an even more sensitive subject: the officially orchestrated Titophobia among today's Serbs. The brainchild of Želimir Žilnik, the film is a sort of documentary in which actor Drajoljub Ljubičić, attired as the late Marshal Tito, walked about Belgrade, interacting with whomever he met. Set up, thus, as a kind of Serbian version of *Candid Camera*, the film records that people were all too ready to talk to "Tito" as if he really were Tito:

"I'm a Serb and you are a Croat," said one man, "but I used to admire you." Another said he had been part of an honor guard at Tito's funeral. "Yes, I remember you," responded Tito encouragingly. The man went on: "You were everything for us, you used to warm us like the sun." But another said: "You are guilty, you are a bandit, you hated Serbs."

One man explained to Tito that now "everyone has their own flag, state and coat of arms. For only two hills, 200–300 boys must die." An old man stopped to accuse him of being pro-American and betraying the Soviet Union in 1948.

Slobodan Stupar, deputy director of Radio B-92, which commissioned the film, says that it is a terrible reflection of Serbia today. "It shows that the common people have lost touch with reality. Everything you tell them through the media they absorb like a sponge."[62]

As a result of the 19 December 1993 elections, Milošević's Socialist Party of Serbia was able to strengthen its hold on parliament, capturing 123 of the 250 seats in the Assembly (as compared with the 101 they controlled in the outgoing Assembly). Since those elections, internal challengers have been clearly weakened, and the chief challenge to Milošević's authority among Serbs has come from the leaders of the Serbian forces in Croatia and Bosnia: Milan Martić, elected president of the Serbian Krajina (occupied Croatia) in March 1994, and Radovan Karadžić, leader of the Bosnian Serb forces.

Desperate for an easing of the U.N. sanctions, Milošević began advocating a negotiated solution already at the onset of 1994 and took pains to portray himself to Western audiences as a man of peace, a moderate. In particular, Milošević urged Karadžić to settle for control of 49 percent of Bosnia's territory—a suggestion that Karadžić found unacceptable. It is a complicated game that Milošević has been playing, for it is his advocacy of a Greater Serbia that has been his single greatest source of legitimation, and any attenuation of his support for that goal could alienate the very groups upon whose support he is dependent. One indication of this dilemma is that as his conflict with Karadžić (to be discussed more fully in Chapter 12) developed, Patriarch Pavle came out in strong support of Karadžić, while the army high command, albeit twice purged, once again showed signs of disquietude. By October 1994, rumors of the impending resignation of the current chief of staff, General Momčilo Perišić, were spreading, thus providing clear evidence of the tenuous authority that Milošević has enjoyed with his army officers.[63]

Milošević consolidated his power by mobilizing society, by exploiting the wider nationalist potential of a reawakening of civil society in Serbia. But this reawakening of civil society did not lead, as some theoreticians would have had it, to the emergence of a democratic system. The reason, as Tomaž Mastnak has insightfully noted, is that "[while] civil society is a necessary condition of democracy, it is not necessarily democratic itself. If there is no democracy without civil society, it is still not impossible to imagine civil society without, or [even] acting against, democracy."[64] One of Milošević's first acts at the end of 1987 was to assert his control over Radio-Television Belgrade and over the Politika publishing, house, which publishes *NIN, Politika*, and *Politika ekspres*. The daily newspaper *Borba* and the weekly magazine *Vreme* remained independent. But in December 1994 Milošević succeeded in placing his information minister, Dragutin Brcin, in charge of *Borba*, thus snuffing out this respected paper's independence.[65] Since Milošević came to power, the number of police in Serbia has doubled to 110,000,[66] and by late 1994, according to opposition politician Zoran Djindjić, authorities were tapping the telephones of virtually anyone of any importance.[67] Serbia has become a police state.

AN INDEPENDENT CROATIA

The seven months of intense fighting that "ended," in a manner of speaking, in February 1992 had taken a bitter toll in Croatia. Between 6,000 and 10,000 persons were dead as a result of the fighting, total material damage was estimated at $18.7 billion, 400,000 were homeless, and one-third of the republic was occupied by hostile forces.[68] Gross industrial production had declined 28.5 percent in 1991 and was to decline another 14.6 percent in 1992. Inflation, which had reached 123 percent in 1991, climbed to 665.5 percent the following year. Net income declined both years, at an accelerating rate, while unemployment rose from 16.4 percent in 1991 to 17.2 percent in 1992. Tourism, the mainstay of the Croatian economy, had crashed by 80.7 percent in 1991 and registered only a meager 5.7 percent revival in 1992.[69] Given all of this, the first priority of the Croatian government in 1992 was to put the economy on a sound footing. Moreover, Croatia confronted this challenge just as the war in Bosnia was raging and as refugees from this new front continued to stream into Croatia. By summer 1994 there were more than 600,000 refugees in Croatia, many of them in Zagreb.

In fact, on most measures Croatia made little headway with its economy in 1993. True enough, Croatia did rebuild its foreign currency reserves and make further progress in reviving its tourist trade, but gross industrial production, exports, and net income all declined that year. As of October 1993, the Croatian economy was on the brink of collapse, and Nikica Valentić, Croatian prime minister since March 1993, now introduced a draconian austerity program that slashed state spending, reformed the currency (pegging it to the German mark), and actually succeeded, by May 1994, in achieving a *negative* inflation rate, as prices started to decline modestly.[70] As the new program began to take effect, Croatia registered its first increase in net income since 1990 and reduced unemployment to the lowest level since 1991.[71]

In late June 1994, Croatia received a significant economic boost from the outside in the form of a World Bank loan for $128 million, to be used to reconstruct buildings and repave roads and streets that had been destroyed in earlier fighting.[72] By August, the monthly inflation rate had been cut to less than 1 percent, and hard currency reserves were pegged at $2 billion and growing. On the other hand, although Croatia had been the first of the Yugoslav successor states to pass legislation concerning privatization,[73] the continuance of the war and efforts on the part of old interest groups to maintain their preexisting privileges have, in tandem, contributed to preserving economic-administrative structures virtually intact.[74] Indeed, as of November 1994, Croatia had succeeded in privatizing only about one-fifth of its social capital.[75] But the tourist sector was expected to bring in $1.3 billion in 1994, which would be a tangible increase over 1993.

It should not be forgotten that the Serbian occupation of one-third of Croatian territory has an enormous impact on the overall economy, even leaving aside the war costs and the burden of refugees.[76] Occupied lands in Slavonia and Baranja include rich agricultural soil, for example, with oil fields at Djeletovci, Privlaka (just south of Vinkovci), and Ilaca, which Serbian forces have been quick to exploit.[77]

There have been at least five issues that have divided the Croatian political elites since 1991: first, the balance of power between the president and the parliament; second, Croatian nationalism, reflected in sundry issues; third, the prosecution of the war; fourth, freedom of the press; and fifth, the status of ethnic and regional peripheries (to be examined in the following section). I shall take these up in sequence.

Presidential vs. Parliamentary Power

From the beginning, it was clear that Franjo Tudjman, elected president in spring 1990, tended to interpret his role as that of "good shepherd" rather than "leading citizen." Indeed, research conducted among Croatian voters by Ivan Šiber at the time found a high degree of authoritarianism among voters, including both those who voted for left-wing parties and those who voted right-of-center.[78] It soon became apparent that the Sabor (the parliament) had little say in matters of the war or of diplomacy, and members of the parliament started to complain about what they called the marginalization of the Sabor.[79] This dispute was personified in a clash between President Tudjman and Stipe Mesić, a high-ranking figure in Tudjman's Croatian Democratic Community (CDC) and the president of the Sabor. Mesić became increasingly frustrated with what he saw as guileless authoritarianism on Tudjman's part and finally, in spring 1994, broke with Tudjman and, together with several other disgruntled figures in the CDC, set up a new party, the Croatian Independent Democratic Party.[80] Moreover, among the opposition generally there was a widespread belief that the electoral units and electoral laws drawn up by the CDC were designed with an eye to assuring and maximizing its victory.[81] Indeed, a CSCE delegation visiting Croatia 30 July–4 August 1992 concluded that "the [2 August] 1992 elections in Croatia cannot be held as a model for what free and fair elections should be."[82]

Croatian Nationalism

Croatia's new nationalism, which enjoys the wholehearted support of Tudjman's CDC, has been expressed in sundry ways, from the publication of a Croatian orthography, which had been prepared originally in the early 1970s but the publication of which had been held up for political reasons,[83] to the erection of a monument to Croatian fighters killed by Tito's partisans at Bleiburg in 1945,[84] to the revamping of the Croatian language with idiosyncratic neologisms and restored archaicisms, for the purpose of building up differences from Serbian.[85] The new currency, the kuna, was chosen for nationalist reasons, the name having a resonance with memories of the medieval Croatian state; unfortunately, the kuna was also the currency of fascist Croatia during World War II—a fact that upset Serbs of Croatia. In April 1992, a dispute concerning references to Yugoslavia in school textbooks led to the resignations of the minister of the interior and the minister of education and culture. The following month, the minister of justice and administration, Bosiljko Misetić, resigned to protest the adoption of legislation extending special status to Serbs in those districts where they constituted an absolute majority.

The new nationalism has been controversial from the start. Stipe Mesić, for example, upon joining the CDC, pointedly advocated that policies be based on the spirit of tolerance.[86] Ivo Banac, a Yale professor who has enjoyed a parallel career engaging in polemics in the pages of Croatian newspapers and magazines, has sharply criticized the Tudjman government for having suppressed any veneration of Ljudevit Gaj and Bishop Josip Juraj Strossmayer.[87] The latter, in particular, is the historical embodiment of "Yugoslavism," melding Croatian nationalism with an embracive attitude toward other South Slavs.[88] Its critics notwithstanding, the CDC pushed ahead with policies ill suited to winning, let us say, Serbian trust;[89] for example, soon after taking power the CDC restaffed the police forces, relieving many Serbs who had been police officers all their lives, and replaced enterprise managers of Serbian ethnicity with Croats.[90] The CDC soon found itself accused of anti-Semitism, Serbophobia above and beyond what was justified by the war, and misogyny. Indeed, given the atmosphere that has prevailed in Croatia since 1990, thousands of Croatian citizens with "un-Croat"-sounding names changed their names to more Croatian variants; most of those concerned were Serbs, changing names like Jovanka and Jovan into Ivanka and Ivan.[91]

The Prosecution of the War

Franjo Tudjman took office with a reputation as a nationalist. Already on the eve of his election, *Borba* quoted a spokesperson for Tudjman as pledging that Croatia would expand into Bosnia-Herzegovina and annex parts of that republic.[92] Tudjman has held firm to this position, telling a press conference on 6 September 1993, "The acceptance of Bosnia-Herzegovina as a unity state would endanger the survival of the Croatian people, as well as the strategic interests of the Republic of Croatia. Therefore, the Croatian people will hold onto those regions in Bosnia-Herzegovina in which Croats constitute a majority."[93]

The Croatian government has held that the pre-July 1991 borders of the Republic of Croatia should be treated as inviolate because they were the administrative borders that had been set down for more than fifty years and because the Serbs constituted a small minority (11.6 percent). On the other hand, Zagreb has wanted to treat the pre-April 1992 borders of the Republic of Bosnia-Herzegovina as open to redefinition, whether by negotiation or by force. This inconsistency is responsibile for a significant portion of the bad press that the Republic of Croatia has received in the United States and England in the years since the breakup of Yugoslavia. Internal critics have realized this. Thus, for example, the independent daily *Novi list* wrote in February 1994: "due to Tudjman's politics, we have almost been put in the same basket with the aggressor and gambled away our victim status like a dumb gambler playing roulette."[94]

In fact, for all of their other disagreements (as noted above), the decisive issue that was responsible for the rupture between Mesić and Tudjman was the prosecution of the war in Bosnia. Mesić (among others) lamented the establishment of the Republic of Herceg-Bosna in southwestern Herzegovina in July 1992, which he held responsible for the outbreak of hostilities between Croatian and Muslim forces.[95] Banac, again, assembled materials to document his argument that Zagreb had pursued a mistaken policy in Bosnia, publishing the resulting text in book form in October 1994.[96]

Freedom of the Press

A 1993 report of the Council of Europe found the Tudjman government guilty of having tried to muzzle and control the press and electronic media and of silencing independent journalists, highlighting his government's use of the governmental Agency for Reconstruction and Development (later renamed the Privatization Fund) in taking over media enterprises.[97] Although some shares have been sold to private investors, it is the government-controlled Privatization Fund that retains most of the shares, giving the government effective control of such "privatized" media concerns.[98] The government takeover of *Vjesnik* and *Večernji list,* suppression of *Start,* suppression and recreation (under new management) of *Danas,* and harassment of *Slobodna Dalmacija* were all symptoms of the Zagreb government's desire to control the information system within the republic. From the beginning, the government used its control of the media to enforce conformity in views. In November 1993, the Croatian Association of Press Reporters took advantage of the continued independence of *Novi list* to publish the following text:

> Lately we have witnessed [a] disturbingly large number of texts and programs in the Croatian media that are crude violations of the laws and fundamental norms of the journalist code.
> Certain editorial offices systematically publish writings in which individuals who have different opinions are insulted, labeled, or called to responsibility, and it is not rare that entire peoples are insulted. It all contributes to the atmosphere of persecution, fear, and insecurity, and the frequency with which certain edito-

rial offices publish these text-warrants of arrest gives rise to the suspicion that it is a matter of a calculated editorial policy.[99]

Perhaps more than any other single issue, Tudjman's treatment of the media has contributed to the impression that he is an old-fashioned authoritarian without much tolerance for diversity.[100]

In combination, these four issues have profoundly alienated a large section of the opposition. For all that, Tudjman remains, at this writing, clearly the most popular politician in Croatia, holding on to 40.5 percent of the votes in an November 1994 opinion poll conducted by *Globus* (up slightly from 38.6 percent in March 1992).[101] This puts him comfortably ahead of his closest challenger, Dražen Budiša, chair of the Croatian Social Liberal Party (20.6 percent in October 1994). Aside from Tudjman and Budiša, no one can claim to be the preference of more than 5.6 percent of the electorate (that tally going to the extreme-right politician, Ante Djapić), according to the *Globus* poll. Ivica Račan, chair of the former Communist Party, who had polled 1.5 percent of the vote in an October survey,[102] talks of rebuilding the left, however, and as of July 1994 was said to be working on a comprehensive sociopolitical program for change,[103] but in the November poll, Račan received no votes at all.

Meanwhile, against the backdrop of economic difficulties and political controversies, the war has continued, not only in Bosnia but also in Croatia, truce or no truce. In January 1993, Croatian forces launched an offensive across U.N. lines into Serb-held Krajina. In March 1993, there was an escalation in fighting when the Croatian army launched an offensive in northern Dalmatia.[104] Fighting continued in occupied areas of Croatia until early 1994, amid rumors that the Croatian and Serbian sides might agree on a swap of land, perhaps exchanging parts of Bosnia occupied by Croatian forces for sections of western Slavonia occupied by Serbian forces.[105] In March 1994, the two sides signed another truce. Throughout all of this, Croatian officials declared themselves "prepared to discuss anything with the Serbs from the occupied regions of Croatia 'except the integrity and sovereignty of the Republic of Croatia' "[106]—code for the possibility of political autonomy for Croatian Serbs—while Croatian Serbs, for their part, persistently rejected any form of cohabitation with Croats, including even in the form of a confederated Croatia (a solution that in any case, went beyond anything that the Croats were prepared to discuss).[107]

But on 2 November the so-called Zagreb contact group, consisting of the U.S. and Russian ambassadors in Zagreb, together with representatives of the U.N. and the EC, presented a new peace plan for Croatia. The plan called for the restoration of the so-called Krajina to Croatian sovereignty, but with autonomous status, and the full reintegration of eastern and western Slavonia into Croatia.[108] Russian ambassador Leonid Keresteianets, however, proposed an amendment to this plan, under which eastern Slavonia and Baranja would also be granted status as an autonomous region. The Croatian press immediately termed the entire package "unacceptable."[109] But while Croatian authorities insisted on the restoration of Croatian sovereignty within the pre-July 1991 borders and while Western and Russian diplomats expressed their usual optimism that their plan might prove acceptable to both sides, Belgrade pointedly declared its unwillingness to countenance any discussion of what it now called the AVNOJ borders.[110]

ETHNIC PERIPHERIES

The war has mobilized ethnic peripheries in both Serbia and Croatia, thus deepening the divisiveness of both political landscapes. In Serbia, the most important ethnic peripheries are the Albanians of Kosovo (1,686,661), the Hungarians of the Vojvodina (345,376), and the Muslims of the Sandžak (237,358).[111] In Croatia, the "Istrians," a regionally defined group composed of Italians, offspring of Italian-Croatian mixed marriages, and Croats living in Istria, have been politically vocal since the election of Franjo Tudjman in 1990, and their largest political party, the Istrian Democratic Party (IDP) captured 72 percent of votes cast in local elections in February 1993.[112] In 1991, there were 19,041 Italians recorded as living in Croatia.[113]

In practice, these ethnic peripheries have received drastically different treatment. In Serbia, for example, the Albanians of Kosovo have been removed from all positions of responsibility; even Albanian physicians have been fired and replaced by Serbs. Although 90 percent of the population of Kosovo is ethnic Albanian, the University of Priština was converted to strictly Serbian language in autumn 1990; at the same time, all Albanian-language instruction from elementary through university was terminated. Albanian-language radio service has been eliminated, the Albanian-language newspaper *Rilindja* was shut down, even the elected parliament was suppressed. Where Kosovo gave indication of its Albanian heritage, until 1992, in the many towns, streets, and public squares bearing Albanian names, these were all changed, beginning in the latter part of that year. Meanwhile, authorities distributed firearms to local Serbian residents, while conducting periodic house searches of Albanian residents, to make certain that they had no firearms of their own.[114] Serbian police have arrested intellectuals and other influential persons in the Albanian community, subjecting them to torture, and beginning in summer 1993 have conducted unwarranted searches, beaten Albanians of all ages, and otherwise terrorized Albanian villagers with the aim of driving them from their homes.[115] By 1992, if not before, most of the Albanians of Kosovo had given up on Serbia and were talking in terms of secession and the creation of an independent state not conjoined (at least in the interim) with Albania.[116]

By contrast, none of the other ethnic peripheries have been treated as cruelly, and none of them have deemed it necessary to push for secession. Both the Hungarians of Vojvodina and the Muslims of the Sandžak have repeatedly petitioned Belgrade to grant regional autonomy—in the case of the Hungarians, requesting no more than the restoration of the status they enjoyed, together with local Serbs, prior to 1989. Yet although both groups have tried to emphasize their loyalty, both have been subjected to active policies of discrimination, harassment, and, according to some sources, "ethnic cleansing."[117] Under these pressures, an estimated 69,000 Muslims had fled the Sandžak by summer 1993, while 60,000 ethnic Hungarians and 40,000 Croats had fled Vojvodina by spring 1994.[118] Meanwhile, Serb authorities have begun settling Serb refugees from Bosnia in Vojvodina, thus changing the ethnic composition of the region and provoking protests on the part of the Federation of Hungarians in Vojvodina.[119]

Finally, there is the case of Istria, a hitherto quiescent region that has become politically aware and that has defined its cultural and political needs as distinct from those of the rest of Croatia. The Istrian Democratic Party has demanded autonomy for Istria, as a protection against "the forcible 'Croatization of Istria' and the imposition of a coarse and fanatical Croatism, as they put it—of the 'Herzegovinan type.' "[120] Furio Radin, an IDP deputy in the Croatian Sabor, has argued that such autonomy is vital for the cultural protection of the Italian minority in Istria.[121] But popular demands for the grant of regional autonomy run deeper and are also voiced by many Croats living in Istria.[122] Hostile to anything smacking of "disunity," the Tudjman government has rebuffed such demands and even set into motion adminstrative "reforms" designed to divide Istria among several juridical units.[123]

CONCLUSION

It is not my purpose here to suggest that the political programs of Croatia and Serbia be equated. To begin with, there is nothing comparable, in Croatia, to the kind of *apartheid* to which the Albanians of Kosovo have been subjected. And while there are some striking similarities in the ideologies of Milošević and Tudjman, most particularly when it comes to Bosnia,[124] they have treated both their political rivals and their ethnic peripheries rather differently. I would add that the ostensible stability of Milošević's rule is deceptive. Although repeated predictions that he was about to be removed from power, or would resign, have all proven mistaken, there is some basis for thinking that he may not be able to survive the conclusion of the war. That is unlikely to hold true for Tudjman.

Setting aside these and other differences, what Serbia and Croatia have in common is that they have become mired in an ethnic war that not only inflames their respective nationalisms and deepens ethnic hatreds but also creates diverse complications for the twin tasks of economic recovery and economic privatization. The war has allowed the respective ruling parties to engage in seductive oversimplifications of complex issues, to marginalize the representatives of minority interests (whether ethnic or otherwise), and to harness nationalism as a false principle of legitimation.[125] This last process is, by its very nature, ill equipped to provide a basis for the construction of democracy. To the extent that one may judge Serbia to be more fully in the grips of nationalism, one may conclude, in that event, that while Croatia's path to democracy is strewn with obstacles, Serbia does not seem to be on that path at all.

As Vesna Pusić has wisely pointed out,

> Reducing the legitimacy of the government to elections is not a way to restrict democracy, but a way to abolish democracy. . . . General programs that are valuated at the elections are far less important for the citizens than the practice of government, the way policies are implemented, the opportunity to supervise the executive, the degree of protection offered to them by the state, and the efficiency of the instruments of protection against the state at their disposal . . . [as well as] "the level of security minorities enjoy."[126]

Failing to measure up to this standard, neither Milošević's Serbia nor Tudjman's Croatia can be said to qualify as democracies, but only, as Pusić puts it, *dictatorships with [the superficial trappings of] democratic legitimacy.*

NOTES

1. Borislav Pekić, *The Houses of Belgrade,* trans. from Serbo-Croatian by Bernard Johnson (Evanston, Ill.: Northwestern University Press, 1994), P. 172; emphases as in original.

2. Ibid., p. 111.

3. Danilo Kiš, *Garden, Ashes,* trans. from Serbo-Croatian by William J. Hannaher (Boston: Faber & Faber, 1978), p. 35.

4. Ibid., p. 50.

5. "The Book of Kings and Fools," in Danilo Kiš, *The Encyclopedia of the Dead,* trans. from Serbo-Croatian by Michael Henry Heim (New York: Penguin Books, 1989), pp. 133–174.

6. Gojko Djogo, *Vunena Vremena* (Belgrade: Srpska Književna Zadruga & Beogradski Izdavačko-grafički zavod, reissued 1992).

7. Radovan V. Karadžić, *Pamtivek* (Sarajevo: Svjetlost Izdavačko Preduzeće, 1971).

8. Details in Leonore Scheffler, "Goli otok. Das Jahr 1948 in den jugoslawischen Gegenwartsliteraturen," *Südost Europa*, Vol. 33, No. 6 (June 1984), pp. 355–356.

9. The remainder of this paragraph and the next paragraph are closely paraphrased from Pedro Ramet, "Apocalypse Culture and Social Change in Yugoslavia,"

in Pedro Ramet, ed., *Yugoslavia in the 1980s* (Boulder, Colo.: Westview Press, 1985), p. 13.

10. Vuk Drašković, *Nož,* 3d ed. (Belgrade: Zapis, 1984).

11. Heinz Klunker, "Die Taubenschlucht öffnet sich," *Theater Heute* (September 1983), p. 20; *Kroatische Berichte*, Vol. 8, No. 1 (1983), p. 7; and *Der Spiegel* (Hamburg) (24 January 1983), pp. 109–110. See also Jovan Radulović, *Braća po materi: savremena proza* (Belgrade: Prosveta, 1987).

12. Details in Sabrina Petra Ramet, *Nationalism and Federalism, 1962–1991,* 2d ed. (Bloomington: Indiana University Press, 1992), pp. 25, 179.

13. Dobrica Ćosić, *South to Destiny*, Vol. 4 of *This Land, This Time* [the English title provided for *Vreme smrti*], trans. from the Serbian by Muriel Heppell (New York: Harcourt Brace Jovanovich, 1981), p. 59.

14. Ibid., p. 41.

15. Ibid., p. 81.

16. Ibid., p. 145. Regarding the role of Ćosić's *Vreme smrti* in mobilizing Serbian nationalism, see Heiko Flottau, "Alle Geschichten, giftige Hetze, verblasene Träume," in *Süddeutche Zeitung-Wochenende* supplement (Munich), 2–3 September 1995, p. 37. Another important Serbian novel about war is Miodrag Bulatović, *Der Krieg war besser,* trans. from Serbo-Croat into German by Fred Wagner (Munich-Carl Hanser, 1968).

17. Danko Popović, *Knjiga o Milutinu* (Belgrade, 1986).

18. *Daily Telegraph* (London) (14 March 1991), p. 12.

19. *Süddeutsche Zeitung* (Munich) (4–5 September 1993), p. 7.

20. *Seattle Times* (29 September 1994), p. A12. An eight-month jail term was later added on a second assault charge. For details, see Tanjug (28 October 1994), in *Federal Broadcast Information Service (FBIS), Daily Report* (Eastern Europe), 31 October 1994, p. 58.

21. *Eastern Europe Newsletter*, Vol. 6, No. 6 (16 March 1992), p. 6.

22. Paul Shoup, "Serbia at the Edge of the Abyss," *RFE/RL Research Report*, Vol. 1, No. 36 (11 September 1992), p. 13.

23. *Süddeutsche Zeitung* (20 May 1992), p. 5.

24. Quoted in Tanjug (28 May 1992), trans. in *FBIS, Daily Report* (Eastern Europe), 29 May 1992, p. 57.

25. *Salzburger Nachrichten* (12 June 1992), p. 4.

26. *Borba* (Belgrade) (12 May 1992), p. 13.

27. *Večernje novosti* (Belgrade) (16 June 1992), p. 6.

28. *Vreme* (Belgrade) (15 June 1992), pp. 18–21.

29. Tanjug (14 June 1992), trans. in *FBIS, Daily Report* (Eastern Europe), 15 June 1992, p. 42.

30. Shoup, "Serbia at the Edge of the Abyss," p. 8.

31. Tanjug (28 April 1992), in *FBIS, Daily Report* (Eastern Europe), 29 April 1992, p. 54; *Neue Zürcher Zeitung* (29 April 1992), p. 1; and *International Herald Tribune* (Paris ed.) (15 July 1992), p. 2.

32. Dobrica Ćosić, in interview with Momčilo Pantelić, editor-in-chief of *Politika*, in *Politika* (Belgrade) (16 October 1992), trans. in *FBIS, Daily Report* (Eastern Europe), 5 November 1992, p. 49.

33. Further details in Douglas E. Schoen, "How Milošević Stole the Elections," in *New York Times Magazine* (14 February 1993). See also *Neue Zürcher Zeitung* (19 December 1992), p. 5; and Milan Panić, *So!* (Belgrade: Plato, 1992).

34. RTB Television Network (Belgrade), 8 December 1992, trans. in *FBIS, Daily Report* (Eastern Europe), 9 December 1992, p. 40.

35. *Vjesnik* (Zagreb) (2 June 1993), p. 9; and *Glas Istre* (Pula) (2 June 1993), p. 16.

36. *International Herald Tribune* (Tokyo ed.) (3 June 1993), pp. 1, 4; *Vjesnik* (4 June 1993), p. 9; *Glas Istre* (6 June 1993), p. 5; *The Times* (London) (7 June 1993), p. 12; *Frankfurter Allgemeine* (8 July 1993), p. 2; and *Süddeutsche Zeitung* (16 July 1993), p. 7. For more extensive discussion, see "Belgrade Demonstrations: Excessive Use of Force and Beatings in Detention," *Helsinki Watch*, Vol. 5, No. 13 (August 1993).

37. Tanjug (26 August 1993), trans. in *FBIS, Daily Report* (Eastern Europe), 27 August 1993, p. 41; and *Süddeutsche Zeitung* (1 September 1993), p. 7.

38. See photo and caption in *Japan Times* (18 April 1994), p. 6.

39. The new Serbian school textbooks also pay virtually no attention to the 1903 constitution and the decade of multiparty democracy that followed it. See *The Woodrow Wilson Center, East European Studies*, Meeting report (November–December 1994), p. 9.

40. Quoted in *The Economist* (London) (9 July 1994), p. 88.

41. *Japan Times* (6 March 1994), p. 10.

42. According to a September 1993 Tanjug report, some 90 percent of inhabitants of the FRY were near or below the poverty line. See Tanjug (3 September 1993), in *FBIS, Daily Report* (Eastern Europe), 3 September 1993, p. 25. See also *Ekonomska politika* (Belgrade), No. 2171 (15 November 1993), pp. 6–9.

43. Regarding crime in Serbia, see *Borba* (24 February 1993), p. 7; *Politika* (11 March 1993), p. 1, and (8 August 1993), p. 7; and *Vreme* (23 August 1993), pp. 33–34.

44. Regarding the "brain drain," see *Borba* (22 March 1993), p. 7.

45. See *Dnevnik* (Ljubljana) (5 February 1993), p. 9, trans. in *FBIS, Daily Report* (Eastern Europe), 2 March 1993, pp. 68–69.

46. *NIN* (Belgrade) (12 February 1993), trans. in *FBIS, Daily Report* (Eastern Europe), 4 March 1993, p. 70.

47. Ibid.

48. *NIN* (20 August 1993), p. 15, trans. in *FBIS, Daily Report* (Eastern Europe), 15 September 1993, p. 50.

49. For an excellent treatment of this question, see M. R. Palairet, "How Long Can the Milošević Regime Withstand Sanctions?" *RFE/RL Research Report* (27 August 1993).

50. Radio Belgrade Network (Belgrade), 30 August 1993, trans. in *FBIS, Daily Report* (Eastern Europe), 31 August 1993, p. 68.

51. Jelica Minić, "The Black Economy in Serbia: Transition from Socialism?" *RFE/RL Research Report* (27 August 1993), p. 26.

52. Tanjug (8 March 1993), in *FBIS, Daily Report* (Eastern Europe), 9 March 1993, p. 58.

53. David Dyker and Vesna Bojičić, "The Impact of Sanctions on the Serbian Economy" in *RFE/RL Research Report* (21 May 1993), pp. 51–52.

54. Regarding the monetary system, see Tanjug (9 November 1993), in *FBIS, Daily Report* (Eastern Europe), 10 November 1993, p. 57. Regarding the state's plundering of its citizens, see *Vreme* (9 August 1993), pp. 28–29, trans. in *FBIS, Daily Report* (Eastern Europe), 31 August 1993, pp. 69–71.

55. *Süddeutsche Zeitung* (4–5 September 1993), p. 7.

56. Tanjug (27 October 1993), trans. in *FBIS, Daily Report* (Eastern Europe), 27 October 1993, p. 30.

57. *Japan Times* (6 March 1994), p. 10.

58. *Eastern Europe Newsletter*, Vol. 8, No. 20 (5 October 1994), p. 8.

59. *Ekonomska politika* (Belgrade) (22 February 1993), p. 13.

60. Quoted in *The Economist* (London) (18 December 1993), p. 80.

61. Ibid.

62. *The Economist* (30 April 1994), pp. 96–97.

63. *New York Times* (25 October 1994), p. A7.

64. Tomaž Mastnak, "From the New Social Movements to Political Parties," in James Simmie and Jože Dekleva, eds., *Yugoslavia in Turmoil: After Self-Management* (London and New York: Pinter, 1991), p. 50.

65. *Welt am Sonntag* (25 December 1994), p. 2.

66. *Financial Times* (7 October 1994), p. 3.

67. *Borba* (28 October 1994), p. 1, trans. in *FBIS, Daily Report* (Eastern Europe), 31 October 1994, p. 59.

68. Casualty figures in *New York Times* (28 February 1992), p. A3. Figure for material damage in *Borba* (23 March 1992), p. 11.

69. *Neue Zürcher Zeitung* (13 July 1994), p. 11.

70. *The European* (London) (1–7 July 1994), p. 20.

71. Unemployment was pegged at 16.5 percent in April 1994, by comparison with 16.4 percent in December 1991. *Neue Zürcher Zeitung* (13 July 1994), p. 11.

72. *Slobodna Dalmacija* (Split) (24 June 1994), p. 11; *Večernji list* (Zagreb) (24 June 1994), p. 3; and *Neue Zürcher Zeitung* (30 June 1994), p. 12.

73. Ivo Bičanić, "Privatization in Croatia," *East European Politics and Societies*, Vol. 7, No. 3 (fall 1993), p. 425.

74. *RFE/RL News Briefs* (11 August 1994), p. 16. See also *Neue Zürcher Zeitung* (20 July 1994), pp. 7–8.

75. *Globus* (Zagreb) (11 November 1994), p. 6. See also *Nedjeljna Dalmacija* (Split) (25 November 1994), p. 23.

76. Regarding refugees in Croatia, see *Danas* (Zagreb) (28 April 1992), pp. 7–10.

77. For details, see *Slobodna Dalmacija* (30 September 1992), p. 7, trans. in *FBIS, Daily Report* (Eastern Europe), 7 October 1992, p. 24.

78. Ivan Šiber, "The Impact of Nationalism, Values, and Ideological Orientations on Multi-Party Elections in Croatia," in Jim Seroka and Vukašin Pavlović, eds., *The Tragedy of Yugoslavia: The Failure of Democratic Transformation* (Armonk, N.Y.: M.E. Sharpe, 1992), p. 167.

79. *Vreme* (25 April 1994), p. 12.

80. *Süddeutsche Zeitung* (25–26 June 1994), p. 8.

81. *Vjesnik* (15 June 1992), p. 10.

82. *Parliamentary and Presidential Elections in an Independent Croatia, August 2, 1992* (Washington, D.C.: CSCE, August 1992), p. 30.

83. *Slobodna Dalmacija* (23 June 1994), p. 8.

84. Ibid., p. 32.

85. *Neue Zürcher Zeitung* (28 May 1994), p. 7.

86. *Novi Vjesnik* (Zagreb) (19 June 1992), p. 5A.

87. Ivo Banac, "Hoće li se Predsjednik Franjo Tudjman uskoro ispricati zbog kune?" *Globus* (Zagreb) (27 May 1994), p. 8.

88. For an elaboration of this aspect of Bishop Strossmayer's career, see Pedro Ramet, "From Strossmayer to Stepinac: Croatian National Ideology and Catholicism," *Canadian Review of Studies in Nationalism,* Vol. 12, No. 1 (spring 1985).

89. This is not to say that Tudjman could have won over the majority of Croatian Serbs even if he had tried, only to suggest that it would have been wise for him to have made a far more serious effort than he did. Certainly, the repeated aspersions cast on Tudjman in the Serbian press would have made it difficult for him, under *any* circumstances, to win the trust of the Serbs. See, for example, "Tudjman— odbrana NDH," *Intervju* (Belgrade), No. 217 (29 September 1989), pp. 49–51.

90. *Human Rights and Democratization in Croatia* (Washington, D.C.: CSCE, September 1993), p. 11.

91. *Borba* (20 January 1993), p. 12.

92. *New York Times* (22 April 1990), p. 11.

93. Quoted in *Vjesnik* (7 September 1993), p. 1.

94. *Novi list* (Rijeka) (13 February 1994), p. 2, trans. in *FBIS, Daily Report* (Eastern Europe), 25 February 1994, p. 51.

95. *Süddeutsche Zeitung* (25–26 June 1994), p. 8.

96. Ivo Banac, *Cijena Bosne,* as discussed in *Ljiljan* (Sarajevo/Ljubljana) (26 October 1994), p. 8.

97. As reported in *Danas* (Zagreb), new series (5 March 1993), trans. in *FBIS, Daily Report* (Eastern Europe), 16 March 1993, p. 52.

98. Vesna Kesić, "The Press in War, the War in the Press: The Press in Croatia," *Uncaptive Minds,* Vol. 6, No. 2 (summer 1993), p. 78. Regarding the government's use of "privatization" to effect *nationalization,* see *Feral Tribune* (Split) (24 October 1994), pp. 6–7, trans. in *FBIS, Daily Report* (Eastern Europe), 16 November 1994, pp. 42–44.

99. *Novi list* (3 November 1993), p. 4, trans. in *FBIS, Daily Report* (Eastern Europe), 8 November 1993, pp. 37–38.

100. For further discussion of the media in Croatia, see Jasmina Kuzmanović, "Media: The Extension of Politics by Other Means," in Sabrina Petra Ramet and Ljubša S. Adamovich, eds., *Beyond Yugoslavia: Politics, Economics, and Culture in a Shattered Community* (Boulder, Colo.: Westview Press, 1995); and Sabrina Petra Ramet, *Social Currents in Eastern Europe: The Sources and Consequences of the Great Transformation,* 2d ed. (Durham, N.C.: Duke University Press, 1995), pp. 427–428.

101. *Globus* (20 March 1992), p. 8, and (25 November 1994), pp. 16, 49.

102. Ibid., (28 October 1994), p. 4.

103. *Feral Tribune* (25 July 1994), p. 9.

104. Radio Belgrade Network (3 March 1993), trans. in *FBIS, Daily Report* (Eastern Europe), 4 March 1993, p. 43; and Tanjug (24 March 1993), trans. in *FBIS, Daily Report* (Eastern Europe), 24 March 1993, p. 47.

105. This is the version repudiated in Radio Belgrade Network (29 October 1993), trans. in *FBIS, Daily Report* (Eastern Europe), 1 November 1993, p. 39.

106. *Vjesnik* (11 October 1993), p. 1.

107. AFP (Paris) (7 September 1993), trans. in *FBIS, Daily Report* (Eastern Europe), 7 September 1993, p. 44; and *Večernje novosti* (Belgrade) (30 January 1994), p. 2, trans. in *FBIS, Daily Report* (Eastern Europe), 2 February 1994, pp. 23–25.

108. *Neue Zürcher Zeitung* (4 November 1994), p. 1.

109. *Nedjeljna Dalmacija* (4 November 1994), p. 3; also *Globus* (11 November 1994), p. 9.

110. See *Die Welt* (Bonn) (5 November 1994), p. 4. But on 2 December Croatian authorities and Croatian Serbs reached an agreement on economic cooperation. See *Süddeutsche Zeitung* (3–4 December 1994), p. 8; also *Evropske novosti* (Belgrade/Frankfurt) (19 November 1994), p. 3.

111. Figures from the 1991 census, as given in "The National Composition of Yugoslavia's Population, 1991," *Yugoslav Survey* (Belgrade), Vol. 33, No. 1, (1992), No. 1, p. 11. In 1991, unlike in previous censuses, separate nationality figures for Kosovo and Vojvodina were not given. It should be kept in mind, therefore, that while most of the Albanians and Hungarians in Serbia live, respectively, in Kosovo and Vojvodina, there may be some living elsewhere in the republic.

112. "Croatia," in *The Europa World Year Book 1994*, Vol. 1 (London: Europa, 1994), p. 886.

113. "National Composition," p. 7.

114. Further details, together with documentation, in Ramet, *Social Currents in Eastern Europe*, 2nd ed., pp. 422–425. See also Elez Biberaj, "Kosova: The Balkan Powder Keg," in *Conflict Studies*, No. 258 (London: Research Institute for the Study of Conflict and Terrorism, February 1993). As of 1990, the Skopje-based *Flaka e Vellazerimit* was the only Albanian-language newspaper being published in Yugoslavia. Later, however, Belgrade allowed the establishment of a new paper in Albanian, *Bujku*, published in Priština.

115. Details and elaboration in *Open Wounds: Human Rights Abuses in Kosovo* (New York: Human Rights Watch, 1993). See also Jens Reuter, "Die politische Entwicklung in Kosovo 1992/93," *Südost Europa*, Vol. 43, Nos. 1–2 (January–February 1994), esp. p. 21.

116. *Rilindja* (Zofingen) (4 March 1993), p. 3, trans. in *FBIS, Daily Report* (Eastern Europe), 18 March 1993, p. 45; *ATA* (Tirana) (23 March 1993), in *FBIS, Daily Report* (Eastern Europe), 24 March 1993, p. 59; and *Süddeutsche Zeitung* (11–12 June 1994), p. 9.

117. For details and documentation of discrimination and harassment in the Vojvodina, see Ramet, *Social Currents in Eastern Europe*, 2d ed., pp. 425–426. For details of discrimination and harassment in the Sandžak, see Commission of Security and Cooperation in Europe, *Sandžak and the CSCE* (Washington, D.C.: CSCE, April 1993); and *Borba* (2 August 1993), p. 13. Regarding charges of "ethnic cleansing" in

the Vojvodina, see *NRC Handelsblad* (Rotterdam) (1 March 1993), p. 5, trans. in *FBIS, Daily Report* (Eastern Europe), 9 March 1993, p. 73. Regarding charges of "ethnic cleansing" in the Sandžak, see *Oslobodjenje* (Sarajevo–Ljubljana) (11–18 February 1994), p. 24, trans. in *FBIS, Daily Report* (Eastern Europe), 16 February 1994, pp. 54–55.

118. "Abuses Continue in the Former Yugoslavia: Serbia, Montenegro, and Bosnia-Hercegovina," *Human Rights Watch Helsinki*, Vol. 5, No. 11 (July 1993), p. 13; CSCE, *Sandžak and the CSCE*, pp. 1, 6; "Human Rights Abuses of Non-Serbs in Kosovo, Sandžak and Vojvodina," *Human Rights Watch Helsinki*, Vol. 6, No. 6 (May 1994), p. 7; and *MTI* (Budapest) (9 September 1993), in *FBIS, Daily Report* (Eastern Europe), 10 September 1993, p. 12.

119. Duna TV (Budapest), 8 November 1994, trans. in *FBIS, Daily Report* (Eastern Europe), 9 November 1994, p. 46.

120. *Vreme* (9 August 1993), p. 30, trans. in *FBIS, Daily Report* (Eastern Europe), 31 August 1993, p. 54.

121. *Glas Istre* (2 June 1993), p. 3.

122. Ibid., p. 4; *Vjesnik* (26 July 1993), p. 4; and *Danas*, new series (6 August 1993), pp. 12–14.

123. Details in *Borba* (26 January 1993), p. 16, trans. in *FBIS, Daily Report* (Eastern Europe), 19 February 1993, pp. 42–43.

124. Discussed and documented in Sabrina Petra Ramet, "Delegitimation and Relegitimation in Yugoslavia and After," in George Andreopoulos, ed., *Security Issues in Eastern Europe* (Westport, Conn.: Greenwood Press, forthcoming).

125. Further elaboration of this point, see ibid.

126. Vesna Pusić, "Dictatorships with Democratic Legitimacy: Democracy Versus Nation," *East European Politics and Societies*, Vol. 8, No. 3 (fall 1994), pp. 397–398. See also Dijana Pleština, "Democracy and Nationalism in Croatia: The First Three Years," in Ramet and Adamovich, *Beyond Yugoslavia*.

CHAPTER ELEVEN

◆

On Their Own: Slovenia and Macedonia Since 1991

Fluellen: *I think it is in Macedon where Alexander is porn. I tell you, captain, if you look in the maps of the 'orld, I warrant you sall find, in the comparisons between Macedon and Monmouth, that the situations, look you, is both alike. There is a river in Macedon; and there is also moreover a river at Monmouth: it is called Wye at Monmouth; but it is out of my prains what is the name of the other river; but 'tis all one, 'tis alike as my fingers is to my fingers, and there is salmons in both.*

—Shakespeare
King Henry the Fifth

It regrettably happened that the Yugoslavs, in their joy at turning out the Turks and becoming masters of Macedonia, pulled down the beautiful mosque that had stood for three centuries in this commanding position, and replaced it by an Officers' Club which is one of the most hideous buildings in the whole of Europe. It is built of turnip-coloured cement and looks like a cross between a fish-kettle and a mausoleum, say the tomb of a very large cod. As my husband received the shock of this building's outline he nearly fell out on the cobbles . . .

—Rebecca West
Black Lamb and Grey Falcon, 1941

DURING A BRIEF VISIT TO LJUBLJANA in September 1989, as I was sitting in a cafe with a group of sociologists from the Institute for Social Research, one of them suddenly turned to me and asked, "Why is it that when fascist states decay, they produce democracy, but when socialist states decay, they produce chaos?" Before I could utter even a syllable in reply, he lunged into an answer of his own: "Fascist states build up the economy first, and decay as a side-effect of economic prosperity. But socialist states only decay under the pressure of economic collapse."

He was right, of course, but only partly. The other half of the story is that fascist states build up a strong center on principles of linear subordination, minimizing challenges to the structures of authority even as system transformation gets underway. Socialist states, including Yugoslavia, on the other hand, frequently divided both authority and administrative responsibility, created complex and overlapping jurisdictions, and founded what, in the Yugoslav case, was a divided and increasingly weak center, on the famed principle of dual subordination—an organizational principle that, as the socialist system disintegrated, provided one of a number of openings for administrative rivalry and organizational challenges. It is telling that two of the stronger parties in Slovenia today—the Liberal-Democratic Party and the Socialist Party (later merged into the Associated List of Social Democrats)—emerged out of the carcasses of official Communist-sponsored "transmission belts" (specifically, the Youth Organization and the Socialist Alliance of Working People) in combination with the former Communists.

The challenges faced by Slovenia and Macedonia have been remarkably similar up to a point, but there have also been some situational differences related in part to Slovenia's better economic position and to Macedonia's diplomatic difficulties vis-à-vis Greece. In broad terms, one may say that the chief challenges the two new states have faced since June 1991 have been: reprivatizing and reviving the economy; demonopolizing the political system and refashioning it along pluralist lines; reorienting trade flows; developing beneficial relations with foreign powers, especially among neighboring states; and staying out of the Yugoslav war. This list is useful up to a point: it at least sets out clearly the basic processes unfolding in the two Yugoslav successor states that have—at least since July 1991—allowed these states to stay out of the fighting between Serbs and non-Serbs in Croatia and Bosnia. But it also glosses over the considerable differences in the challenges facing these two states at each of these levels. Certainly, Macedonia comes out behind in any comparison with Slovenia, at any level. An example may illustrate this: the entire Macedonian Foreign Ministry—so I was told—had only one photocopying machine and only one fax machine even in 1993; needless to say, the Slovenes have not suffered from any comparable lack of equipment.

But there are at least two other factors that further complicate the picture for the Macedonians, which are not subsumed under any of the challenges listed above. The first is that between 21 and 40 percent of the population of Macedonia consists of ethnic Albanians living in compact areas adjoining Albania;[1] their devotion to the new Macedonian state may be open to question. The second complication for Macedonia is that of its four immediate neighbors—Serbia, Bulgaria, Greece, and Albania—only one, Albania, allows that the Macedonian people are entitled to call themselves

Macedonians. Most Bulgarians, including both political leaders and academics, view the Macedonians as "west Bulgarians" who speak a Bulgarian dialect. The Greek government, on the other hand, has long made a policy of describing Macedonians, at least those living within its borders, but by implication also those living in the Republic of Macedonia, as Slavophone Greeks; precisely which Slavic language these "Slavophone Greeks" speak is a matter of indifference to the Greek government, just so long as they don't speak it in public. The Serbian (FR Yugoslav) government has generally kept quiet about the question of Macedonian nationality, except to express its unqualified "understanding" for the Greek position; but virtually the entire Serbian Orthodox Church hierarchy and priesthood, along with many Serbs associated with the most prominent parties (those of Milošević, Šešelj, and Drašković) hold onto the interwar (1918–1941) designation, which held that the Macedonians should be viewed as "south Serbs." Needless to say, the Macedonian government has read irredentist yearnings into these rival "interpretations."

SLOVENIA'S TROUBLED PATH TO PROSPERITY

It was only in 1989 that the question of Slovenia's relation to the Yugoslav federation was first posed, with the drafting of controversial amendments that gave Slovenian authorities more control over the disposition of armed forces within their own republic. But through much of 1990, Slovenian politicians clung to the hope of preserving some connection with the other Yugoslav republics, joining Croatia in putting forward a draft treaty of confederation in October of that year.[2] In July, Slovenian Prime Minister Peterle told an Austrian weekly magazine that confederation, rather than independence, was Slovenia's first choice.[3] And as late as November, Dimitrij Rupel, then Slovenian foreign minister, confirmed that position.[4] But Slovenes were, even then, increasingly convinced, as Slovenian President Milan Kučan put it that same month, "that the interests, and even the survival of the Slovenian people, have been jeopardized in the insupportable relations in Yugoslavia."[5] An opinion poll taken that month found that 64.3 percent of Slovenes wanted Slovenia to declare its independence,[6] and beginning in early autumn, formal institutional connections between Slovenia and the Yugoslav federation were severed, one by one.[7] The act of "disassociation" was submitted to the Slovenian parliament already on 20 February 1991, making it all the more preposterous that so many high-ranking U.S. and West European politicians expressed surprise when the Slovenes in fact seceded four months later. Secession might have been carried out sooner except that, as of early 1991, only part of the military in Slovenia was under Slovenian command, and Ljubljana authorities needed time to try to change this.[8] Ironically, as the deadline for secession neared, some Slovenes got cold feet, as an opinion poll conducted by the daily newspaper *Delo* 27–28 March 1991 showed. The *Delo* poll found that only 45.3 percent of respondents were prepared for independence, with another 31.2 percent feeling that such a move was hasty and that Slovenia was not yet prepared for independence.[9]

As Slovenia approached independence day, strange ideas started to seem plausible to some portions of the Slovenian population. For example, there was the Republican Party of Slovenia, whose founding was announced in July 1990 and which pledged itself to work for annexation to the United States as the fifty-first state.[10] Then there were the various rumors of new political unions, one of the more imaginative suggesting the creation of a new federation which would include not merely Slovenia and Croatia but also Furlania, the northern part of Italy.[11] A variant of this xenophilia held that Slovenia's best option was annexation to Austria, and in March 1991, the Serbian daily newspaper *Politika* claimed that 13 percent of Slovenes in fact preferred this outcome.[12] With independence, there were new rumors, such as one in August—after the cease-fire between the Yugoslav Army and the Slovenian territorial defense forces—which held that the chief of staff of the Yugoslav Army had held a secret meeting on 5 August in which it agreed to delay its withdrawal from Slovenia, to infiltrate Slovenian territorial defense forces, to blow up the Krško nuclear plant, and to conduct aerial strikes against Maribor and Ljubljana.[13] These rumors were important as indicators of the extreme uncertainty that Slovenes felt at the time.

But independence also brought new problems. In the short run, the loss of the Yugoslav market hurt the Slovenian economy and contributed to putting additional people out of work.[14] And there were new problems in foreign relations, as the Slovenes suddenly discovered that they had a border dispute with Croatia.[15] Moreover, the reluctance of the West Europeans to extend diplomatic recognition to these new republics had economic as well as political consequences, and it was indicative that among the first states to recognize Slovenian statehood were Lithuania, Georgia, and Latvia—themselves newly established states.[16] And finally, there were problems of adjustment, as three successive privatization plans were drawn up and then scuttled for lack of consensus. The last two issues (foreign policy and privatization) became the clubs with which Slovenian Prime Minister Peterle was beaten by his critics, and by February 1992, after the dissolution of the Demos coalition, which had brought Christian Democrat Peterle to power, Slovenia was in the grips of a full-blown governmental crisis.[17]

Foreign Relations

As a result of a combination of internal economic pressures, the repercussions of the federal breakup, and ostracism by the West, Slovenia began its

independence with an economic nosedive, and by October 1991 its indus-
trial production stood at 17 percent less than the previous October.[18]
Already in August, bank representatives from Slovenia issued a plea to West
European banking institutions and politicians to resume normal banking
and financing; this call was aimed most especially at Italy, Austria,
Switzerland, France, and the United States.[19] But in spite of strong support
from Germany, Austria, and Italy, other EC states, most especially Britain,
France, and Spain, insisted on a policy of diplomatic and economic isolation of Slovenia and Croatia as long as possible.[20] The Russians stepped in
to fill the breach, and on 12 December, even before the EC had finally
agreed to recognize Slovenia, Moscow and Ljubljana signed their first trade
agreement, under which the Russians promised to deliver 700,000 tons of
oil and 450,000 tons of oil derivatives and coal to Slovenia in exchange for
medicines, footwear, bakery equipment, and other machine equipment.[21]
Most of the West European states extended recognition between December
1991 and January 1992; in fact, among major West European states,
Serbophile France was the last to do so, waiting until 23 April, more than
two weeks after the belated U.S. recognition of Slovenia.[22]

With diplomatic recognition, economic contacts quickly rebounded.
Economic ties between Slovenia and northern Italy revived,[23] Austrian
banks once again invested in Slovenia,[24] and economic relations were soon
established with the Benelux countries, Iran, and China,[25] alongside
Slovenia's traditional trading partners. Slovenian exports increased 8 percent in the period 1991–1992, finding their largest markets in Germany
($1.19 billion), Croatia ($891 million), Italy ($732 million), and Austria
($281).[26] Slovenia also signed defense accords with Austria (in November
1992) and with Hungary (in January 1993).[27]

Slovenia's relations with Croatia and Italy have remained complicated,
however. The Slovene–Croat dispute over fishing rights was supposedly resolved by an agreement in April 1992,[28] but difficulties in this sphere continued.[29] Moreover, by 1993 Slovenes and Croats were quarreling over ownership of the Krško nuclear plant, of which Slovenia demanded full
ownership, although Croatia had been joint owner of the plant.[30] There
have even been allegations in the Croatian press that certain Slovenian
politicians (specifically Zoran Thaler, Dimitrij Rupel, and Zmago Jelinčić)
have demanded the transfer of certain parts of Istria to Slovenia.[31] As for
Italy, an unresolved dispute over property rights in the Istrian peninsula
sabotaged bilateral talks in October 1994, resulting in an Italian threat to
veto Slovenia's application to join the European Union.[32]

Meanwhile, Slovenia gradually entered a series of international organizations, including the World Bank in February 1993[33] and the Council of
Europe, and in October 1994 became a signatory to the General Agreement
on Tariffs and Trade (GATT).[34] Slovenia also signed trade agreements with

the European Free Trade Association (EFTA) in May 1992 and with the European Community in April 1993.[35]

Domestic Affairs

Four issues dominated political discussions in Slovenia in the months following secession: the constitutional and legal restructuring of the system; the continued state control of Radio-Television Slovenia (and the advantage which the new officeholders suddenly saw in this arrangement); privatization and how to go about it; and the role of Catholic values in the political system. I have described some of these elsewhere[36] and will restrict myself here to a brief discussion of the fourth issue aforementioned before taking up an assessment of the challenges faced by the Slovenian government in the economic and political sectors more broadly.

In a word, the Catholic Church, which claims the allegiance of the vast majority of religiously oriented Slovenes, decided to take advantage of the collapse of communism to push for the delegalization of abortion and for the introduction of (Catholic) religious instruction as a mandatory subject in elementary and middle schools. The Slovenian parliament's refusal to strike from the constitution a clause guaranteeing a woman's right to an abortion no doubt lay behind the episcopal conference's statement, in November 1992, calling for the dissolution of the parliament, "since it has preserved certain characteristics from the nondemocratic times."[37] In fall 1992, the Catholic Church campaigned actively for Christian Democratic candidates and tried to mobilize its members to vote "Christian." In this the Church failed, however, and the Liberal Democratic Party, a secular-progressive grouping, maintained the predominance it had gained in early 1992; and in August 1994 the Liberal Democrats dealt the Church its second setback, ruling against any introduction of religious instruction into the schools.[38]

In the economic sector, 1993 showed the first signs of real economy recovery. In the years 1987–1992, the Slovenian GDP had declined some 23 percent (6.5 percent between 1991 and 1992 alone).[39] Personal consumption declined 24 percent between 1990 and 1992, while gross fixed investment declined 34 percent in the same period.[40] But production staged a robust 4.7 percent rebound in 1993, and by December of that year unemployment was starting to contract, shrinking from a high of 15.5 percent to 15.1 percent.[41] Inflation was also slowed in 1993.

Yet the dissolution of Yugoslavia has inflicted some hardship on the Slovenian economy permanently. Quite apart from the shift of trade that has accompanied the Yugoslav breakup, Slovenia suffered from the nationalization in February 1992 of branches of Slovenian enterprises operating in Serbia,[42] not to mention the unexpected confiscation by the Yugoslav Army (at the time of its evacuation from Slovenia in October 1991) of all radar and air traffic communications equipment.[43] Then there is the impact of the war. Already in April 1992, Slovenia had given refuge to some 5,000 displaced persons from Croatia, as well as another 11,000 refugees from Bosnia-Herzegovina; the situation was, even then, described as "becoming increasingly serious for our republic."[44] But by June this figure had risen to somewhere between 50,000 and 60,000,[45] resulting in Slovenia's closing its doors to any further refugees. But however complicating these developments have been, Slovenia's economic prognosis remains good, thanks both to its solid industrial and agricultural infrastructure and to its strong and growing reputation for high quality manufactures.[46]

In the political sphere, however, challenges have been more subtle. It is one thing to adopt a good constitution and to arrange successfully for the passage of literally hundreds of laws to convert the system from socialism to pluralism; it is another thing to safeguard that pluralism and to make sure that it operates according to its nominal principles. Some people fear that the system has been slow to complete its transformation. For example, in August 1993, writers Drago Jančar and Rudi Šeligo were among fourteen signatories to a protest article which alleged that Communist vestiges still dominated Slovenia through cliques and informal groupings said to have been responsible for "a whole series of scandals and deviations."[47] Then there is the case of Rudi Rizman, an internationally renowned professor of sociology at the University of Ljubljana, who has become the victim of a witch hunt. Rizman, an outspoken critic of Janez Janša (the head of the Social Democratic Party, who was dismissed as defense minister in March 1994[48]), warned in newspaper articles that Janša did not respect constitutional principles and was trying to make a bid for (dictatorial) power. Then on 26 March 1994 the state television quoted extensively from two private letters that Rizman had sent to friends in Germany and the United States, in which Rizman had criticized Janša.[49] Rizman and his family started to receive death threats and to become victims of other forms of intimidation. Then in November 1994 Janša used his personal connections to arrange for the public prosecutor to serve Rizman with a summons to appear before the Division of Security Matters in the Ministry of Defense in order to respond to charges that he had betrayed an "official secret." Quite apart from the fact that Rizman's characterization of Janša as megalomanic was a matter of private opinion based on open materials and expressed in *private* correspondence, by terming it an official secret the public prosecutor seemed to be admitting the truth of Rizman's description of Janša.[50]

Add to these disquieting signs the continued instability in political parties, as parties continue to split and recombine with other parties,[51] the unresolved question of media freedom, and the marginalization of women's rights (to be taken up in Chapter 12), not to mention the likelihood of continued pressure by the Catholic Church in its efforts to desecularize the political sector, and there are grounds enough for concern about the eventual outcome of Slovenia's efforts at democratization.

MACEDONIA—RELUCTANTLY INDEPENDENT

The Macedonians were not prepared for independence when Slovenia and Croatia seceded, and for a while Macedonian President Gligorov continued to think in terms of Macedonia remaining in federal union with Serbia and Montenegro.[52] But as the reality of Yugoslavia's death sank in, Macedonian authorities brought the inevitable question before the public and asked them to vote in a referendum on independence held 9 September. Three-quarters of those voting declared for Macedonian independence. Nine days later, the Macedonian Assembly issued a declaration of independence, but in a new constitution drafted shortly thereafter and adopted on 29 November the Assembly pointedly left open the possibility that Macedonia might join another state.[53]

As Belgrade sent its military juggernaut first against Slovenia, then against Croatia, the Macedonians gave in to deep apprehensions, and Macedonian authorities expressed concern on numerous occasions that the war might spread to their republic. But in January 1992 Macedonia completed its withdrawal from the federation with the removal of all its of its representatives and officials from federal organs and bodies.[54] And in the course of the following two months, the Yugoslav National Army completed its withdrawal from its bases in Macedonia, though not without removing most of the military technical equipment and the main radar system at Petrovec airport, and even attempting to dismantle and remove the telephone equipment in the 4 July barracks in Stip—both in contravention of a prior agreement with Macedonian authorities.[55]

Alone at last, Macedonia remained diplomatically isolated until 15 January 1992, when Bulgaria became the first state to accord full recognition to the Republic of Macedonia. Slovenia and Croatia followed in February. But while Macedonia struggled to overcome what amounted to a diplomatic quarantine, its small Serbian minority started to register complaints that sounded all too reminiscent of complaints voiced by Serbs in Croatia and Bosnia before hostilities broke out in those republics. Understandably, Macedonian authorities did not take these complaints lightly.

Foreign Relations

By summer 1992, Macedonia had succeeded in establishing diplomatic ties with only seven countries: Bulgaria, Croatia, Slovenia, Turkey, Bosnia-Herzegovina, Lithuania, and the Philippines. Russia had recognized Macedonian independence in mid-May but had indicated that it would wait until the EC had granted diplomatic recognition before exchanging ambassadors. But the United States and the members of the European Community delayed recognition pending resolution of a dispute that flared up between Greece and Macedonia immediately after Macedonia had declared its independence. In a word, the Greek government declared that Macedonia had no right to its name, flag, or coat of arms, demanded that the Macedonians explicitly forswear any interest in reunion with those parts of southern Macedonia that Greece had annexed in 1913, and soon suggested to the Macedonians that they call their state the Republic of Skopje. The Greeks even started referring to the Macedonians as Skopjans, even though within Macedonia that designation seemed appropriate only to residents of the city of Skopje, and even then not in an ethnic or national sense. The EC met on 16 December 1991 and laid down three conditions for recognition to Macedonia: the passage of constitutional amendments guaranteeing respect for existing borders; an explicit declaration that Macedonia harbored no territorial pretensions against its neighbors; and a promise not to interfere in Greece's internal affairs.[56] Obediently, the Macedonian Assembly met on 6 January 1992 and in unceremonious haste adopted amendments affecting articles 3 and 49 of the constitution, explicitly declaring Macedonians' commitment to respect existing borders and to abstain from interference in the internal affairs of their neighbors. The Macedonians also declared that they had no aspirations to territorial expansion. These unusual provisions (not normally considered necessary to be given explicit formulation, least of all by a militarily weak and economically endangered country) were passed amid sarcastic comments from the legislators themselves.[57]

But the Greeks were not satisfied. They claimed that the name "Macedonia" was the historical property of the Greek people and insisted that their northern neighbor omit any derivative or variant of this word in the republic's eventual designation. They also claimed to fear an armed attack by Macedonia, although the figures in Table 11.1 cast considerable doubt on the plausibility of any such scenario. Two factors underlay the Greek response. The first was the calculated fear of the Greek government that the authorities in Skopje, who had long championed the rights of the culturally repressed Slavophone Macedonian minority in Greece, a group described by the Athens government as "Slavophone Greeks" and denied education in their own language,[58] would continue to act as guardians of Greece's 20,000–50,000 Macedonians.[59] If its independence should be recognized and consolidated, an independent Macedonia could become a magnet for Greece's Macedonians, thus stimulating protests and internal disorder. The second factor was the strong nationalist response that took ahold of the Greek public. The Greeks assumed what has never been proven, namely, that no two peoples can ever have any cultural artifacts, history, symbols, historical figures, or images in common. If the Greek as-

TABLE 11.1   Military Strength of Macedonia and Greece (1993)

	Macedonia	Greece
Army troops	11,000–12,000	113,000
Reservists	120,000	34,000
Tanks	4	1,842
Aircraft	0	855
Heavy artillery pieces	0	2,151
Missiles	0	AGM-12 Bullpup, AGM-65 Maverick, AIM-7 Sparrow, AIM-9 Sidewinder, R-550 Magic systems
Navy	0	19,500
Helicopters	0	173

SOURCES: Macedonian figures from Duncan M. Perry, "Crisis in the Making? Macedonia and Its Neighbours," *Südost Europa*, Vol. 43, Nos. 1–2 (January–February 1994), pp. 40, 45. Greek figures from International Institute for Strategic Studies, *The Military Balance 1993–1994* (London: Brassey's, October 1993), pp. 40–50.

sumption is correct, then it is time for France and Germany to go to war over the question as to whether Charlemagne was French or German.

To the Macedonians' surprise, the EC honored Greek reservations for more than two years, and it was only in December 1993 that the West European states finally accorded recognition to Macedonia, followed in short order by Japan and by an exchange of ambassadors with Russia. Macedonia was even admitted to the U.N., albeit under the inelegant name, "the Former Yugoslav Republic of Macedonia."

By 1992, the Greeks had blockaded shipments to Macedonia passing through Salonika, stimulating shortages of food, oil, and medicine in that landlocked republic. The Greeks lifted the embargo in the course of 1993, as bilateral talks between Greece and Macedonia began to show some promise. But in October 1993 Andreas Papandreou returned to the prime ministership and these bilateral talks were abruptly terminated. Then, a week after the United States declared its intention to extend full diplomatic recognition to the Republic of Macedonia,[60] Papandreou declared the reimposition of a trade embargo against Macedonia, indeed of a tougher embargo than the Macedonians had seen in 1992–1993.[61] Meanwhile, Senator Paul Sarbanes of Maryland, Representative Michael Bilirakis of Florida, and several other prominent Greek-Americans with links to the Democratic Party started to turn up the heat at the White House. Exactly a month after the State Department announcement, Clinton, Vice President Al Gore, and National Security Adviser Anthony Lake met between closed doors with Sarbanes, Greek Orthodox Archbishop Iakovos, Greek-American lobbyist

TABLE 11.2   Population of Macedonia, by Nationality (1991, 1994)

	1991		1994	
Macedonians	1,314,283	64.62%	1,288,333	66.93%
Albanians	427,313	21.01%	434,033	22.55%
Turks	97,416	4.79%	74,267	3.88%
Gypsies (Roma)	55,575	2.73%	43,732	2.27%
Serbs	44,159	2.17%	39,624	2.04%
Others	95,218	4.68%	45,229	2.33%
Total	2,033,964	100%	1,925,011	100%

SOURCES: Figures from the 1991 census as reported in *Broj i struktura na nesele-nieto vo Republika Makedonija po opštini i nacionalna pripadnost* (Skopje: Repub-lički zavod za statistiku, 1991), p. 6. Percentages for the 1991 distribution as reported in *Vreme* (Belgrade) (9 May 1994), p. 16. Figures and percentages from the 1994 census as reported in *Nova Makedonija* (Skopje) (13 November 1994), p. 3, trans. in *FBIS, Daily Report* (Eastern Europe), 15 November 1994, p. 52.

Andrew Manatos, and thirteen other prominent Greek-Americans. After the meeting (at which no one from the State Department was present), Clinton announced the abrogation of the earlier statement recognizing Macedonia.[62]

Greece's European partners tried to pressure the Greeks to lift the embargo and even threatened the Greeks with legal action unless the embargo was lifted. When the Greeks ignored a 13 April 1994 deadline to fall into line, the European Union took the case to the European Court of Justice. But on 30 June the Court ruled that since the Greek action did not harm the interests of any members of the European Union, the Greeks could not be ordered to lift the embargo.[63]

But if the Macedonians could scarcely feel reassured by these developments, they could nonetheless take solace not only in the firm economic support they were getting from Bulgaria and Turkey but also from the stationing of a U.N. protective force along Macedonia's border with Serbia in July 1993. Given certain troop movements on the Serbian side of the border in 1993 and the repeated Serbian armed provocations along the Macedonian border during 1994, including several armed incursions across the border,[64] the stationing of this force, which consisted of some 1,300 U.N. troops as of October 1994,[65] seemed to offer some reassurance. Moreover, in November the United States signed an agreement with Macedonia under which Macedonian officers could attend U.S. military academies.[66]

By August 1994, mediation by Germany and France in the Greek–Macedonian dispute was starting to show results, Greek Foreign Minister Papoulias was showing flexibility, and diplomats were expressing optimism that the dispute between Greece and Macedonia might finally be settled by early 1995.[67]

Domestic Affairs: Nationalities

In March 1991, on the eve of the formal disintegration of Yugoslavia, a census was conducted in Macedonia which found that nearly 65 percent of the republic's inhabitants were Macedonians, with just over 20 percent being Albanians (see figures in Table 11.2). No other group accounted for even 5 percent of the population, and aside from the Turks, all other groups accounted for less than 3 percent of the population each. But there was widespread agreement that the 1991 census was "unreliable," and representatives of at least two nationality groups challenged the census, claiming that the numerical strengths of their respective groups had been underestimated. Albanian spokespersons generally held that their group accounted for some 40 percent of the republic's population,[68] while local Serbs claimed to number at least 300,000, if not 400,000—that is to say, eight to ten times the official estimate.[69] Since these claims held political significance across several policy areas, Macedonian authorities soon began organizing a second census, to be conducted under international supervision. After nearly two years of preparations, the second census was held in June–July 1994. What is interesting about the new figures is that all nationality groups, except the Albanians, were smaller now than in 1991, although the growth in the Albanian figure does not nearly approach the claims made by Albanian spokespersons after the first census. Indeed, what is striking about the two censuses is how similar the results were each time—a feature that is unlikely to be pleasing to local Albanians or Serbs. In fact, several Albanian political parties had already prepared the ground for continued challenges to the census results by calling, on the eve of the second census, for an Albanian boycott of this census as well.[70] How many did in fact boycott the census is impossible to say.

The most important political force among Macedonia's Albanians is the Party for Democratic Prosperity (PDP), headed since July 1994 by Abdurahman Aliti. Moderate in political orientation, the PDP has pursued a policy of cooperation and negotiation with ethnic Macedonian parties and leaders and, prior to the elections of October 1994, had twenty-two seats in the Macedonian parliament. In the period 1993–1994, there were five ethnic Albanians among twenty-two cabinet ministers. Other ethnic Albanian parties active in Macedonia include the Democratic People's Party, the Democratic Alliance of Albanians/Liberal Party, and the Party of Democratic Action.

Even before independence, ethnic Albanians in Macedonia were presenting petitions, requesting the opening of cultural institutions, schools, and other facilities that would conduct their business in Albanian, and the reinstatement of teachers suspended for having allegedly indoctrinated their students with Albanian nationalist ideas.[71] Failing to make any headway in at least some of these areas and drawing inspiration from Titoist practices, which always sought to solve problems by dividing jurisdictions and creating new autonomous zones (whether provinces, republics, or whatever), Macedonia's Albanians began likewise to think in terms of autonomy.

The Albanian population of Macedonia in fact staged a referendum on ethnic-regional autonomy in early January 1992, in spite of government warnings that it considered any such referendum illegal. But the government in fact did little to impede the progress of this referendum, which was conducted publicly at more than 500 polling stations. Some 276,921 Albanians took part in the referendum, with 74 percent voting in favor of autonomy.[72] The government declined to take up the question of autonomy, however, fearing that the results could be highly destabilizing. But in reply, ethnic Albanians from all over Macedonia assembled in downtown Skopje on 31 March for a peaceful protest. The meeting was organized by the PDP, whose president at that time, Nevzet Halili, told those assembled that, as "a constituent element in the new Macedonian state," the Albanians of Macedonia were entitled to "territorial, political, and cultural autonomy."[73] The government maintained, however, that autonomy would not in fact serve Albanians' interests but would, on the contrary, result in the creation of a "ghetto," cutting them off from mainstream Macedonian public life.[74] Frustrated with the government's response, a small group of Albanian nationalists in fact declared the creation of an "Ilirida Republic" in the area around Struga in early April 1992, but the declaration was purely demonstrative, without any practical effect.[75]

The government did propose to establish an Albanian quota at the University of Skopje, in effect institutionalizing a form of "positive discrimination," but university officials balked.[76] Later, in November 1994, a session of the Tetovo city assembly gave support to an initiative to establish an Albanian-language university in Macedonia, though not without some of its members noting that such a move lay far outside the nominal jurisdiction of a city assembly.[77]

But there have also been tensions, including violent clashes between Albanians and Macedonian police in November 1992, fist fights between Albanian and Macedonian young people in June 1994, and the arrest of nine high-ranking Albanian officials in November 1993, on suspicion of smuggling weapons, organizing paramilitary organizations, and preparing for the overthrow of the state.[78] Within the generally moderate PDP, moreover, there is a radical wing, led by soft-spoken Arben Xhaferi. As of early 1994, these radicals were openly advocating armed revolt and backed off only after Albanian President Sali Berisha personally asked them to tone down their rhetoric.[79] Still, for all that, there is some basis for Duncan Perry's optimistic conclusion that "Macedonia's Albanians, economically better off than their cousins in Albania or Kosovo, seem to recognize that they are a culture apart from other Albanians and that their lot is better cast with Macedonia."[80] That does not, however, solve the question of autonomy.

The third largest nationality group in Macedonia is the Turks, but despite the existence of several Turkish parties, they have little chance of bringing their concerns to center stage. They are simply too few. Still, despite their sincere protestations of loyalty,[81] there have been expressions of discontent with problems encountered in education, culture, and economic life.[82]

The Serbs, who number less than 40,000 according to the 1994 census, are the fifth largest nationality group, after the Macedonians, Albanians, Turks, and Gypsies. Only 2 percent of Macedonia's inhabitants are Serbs. But because of their powerful neighbor to the north, Macedonia's Serbs have been in the position to raise a great deal of clamor, demanding autonomy, demanding to be listed as one of the "state-constituent" peoples of Macedonia in the constitution, demanding education in their own language, characterizing themselves as "socially threatened,"[83] and demanding the erection, by the state, of a Serbian National Theater, a cultural association for Macedonia's Serbs, a weekly magazine for the small community, and Serbian broadcasts on state radio.[84] The fact that they expect the state to provide everything, rather than thinking in terms of setting up these institutions themselves, is a telling legacy of socialism.

But again, the Macedonian state authorities have made serious efforts to reach negotiated solutions to these questions. Thus, for example, in August 1993 Macedonian authorities met with Bora Ristić, representative of Macedonia's Serbian community, and agreed to guarantee to Serbs the right to primary education in the Serbian language, provided that there are at least fifteen children enrolled in the class, and to secondary education in Serbian, given a minimum class enrollment of twenty-five students.[85]

Domestic Affairs: Economics and Politics

With declines in the social product of 9.5 percent in 1990, 10.0 percent in 1991, and yet another 14.7 percent in 1992, and parallel declines over those years of 10.6, 17.2, and 11.0 percent in industrial production, Macedonia's economy got off to a bad start.[86] Moreover, the imposition of the U.N. trade embargo against Serbia had serious negative effects on Macedonia, as did the combined effect of the Greek closure of its border and the obstruction to trade given by the war itself. These three factors cost Macedonia about 60 percent of its trade, according to President Gligorov.[87] The result is that unemployment rose to 17 percent by summer 1994, basic supplies (of oil, food, medicine, etc.) have remained scarce, and Macedonia's economy has slid downward, coming to resemble that of a third world country more than anything else.

But economics sometimes seems shunted to second place, as the Greek blockade, suspicions of Serbian intentions, and concerns about internal interethnic relations all take priority on the daily agenda.

In the first multiparty elections of 1990, Ljupčo Georgievski's Internal Macedonian Revolutionary Party–Democratic Party of Macedonian National Unity (IMRO–DPMNU) had taken the largest number of votes and initially participated in the formation of a coalition government. But IMRO-DPMNU's strong differences with its coalition partners led to its withdrawal from the coalition, and the Party for Democration Prosperity took IMRO-DPMNUs place in the coalition. The result was a new coalition government involving the Social Democratic Union (the former Communists), the Liberal Party, the Socialist Party, and the (ethnic Albanian) Party for Democratic Prosperity. Kiro Gligorov of the Social Democratic Union became president of the republic.

In preparing for the 1994 elections, the three Macedonian parties of the ruling coalition formed a union called Alliance for Macedonia, which now outpolled Georgievski's party, taking 95 of the 114 parliamentary seats up for election.[88] Gligorov's party won 58 seats, with the other 37 seats divided between the other two Alliance parties. In the presidential race, Gligorov was reelected with 52.4 percent of the vote, easily defeating Ljubiša Georgievski, a theater director, who ran as the standard-bearer for IMRO-DPMNU in place of the party's under-age president, Ljupčo Georgievski. Ljubiša Georgievski attracted only 14.4 percent of the vote.[89]

Georgievski and other opposition leaders staged protest meetings on 19 October (after the first round of voting, with about 20,000 persons attending) and again on 26 October (after the second round). Petar Gošev, leader of the opposition Democratic Party, told the second meeting that the elections had been rigged and promised to continue to struggle against the system.[90] Opposition supporters lit candles to signify, as they put it, "the burial of democracy" in Macedonia and chanted "Macedonia is ours," and "Death to communism!"[91]

CONCLUSION

Although the Liberal-Democratic Party, which won the Slovenian elections of 6 December 1992 with a plurality of 23.3 percent of the vote,[92] has not been accused of rigging the elections, both Slovenia and Macedonia still betray some of the debilities and vulnerabilities inherent in new systems. Their citizens (especially in Macedonia) are not entirely used to democratic politics and are still apt to have some expectations better suited to Communist times. The conversion to new systems is not yet complete in either case, and among the new laws and procedures that have already been laid down some will most certainly be in need of refinement and adjustment in the coming months and years. The common challenge to both of them, in this time of transition, is to use discretion and judgment in appraising the legacy of communism and not to assume that everything ever done by the Communists was wicked and reprehensible. The challenge, as the quotation from Rebecca West at the outset of this chapter might suggest, is to know when it is better to preserve the artifacts of what is ever an ambiguous past, rather than to bulldoze the national heritage and replace it with a "tomb to an unknown cod."

NOTES

1. The official government estimate is 21 percent, as given in *Broj i struktura na naselenieto vo Republika Macedonija po opštini i nacionalna pripadnost* (Skopje: Republički zavod za statistika, 1991), p. 6. The figure claimed by Albanian activists in Macedonia is 40 percent.

2. Zagreb Domestic Service (11 October 1990), trans. in *Foreign Broadcast Information Service (FBIS), Daily Report* (Eastern Europe), 12 October 1990, p. 51.

3. *Profil* (Vienna) (30 July 1990), p. 37, trans. in *FBIS, Daily Report* (Eastern Europe), 1 August 1990, p. 58.

4. *Borba* (Belgrade) (10–11 November 1990), p. 5.

5. Tanjug (10 November 1990), in *FBIS, Daily Report* (Eastern Europe), 13 November 1990, p. 71.

6. *Delo* (Ljubljana) (17 November 1990), pp. 1, 3, as summarized in *FBIS, Daily Report* (Eastern Europe), 30 November 1990, p. 72.

7. E.g., in October, the Council of the Federation of the Free Trade Unions of Slovenia severed its connection with its Yugoslav federal counterpart. See Tanjug (29 October 1990), trans. in *FBIS, Daily Report* (Eastern Europe), 30 October 1990, p. 59.

8. *Die Presse* (Vienna) (16 January 1991), p. 4.

9. *Delo* (30 March 1991), pp. 1, 3, summarized in *FBIS, Daily Report* (Eastern Europe), 15 April 1991, p. 55.

10. *Borba* (30 July 1990), p. 14.

11. *Vjesnik* (Zagreb) (6 September 1990), p. 5.

12. *Politika* (Belgrade) (28 March 1991), p. 19.

13. *Neue Kronen-Zeitung* (Vienna) (10 August 1991), pp. 2–3, trans. in *FBIS, Daily Report* (Eastern Europe), 12 August 1991, p. 28.

14. Radio Slovenia Network (Ljubljana), 17 September 1991, trans. in *FBIS, Daily Report* (Eastern Europe), 18 September 1991, p. 30.

15. For details, see Tanjug (22 January 1992), in *FBIS, Daily Report* (Eastern Europe), 22 January 1992, p. 33.

16. Regarding Lithuania, see *Baltfax* (Moscow) (5 July 1991), in *FBIS, Daily Report* (Soviet Union), 9 July 1991, p. 54; and Radio Vilnius Network (Vilnius) (30 July 1991), trans. in *FBIS, Daily Report* (Soviet Union), 31 July 1991, p. 73. Regarding Georgia, see TASS International Service (Moscow) (12 August 1991), trans. in *FBIS, Daily Report* (Soviet Union), 13 August 1991, p. 59; Radio Slovenia Network (12 August 1991), trans. in *FBIS, Daily Report* (Eastern Europe), 13 August 1991, p. 32;

and *Neue Zürcher Zeitung* (15 August 1991), p. 2. Regarding Latvia, see Tanjug (3 August 1991), trans. in *FBIS, Daily Report* (Soviet Union), 4 September 1991, p. 73.

17. *Neue Zürcher Zeitung* (1 February 1992), p. 4.

18. *Neodvisni dnevnik* (Ljubljana) (26 November 1991), p. 5, trans. in *FBIS, Daily Report* (Eastern Europe), 10 December 1991, p. 47.

19. *Financial Times* (2 August 1991), p. 2.

20. Tanjug (12 December 1991), in *FBIS, Daily Report* (Eastern Europe), 13 December 1991, p. 25.

21. Tanjug (12 December 1991), in *FBIS, Daily Report* (Eastern Europe), 13 December 1991, p. 23. See further reports on Russian–Slovenian trade in *Delo* (3 October 1992), p. 2; and *Slovenec* (Ljubljana) (19 February 1993), p. 1.

22. Tanjug (23 April 1992), trans. in *FBIS, Daily Report* (Eastern Europe), 24 April 1992, p. 29.

23. *Il Piccolo* (Trieste) (26 March 1992), p. 8.

24. *Slobodna Dalmacija* (Split) (22 March 1992), p. 7.

25. Regarding the Benelux, see *Informacije iz Slovenije* (Ljubljana) (2 March 1992), pp. 2–7, trans. in *FBIS, Daily Report* (Eastern Europe), 1 May 1992, pp. 35–39. Regarding Iran, see Tanjug (10 March 1992), trans. in *FBIS, Daily Report* (Eastern Europe), 11 March 1992, p. 45. Regarding China, see *Delo* (27 February 1992), p. 3, trans. in *FBIS, Daily Report* (Eastern Europe), 6 March 1992, p. 43; and Radio Slovenia Network (11 May 1992), trans. in *FBIS, Daily Report* (Eastern Europe), 12 May 1992, p. 35.

26. Tanjug (12 February 1993), trans. in *FBIS, Daily Report* (Eastern Europe), 16 February 1993, p. 55.

27. Regarding Austria, see Radio Slovenia Network (4 November 1992), trans. in *FBIS, Daily Report* (Eastern Europe), 5 November 1992, p. 43. Regarding Hungary, see *MTI* (Budapest) (21 January 1993), in *FBIS, Daily Report* (Eastern Europe), 22 January 1993, p. 31.

28. *Dnevnik* (Ljubljana) (15 April 1992), p. 24, trans. in *FBIS, Daily Report* (28 April 1992), p. 36.

29. Tanjug (6 October 1992), trans. in *FBIS, Daily Report* (Eastern Europe), 7 October 1992, p. 25.

30. *Vjesnik* (10 November 1993), p. 11, trans. in *FBIS, Daily Report* (Eastern Europe), 16 November 1993, p. 41.

31. *Večernji list* (Zagreb) (18 June 1994), p. 7, reprinted from *Slobodna Dalmacija*.

32. *The European* (London) (28 October–3 November 1994), p. 2.

33. *Delo* (26 February 1993), p. 1, trans. in *FBIS, Daily Report* (Eastern Europe), 23 March 1993, p. 35.

34. *Neue Zürcher Zeitung* (2 November 1994), p. 11.

35. Regarding EFTA, see Radio Slovenia Network (21 May 1992), trans. in *FBIS, Daily Report* (Eastern Europe), 22 May 1992, p. 26. Regarding. the EC, see *Neue Zürcher Zeitung* (7 April 1993), p. 13.

36. See Sabrina Petra Ramet, "Slovenia's Road to Democracy," *Europe-Asia Studies,* Vol. 45, No. 5 (1993), pp. 879–883.

37. Tanjug (26 November 1992), in *FBIS, Daily Report* (Eastern Europe), 30 November 1992, p. 48.

38. *Süddeutsche Zeitung* (Munich) (13–15 August 1994), p. 6.

39. Egon žižmond, "Slovenia—One Year of Independence," *Europe-Asia Studies,* Vol. 45, No. 5 (1993), p. 887.

40. Ibid., p. 888.

41. Georg Witschel, "Sloweniens Wirtschaftslage im Frühjahr 1994," *Südost Europa,* Vol. 43, No. 1 (January 1994), pp. 60–61.

42. Radio Slovenia Network (27 February 1992), trans. in *FBIS, Daily Report* (Eastern Europe), 3 March 1992, p. 41.

43. Michael Moran, "A Year Later: The State of Slovenia," *The New Leader* (10–24 August 1992), p. 8.

44. *Delo* (25 April 1992), p. 2, trans. in *FBIS, Daily Report* (Eastern Europe), 8 May 1992, p. 24.

45. *Die Presse* (16 June 1992), p. 3; and *Die Furche* (Vienna) (18 June 1992), p. 1.

46. For a recent example, see *The European—élan* (London) (15–21 April 1994), p. 4.

47. *Delo* (24 August 1993), p. 2, trans. in *FBIS, Daily Report* (Eastern Europe), 17 September 1993, p. 58.

48. *Frankfurter Allgemeine* (30 March 1994), p. 2.

49. *Eastern Europe Newsletter,* Vol. 8, No. 8 (13 April 1994), pp. 7–8. For background, see *Eastern Europe Newsletter,* Vol. 8, No. 7 (29 March 1994), pp. 1–2.

50. For some background, see Rudi Rizman's open letter in *Frankfurter Rundschau* (17 October 1994), p. 20.

51. A recent example involves the Green Party of Dušan Plut, which split into left and right factions in March 1993. See *Delo* (18 March 1993), p. 2, trans. in *FBIS, Daily Report* (Eastern Europe), 13 April 1993, p. 27.

52. Details in Sabrina Petra Ramet, *Nationalism and Federalism in Yugoslavia, 1962–1991,* 2d ed. (Bloomington; Indiana University Press, 1992), pp. 256–257.

53. *Eastern Europe Newsletter,* Vol. 8, No. 20 (5 October 1994), p. 5.

54. Radio Belgrade Network (22 January 1992), trans. in *FBIS, Daily Report* (Eastern Europe), 23 January 1992, p. 59.

55. Radio Belgrade Network (5 February 1992), trans. in *FBIS, Daily Report* (Eastern Europe), 6 February 1992, p. 25; Tanjug (13 February 1992), trans. in *FBIS, Daily Report* (Eastern Europe), 14 February 1992, p. 41; Tanjug (21 February 1992), trans. in *FBIS, Daily Report* (Eastern Europe), 24 February 1992, p. 37; Radio Macedonia Network (Skopje), 24 February 1992, trans. in *FBIS, Daily Report* (Eastern Europe), 25 February 1992, p. 47; and Tanjug (26 March 1992), trans. in *FBIS, Daily Report* (Eastern Europe), 27 March 1992, pp. 49–50.

56. *Neue Zürcher Zeitung* (28 April 1992), p. 4.

57. Radio Belgrade Network (6 January 1992), trans. in *FBIS, Daily Report* (Eastern Europe), 6 January 1992, p. 57; and *Politika—International Weekly* (Belgrade), (11–17 January 1992), p. 4.

58. For more details, see Sabrina Petra Ramet, "The Macedonian Enigma," in Sabrina Petra Ramet and Ljubiša S. Adamovich, eds., *Beyond Yugoslavia: Politics, Economics, and Culture in a Shattered Community* (Boulder, Colo.: Westview Press, 1995).

59. As estimated by Duncan M. Perry in his article, "Crisis in the Making? Macedonia and Its Neighbors," *Südost Europa,* Vol. 43, Nos. 1–2 (January–February

1994), p. 44. The Macedonian government says there are 230,000 Macedonians in Greece.

60. ET-1 Television Network (Athens), 9 February 1994, trans. in *FBIS, Daily Report* (Eastern Europe), 10 February 1994, p. 38; and *U.S. Department of State Dispatch,* Vol. 5, No. 8 (21 February 1994), p. 98.

61. *Japan Times* (18 February 1994), p. 5.

62. This account is based on Hanna Rosin, "Why We Flip-flopped on Macedonia: Greek Pique," *The New Republic* (13 June 1994), p. 11.

63. *Mainichi Daily News* (Tokyo) (23 February 1994), p. 3; *Japan Times* (23 February 1994), p. 5, and (9 April 1994), p. 7; *The European* (8–14 April 1994), p. 2, and (1–7 July 1994), p. 2; *Financial Times* (11 April 1994), p. 30; *New York Times* (1 July 1994), p. A4.

64. *The Times* (London) (13 June 1994), p. 15; and *Neue Zürcher Zeitung* (17 June 1994), p. 5.

65. *The Observer* (London) (16 October 1994), p. 17.

66. *Ljiljan* (Sarajevo–Ljubljana) (23 November 1994), p. 9.

67. *Süddeutsche Zeitung* (13–15 August 1994), p. 6; *Neue Zürcher Zeitung* (24 September 1994), p. 7, and (27 September 1994), p. 4.

68. *Süddeutsche Zeitung* (5–6 December 1992), p. 10. For a wide-ranging survey of the historical, demographic, and geographic context of Macedonia's Albanians, see Jovan Trifunoski, *Albansko stanovništvo u Socijalističkoj Republički Makedoniji* (Belgrade: Književne novine, 1988).

69. *Neue Zürcher Zeitung* (27 June 1992), p. 5; also *Dijaspora* (a Serbian publication targeting Serbs outside Serbia), as summarized in *Vjesnik* (1 August 1994), p. 9, trans. in *FBIS, Daily Report* (Eastern Europe), 17 August 1994, p. 38.

70. *Neue Zürcher Zeitung* (23 June 1994), p. 3.

71. Tanjug (28 August 1990), trans. in *FBIS, Daily Report* (Eastern Europe), 29 August 1990, p. 73.

72. Tanjug (11 January 1992), trans. in *FBIS, Daily Report* (Eastern Europe), 13 January 1992, p. 57; *Borba* (13 January 1992), pp. 1–2; Radio Belgrade Network (15 January 1992), trans. in *FBIS, Daily Report* (Eastern Europe), 15 January 1992, pp. 58–59; Tanjug (15 January 1992), trans. in *FBIS, Daily Report* (Eastern Europe), 16 January 1992, p. 59; and Perry, "Crisis in the Making," p. 36.

73. Tanjug (31 March 1992), trans. in *FBIS, Daily Report* (Eastern Europe), 1 April 1992, p. 52.

74. See, for example, *Nova Makedonija* (Skopje) (20 November 1993), p. 4, trans. in *FBIS, Daily Report* (Eastern Europe), 30 November 1993, p. 59.

75. Tanjug (9 April 1992), in *FBIS, Daily Report* (Eastern Europe), 10 April 1992, p. 51.

76. *Borba* (25–26 April 1992), p. 6.

77. *Nova Makedonija* (5 November 1994), p. 4, trans. in *FBIS, Daily Report* (Eastern Europe), 10 November 1994, p. 48.

78. *MIC* (Skopje) (10 November 1993); *Nova Makedonija* (11 November 1993), pp. 1, 4; and Radio Macedonia Network (Skopje) (11 November 1993)—all trans. in *FBIS, Daily Report* (Eastern Europe), 12 November 1993, pp. 62–63, 65–66; *RFE/RL News Briefs* (8–12 November 1993), p. 13; and *The Economist* (London) (20 November 1993), p. 46.

79. *The Globe and Mail* (Toronto) (5 July 1994), p. A7.

80. Perry, "Crisis in the Making," p. 37.

81. See, for example, *Nova Makedonija* (4 January 1992), p. 15, trans. in *FBIS, Daily Report* (Eastern Europe), 29 January 1992, pp. 41–44.

82. Comments by Erdogan Šarac, president of the Democratic Party of Ethnic Turks, as reported in Tanjug (31 October 1992), trans. in *FBIS, Daily Report* (Eastern Europe), 2 November 1992, p. 42.

83. *Politika* (5 October 1992), p. 5.

84. *Nova Makedonija* (23 January 1993), trans. into German as "Die serbische Minderheit in Makedonien," *Osteuropa,* Vol. 43, No. 9 (September 1993), p. A525. These desiderata are confirmed in Tanjug (20 March 1993), trans. in *FBIS, Daily Report* (Eastern Europe), 22 March 1993, p. 73.

85. *MILS NEWS, Dnevni vesti* (Skopje) (27 August 1993), trans. in *FBIS, Daily Report* (Eastern Europe), 30 August 1993, p. 70. For forther discussion of interethnic relations in postcommunist Macedonia, see Sabrina Petra Ranet, "All Quiet on the Southern Front? Macedonia Between the Hammer and the Anvil," in *Problems of Post-Communism* (November/December 1995).

86. Data from *Neue Zürcher Zeitung* (12 May 1993), p. 19.

87. See his interview with *Die Zeit* (Hamburg) (19 August 1994), p. 8, trans. in *FBIS, Daily Report* (Eastern Europe), 19 August 1994, p. 35.

88. *Nova Makedonija* (15 November 1994), pp. 1, 4, trans. in *FBIS, Daily Report* (Eastern Europe), 16 November 1994, p. 45. See also *Slobodna Dalmacija* (Split), 20 October 1994, p. 10.

89. *Süddeutsche Zeitung* (22–23 October 1994), p. 9. See also *Slobodna Dalmacija* (19 October 1994), p. 11.

90. *Večer* (Skopje) (27 October 1994), p. 4, trans. in *FBIS, Daily Report* (Eastern Europe), 28 October 1994, p. 34.

91. AFP (Paris) (30 October 1994), in *FBIS, Daily Report* (Eastern Europe), 31 October 1994, p. 53.

92. The second-place Christian Democrats took 14.5 percent, the Social Democratic Party of Renewal (former Communists) came in third with 13.6 percent, and the right-of-center National Party placed fourth with 9.9 percent of the vote. The radical-right Slovenian People's Party was in fifth place with 8.8 percent of the vote, while the once formidable Democratic Party managed to attract only 5 percent of the votes. As a result of the voting, Liberal-Democratic leader Janez Drnovšek retained the prime ministership. See *Neue Zürcher Zeitung* (10 December 1992), p. 2. For background, see *Neue Zürcher Zeitung* (25 April 1992), p. 2.

CHAPTER TWELVE

◆

The Struggle for Bosnia

MUSLIMS, SERBS, AND CROATS HAD LIVED in peace for most of the 500 years they cohabited in Bosnia-Herzegovina. The intercommunal violence that accompanied World War II was an important deviation from this pattern, but even then the situation was complicated. Muslims and Croats, for example, were found in the ranks of both the Ustasha and the Communist-led partisans, while Serbs fought with both Mihailović's Chetniks and Tito's partisans. The current war is different in that, with the exception of the defenders of Sarajevo, the respective sides have tended to recruit exclusively from the nationality each claims to represent.

No civil war—or if one prefers, "ethnic" war—erupts until the seeds of intercommunal hatred have been sown. In many cases, it has been the religious organizations that have played the most crucial role in sowing such hatreds; and in the case of Yugoslavia, the Serbian Orthodox Church certainly deserves credit for having done much to embitter Serbs against Albanians, in the first place, and subsequently against Croats. There had been some difficulties in Bosnia throughout the years after World War II, but there were always countervailing tendencies, self-designated "Yugoslavs," threads of Titoism, and a sense and understanding that Bosnia was a community in its own right.

That sense of Bosnianness began to unravel in the latter half of the 1980s, and by 1989 the deterioration of interethnic relations in Bosnia became sufficiently visible to be mentioned in the local press[1]. A well-publicized brawl between Serbs and Muslims in the village of Kožja Luka, near Foča, in August 1990 alerted the Yugoslav public to the growing disintegration of social harmony in that republic,[2] and soon after—in September or October of that year—Bosnian Serbs began setting up illegal military formations in Bosnia, formations that were supplied and trained, on a clandestine basis, by the Serb-controlled JNA.[3] These formations were set up, thus, *before* the elections that would place Muslim leader Alija Izetbegović in the presidency and cannot, therefore, be portrayed as a response to his election.

The census of April 1991 recorded that 43.77 percent of the residents of Bosnia-Herzegovina were "ethnic Muslims," 31.46 percent were Serbs, and 17.34 percent were Croats.[4] There were especially large concentrations of Serbs in western Bosnia—far from the Republic of Serbia—and of Muslims in eastern Bosnia, along the Serbian border. But the picture was rendered even more complex by the fact that in only 32 of Bosnia-Herzegovina's 109 districts did one of the three ethnic groups constitute 70 percent or more of the local population.[5] Muslims constituted the majority group in 11 of these districts, Serbs in another 11, and Croats in 10. Under the circumstances, all three communities had long shared the view that any partition of the republic was entirely out of question,[6] quite apart from its being injurious to the sense of Bosnian community.

Shortly after the war in Croatia began, the Yugoslav Army's high command commissioned a study of likely international responses to the war. The committee entrusted with this assignment studied Western responses to Iraqi threats and to the eventual Iraqi invasion of Kuwait and specifically ruled out any conclusion that a similar Western response might be anticipated in the cases of Croatia or Bosnia. Some of the findings were published in the army journal, *Vojno delo*, in October 1991. In a key contribution to this issue, Milan Radaković summarized the army experts' consensus "that there was little reason to expect international armed intervention in Yugoslavia. That conclusion was based on the recognition that the EC countries, through the Western European Union, could not engage in meaningful military operations without U.S. support, which, because the United States was not significantly involved, was lacking."[7]

Vojno delo also correctly identified the need for international consensus, especially within the U.N. Security Council, as a critical weakness that could be exploited. One of the tactics that Belgrade adopted in order to exploit this weakness was to play on American tendencies to see trouble spots as potential "Vietnams."[8] Nor was there anything subtle about the Serbian approach, as Bosnian Serb leader Radovan Karadžić, then-Prime Minister Milan Panić, and others explicitly warned that any U.S. involvement would lead to a Vietnam-type situation, dragging on for years.[9]

There were isolated calls for a forceful Western response to the Serbian seizure of some 30 percent of Croatia's territory in the months between July 1991 and January 1992. But in spite of both this and the unmistakable evidence of Serbian military preparations for armed action in Bosnia,[10] the only Western response during 1991 to the growing tensions within Bosnia was to include Bosnia-Herzegovina in the general arms embargo imposed on all five Yugoslav successor-states via the U.N. Security Council on 25 September 1991.[11] During the months between October 1990 and March

1992, as explained in Chapter 3, the illegally established Serbian militias loyal to Bosnian Serb politician Radovan Karadžić benefited from a steady infusion of armaments, including tanks and heavy artillery, from the Yugoslav Army. Bosnia's Croat and Muslim communities were constrained to look elsewhere for arms and, thanks at least in part to the arms embargo, were able to obtain much less in the way of military hardware than the Serbs; this was especially true of the Muslims. The net effect of the arms embargo, thus, was to encourage Serbian aggression in Bosnia and to facilitate the success of that aggression once it finally came.

Four Serb autonomous regions were established in Bosnia and in September 1991 requested assistance from the FRY army. Well over 5,000 Yugoslav Army troops were dispatched in response to this request and had secured the borders of a self-designated "Serb Autonomous Region of Herzegovina" by the end of the month.[12]

Between 31 December 1991 and 2 January 1992, the governments of rump Yugoslavia and of Croatia and officials of the Yugoslav Army and of the Croatian National Guard agreed to a cease-fire in place and to a plan, brokered by U.N. special envoy Cyrus Vance, that called for the withdrawal of the Yugoslav Army from the Republic of Croatia and for the emplacement of some 10,000 (later increased to 13,500) U.N. peacekeeping troops in Croatia. This truce set the stage for the expansion of the war into Bosnia.

THE BOSNIAN WAR, TO APRIL 1993

On 12 November 1991, Bosnian President Izetbegović had warned of the danger of "total war" breaking out in his republic and had requested the immediate dispatch of U.N. peacekeeping forces to head off the impending conflict.[13] On 20 December, three months after Karadžić and Milošević had met to coordinate plans for the Serbian assault on Bosnia-Herzegovina,[14] the Bosnian presidency requested diplomatic recognition from the European Community. On the next day, an insurgent Assembly of Bosnian Serbs proclaimed the creation of the Serbian Republic of Bosnia-Herzegovina. This was followed, on 22 December, by Izetbegović's appeal to the U.N. to deploy a peacekeeping force along Bosnia's borders.[15] The U.N. failed to respond, however, and on 9 January 1992, less than a week after the cease-fire in Croatia had taken effect, the Bosnian Serb minority proclaimed the independence of this Bosnian Serb Republic. It was clear to all observers that Bosnia's fragile and tenuous stability was crumbling and that there was a high risk of hostilities. Meanwhile, pressed by the EC's Badinter Commission to let the people of Bosnia vote on their political future, the elected government of Bosnia-Herzegovina held a referendum on independence 29 February–1 March 1992. Karadžić told Bosnian Serbs that it was their duty to boycott the referendum, and the Yugoslav air force assisted by dropping leaflets urging Serbs to stay home.[16] The Bosnian Serbs, who had already declared their secession from Bosnia, protested, claiming that by calling for a vote the government of Sarajevo had violated certain unwritten "rules of the game." The Serbs boycotted the referendum, but with nearly unanimous support from local Croats and Muslims the mandate for independence was easily obtained, with 62.7 percent of the total number of eligible voters (whether voting or not) declaring themselves in favor of the measure.

Zagreb seems to have been confused as to its goals or strategies at this time. On the one hand, Croatian officials are known to have held secret talks about this time with their Serbian counterparts concerning a possible partition of Bosnia.[17] On the other hand, Josip Manolić, chief of the Secret Service of the Republic of Croatia, warned the Serbs in mid-March that in the event that the war should spread to Bosnia, Croatia would not be able to stand aside,[18] and when the Serbs ignited hostilities in April, the Croats began selling war materiel to the Bosnian Army.[19]

The day after the Bosnian referendum on independence was held, the Serbs set up barricades in Sarajevo. Undeterred, the Sarajevo government, under the presidency of Alija Izetbegović, declared Bosnian independence on 3 March. By this point, Bosnian Serb leader Karadžić was talking openly of a war to keep Serbian regions of Bosnia attached to the FRY.

It was now, at the proverbial "last minute," that the EC made an all-too-feeble attempt at achieving a compromise, proposing a "cantonization" scheme that would have divided Bosnia-Herzegovina into several dozen ethnic-based cantons.[20] (A partition assigning eastern Bosnia to Serbia, southwestern Herzegovina to Croatia, and the rest to the Muslims, if accompanied by extensive population exchanges, might have had much better prospects of avoiding bloodshed.) But all three communities rejected this scheme, and as the month progressed there were ever more serious incidents and confrontations between Serbs and non-Serbs in Bosnia.[21] On 3 April, for instance, there were serious clashes in the towns of Bosanski Brod and Kupres between Serbian irregulars (backed by the Yugoslav Army) and Bosnian Muslims and Croats. Finally, on 6 April, Bosnian Serbs opened a military front in the eastern part of the republic and began to push westward. Within five weeks, the Serbian insurgents controlled more than 60 percent of Bosnia.[22] In May, responding to international protests, Milošević demonstratively ordered the withdrawal of the Yugoslav Army, which had played a central role in the fighting. But the move was largely cosmetic: of the 89,000 Yugoslav Army troops that had been fighting alongside Karadžić's irregulars, only about 14,000 were actually withdrawn. The rest were transferred to Karadžić's command and renamed the Army of the Serbian Republic of Bosnia-Herzegovina.[23] By the end of the year, Bosnian Serbs controlled 70 percent of the territory of Bosnia-Herzegovina.

The United States, Western Europe, and the Islamic nations were the powers most directly concerned with debates about the growing Bosnian crisis. The Islamic community realized that any move on its part, even if on a multilateral basis, could actually hurt the Bosnian Muslims by allowing the West to view the conflict as a showdown between the Christian West and "fundamentalist" Islam (as Serbian propaganda portrayed the conflict). The Islamic nations therefore deferred to the West and restricted themselves to periodic conferences on Bosnia, protests against Western inaction, and demands for a lifting of the arms embargo. The United States, for its part, first under Bush and then (albeit rather inconsistently) under Clinton, chose to leave it to the (West) European Community to sort out, on the reasoning that genocide in Europe was a "European problem."[24] The European states themselves were divided between traditional friends of the Croats (Germany and Austria), traditional friends of the Serbs (France and Russia), and the traditionally apathetic (Great Britain and the Netherlands). Because of these factors, the international community was slow to react.

Only on 30 May 1992, nearly two months after the opening of full-scale warfare in Bosnia-Herzegovina, did the UN Security Council vote to impose trade sanctions on Serbia. Thanks to obstruction by Serbia's friend, Russia, the Conference on Security and Cooperation in Europe (CSCE) was even slower to act and voted merely to suspend Serbia (the FRY) from its ranks for three months, taking that vote only on 8 July.

Earlier, in December 1991, the U.N. Security Council had adopted Resolution #724, affirming that the conditions for introducing U.N. peace-keeping forces in former Yugoslavia did not yet exist.[25] Later, in April 1992, by which time U.N. peacekeepers had been introduced in Croatia, U.N. Secretary-General Boutros Boutros-Ghali had rebuffed calls for an extension of the U.N. mandate in Croatia to include Bosnia. In a report to the U.N. Security Council on 13 May, Marrack Goulding, head of the U.N. Department of Peacekeeping Operations, had warned against any such deployment in wartorn Bosnia.[26] In spite of this warning, the Security Council decided on 8 June to authorize a U.N. Protection Force (UNPROFOR) to take control of Sarajevo airport. The UNPROFOR presence in Bosnia expanded rapidly in the weeks and months thereafter.[27] Boutros-Ghali had by then become enamoured of the idea of using U.N. forces in this way, and in a policy statement entitled "An Agenda for Peace" Boutros-Ghali claimed to see an opportunity to "achieve the great objectives of the [U.N.] Charter—a United Nations capable of maintaining international peace and security, of securing human rights and justice and of promoting . . . social progress and better standards of life in larger freedom."[28]

Meanwhile, the Bosnian Croats placed their stress, from the beginning, on consolidating their hold on western Herzegovina, where in early July they proclaimed the creation of Herceg-Bosna (already mentioned in

Chapter 10), as a nominally independent Bosnian Croat state whose intended future clearly lay in absorption into Croatia.[29]

Only in August 1992, by which point there were already 50,000 dead (mostly civilians) and more than 2 million homeless as a result of Serbian aggression in both Croatia and Bosnia, did the EC convene the so-called London Conference. The London Conference recognized the territorial integrity of Bosnia-Herzegovina and identified Serbia and Montenegro as aggressors, calling for the introduction of U.N. peacekeeping forces into Bosnia in order to maintain a cease-fire in the area.[30]

The Geneva Peace Conference, which began its work the following month, was tasked to find mechanisms to implement the principles laid down at the London Conference. However, guided by cochairmen Lord David Owen (for the EC) and Cyrus Vance (for the U.N. secretary general), the Geneva Conference in effect repudiated its mandate. Instead of honoring the London Conference's recognition of Bosnian territorial integrity and the Western powers' recognition of the elected government of Alija Izetbegović as having, by that virtue, a status higher than that of insurgent forces, Vance and Owen introduced the notion of "three warring factions." This placed the government of Sarajevo on the same level with the Croat and Serbian insurgents. This, in turn, laid the basis for negotiating the partition of Bosnia, which entailed, in turn, the decision to reward Serbian aggression. The U.N. and EC mediators, along with the Western media, began to treat the Bosnian government as if it represented only Muslims, even though, as of 12 February 1993, the Bosnian cabinet still included six Serbs and five Croats, alongside nine Muslims.[31]

Indeed, as already noted, the Croats, who had at first supported the Izetbegović government, had decided to go it alone and seized about 20 percent of Bosnia's territory, including much of southwestern Herzegovina. The war had become a three-cornered conflict, and the Izetbegović government, despite the continued presence of some Croats and Serbs in its ranks, and although legitimately elected as the government of all the peoples of Bosnia-Herzegovina, was increasingly seen as the government of Bosnian Muslims only.

By this point the Muslims were scarcely able to feed themselves, and the West undertook to send regular food shipments to the besieged Muslims in several cities, most notably Sarajevo. In order to protect aid convoys, some 8,000 U.N. soldiers were dispatched to Bosnia in October 1992 and advised that they were allowed to use force only in the event that an aid convoy was actually attacked.

Vance and Owen were appointed to serve as international *mediators*, but they soon found mediation impossible: the warring sides were simply unable to agree on *any* fundamental principles. In particular, while Bosnian President Izetbegović held fast to the principle that the unity of the Bosnian state had to be preserved, Bosnian Serb leader Radovan Karadžić followed Serbian President Milošević in insisting that any area inhabited by Serbs (even if Serbs were only a minority in that area) had the right to be conjoined with the larger Serbian state being created.

Instead of recommending forceful military action on the part of the West to halt the continued aggression being waged against the underarmed Muslims—an option to which Russia had expressed its decided opposition[32]—Vance and Owen proceeded on the premise that parties could engage in meaningful peace negotiations in good faith, in the absence of a cease-fire or any curtailment of genocidal policies euphemistically dubbed "ethnic cleansing." As it proved impossible to stage meaningful peace negotiations, Vance and Owen eventually ignored the warring sides and worked out their own peace plan in October 1992. This was quite appropriately called the Vance-Owen Plan because it represented little beside the optimistic hopes and private notions of Lord Owen and Cyrus Vance.

The Vance-Owen Plan would have divided Bosnia into ten ethnic cantons, but it proposed to do so in such a way as to produce a patchwork quilt in which Muslim cantons would be separated from other Muslim cantons, Serb cantons from other Serb cantons, etc. Bosnian Croat leader Mate Boban accepted the plan, which gave the Bosnian Croats much of southwestern Herzegovina, which was the Croats' principal desideratum. Bosnian President Izetbegović resisted at first but under persistent Western pressure eventually caved in and agreed, on behalf of the Bosnian government, to accept it. The Bosnian Serbs, however, explicitly rejected the plan as early as 12 January 1993.

Many observers pointed out that the Vance-Owen Plan had no detectable prospects for long-term stability and would serve only to legitimate the principle that international borders could be redrawn by force (thus repudiating the Helsinki Accords of 1975).[33] But the European Community insisted all the same on obtaining the Vance-Owen Plan—first, because it enabled the EC to reject calls for a military response; and second, because the EC did not believe that its interests ultimately extended beyond wanting to dam up the flow of refugees out of the country.

The Vance-Owen Plan in fact made a dramatic break with past diplomatic practice and in one swoop annulled a key principle of international law that had been agreed upon in the interests of fostering stability in political transitions. Known as *uti possidetis, ita possidetis* (you may keep what you had before), the principle established that when colonial possessions became independent or when existing states broke up, internal administrative borders should be treated as legitimate. As Rein Mullerson notes,

the *uti possidetis* emerged in the context of the decolonization of Latin America and was later applied in Africa. The Chamber of the International Court of Justice in its decision on the frontier dispute between Burkina Faso and Mali of December 22, 1986 established that *uti possidetis* constituted a general principle which is logically related to the achievement of independence whenever it occurs. Likewise, the Arbitration Commission on Yugoslavia in its opinion of January 11, 1992 declared that, in the absence of an agreement stating otherwise, previous limitations acquire the character of frontiers protected by international law.[34]

With the Vance-Owen Plan, the EC began its slide away from *uti possidetis* and opened the door to the partial recognition of conquests.

On 6 April, the foreign ministers of the EC states adopted a "Declaration on Former Yugoslavia," indicating that in the event that the Bosnian Serbs failed to sign the Vance-Owen Plan both they and the Serb-Montenegrin federation would be subjected to long-term international isolation, branded as a pariah state.[35]

On 17 April 1993, the U.N. Security Council approved a resolution (with thirteen votes in favor and only Russia abstaining), calling for a toughening of the hitherto largely ineffectual economic sanctions against Serbia.[36] Lord Owen met with Karadžić on 23 April and offered to press for further concessions to the Serbs, but the following day Karadžić reiterated his earlier rejection of the plan. The West also began, for the first time, to consider a military option against the FRY and the Bosnian Serbs. It was at this point that the United States became actively, albeit only briefly, involved in the efforts to stop the fighting. U.S. President Clinton met with various members of Congress on 27 April to sound them out about air strikes against Bosnian Serbs, and the Pentagon began to collect intelligence on Bosnia, specifically identifying appropriate targets for aerial strikes.[37]

Milošević and Karadžić now conspired to confuse and derail the West. First, Karadžić pretended to cave in and signed the Vance-Owen Plan on 2 May. The West immediately called off further military preparations. The Bosnian Serb parliament was scheduled to convene to ratify the plan at its 6 May session, and in these crucial days the West lost its momentum, as Britain and France began to place their hopes once more in "easy" solutions. The Bosnian Serb parliament in due course rejected the plan. But now Milošević and Karadžić played out the second part of their plan—a variation on the familiar "good cop, bad cop" strategy. Karadžić held fast to a rejectionist stance, while Milošević issued a strongly worded condemnation of the Bosnian Serbs and promised to cease supplying them with arms and other equipment (finally conceding what he had denied up to now, i.e., that supplies from Serbia were crucial to the Bosnian Serb war effort).[38] Meanwhile, Karadžić referred the question to a referendum on which the West appeared to pin some vaguely formulated hopes. On 15 May the referendum was held and the Bosnian Serbs overwhelmingly rejected the Vance-Owen Plan.

The United States now backed off, declaring that it had no vital interests at stake in Bosnia;[39] the EC dropped the Vance-Owen Plan and advised Lord Owen to resume negotiations with the three warring parties.

THE DIPLOMACY OF ACCOMMODATION—SECOND PHASE

The Croats were astounded at the sudden evanescence of Western resolve. Subsequently, when foreign ministers from the United States, Russia, Britain, France, and Spain (but not Germany[40]) met in Washington, D.C., and timidly proposed to guarantee six "safe havens" to the Bosnian Muslims, *Vjesnik* commentator Nenad Ivanković described the Western response as "the final 'capitulation' of the international community before Serbian aggression."[41] About this time there started to be serious frictions between Croats and Muslims—frictions later blamed, by Croatian sources, on specifically British orchestration and machinations. These frictions prepared the stage for changes in political alignment, while the limpness of the Western reaction to Serbian obstruction convinced the Croats that it was time to make a deal with the Serbs. It is for this reason that the failure of April–May 1993 constituted a turning point in the Bosnian war. It was a straight line from the collapse of Western resolve in April–May 1993 to the forging of an anti-Muslim coalition between Bosnian Croats and Serbs in June. The immediate results included the virtual cessation of fighting between Croats and Serbs in Bosnia, the concentration of Bosnian Croat firepower against the Muslims, a direct meeting between Croatian President Franjo Tudjman and Serbian President Milošević on 16 June, and the formulation of a joint Serb-Croat plan for the partition of Bosnia-Herzegovina. Lord Owen and Thorvald Stoltenberg, who had replaced Vance as U.N. mediator in May 1993, accommodated themselves to the new reality of a Serb-Croat coalition, and the Owen-Stoltenberg Plan, presented to the warring parties on 20 August, closely followed the Serb-Croat plan: as modified by Owen and Stoltenberg, this second peace plan proposed to assign 52 percent of Bosnian territory to the Bosnian Serbs, 30 percent to the Muslims, and 18 percent (mostly in the southwest) to the Croats.[42] Western mediators at first expressed "optimism" at the prospects for Muslim acceptance of what was, in effect, a Serb-Croat plan, and described the ultimate Muslim rejection of the plan as "unexpected."[43]

Throughout 1992 and 1993, the Bosnian government, supported intermittently by the United States and Germany and steadfastly by the Islamic states, tried to persuade the U.N. Security Council to lift the arms embargo. Britain and France obstinately insisted on keeping the arms embargo in place, leading U.S. State Department officials to speculate that despite their protestations to the contrary the British and French actually hoped for a

Serbian victory.[44] British Foreign Secretary Douglas Hurd observed, rather transparently, that giving the Muslims access to weaponry would "only prolong the fighting"[45]—a rather obvious point that did not, in and of itself, explain why Secretary Hurd preferred the "quicker" result obtainable via total Serbian victory. In June 1993, the United States, with the active support of several Islamic states, introduced a resolution in the U.N. Security Council to lift the arms embargo. Eight votes were required for adoption, but with Britain, France, Russia, and six other members abstaining, the resolution obtained only six votes and died on the table. Later, in December, the U.N. General Assembly passed a resolution calling on the Security Council to lift the arms embargo against the Muslims. Britain and France brandished their veto powers within the Security Council and effectively scuttled the initiative.

Thanks to the Western arms embargo, it took months before the Muslims were able to arm themselves decently (though not impressively). A key breakthrough came in May 1993, when Muslim forces daringly attacked a Serbian column and captured some 15,000 weapons. These were mostly small arms but also included some anti-armor rockets and a number of mortars.[46] In addition, despite the loss to Bosnian Serbs of a vital arms factory in Banja Luka, the Muslims have continued to hold onto Travnik, where the Bratstvo ("Brotherhood") ammunition factory produced necessary ammunition. (This factory was the target of a Croatian rocket attack on 13 January 1994, however.[47]) With these modest resources, the Bosnian Muslims managed to defend their remaining positions (amounting in 1993 to less than 10 percent of the republic's territory) and to score some successes against both Croatian and Serbian forces.

Yet a June 1993 assessment of the military situation indicated that the Bosnian (Muslim) army had, at that point, 120,000 active troops and an additional 80,000 reserves, with perhaps about 2,500 Muslim guerrillas operating hit-and-run raids on the model of Tito's partisans. Against this, the Bosnian Serb army was fielding only 60,000 troops, albeit much better armed, supplemented by up to 20,000 Yugoslav Army troops.[48] It is a well-known maxim that in military conflict, the defender enjoys a natural advantage. When the defender also disposes of an army twice as large as that of the invaders, the normal expectation would be the defeat of the invaders—unless, of course, the invaders enjoyed vast superiority in arms (in this case, for example, with Bosnian Serbs holding 350 tanks and 35 aircraft, facing Bosnian Muslim forces with 40 tanks and 1 aircraft).[49] The Bosnian Serbs, it seems painfully obvious, could not have achieved such dramatic success or been in the position to inflict so much suffering had it not been for the Western arms embargo.[50]

Given their vast inferiority in arms, thus, the Bosnian Muslims had initially agreed "in principle" to the Owen-Stoltenberg Plan on 30 July 1993, but efforts to flush out the details soon bogged down. In the meantime, Bosnian Serb militias tightened their stranglehold on Sarajevo and continued the bombardment of the city. Once more the West discussed the possibility of aerial strikes against selected Bosnian Serb targets, and Clinton administration officials announced that plans for such strikes were being developed. On 2 August, U.S. officials tried, during lengthy negotiations with other NATO ministers, to obtain agreement to launch aerial strikes against the Bosnian Serbs; objections by the Canadian delegate held up any consensus for the time being. A week later, after further discussions and ensuing compromises, NATO officials agreed on an elaborate and complex set of procedures for conducting aerial strikes against the Serbs, requiring approval from Lieutenant General Jean Cot of France (the commander of U.N. "peacekeeping" forces in the Balkans), U.N. Secretary-General Boutros Boutros-Ghali, and all sixteen members of NATO.

There ensued a series of disagreements between General Cot and Boutros-Ghali when the latter reportedly rebuffed requests by General Cot for authorization for aerial strikes. U.N. Secretary-General Boutros Boutros-Ghali increasingly found himself at the center of controversy and (in December 1993), in an effort to extricate himself, appointed Yasushi Akashi, a Japanese national with U.N. experience in Cambodia, to take the position of chief of the U.N. "peacekeeping" mission.[51] Akashi now inherited Boutros-Ghali's authority to approve requests for NATO air strikes against Bosnian Serbs and put it to use by repeatedly (although not consistently) vetoing NATO requests to conduct punitive strikes against the Serbs.[52]

In these circumstances, it is not surprising that a group of Muslims controlling the Bihać enclave in northwestern Bosnia decided, in October 1993, to break with the Izetbegović government and establish a working relationship with Karadžić instead. Their understanding was formalized on 7 November, and Bihać leader Fikret Abdić subsequently received artillery and other weaponry from Bosnian Serb arsenals. The Izetbegović government was, in turn, compelled to divert part of its war effort to fighting the Bihać secessionists. By early August 1994, however, Bosnian government loyalists turned the tide in their struggle against Abdić, and at least 5,100 civilians and 1,600 soldiers loyal to Abdić fled to Serbian-held parts of Croatia.[53]

U.S., RUSSIAN, AND OTHER FOREIGN RESPONSES

During 1993, Britain and France began lodging recriminations against the United States for not sending U.S. troops to join the so-called peacekeeping force in the war zone. Ironically, at the same time that Britain and France were demanding that the United States send in troops, they started talking about pulling out their own troops, regardless what the United States might do.[54] The United States has consistently resisted British and French pressure to commit U.S. ground forces to Bosnia. Instead of involving itself with the Anglo-French concept of "peacekeeping" in a war zone, the Clinton administration preferred to press for lifting the arms embargo and, aside from that, to emphasize containment. Repeated visits by congressmen and other high-level officials to Kosovo, Albania, Bulgaria, and Macedonia are one reflection of this policy. As early as July 1993, the United States dispatched a small contingent of peacekeeping troops to Macedonia to help to monitor activity along that republic's border with Serbia—a contingent that grew to more than 500 by April 1994. Then, on 8 October 1993, the United States signed an agreement with Albania, providing for military assistance, including U.S. training for Albanian officers and high-level meetings to discuss international security.[55] In early 1994, the CIA began flying unmanned surveillance missions over Serbia and Bosnia from Gjader air base in Albania. Albanian President Sali Berisha publicly offered to make available "airport facilities that NATO may need to accomplish its missions within the U.N. framework,"[56] although the Pentagon denied harboring any intention of building a military base in Albania.[57]

Russia has experienced deep ambivalence in connection with the war in Bosnia, torn between its desire to reinforce its financially rewarding relationship with the West and its confessionally rooted affinity for the Serbs. Already In April 1993, the Russian parliament had adopted a resolution calling on the government to use its Security Council veto to block any proposed U.N. military action against Bosnian Serbs—a move only partly mitigated by Deputy Foreign Minister Vitaly Churkin's reassurance that the government intended to ignore the vote.[58]

In spite of these reassurances, Russia has provided assistance at a variety of levels, including both diplomatic and military. In May 1994, the Russian Writers' Union even bestowed the Mikhail Sholokov prize on Radovan Karadžić, in recognition of "the aesthetic value of his work and of his high moral principles."[59] The previous year, Karadžić had been awarded the most prestigious Montenegrin prize for literature for his collection of poetry, *The Slavic Guest*.[60] In bestowing these prizes on Karadžić, the prize-givers were engaging in the diplomacy of cultural symbology, using the prestige of literary prizes to try to build up an alternative image for the Bosnian Serb leader.

In the military sphere, high-ranking Russian officials signed a secret deal on 22 January 1993, agreeing to supply Serbian forces in Croatia and Bosnia with T-55 tanks and anti-aircraft missiles, according to British defense analysts. The deal was said to have been worked out between Russian army and intelligence service officials and Serbian military authorities.[61] A senior Russian Trade Ministry official later acknowledged sales of Russian missiles and other weaponry to Bosnian Serbs but denied that the Russian government was involved.[62] Bosnian Radio also reported on the flow of Russian arms to the Bosnian Serbs, noting in particular a large convoy of eight trailers, stocked with arms, that was said to have reached Karadžić's forces in January 1994.[63] More recently, there have been signs of growing Russian impatience with Bosnian Serb refusal to accept a compromise, but at this writing Russia remains opposed to the use of aerial strikes to combat Bosnian Serb aggression.[64] Impatient or not, the Russians have continued to make available, to the Bosnian Serbs, sophisticated weaponry, including eighty-three 122 mm. caliber howitzers, mobile SA-6 surface-to-air missiles, and ultra high-tech S-300b anti-aircraft missiles. Indeed, in the latter months of 1994, more than 4,000 Russian freight cars loaded with war materiel were sent to the Balkans.[65]

Ironically, 1993 also saw continued calls in the international community for a lifting of the U.N. economic embargo against *Serbia*—at the very point when it appeared to be *slowly* shaking the Milošević regime's will to continue the war. Romania, Bulgaria, and Greece had been bridling at the reins all along, pointed out the costs of the embargo to their own economies, and in November 1993 joined ranks to make a joint appeal to have the U.N. economic embargo against Serbia lifted as soon as possible.[66] About the same time, France and Germany proposed to lift international sanctions against Serbia if the latter conceded some additional territory to the Muslims at the negotiating table in Geneva.[67] The Bosnian Muslim government of Alija Izetbegović took umbrage at this proposal, but in any case, two days later, at a meeting of NATO ambassadors, the U.S. publicly rebuked France and Germany for this initiative.[68] Meanwhile, some Church circles in the West started to become nervous about the effects of the embargo on Serbia's population. In mid-October 1993, for example, the Central Conference of Methodist Churches from Central and Southern Europe criticized the U.N. sanctions, blaming them for contributing to additional injustice in the region.[69] At the end of the same month, the Ecumenical Council of Churches and the Conference of European Churches issued a statement criticizing U.N. sanctions against Serbia and Montenegro as "unfair" and "one-sided."[70]

Islamic states, by contrast, have overwhelmingly opposed the continuation of the arms embargo against the Bosnian Muslims and have used international conferences and forums to express their outrage at both Serb aggression against Muslim communities and Western inaction. As early as May 1992, King Fahd of Saudi Arabia authorized emergency aid amounting to $5 million for the Bosnian government, increasing that figure to $8 million the following month. In July, Saudi Arabia began relief shipments to Sarajevo.[71] Iran also began sending food, medicine, and other staples to the Bosnian state about this time and assumed a role coordinating assistance from the Islamic world.[72] In September of that year, Islamic countries used the nonaligned meeting in Djakarta, Indonesia, to obtain a collective condemnation of the Bosnian Serbs. That same month, Iran staged a nationwide rally to protest Serbian atrocities. Later, in May 1993, members of the Organization of the Islamic Conference pledged some $85 million in additional aid for Bosnia and reiterated their earlier demand for a repeal of the arms embargo against the Muslims.[73]

The Islamic countries lobbied hard at the U.N. for a lifting of the arms embargo against Bosnia. Their efforts culminated in the aforementioned abortive Security Council vote in June 1993. As Islamic hopes for a Western reassessment faded, Iran authorized an additional $1.7 million in aid to the Bosnian Muslims and Teheran Radio began broadcasting to Bosnia in Serbo-Croatian.[74]

Turkey, with ambitions to expand its influence in the Balkans, has been especially concerned about the war in Bosnia and became one of the first states to extend diplomatic recognition to Bosnia-Herzegovina. Shortly thereafter, the Turkish government signed an economic and technological assistance pact with Bosnia. In August 1992, just four months after the outbreak of open warfare in Bosnia, the Ankara government outlined a plan for solving the crisis, which included limited air bombardment of Bosnian Serb military positions.[75]

There have been repeated popular demonstrations in Turkey on behalf of the Bosnian Muslims, alongside repeated efforts by the Ankara government to contribute to a solution. An important Turkish initiative came on 12 November 1993, when Ankara endeavored (evidently with some success) to mediate the temporary conflict between the Muslims and the Croats.[76] Later, in February 1994, Pakistan's Prime Minister Benazir Bhutto joined Turkish Prime Minister Tansu Ciller in paying a demonstrative visit to Sarajevo that culminated in a tripartite Agreement of Mutual Friendship and Cooperation.[77] But when the first Turkish contingents arrived in Bosnia in May and June 1994, as part of the U.N. Protection Force,[78] Serbs were quick to draw parallels with the by-gone Ottoman Empire.

In the course of 1994, the Bosnian Army received arms and war materiel from Iran, Pakistan, and Sudan, as well as from nongovernmental sources in Tunisia, Afghanistan, and Saudi Arabia.[79] Serbian sources claim that Ukraine has also supplied Bosnian Muslim forces with weaponry, ammunition, and military equipment,[80] but this may amount to no more than a Serbian effort to exploit traditional Russian–Ukrainian enmity.

THE EUROPEAN UNION PLAN OF JUNE 1994

The Bosnian war moved into a new phase in spring 1994, when the Bosnian Croats abandoned their unreliable Serbian allies and, responding to U.S. mediation efforts, agreed to mend their fences with the Muslims. The Bosnian Croats and Muslims in fact had agreed in February to establish a joint federation and the following month announced the merger of their armies. The new joint parliament promptly elected the talented Bosnian Prime Minister Haris Silajdžić to serve as prime minister of the Bosnian Croat-Muslim federation.[81]

By this point the Croats and Muslims had benefited from a large infusion of arms from Iran and displayed a new confidence.[82] In late May Bosnian government troops, backed up by tanks and heavy artillery, launched a major offensive to retake ground from Serbian forces west of Tesanj in northern Bosnia. In early July, after some initial successes, the Bosnian government army staged a massive assault against Serb positions around Mount Ozren in central Bosnia, but the Bosnian Serbs eventually repulsed the attack, inflicting 2,500 casualties on Bosnian government forces.[83] This setback ended the first Bosnian offensive of 1994.

Meanwhile, U.N. and European Union "mediators" devised a third partition plan, which they presented in June with the support of the United States and Russia. The plan proposed to assign 51 percent of Bosnian territory to the Croat-Muslim federation and 49 percent to the Bosnian Serbs.[84] The Western powers now signaled that if the Bosnian Serbs accepted the plan, the economic sanctions against Serbia and Montenegro would be lifted. On the other hand, the Western powers threatened to lift the arms embargo against the Muslims and Croats if the Serbs rejected the plan.[85] The threat was only a bluff, however, and the Bosnian Serbs called the bluff by rejecting the plan.[86] While the "contact group" met to decide what to do next, the Bosnian Serbs stepped up the sniping of civilians in Sarajevo, in effect thumbing their noses at the West. In response, U.N. officials quickly ruled out aerial strikes of any significant scope because the U.N.'s "peace-keeping" troops on the ground would be exposed to Serbian retaliatory strikes. Others advised inaction on the grounds that "the time for the West to fight a just war was two years ago, not now."[87]

The scenario of April 1993 was then reenacted. Karadžić referred the question to the Bosnian Serb Assembly, which in turn rejected the plan altogether (on 3 August). But the Assembly in turn called for a general referendum among Bosnian Serbs on 27–28 August, although this one was no more likely than the referendum of 15 May 1993 to reverse the decision of the Bosnian Serb leadership. Finally, as before, rumors were quickly circulated about a fresh rift between Milošević and Karadžić, as Milošević ostentatiously declared his borders closed to arms traffic to Bosnia.[88] Western observers were tantalized by the launching, in the Serbian media, of a defamatory campaign against Karadžić and other Bosnian Serb leaders, portraying them as drunkards, gamblers, and womanizers. This disinformation campaign notwithstanding, arms, ammunition, and fuel continued to flow across the Drina from Serbia to Bosnian Serb territory; indeed, the fact that Russia considered it necessary to use its Security Council veto (for the first time in the Yugoslav war) to kill a proposal to block fuel from crossing Serbia to the Bosnian Serbs[89] showed how porous this self-declared "embargo" was.

WAR CRIMES

As early as 16 December 1992, Acting Secretary of State Lawrence Eagleburger called for the establishment of a war crimes tribunal to try war criminals in the Bosnian war, specifying, among others, Serbian President Milošević, Bosnian Serb President Karadžić, Bosnian Serb commander General Ratko Mladić, Serbian Radical leader Vojislav Šešelj, and paramilitary leader Željko Raznjatović ("Arkan").[90] Like other supporters of this proposal in the United States, Germany, and elsewhere, Eagleburger thought chiefly in terms of *Serbian* offenders.

The first, albeit hesitant step in this direction had come earlier, on 13 July 1992, when the U.N. Security Council had affirmed that all parties to the war in Bosnia were bound by the provisions of the Geneva Conventions of August 1949 and other provisions of international humanitarian law. Subsequently, on 13 August, the U.N. Security Council passed a resolution (No. 771) expressing alarm at reports of atrocities in Bosnia, which clearly contravened these conventions.[91] Among other things, Resolution No. 771 underlined the "mass forcible expulsion and deportation of civilians, imprisonment and abuse of civilians in detention centers, deliberate attacks on noncombatants, hospitals and ambulances, impeding the delivery of food and medical supplies to the civilian population, and wanton devastation and destruction of property."[92] Finally, on 22 February 1993, the Security Council adopted a resolution establishing an international tribunal "for the prosecution of persons responsible for serious violations of international humanitarian law committed in the territory of the former Yugoslavia since 1991."[93]

A specific feature of the Bosnian war has been the incidence of organized systematic rape—or rather, forced impregnation, since pregnancy was a conscious goal of the Serbs. An EC investigative mission produced a report in January 1993 estimating that some 20,000 Bosnian Muslim women had been raped by Bosnian Serb men in what could be called "rape camps."[94] In a cogently argued piece about the use of rape in the Bosnian war, Dorothy Thomas and Regan Ralph noted that, in warfare, "rape is neither incidental nor private. [On the contrary,] it routinely serves a strategic function in war and acts as an integral tool for achieving particular military objectives. In the former Yugoslavia, rape and other grave abuses committed by Serbian forces rid villages of the non-Serb population."[95] Serbian sources have, predictably, routinely denied allegations of any campaign of systematic rape.[96]

In June 1994, a U.N. commission on war crimes completed a study of the Prijedor district in northwest Bosnia, concluding that Serbian forces had killed or deported 52,811 persons *from that district alone*.[97] Despite considerable interest in the tribunal,[98] preparations for judicial procedures unfolded slowly, and it was only in October 1994 that the U.N.-sponsored tribunal in The Hague was finally ready to take up its first case: a former Bosnian Serb prison guard, Dušan Tadić, arrested in Germany and later charged with genocide.[99] In a transparently political gesture, the Serbs staged their own "war crimes" trial in Šabac in the second half of November; the accused, Dušan Vučković, a Serb paramilitary, was charged with having shot several Muslim prisoners to death in 1992. But observers confidently predicted that the defense, which sought to portray Vučković as a psychopath, would have its way—meaning that the accused would be confined to a mental institution for the rest of his life.[100]

BELGRADE'S FRIENDS IN THE WEST

From the beginning, Serbia has had its supporters in the West. In the case of the French, Serbophilia is "traditional," reflecting, in part, a French desire to counter German friendship for Croatia. Moreover, French businessmen have been eager to resume economic cooperation with Serbia and have maintained contact with their Serbian counterparts throughout the war.[101] The British advocacy of "not-so-benign neglect" during the Bosnian war seems at first harder to explain but is probably the result of a combination of English Islamophobia,[102] English loathing of secessionist movements insofar as they mirror certain currents in Scotland and Northern Ireland, and a more general antipathy toward fragmentation. The repeated comments by British Prime Minister John Major and Foreign Secretary Hurd that there were enough weapons in the area (even though the overwhelming majority of heavy weaponry was in the hands of the aggressors) and to the effect that any further infusion of arms could only prolong the war can only be seen as veiled revelations of a covert British government sympathy for the Serbs, albeit set against a history of British diplomatic apathy, sometimes carried to the point of bungling.[103]

The Serbs have had their advocates in the United States as well. Serbia's American friends have diverse motivations. For many of the post-Watergate, post-Vietnam generation, it is no longer believable that there are any "pure aggressors" or "pure victims." Everything is relativized to the point where everyone becomes equally guilty. In consequence, the only "rational" response seems, to relativists, to be total indifference or studied "evenhandedness." Carl Jacobsen is a good example of this trend. In an article for

Mediterranean Quarterly, Jacobsen mysteriously claims that "foreigners" have invaded Serbia (where and when he does not say),[104] calls for putting Bosnian President Izetbegović on trial for "war crimes,"[105] and even offers the dubious assertion that "Bosnia was historically Serb"[106] (a proposition that even if it were true, would not entitle twentieth-century Serbs to expel non-Serbs from their land). Jacobsen's recipe calls for a nonpunitive attitude toward Serbia and Bosnian Serbs, regardless of their behavior.

Other writers[107] accuse the U.S. media of bias and one-sided reporting because the media have devoted more time to reportage of Serbian atrocities against non-Serbs than vice versa. No doubt there were those, in World War II, who considered it "biased" that the American media devoted so little attention to discussing the "atrocities" perpetrated by the Polish resistance against Nazi occupation forces.

Still others, offering themselves as steeled "realists," argue for a full rehabilitation of Serbia. In a bold statement of this position, Marten van Heuven, a retired U.S. Foreign Service officer, argued, in the fall 1994 issue of *Foreign Policy,* for a gradual lifting of U.N. sanctions, a restoration of Serbian membership in international organizations, and the extension of IMF and other international financial assistance to Serbia, as incentives to obtain some limited concessions from Serbia: respect for negotiated borders with Croatia and Bosnia, respect for the independence of Macedonia, and adequate guarantees for human rights for the Albanian population of Kosovo.[108]

Still others, likewise thinking of themselves as "realists," took to asserting that it was "too late" for aerial strikes against Bosnian Serb positions (even though non-Serb communities were still being subjected to bombardment by Serbs, and even though Croats and Muslims still fielded armies), "too late" to do anything for Bihać (even before Bihać had fallen), "too late" to do anything except pull out.[109] This orientation lent itself to a view of the Serbs as "invincible."

Finally, there are those such as Fareed Zakaria and Karen Elliott House who have been motivated by a deeply ingrained distrust of U.S. government rhetoric and purposes. For these writers, calls for action to bring an end to genocide and mass rape only reflect a grand megalomania born of naiveté and crystalized in an arrogation to self of the role of "masters of the universe."[110] In their view, advocates of countermeasures are deluded idealists who dream of a new world order of democracy and harmony and view the war in Bosnia as an obstacle to their aspirations.[111] In their view, such advocates are guilty of the arrogance of power.

But there is also the argument that power brings certain responsibilities and hence that the United States is morally bound to take the lead in combatting genocide and other crimes against humanity. In an articulate statement of this position, syndicated columnist Hodding Carter wrote, "Former senator William Fulbright, Clinton's fellow Arkansan and occasional mentor, once spoke wisely of the 'arrogance of power' as applied most notably to U.S. policy in Vietnam. But there are two possible kinds of arrogance. One is to have power and influence and [to] abuse them. The other is to have both and, in a situation that cries out for their application, fail to use them."[112]

THE END OF THE EMBARGO?

On 11 August 1994, President Clinton announced that he was setting a deadline of late October for the Bosnian Serbs to accept the new peace plan. If the Serbs still refused to cooperate, Clinton promised to "seek" to have the arms embargo against the Muslims lifted.[113] The Bosnian Serbs, in fact, did not take so qualified a threat at all seriously. Indeed, the Bosnian Serbs have repeatedly shown their utter disrespect for the U.N. and West. They have repeatedly disarmed and humiliated U.N. troops, taken pot shots at them, and stolen heavy weapons held under U.N. guard. In April 1994 they even placed some forty U.N. military observers under "virtual house arrest" for several days, posting sentries outside their doors—a tactic they repeated in November 1994, capturing a number of U.N. "peacekeepers." They have repeatedly violated the U.N.-proclaimed "no-fly zone" in Bosnia, as well as the heavy weapons' exclusion zones around Sarajevo and Goražde. They have dragged their feet in meeting supposedly strict U.N. deadlines, have violated cease-fires, and have treated promises as tools of deception, not as words of honor. And yet, for all that, the West continued to show infinite patience, continued to pursue a diplomacy of accommodation. Indeed, by late August there were ever more voluble rumors that the West was preparing to pull out of Bosnia-Herzegovina altogether, lifting the arms embargo, and simply washing its hands of the entire affair.

On 11 November, the United States belatedly declared that it would no longer enforce the arms embargo and withdrew its two ships from embargo enforcement in the Adriatic. But NATO continued to operate sixteen other ships in the Adriatic for purposes of enforcing the embargo.[114] Britain and France howled in protest, but in fact the embargo had increasingly become a chimera, as Serbs found it relatively easy to obtain weapons from Russia (shipped through Romania) and even from sources in Germany,[115] and as Islamic states, fed up with the West's pusillanimity and lack of resolve, stepped up arms aid to the Croat–Muslim alliance.[116] That alliance, as Croatian Defense Minister Gojko Šušak conceded, was enjoying increasing success in purchasing arms in Pakistan, Iran, Germany, Poland, Bulgaria, even Russia. Some of these arms, including antitank weapons and ammunition for mortars, cannons, and machine guns, were passed on to the Muslims.[117] In addition, the Croats had succeeded, by 1994, in building up a formidable arms industry and were manufacturing their own tanks, fighter aircraft (the MiG-21), and other weaponry.[118]

After the Bosnian Serb rejection of the third EC plan in August, the Geneva process lost momentum. At the same time, there was an escalation of fighting both in the northwestern corner of Bosnia and in central Bosnia. In the northwest, Bosnian government troops succeeded in overcoming the forces loyal to Fikret Abdić in the Bihać enclave, and by late August the number of civilians to have taken flight from Bihać had increased to 20,000.[119] But although strengthened by a recent infusion of light arms, the Bosnian army lacked either the equipment or the technical support for strategic operations. Thus, most of the Bosnian army's battlefield gains were in the countryside; at this point in time, the Bosnian army did not attempt to retake occupied towns and cities.[120]

Having rejected the EC-brokered peace plan, which the Croats and Muslims had accepted, Bosnian Serbs defied international negotiators and the entire Geneva peace process by proclaiming, on 18 August, their intention to seek to link their territories with the FRY and Serb-occupied areas of Croatia,[121] an announcement that should not have come as a surprise to anyone aware of Karadžić's earlier programmatic statements.[122] Consistent with previous French actions, French Foreign Minister Alain Juppe declared, shortly thereafter, that the Bosnian Serbs had every right to link their conquests with the FRY.[123] Yet even as Juppe offered his support to the Bosnian Serbs, the latter continued to expel Gypsies, Muslims, and Croats from Banja Luka, Bijeljina, Janja, and other areas long secured by Serbian forces. These expulsions of noncombatants began in May 1994. Between mid-July and mid-September alone, more than 6,000 Muslims living in these Serb-occupied towns were driven from their homes by Serb forces. A Bosnian government official said that the Serbs had promised to expel another 6,000 before the end of the year.[124] Bosnian Serbs have raped non-Serb women and girls in Banja Luka on a wide scale, have used force to evict non-Serbs from their homes, have orchestrated the mass dismissal of non-Serbs from their jobs, and have even recruited non-Serbian men into slave labor brigades.[125] The resultant changes in the ethnic composition of Bosnian Serb-held territory are shown in Table 12.1.

Yet, at the very moment when Bosnian Muslim forces were showing a new strength, Western diplomats signed an agreement with Slobodan Milošević, offering to reward Milošević for his break with Karadžić and agreeing to ease international trade sanctions in exchange for his agreement to the stationing of 135 civilian observers to monitor the FRY-Bosnian border.[126] On 8 September, however, Serbian forces in Croatia and Bosnia launched a joint campaign against Bosnian government forces in Bihać. More than 1,000 Croatian Serb forces were deployed in the action, backed by tanks and heavy artillery.[127] Croat and Bosnian government forces

TABLE 12.1   Ethnic Composition of Bosanska Krajina (1991, 1994)

	1991	1994
Serbs	625,000	875,000
Croats and Muslims	550,000	50,000

SOURCE: "War Crimes in Bosnia-Hercegovina: U.N. Cease-Fire Won't Help Banja Luka," *Human Rights Watch Helsinki*, Vol. 6, No. 8 (June 1994), p. 5.

replied by launching a counteroffensive, driving the Serbs back on three fronts. By the end of October, Bosnian government forces had retaken 100–150 square kilometers of territory to the east and southeast of Bihać, setting Bosnian Serb soldiers and civilians to flight and capturing four tanks and dozens of mortars, abandoned by the Serbs.[128] But when units of the Bosnian Army succeeded in crushing a Serbian battalion (killing twenty Serb troops) in battle action around Sarajevo, U.N. troops intervened (on 7 October) to expel more than 500 Bosnian troops. That same day, Yasushi Akashi, Boutros-Ghali's special envoy to Bosnia, visited Bosnian President Izetbegović and issued an acidic protest, threatening the Bosnian government with serious counter-measures in the event of a recurrence.[129]

The United States was, by now, lobbying hard for more resolute military action against the Bosnian Serbs. U.S. Defense Secretary William Perry, for example, said on 28 September that he wanted NATO to use "compelling force" against Bosnian Serb forces.[130] But the British and French remained opposed. Lieutenant General Sir Michael Rose, UNPROFOR commander in Bosnia, responded to U.S. pressures by emphasizing his concept of "peace-keeping" as self-limiting in the means employed.[131] Rose demonstrated what he meant by authorizing pin-prick strikes against a Bosnian Serb tank near Sarajevo (on 22 September) and against a runway at Udbina (in occupied Croatia, on 21 November), the latter coming as a response to an attack by two Serbian Orao fighters from Udbina base on civilians at Bihać and Cazin.[132] The Bosnian Serb military command issued a cocky riposte: "This means that UNPROFOR and NATO forces are [now] legitimate targets. We reserve the right to retaliate how and when we see fit."[133] Unintimidated by the U.N.-NATO approach, the Bosnian Serbs even attacked a U.N. aid convoy on 18 October.[134] As for the Bosnian Muslims, they called on the U.N. to remove Sir Michael Rose as commander of U.N. forces in Bosnia, accusing him of favoring the Serbs and of executing British, rather than U.N., policy.[135]

The U.N. commitment was, by then, flagging. The British and French, in particular, were increasingly impatient to terminate their participation in the ill-conceived "peacekeeping" forces, although they remained steadfastly opposed to any arming of the Muslims—betraying all too clearly the pro-Serbian attitude that underlay British and French policy statements. In late

TABLE 12.2 Troop Strengths of the Rival Forces (November 1994)

Estimate Source	Bosnian Serbs	Bosnian Muslims	Bosnian Croats
McNeil-Lehrer	80,000	100,000	50,000
Die Welt	60,000	210,000	n/a
Jane's Defence Weekly	102,000	164,000	50,000*
Nedjeljna Dalmacija	80,000	120,000	n/a

*1993, from *The Military Balance*.

SOURCES: McNeil-Lehrer News Hour, 4 November 1994; *Die Welt* (Bonn) (4 November 1994), p. 4; *Jane's Defence Weekly*, as cited in *The Sun* (Baltimore) (6 November 1994), p. 11A; International Institute for Strategic Studies, *The Military Balance 1993–1994* (London: Brassey's, October 1993), p. 74; and *Nedjeljna Dalmacija* (Split) (4 November 1994), p. 21.

July, U.N. Secretary-General Boutros Boutros-Ghali recommended to the U.N. Security Council that the UN "peacekeepers" in Croatia and Bosnia be withdrawn.[136]

The Croat-Bosnian offensive pressed forward until mid-November, capturing the town of Kupres on 3 November, dislodging Bosnian Serbs from several locations in the mountains overlooking Sarajevo, and tightening a noose around Trnovo, a key town whose capture could relieve Bosnian Serb pressure on several Muslim-held towns.[137] In a misdirected retaliation that hit civilians only, Bosnian Serb forces fired seven missiles into Bihać on 3–4 November. One of these hit a school, wounding a woman and six children.[138] Bosnian Serb forces also continued to shell suburban Sarajevo, provoking a strange comment by French Lieutenant General Bertrand de Lapresle, commander of U.N. troops in the Balkans, saying that the Bosnian Serbs forces should be shown more "support" and "understanding" by the U.N. and the West.[139] The military strength levels of the Muslim, Bosnian Croat, and Bosnian Serb forces are shown in Tables 12.2 and 12.3.

But the Bosnian Serbs rallied, as rebel Serb forces from neighboring Croatia crossed the border to join in the fighting. The Serbs began to regain the upper hand in the first half of November, recaptured about 80 percent of the territory lost earlier to the Muslims, and by the end of the month, were encircling the town of Bihać and pushing toward its center.[140]

NATO ambassadors met on 24 November to consider the possibility of further aerial strikes against Bosnian Serbs but failed to reach an agreement.[141] Three days later, a morose U.S. Defense Secretary Perry declared the Serbs "unstoppable" and opined that further NATO air strikes could not make any difference.[142] A despondent Boutros-Ghali, conscious of his utter lack of credibilty with any of the parties to the conflict, announced at the end of the month that it may be time to pull U.N. "peacekeepers" out.[143] The following day, perhaps more to show contempt for the U.N. and NATO

TABLE 12.3   Armaments Possessed by the Combatants in Bosnia (November 1994)

	Tanks	Artillery Pieces	Armored Personnel Carriers	Aircraft*
Bosnian Serbs	330	800	400	37
Bosnian Muslims	40	a few*	30	0
Bosnian Croats	75	200	n/a	0

*1993.

SOURCES: McNeil-Lehrer News Hour, 4 November 1994; and International Institute for Strategic Studies, *The Military Balance 1993–1994* (London: Brassey's, October 1993), pp. 74–75.

than anything else, Bosnian Serbs crossed into Croatia and seized seven Ukrainian soldiers assigned to U.N. "peacekeeping" duty.[144] Taking stock of NATO's miserable performance in Bosnia, a *New York Times* editorial writer pronounced NATO dead, pointing to Anglo-French obstructionism as the source of NATO's seeming impotence.[145]

Meanwhile, the United States began taking the first steps toward belatedly arming the Croats and Muslims. In mid-October, officials announced that a U.S. military mission consisting of fifteen officers and headed by retired General John Galvin would soon arrive in Sarajevo to help integrate the joint Muslim-Croat forces and train them for combat.[146] The Pentagon drew up a plan to provide military training and as much as $5 billion in weapons to Bosnian government forces.[147] Meanwhile, CIA operatives were dispatched to Bosnia to begin training Bosnian government troops.[148] Americans were also said to be involved in the construction of a secret airfield in an isolated valley in central Bosnia, between Visoko and Kakanj; the airstrip was said to be designed to receive air shipments of weaponry.[149] Finally, on 29 November, U.S. Defense Secretary Perry received his Croatian counterpart and signed a "Memorandum of Cooperation on Defense and Military Relations" between the United States and Croatia. The text did not mention arms supplies but called for an expansion of defense contacts and bilateral cooperation, to include periodic meetings of officials, exchanges of delegations, and military training for Croatia forces, to be provided by the U.S. International Military Education and Training Program.[150]

As late as the first week of December, France and Britain held to their plan to pull their troops out of Bosnia.[151] Since British and French forces accounted for about a third of UNPROFOR's total strength in Bosnia (see Table 12.4), their withdrawal would have compelled the U.N. to terminate its mission in Bosnia. Russian Foreign Minister Kozyrev quickly announced that his country might maintain its military presence in Bosnia even after the termination of the UNPROFOR mandate—an announcement that had

TABLE 12.4   Composition of UNPROFOR Troops Stationed in Bosnia
(December 1994)

Country of Origin	Number of Troops
France	3,646
Britain	3,390
Pakistan	3,016
Netherlands	1,650
Malaysia	1,544
Turkey	1,462
Spain	1,259
Bangladesh	1,235
Sweden	1,051
Canada	863
Norway	663
Ukraine	581
Russia	506
Egypt	426
Denmark	286
Belgium	276
New Zealand	249
Jordan	100
United States*	5
Total	22,208

*Part of U.N. headquarters in Sarajevo; fifteen more are attached to relief agencies and other units.

SOURCE: *USA Today* (9–11 December 1994), p. 5A.

no visible effect on either the British or the French. But on 6 December Bosnian President Izetbegović announced that a number of Islamic countries had pledged to send "replacement" forces in the event that UNPROFOR troops were withdrawn.[152] Within a few days of this announcement, the French performed an about-face and not only announced their intention to keep their troops in Bosnia after all but even called for an expansion of the UNPROFOR mission.[153] In fact, the French have clearly taken a great interest in the conflict, taking part in meetings of NATO defense ministers in 1994 for the first time in twenty-eight years[154] and repeatedly demanding concessions for the Serbs.[155] For that matter, the Bosnian Serbs were not too pleased about talk of the removal of U.N. troops, since UNPROFOR had been allowing Bosnian Serb forces to skim off nearly 50 percent of all food brought in for "humanitarian" purposes and nearly 40 percent of all fuel.[156] As the *Christian Science Monitor* put it, "the Karadžić war machine is literally fueled by U.N. aid."[157]

The relationship between the Anglo-French use of the U.N. Protection Force as a supplier of the Bosnian Serbs and their insistence on maintaining the arms embargo against the Muslims, not to mention their earlier efforts to suffocate Slovenian and Croatian independence, was not generally understood in the United States. Yet this background sets the context for understanding the Anglo-French initiative of 3 December 1994, which scrapped the supposedly sacrosanct principle of the integrity of Bosnia's borders (even if compromised with formulas of cantonization and ethnic sectors) and offered Bosnian Serbs the prospect of international recognition of their political union with Serbia proper.[158]

CONCLUSION

Casualties have continued to rise. As of December 1994, between 200,000 and 400,000 people had died since June 1991 as a result of the war between Serbs and non-Serbs, and at least 2.7 million people had been reduced to refugees.[159] An estimated 20,000–50,000 Bosnian Muslim women had been raped by Bosnian Serb soldiers in a systematic campaign of humiliation and psychological terror.[160]

Moreover, the war is having an impact far greater than skeptics were prepared to believe back in 1991 or even in 1992. To begin with, the West has declined to defend either the Helsinki Accords, the Geneva Conventions, or the Genocide Convention of 1948,[161] suggesting that the West either considers it impossible to defend these accords or no longer values them. Second, the long-established principle of international law known as *uti possidetis* and mentioned earlier, under which new states that emerged from the fracturing of larger states were recognized within their preexisting administrative boundaries, however they might have been drawn, has now been scuttled in favor of the principle that aggression should be rewarded.[162] Third, given NATO's timidity and the eagerness of the West to place it under U.N. authority, questions have now been raised as to whether NATO has any practical military utility at all. Fourth, as David Rieff has suggested, with the obvious failure of the U.N. in Bosnia, it may be that only unilateral action by the great powers can effectively impose stability in unstable societies.[163] Finally, as many observers have pointed out, if, despite so much clamor and so many threats, neither the U.N. nor the West is able to defend either moral principles or political order, then it is not clear why either should be regarded with respect.

One of the problems that has afflicted much Western grappling with the question of Bosnia has to do with the notion of democracy. In the West, democracy is taken to be operative when fair elections and referenda are held and when duly elected officials take office and policies endorsed by the majority are put into effect. In the case of Bosnia, however, many Westerners have accepted the principle that an ethnic numerical minority, even if not inhabiting a compact area, need not feel bound by the will of even two-thirds of the citizens and may resort to force, including "ethnic cleansing," in order to resist and combat the will of the majority.[164] If those in the West have such a poor grasp of the concept of democracy—the very core of which is majority rule[165]—then no one need be surprised when fundamental social and political changes that subvert democracy *in the West* are not even recognized by most of those directly affected.

NOTES

This is a revised and expanded version of "The Bosnian War and the Diplomacy of Accommodation," which appeared originally in *Current History*, Vol. 93, No. 586 (November 1994). The author is grateful to the editors of *Current History* for permission to reuse this material here.

1. See Chapter 3 of this book.
2. See *Večernji list* (Zagreb) (30 August 1990), p. 4.
3. *Vjesnik* (Zagreb) (15 October 1990), p. 14.
4. *Popis stanovništva, domaćinstva, stanova i poljoprivrednih gazdinstava 1991. Prvi rezultati za republiku i po opštinama,* S.R. Bosna i Hercegovina, Statistički bilten, No. 219 (Sarajevo: Republički Zavod za Statistiku, May 1991), p. 11.
5. According to figures from the 1981 census, as reported in Ante Markotić, "Demografski aspekt promjena u nacionalnoj strukture stanovništva Bosne i Hercegovine," *Sveške,* Vol. 16–17 (1986), p. 299, and fold-out facing p. 302.
6. Some close observers even suggested that the sheer heterogeneity of Bosnia's population was a guarantee against interethnic war. For one example, see interview (February 1991) with Svetozar Stojanović, "Optimistic About Yugoslavia: Interview with Svetozar Stojanović," *East European Reporter*, Vol. 4, No. 4 (spring–summer 1991), p. 14.
7. James Gow, "One Year of War in Bosnia and Herzegovina," *RFE/RL Research Report* (4 June 1993), p. 6, summarizing Milan Radaković, "The European Community: The Possibility of Military Integration" [title as given in Gow], *Vojno delo*, Nos. 4–5 (July–October 1991), pp. 188–203.
8. Gow, "One Year of War," p. 6.
9. For further discussion of this point, see Sabrina Petra Ramet, "The Yugoslav Crisis and the West: Avoiding 'Vietnam' and Blundering into 'Abyssinia,' " *East European Politics and Societies*, Vol. 8, No. 1 (winter 1994).
10. See Chapter 3 of this book; and Branka Magaš, *The Destruction of Yugoslavia: Tracking Yugoslavia's Break-up, 1980–92* (London: Verso, 1993), pp. 261, 311, 333.
11. *New York Times* (26 September 1991), p. A3. The five successor states are Slovenia, Croatia, Bosnia-Herzegovina, Macedonia, and the Federal Republic of Yugoslavia (the last-mentioned consisting of Serbia and Montenegro).
12. Noel Malcolm, *Bosnia: A Short History* (New York: New York University Press, 1994), pp. 227–228.
13. Tanjug (12 November 1991), trans. in *Foreign Broadcast Information Service (FBIS), Daily Report* (Eastern Europe), 13 November 1991, p. 41.
14. *Vreme* (Belgrade) (30 September 1991), p. 5.

15. *New York Times* (28 December 1991), p. 4.

16. Robert J. Donia and John V.A. Fine, Jr., *Bosnia and Hercegovina: A Tradition Betrayed* (New York: Columbia University Press, 1994), p. 238.

17. See *Daily Telegraph* (London) (29 February 1992), p. 8.

18. *Der Standard* (Vienna) (17 March 1992), p. 2.

19. *New York Times* (6 November 1992), p. A4.

20. *Večernji list* (19 March 1992), p. 9, and (26 March 1992), p. 7.

21. See, for example, *Salzburger Nachrichten* (28 March 1992), p. 4; and *Die Presse* (Vienna) (28–29 March 1992), p. 1.

22. *Neue Zürcher Zeitung* (15 May 1992), p. 1.

23. Donia and Fine, *Bosnia and Hercegovina*, pp. 243–244; confirmed in *L'Orient–Le Jour* (Beirut, Lebanon) (9 May 1992), p. 1.

24. See *The Times* (London) (21 June 1993), p. 9.

25. Amy Lou King, "Bosnia-Herzegovina—Vance-Owen Agenda for a Peaceful Settlement: Did the U.N. Do Too Little, Too Late, to Support This Endeavor?" *Georgia Journal of International and Comparative Law*, Vol. 23, No. 2 (1993), p. 354.

26. David Rieff, "The Illusions of Peacekeeping," *World Policy Journal*, Vol. 11, No. 3 (fall 1994), p. 1.

27. Ibid., p. 2.

28. Quoted in ibid., p. 4.

29. *Financial Times* (6 July 1992), p. 12. For a more recent report on Herceg-Bosna, see *Nedjeljna Dalmacija* (Split) (22 June 1994), p. 7.

30. Kasim Trnka, "The Degradation of the Bosnian Peace Negotiations," in Rabia Ali and Lawrence Lifschultz, eds., *Why Bosnia? Writings on the Balkan War* (Stony Creek, Conn.: Pamphleteer's Press, 1993), pp. 203, 203n.

31. Donia and Fine, *Bosnia and Hercegovina*, p. 6, also pp. 261–263.

32. ITAR-Tass World Service (Moscow) (26 June 1992), trans. in *FBIS, Daily Report* (Central Eurasia), 1 July 1992, pp. 15–16.

33. E.g., letter to the editor from Flora Lewis, *Foreign Affairs*, Vol. 72, No. 3 (summer 1993), p. 221.

34. Rein Mullerson, "New Developments in the Former USSR and Yugoslavia," *Virginia Journal of International Law*, Vol. 33, No. 2 (winter 1993), p. 313.

35. *Borba* (Belgrade) (7 April 1993), p. 4.

36. *New York Times* (18 April 1993), p. 1; *Politika* (Belgrade) (19 April 1993), pp. 1–2; and *Washington Post* (27 April 1993), p. A1.

37. *Los Angeles Times* (10 May 1993), p. A18.

38. *Süddeutsche Zeitung* (Munich) (8–9 May 1993), p. 2.

39. *Glas Istre* (Pula) (4 June 1993), p. 6.

40. Germany subsequently protested her exclusion from this meeting.

41. *Vjesnik* (23 May 1993), p. 5.

42. *Danas* (Zagreb), new series (24 August 1993), p. 33.

43. *New York Times* (2 September 1993), pp. A1, A8.

44. These speculations are reported in *The Times* (12 May 1993), p. 1.

45. Quoted in Malcolm, *Bosnia: A Short History*, p. 244.

46. Gow, "One Year of War," p. 9.

47. *International Herald Tribune* (Tokyo ed.) (15–16 January 1994), p. 2.

48. Gow, "One Year of War," p. 2.

49. Ibid.

50. Western military experts reportedly agree with this assessment and have attributed the Serbian military victories in Bosnia directly to the Western arms embargo against Muslims and Croats. See *Frankfurter Allgemeine* (28 August 1993), p. 5.

51. *Japan Times* (4 December 1993), p. 1.

52. See, for example, *Kyodo* (Tokyo) (11 February 1994), trans. in *FBIS, Daily Report* (Eastern Europe), 14 February 1994, p. 34; and again, *The Globe and Mail* (Toronto) (1 June 1994), p. A7.

53. Tanjug (8 November 1993), in *FBIS, Daily Report* (Eastern Europe), 9 November 1993, p. 36; and *The Globe and Mail* (10 August 1994), p. 1.

54. Regarding British demands that the United States commit ground troops to Bosnia, see *Sunday Telegraph* (London) (9 May 1993), p. 2; editorial comment in *New York Times* (12 May 1993), p. A10; *Washington Post* (14 November 1993), p. A25; and *Japan Times* (2 February 1994), p. 5. Regarding French demands to the same effect, see *New York Times* (6 January 1994), p. A8; and *Japan Times* (27 January 1994), p. 5. Regarding British and French discussions about withdrawing their forces (and parallel declarations on the part of Canada and Spain), see *The Times* (28 December 1993), p. 8; and *Mainichi Daily News* (Tokyo) (23 January 1994), p. 1.

55. *International Herald Tribune* (Tokyo ed.) (21 October 1993), p. 2.

56. TVSH Television Network (10 February 1994), trans. in *FBIS, Daily Report* (Eastern Europe), 14 February 1994, p. 10.

57. *Philadelphia Inquirer* (15 May 1994), p. A17.

58. *The Times* (1 May 1993), p. 10.

59. Quoted in *Frankfurter Allgemeine* (2 June 1994), p. 2.

60. *Süddeutsche Zeitung* (21–22 August 1993), p. 7.

61. *The Times* (2 March 1993), p. 14.

62. *Kyodo* (1 October 1993), in *FBIS, Daily Report* (Eastern Europe), 5 October 1993, p. 42.

63. Radio Bosnia-Herzegovina (Sarajevo) (23 February 1994), trans. in *FBIS, Daily Report* (Eastern Europe), 23 February 1994, p. 34.

64. See, for example, *Boston Sunday Globe* (31 July 1994), p. 2; and *Die Welt* (Bonn) (4 November 1994), p. 4.

65. DDP/ADN (Berlin) (12 November 1994), trans. in *FBIS, Daily Report* (Eastern Europe), 14 November 1994, p. 37; and *Manchester Guardian Weekly* (18 December 1994), p. 3.

66. *Frankfurter Allgemeine* (18 November 1993), p. 9.

67. *International Herald Tribune* (Tokyo ed.) (9 November 1993), p. 2.

68. *International Herald Tribune* (15 November 1993), p. 5.

69. *Süddeutsche Zeitung* (15 October 1993), p. 8.

70. *Süddeutsche Zeitung* (30–31 October–1 November 1993), p. 8.

71. Tetsuya Sahara, "The Islamic World and the Bosnian Crisis," *Current History*, Vol. 93, No. 586 (November 1994), p. 387.

72. *Ljiljan* (Sarajevo–Ljubljana) (23 November 1994), p. 25.

73. Sahara, "The Islamic World," pp. 387–388. See also *Malaysian Digest* (Kuala Lumpur) (October 1992), p. 1.

74. *The Times* (2 June 1994), p. 12.

75. Sahara, "The Islamic World," p. 389.

76. *Süddeutsche Zeitung* (13–14 November 1993), p. 2.

77. *Oslobodjenje—European edition* (18 February 1994), trans. into English in *Oslobodjenje*, 1st English ed. (Sarajevo–Washington, D.C.) (April 1994), p. 15.

78. *Neue Zürcher Zeitung* (22–23 May 1994), p. 1; and *The European* (London) (17–23 June 1994), p. 1.

79. *Daily Telegraph* (London) (16 November 1994), p. 13.

80. Tanjug (28 October 1994), in *FBIS, Daily Report* (Eastern Europe), 31 October 1994, p. 44.

81. *Večernji list (24 June 1994), p. 7.*

82. *Seattle Times* (13 May 1994), p. A3; and *The Sunday Times* (London) (15 May 1994), p. 17.

83. As reported later in *Washington Post* (3 November 1994), p. A31.

84. *Boston Sunday Globe* (19 June 1994), p. 6; *Večernji list* (21–22 June 1994), p. 8; and *La Repubblica* (Rome) (1 July 1994), p. 13.

85. *Financial Times* (8 July 1994), p. 13.

86. On 21 July 1994, by attaching so many conditions as to render it null and void.

87. A senior Western military official in Bosnia, as quoted in *Independent on Sunday* (London) (31 July 1994), p. 11.

88. "Das Duell der Kriegsverbrecher," *Stern* (Hamburg) (11 August 1994), pp. 102–105.

89. *New York Times* (4 December 1994), p. 11.

90. "The Relentless Agony of Former Yugoslavia: 1. Naming War Criminals in Bosnia-Herzegovina," *Foreign Policy Bulletin* [The Documentary Record of United States Foreign Policy], Vol. 3, Nos. 4–5 (January–April 1993), p. 57.

91. "United Nations: Secretary-General's Report on Aspects of Establishing an International Tribunal for the Prosecution of Persons Responsible for Serious Violations of International Humanitarian Law Committed in the Territory of the Former Yugoslavia" [3 May 1993], *International Legal Materials*, Vol. 32, No. 4 (July 1993), p. 1165.

92. Quoted in "War Crimes and the Menace of Winter in Former Yugoslavia," *Foreign Policy Bulletin*, Vol. 3, No. 3 (November–December 1992), p. 49.

93. Quoted in "United Nations: Secretary-General's Report," p. 1164.

94. Dorothy Q. Thomas and Regan E. Ralph, "Rape in War: Challenging the Notion of Impunity," *SAIS Review*, Vol. 14, No. 1 (winter–spring 1994), p. 93.

95. Ibid., p. 85. For further discussion, see Alexandra Stiglmayer, ed., *Mass Rape: The War Against Women in Bosnia-Herzegovina*, including translations by Marion Faber (Lincoln: University of Nebraska Press, 1993).

96. See, for example, *Politika* (10 February 1993), p. 22, and (23 February 1993), p. 6; and *NIN* (Belgrade) (19 February 1993), pp. 26–28. Also interview with Dobrica Ćosić in *Adevarul* (Bucharest) (24 February 1993), pp. 1, 8, trans. in *FBIS, Daily Report* (Eastern Europe), 1 March 1993, p. 43.

97. *The Times* (2 June 1994), p. 12.

98. See, for example, Jeri Laber and Ivana Nizich, "The War Crimes Tribunal for the Former Yugoslavia: Problems and Prospects," *The Fletcher Forum of World Affairs*, Vol. 18, No. 2 (summer–fall 1994).

99. *Frankfurter Allgemeine* (15 October 1994), p. 1; *Slobodna Dalmacija* (Split) (20 October 1994), p. 10; *The European* (21–27 October 1994), p. 13; and *Philadelphia Inquirer* (9 November 1994), p. A4.

100. *Boston Sunday Globe* (20 November 1994), p. 10.

101. *Ekonomska politika* (Belgrade) (1 March 1993), p. 14.

102. See comments by Bosnian Vice President Ejup Ganić in *International Herald Tribune* (Tokyo ed.) (26–27 June 1993), p. 2; also *Ljiljan* (23 November 1994), p. 9.

103. For specifics, see Ramet, "The Yugoslav Crisis and the West."

104. Carl G. Jacobsen, "Yugoslavia's Wars of Secession and Succession: Media Manipulation, Historical Amnesia, and Subjective Morality," *Mediterranean Quarterly*, Vol. 5, No. 3 (summer 1994), p. 35.

105. Ibid., p. 39.

106. Ibid., p. 26. For a corrective, see Malcolm, *Bosnia: A Short History*.

107. See Peter Brock, "Dateline Yugoslavia: The Partisan Press," *Foreign Policy*, No. 93 (winter 1993–94).

108. Martin van Heuven, "Rehabilitating Serbia," *Foreign Policy*, No. 96 (fall 1994), p. 40.

109. For example, in August 1993, John Lampe, director of East European Studies at the Wilson Center, Washington, D.C., asserted that "it may be too late to reverse the majority of Serb gains in Bosnia." As reported in *Digest of the Helsinki Commission*, Vol. 16, No. 4 (August 1993), p. 3.

110. Karen Elliott House, "The New Masters of the Universe," *Wall Street Journal* (4 May 1993), p. A18.

111. Fareed Zakaria, "Bosnia Explodes 3 Myths," *New York Times, Weekly Review* (international ed.) (26 September 1993), p. 7.

112. Hodding Carter, "Punishing Serbia," *Foreign Policy*, No. 96 (fall 1994), p. 55.

113. *New York Times* (12 August 1994), p. A3.

114. *Süddeutsche Zeitung* (12–13 November 1994), p. 1. Regarding continued U.S. efforts to lift the arms embargo, see *Ljiljan* (2 November 1994), p. 9; and *Evropske novosti* (Belgrade–Frankfurt) (19 November 1994), p. 9.

115. Regarding Serbia's ability to obtain Russian weapons from what had been the GDR, see *Der Spiegel* (Hamburg) (14 November 1994), pp. 65, 68, 70.

116. See Ibid., p. 154.

117. *The Sun* (Baltimore) (6 November 1994), pp. 1A, 11A.

118. Ibid., p. 1A.

119. *Neue Zürcher Zeitung* (23 August 1994), p. 2.

120. See comments by Brigadier General Mustafa Hajrulahović of the Bosnian General Staff in *Daily Telegraph* (20 August 1994), p. 13.

121. *New York Times* (19 August 1994), p. A2.

122. See, for example, Karadžić's indication, on 18 October 1993, that his goal was to adjoin Serb-conquered areas in Bosnia-Herzegovina to a "Greater Serbia." *Süddeutsche Zeitung* (19 October 1993), p. 6.

123. *Neue Zürcher Zeitung* (7 September 1994), p. 1.

124. These figures are reported in *Boston Sunday Globe* (18 September 1994), p. 15. See also *New York Times* (5 September 1994), p. 5; and *The Globe and Mail* (20 September 1994), p. A8. Regarding the use of police to expel non-Serbs, see AFP (Paris) (28 October 1994), in *FBIS, Daily Report* (Eastern Europe), 1 November 1994, p. 33.

125. "War Crimes in Bosnia-Hercegovina: U.N. Cease-Fire Won't Help Banja Luka," *Human Rights Watch Helsinki*, Vol. 6, No. 8 (June 1994), pp. 1–3, 13–21, 30–31.

126. *New York Times* (9 September 1994), p. A1; *Boston Sunday Globe* (25 September 1994), p. 23; *Neue Zürcher Zeitung* (16 September 1994), p. 2; *Daily Telegraph* (17 September 1994), p. 14; and *Welt am Sonntag* (25 September 1994), p. 6.

127. *New York Times* (9 September 1994), p. A7; and *Globus* (Zagreb) (23 September 1994), pp. 2–3.

128. The 100 square kilometer estimate comes from *The Globe and Mail* (28 October 1994), p. A7; the 150 square kilometer estimate comes from *Süddeutsche Zeitung* (29–30 October 1994), p. 1; other facts from *New York Times* (28 October 1994), p. A1.

129. *Bosna Press* (Frankfurt), in Croatian (13–20 October 1994), p. 3; and *The Globe and Mail* (8 October 1994), p. A12.

130. *The Globe and Mail* (29 September 1994), p. A8.

131. *New York Times* (29 September 1994), p. A4.

132. *Ljiljan* (23 November 1994), p. 5. Regarding demands by several commentators that NATO forces bomb the Bosnian Serb capital of Pale, see *Ljiljan* (30 November 1994), p. 9.

133. Quoted in *Sunday Telegraph* (25 September 1994), p. 31.

134. See details in *Neue Zürcher Zeitung* (20 October 1994), p. 2.

135. *The Times* (26 October 1994), p. 15.

136. *Neue Zürcher Zeitung* (27 July 1994), pp. 1, 3; and *Ljiljan* (27 July 1994), p. 16.

137. *Neue Zürcher Zeitung* (2 November 1994), p. 2; *Philadelphia Inquirer* (4 November 1994), p. A2; and *The European* (4–10 November 1994), p. 2.

138. *Washington Post* (5 November 1994), p. A17.

139. U.S. Defense Secretary William J. Perry rebutted de Lapresle's comments, declaring, "I don't think myself that understanding is the appropriate response to aggressive military actions." Both quoted in *Philadelphia Inquirer* (2 November 1994), p. A4.

140. AFP (Paris) (14 November 1994), trans. in *FBIS, Daily Report* (Eastern Europe), 14 November 1994, p. 36; *Philadelphia Inquirer* (15 November 1994), p. A4, (16 November 1994), p. A8, and (18 November 1994), p. A32; *La Stampa* (Torino), 22 November 1994, pp. 1, 9; *La Repubblica* (22 November 1994), pp. 1, 14–15; *Nedjeljna Dalmacija* (25 November 1994), pp. 15–16; and *Chicago Tribune* (25 November 1994), p. 3.

141. *Pittsburgh Tribune-Review* (25 November 1994), p. A1.

142. *Los Angeles Times* (28 November 1994), p. A1.

143. *The Globe and Mail* (1 December 1994), p. A1.

144. *Seattle Post-Intelligencer* (2 December 1994), p. A2.

145. *New York Times* (28 November 1994), p. A15.

146. *New York Times* (21 October 1994), p. A4.

147. *Daily Telegraph* (London) (19 November 1994), p. 14.

148. *The European* (18–24 November 1994), p. 1; confirmed in *The European* (25 November–1 December 1994), p. 4.

149. *The European* (18–24 November 1994), p. 1.

150. From the authentic English text, courtesy of the Embassy of the Republic of Croatia.

151. *The European* (2–8 December 1994), p. 1.

152. *RFE/RL Daily Report* (7 December 1994).

153. *New York Times* (13 December 1994), p. A1.

154. *Neue Zürcher Zeitung* (1 October 1994), p. 1.

155. *Neue Zürcher Zeitung* (1 December 1994), p. 5.

156. *Christian Science Monitor* (20 December 1994), p. 18.

157. Ibid.

158. *Sunday Telegraph* (London) (4 December 1994), p. 2.

159. The estimate of the number of refugees is provided by the Stockholm International Peace Research Institute for autumn 1992, as reported in *SIPRI Yearbook 1993: World Armaments and Disarmament* (Stockholm, 1993), p. 5.

160. Slavenka Drakulić, "Women Hide Behind a Wall of Silence," in Ali and Lifschultz, *Why Bosnia?*, p. 118. The Sarajevo State Commission for the Investigation of War Crimes estimated that some 50,000 Muslim women had been raped by Serbs between April 1992 and October 1992 alone.

161. Regarding the Convention on the Prevention and Punishment of the Crime of Genocide, adopted by the U.N. General Assembly on 9 December 1948, see John Webb, "Genocide Treaty, Ethnic Cleansing, Substantive and Procedural Hurdles in the Application of the Genocide Convention to Alleged Crimes in the Former Yugoslavia," *Georgia Journal of International and Comparative Law*, Vol. 23, No. 2 (1993).

162. See Mullerson, "New Developments," pp. 313–315, 320–322; and Rein Mullerson, "The Continuity and Succession of States, by Reference to the Former USSR and Yugoslavia," *International and Comparative Law Quarterly*, Vol. 42, Pt. 3 (July 1993).

163. Rieff, "Illusions," p. 18.

164. See, for example, Robert M. Hayden's mockery of majority rule as a so-called superior right in his article, "The Constitution of the Federation of Bosnia and Herzegovina: An Imaginary Constitution for an Illusory 'Federation,' " *Balkan Forum*, Vol. 2, No. 3 (September 1994), p. 79.

165. Norberto Bobbio, *The Future of Democracy*, trans. from Italian by Roger Griffin (Cambridge: Polity Press, 1987), p. 63.

———————————— ◆ ————————————

CHAPTER THIRTEEN

Repercussions of the War in Religion, Gender Relations, and Culture

The three rivers of the ancient world of the dead—the Acheron, the Phlegethon, and the Cocytus—today belong to the underworlds of Islam, Judaism, and Christianity; their flow divides the three hells—Gehenna, Hades, and the icy hell of the Mohammedans—beneath the one-time Khazar lands. And there, at the junction of these three borders, are confronted the three worlds of the dead: Satan's fiery state, with the nine circles of the Christian Hades, with Lucifer's throne, and with the flags of the Prince of Darkness; the Moslem underworld, with the kingdom of icy torment; and Gebhurah's territory, to the left of the Temple, where the Hebrew gods of evil, greed, and hunger sit, in Gehenna, under Asmodeus' rule. . . . In the Jewish hell, in the state of Belial, the angel of darkness and sin, it is not Jews who burn, as you think. Those like yourself, all Arabs or Christians, burn there. Similarly, there are no Christians in the Christian hell—those who reach the fires are Mohammedans or of David's faith, whereas in Iblis' Moslem torture chamber they are all Christians and Jews, not a single Turk or Arab.

Milorad Pavić
Dictionary of the Khazars, 1988

SERBIAN NOVELIST MILORAD PAVIĆ probably was not thinking about a future Yugoslav ethnic war when he wrote the lines quoted above, but what he understood all too clearly is that religion has often functioned historically as a mechanism for consigning enemies of the ethnoconfessional group to hell—whether a supernatural hell or a natural-secular hell, or both. He understood, too, that religion has the capacity to sacralize violence, deception, land grabs, even genocide.[1]

In fact, not only have religious organizations contributed to preparing the ground for war but so too has the cultural sector. By the same virtue, the war has had repercussions for the religious sphere, as well as for gender relations and the cultural sector. This chapter will examine these sectors and show how the war has affected them, noting, where appropriate, how prominent figures in these sectors have responded to the tide of hate that has overcome a country that once boasted of its "brotherhood and unity."

IN THE NAME OF GOD

The Serbian Orthodox Church played a significant role in weaving the tapestry of hate that eventually covered all of Serbia. The Church's strong response to the Albanian riots of 1981 (discussed in Chapter 8) and one-sided manipulation of the distorted memories of World War II[2] only foreshadowed the explicit irredentism that, dressed up as cultural history, had crept into the pages of the patriarchal organ, *Pravoslavlje*, by 1991.[3]

As interethnic relations in Yugoslavia soured, interconfessional relations did likewise. In early 1990, Serbs scrawled anti-Muslim graffiti (such as "Death to Muslims!") on Islamic buildings.[4] Catholic–Orthodox dialogue broke down, even at the highest levels, while anti-Catholic propaganda continued unabated in Orthodox Serbia. The publication of Vladimir Dedijer's anti-Catholic diatribe, *Vatikan i Jasenovac*,[5]set the tone for a proliferation of theories about alleged Vatican conspiracies, in league with Croats and Germans, directed against the always blameless Serbs.

While the Serbs prepared for war, in the period 1990–1991, the Croats were focused on their own internal programs, as the election of the first noncommunist government in spring 1990 led immediately to a need to draft new legislation across a wide array of policy spheres. The Catholic Church exerted pressure on the government to strike from the constitution a provision prohibiting the formation of associations based on religious affiliation.[6] The Catholic Church also pushed for the reintroduction of Catholic religious instruction into state schools, in the face of resistance from non-Catholic parents. But Catholic religion was quickly becoming a badge of Croatian national identity, hence the restoration of religious instruction took on some of the character of a nationalist cause.

During the final year before the breakup of Yugoslavia, interconfessional relations soured monumentally across the country, as already mentioned. In Croatia, Orthodox (Serb) bystanders pelted buses carrying Catholic (Croatian) pilgrims with stones. While the Serbian Orthodox Church engaged in a campaign to defame the Catholic Church's role in World War II, the Catholic weekly newspaper *Glas koncila* started a series in March 1990, based on newly available archival material, revealing the Serbian Orthodox Church's collaboration with the Nazi-installed Nedić regime in Belgrade during that same war.[7] As the country veered toward the brink, the hierarchy of the Serbian Orthodox Church in Croatia, meeting in Pakrac, issued a statement encouraging Serbs "to secure for themselves the right to life on their age-old hearths in Croatia by [setting up] armed sentinels [and] barricades."[8] The Serbian Orthodox patriarchate in Belgrade endorsed this statement and in March 1992 offered that "in this new independent state of Croatia, as in the earlier one, there is no life for Orthodox Serbs."[9] The previous month in Banja Luka, in an ominous anticipation of impending events, unknown persons had vandalized a mosque and an Islamic burial chamber.[10]

Even when, in response to the expansion of the war into Bosnia, the Synod of Bishops of the Serbian Orthodox Church began demanding that Milošević resign, it nonetheless continued to purvey a self-righteously sketched portrait of Serbia as the great victim of history.[11] When, after Pavle succeeded German as patriarch of the Serbian Church, ecumenical contacts between the Orthodox and Catholic Churches resumed, it was effectively too late for the Churches to dampen the hatreds stirred up most especially from 1987 on. Nor was Pavle himself able to rise above the situation: on meeting with Roman Catholic Franjo Cardinal Kuharić and Islamic Reis-ul-ulema Jakub Selimoški in November 1992, he made a point of telling his Islamic counterpart that Bosnian Serb massacres and expulsions of the Muslims from their lands were "justified" because, as he put it, Serbs were themselves endangered in Bosnia-Herzegovina.[12]

Serbian polemicists and publicists have repeatedly construed the war as religious in character, in an effort to use confessional difference to concentrate Serbian prejudice and hatred. Catholic prelates, however, have repeatedly denied that the conflict can legitimately be construed as a "religious war."[13] In fact, the war was ignited by rising tempers of ethnic hatreds and did not at first have the character of a "religious" war, but as time has passed, this war has taken on ever more religious characteristics. Imams and Christian clergy have followed the troops into battle, blessing them and praying for their success in battle. (Some forty-eight imams had died in battle by September 1994, according to official figures of the Islamic community.[14]) Catholic religious instruction was introduced in Croatia in 1991[15] — a policy move that provoked complaints that such instruction was being used to Catholicize Serb children of Orthodox faith.[16] Later, after the war spread to Bosnia, Islamic religious instruction was introduced in schools run by the Bosnian government.[17] In areas controlled by the Bosnian Serbs, the Serbian Orthodox Church was allowed likewise to introduce religious instruction into the secular schools.[18] While such religious instruction was at least formally nonobligatory in Croatia, for example,[19] the Serbian Orthodox Church made a big push in 1992 and again in 1994 to have *mandatory* Orthodox religious instruction introduced in state schools in the Federal Republic of Yugoslavia, only to be rebuffed by the Federal Assembly.[20]

As religion became politicized, imams were found telling Bosnian Muslims, by autumn 1994, that they should try to avoid marrying non-

Muslims, and there were increasing incentives to Muslim women to cover their heads in public. In Mostar, instruction in Arabic was introduced in Muslim-run schools, in token of the Bosnian Muslims' growing tendency to look East for friends, rather than West.[21] Ironically, by driving more conservative rural Muslims into the cities, Bosnian Serbs have given the towns a more conservative cast, underpinning and reinforcing Islamic consciousness in the cities.[22]

Inexorably, waxing Serb hatred of Catholics and Muslims came to be expressed in efforts to extirpate all traces of multiconfessionality in areas occupied by Bosnian Serb forces. By June 1994, Bosnian Serbs had succeeded in destroying 45 percent of Catholic churches in the Vrhbosanska-Sarajevo Archbishopric, 50 percent of Catholic churches in the Bishopric of Banja Luka, and more than forty Catholic churches and church edifices in the Bishopric of Mostar; in addition, they caused serious damage to an additional 30 percent of Catholic churches in Vrhbosanska and an additional 45 percent in Banja Luka.[23] In Serb-occupied areas of Croatia, Serb forces destroyed an additional 115 Catholic parish churches.[24] That this destruction was premeditated and calculated is evident both from subsequent Serb claims, in many regions, that no non-Serbs had ever lived in the region and that no non-Orthodox church or mosque had ever existed there and from the fact that many of these edifices were dynamited after the Serbs had taken control of the towns in question. In Serb-held Banja Luka, for example, which at one time boasted a large number of mosques, Bosnian Serb authorities dynamited two mosques of considerable aesthetic and historical importance in May 1993—the ornate Ferhad Pasha mosque (built in 1583) and the Arnaudija mosque (built in 1587)[25]—and destroyed the last three remaining mosques in the town in September 1993.[26] By August 1994, Bosnian Serb forces had destroyed or ruined some 650 mosques across Bosnia-Herzegovina.[27] In addition, Catholics (all of Slovenian, Croatian, or Hungarian extraction) living in the Archbishopric of Belgrade have repeatedly been harassed by local Serbs since about 1989, and between 1990 and 1993 the number of Catholics remaining there dropped from 34,000 to fewer than 9,000.[28]

To some extent Croatian forces have replied in kind —in the process providing grist for Serbian propaganda.[29] But in Bosnian government-controlled Sarajevo, by contrast, "Serb Orthodox churches stand untouched (unlike mosques burned down in Serbian-captured territory)."[30] Far from being the hotbed of Islamic fundamentalism painted by Serbian propaganda, thus, Sarajevo has continued to display a unique degree of religious tolerance. In one token of this, a new Catholic school center opened in Sarajevo in autumn 1994.[31]

Not surprisingly in these circumstances, religious figures assumed an unusual prominence in their respective societies. For example, a poll conducted by the weekly newspaper *Globus* in September 1994 found that the most respected person in Croatia was Franjo Cardinal Kuharić, with a 30.7 percent rating—well ahead of second-place Franjo Tudjman (21.6 percent) and third-place Nikica Valentić (the prime minister, 14.6 percent), let alone opposition politician Dražen Budiša (with a 2.0 percent rating).[32] Similarly, when asked whom they hated, 68.4 percent of Croats named Patriarch Pavle (but 96.1 percent also named Serbian President Milošević).[33]

THE POLITICS OF SERBIAN ORTHODOXY

When socialist Yugoslavia disintegrated, Serbian Orthodox hierarchs were quick to sketch out programs for a restoration of the privileges they had enjoyed in the interwar Kingdom of Yugoslavia (1918–1941). Despite some setbacks, such as the government's refusal to introduce obligatory religious education in the schools and, for that matter, the federal government's refusal to establish Christmas, Easter, and St. Vitus' Day as state holidays,[34] the Orthodox Church has, in fact, prospered under Milošević. Quite apart from the revival of its publishing activity, the Church also obtained permission to restore the historic Gradac monastery in central Serbia and was able to continue construction of the Church of St. Sava (resumed only in 1984, after having been suspended forty-three years earlier). Beyond that, the Serbian Orthodox Church has embarked on an ambitious church construction program, erecting monasteries on the territory of the Bosanska Srpska Republic[35] and giving especial stress to the architectural "reconquest" of Kosovo. Thus, as the Slovenian daily newspaper *Delo* reported in 1993, "there is almost not a village in Kosovo where some church facility (church, monastery, parish) is not being built."[36] When, however, the Church took possession of a hitherto state cultural facility in Priština, the Presidency of the Kosovo Democratic Alliance issued a statement of protest.[37] In another equally hazardous move, the Serbian Orthodox patriarchate continued to press its claims to ecclesiastical jurisdiction in Macedonia,[38] even after the Republic of Macedonia had declared its independence. In a sharply worded statement issued on 17 December 1992, Metropolitan Jovan of Zagreb-Ljubljana reiterated the Serbian Church's traditional position that it retained legitimate "title" to all ecclesiastical structures in Macedonia but added a new point by claiming the right of the Serbian Church to organize parallel structures in Macedonia to cater to the small Serbian minority in that republic. "We are obliged to protect our believers and the numerous Serbian shrines in that republic," Metropolitan Jovan said,[39] without specifying against what threat such protection was thought to be necessary.

Within rump Croatia, Serbian Orthodox clerics have sounded the alarm, claiming that because of the drastic impoverishment of their Church there was a growing danger that the Croatian state might simply "nationalize"

Serbian Orthodox churches and monasteries on Croatian territory.[40] This, in turn, contributed to an appeal from the Holy Synod to its believers to rally to the Church and to raise funds for its use, not just in Croatia but throughout former Yugoslavia.[41]

The Serbian Orthodox Church would like very much to play a greater role in Serbian society, but a 1994 survey found that only 48 percent of women and 37 percent of men in Serbia consider themselves religious. Among supporters of Milošević's ruling Serbian Socialist Party, only 42 percent are believers.[42] This is not a sufficiently broad base upon which to establish some of the policies and programs that the Church would like to see.

Nonetheless, the Church has continued, to build a presence through its political engagement, receiving foreign visitors from Greek Prime Minister Konstantin Mitsotakis,[43] to Vladimir Zhirinovsky, leader of the radical-right Liberal Democratic Party of Russia,[44] passing judgment in April 1993 on the Vance-Owen Plan,[45] and speaking out against Milošević when he announced the imposition of a blockade against the Bosnian Serbs in August 1994.[46] By contrast with the Roman pontiff, who aspired to address himself to all nations, including all three parties to the Yugoslav conflict, Patriarch Pavle has not once presumed to look beyond his Serbian flock. This attitude provoked the Bosnian newspaper *Oslobodjenje* to complain:

> Patriarch Pavle last year came to Pale to bless the Serbian barbarians and devout criminals. He did not come to Sarajevo, where even today there are five times as many Serbs as there are in Pale. Never once did he condemn the monstrous Serbian crimes committed against the Bosnian Muslims. He made no mention of the destruction of their oldest and most beautiful mosques, he remained mute about the wiping out of all traces of Islamic culture and civilization in these areas.[47]

On the contrary, in an interview with *Evropske novosti* in December 1994, Patriarch Pavle waxed rapturous about those individuals who had allegedly earned for Serbs the epithet "heavenly Serbia."[48]

A PAPAL VISIT

From the very beginning of the conflict, Pope John Paul II has spoken out—calling for tolerance, peace, and a setting aside of nationalist passions. Although the Vatican was one of the first countries to accord diplomatic recognition to the newly independent republics of Slovenia and Croatia, Pope John Paul II has directed his pastoral concern to all peoples of Serbia, Croatia, and Bosnia alike. Thus when in 1994 the Pope began to plan his "pilgrimage for peace" to the region, he requested permission from Serbian authorities to include Belgrade in his itinerary and indicated an especial interest in having talks with Serbian Patriarch Pavle.[49] Pavle, however, deemed a papal visit "inopportune"[50] and Belgrade refused permission.[51]

Despite this setback, the pontiff proceeded with plans to visit the capitals of the two other combatants, Sarajevo and Zagreb. Both Bosnian President Izetbegovic and Croatian President Tudjman expressed considerable enthusiasm at the prospect of a papal visit, the former seeing in it the potential for awakening the international community's slumbering conscience.

Then the problems began. The Bosnian Serbs refused to guaranteee the Pope's security and even made vague threats, implying that they were prepared to blame the Muslims for any mishap.[52] With the visit to Sarajevo scheduled for 10 September, the Pope held fast to his plans until Yasushi Akashi, evidently prodded by Britain and France, sent the Pope a letter on 7 September indicating that the U.N. could not guarantee the pontiff's security and advising that he cancel his projected visit.[53] This letter culminated several weeks of pressures by U.N. officials on the Pope to cancel his visit[54] and now, at the last minute, Pope John Paul II bowed to what was starting to seem like fate and canceled his visit. The cancelation evoked despondency in Sarajevo among both Catholics and Muslims.

But plans proceeded for a papal visit to Zagreb, scheduled for 10–11 September, a visit that culminated Vatican efforts over more than twenty years to obtain permission for a trip to Croatia.[55] As with his earlier visits to Poland, Pope John Paul's visit to Croatia was transparently political in nature. On his arrival in Zagreb, the Pope praised the late Alojzije Cardinal Stepinac, whom Serbs have sought to portray as a Nazi collaborator, and spoke of the tragedy inflicted on the Croatian towns of Vukovar, Dubrovnik, and Zadar by besieging Serbian forces. He also talked of Sarajevo, calling it "a martyred town, which I as a pilgrim of peace and hope wanted fervently to visit."[56] The next day, more than a million people gathered to hear the Pope speak. Setting himself squarely against Croatian President Tudjman's efforts to harness Catholicism as an element in official nationalism, the Pope warned (in fluent Croatian) about "the risk of idolizing a nation, a race, [or] a party and justifying in their name hatred, discrimination, and violence."[57] Urging his listeners to put aside notions of vengeance and hatred, he called on Croatian Catholics to "become apostles of [a] new concord between peoples."[58] While condemning the "inhuman practice of so-called ethnic cleansing," he offered a "kiss of peace" to leaders of the Serbian Orthodox Church.[59]

Among Muslims there was praise for the Pope, both for his criticism of some of Tudjman's policies in Bosnia-Herzegovina and for his commitment to end the suffering of the peoples of all three republics.[60] The Pope's visit, if anything, confirmed the confidence expressed by Sefko Omerbašić, president of the Mesihat (council of Islamic elders) for Croatia and Slovenia, in

February 1993, when, acknowledging the Catholic Church's role in providing humanitarian assistance to all victims of Serbian aggression, he told *Delo*, "I am convinced that with this war the Catholic Church has gained lasting [esteem], which we Muslims will know how to foster and develop. That quality is actually also the biggest guarantee that it will be possible to resolve the Croatian–Muslim dispute considerably more easily than it appears at this moment."[61]

Two months after his visit, Pope John Paul elevated thirty bishops to the College of Cardinals, among them, Vinko Puljić, the archbishop of Sarajevo. The forty-nine-year-old Puljić became the youngest member of the College of Cardinals.[62] The Pope took advantage of Puljić's elevation to draw attention once again to the suffering in Bosnia and to bemoan the elusiveness of peace in the region.

THE NEW PATRIARCHY

In early 1990, members of the lesbian and gay community in Belgrade formed a lesbian and gay lobby, Arkadia, which began holding public discussions and writing articles for the press. In September 1990, Arkadia issued an open letter, responding to one of the leaders of the Serbian Renaissance Party who had urged Serbian women to concentrate their energies on "reproduc[ing] the greater Serbian nation."[63] The letter showed a keen awareness of the dangerous waters into which the Serbian ship of state was sailing: "One supposes," the letter stated, "that young Serbian foetuses will be immediately baptised, conditioned to hate, and lead the war against the many Enemies of the Serbian nation."[64]

Two months later, on the eve of Serbian national elections, a group of Belgrade women, among them žarana Papić and Lina Vušković, formed a Women's Party. The party favored a nonauthoritarian system based on a mixed economy, with free medical care and emphasis on education and environmental protection. They campaigned against Milošević in the December elections and urged voters to avoid candidates who appealed to nationalist or chauvinist sentiments. By January 1991 the party had 500 members, but they labored under the difficulty that the regime had already succeeded in stigmatizing the appellation "feminist," with the result that they felt constrained to define themselves more elliptically.[65] In the event, they had little, if any, impact on the outcome of the elections, and the Serbian parliament elected in December 1990 consisted of only 1.6 percent women, the lowest representation of women in any European parliament. In response to this low representation, Serbian feminist activists formed an opposition "Women's Parliament" on 8 March 1991 (8 March being the traditional day designated for honoring women and women's equality in many European countries). They also took up the pacifist banner and on 9

October 1991 protested on the streets of Belgrade against the war against Croatia.

In August 1990, Belgrade's feminists had appealed for the "demilitarization" of Yugoslavia, and in December of that year they issued a protest against new textbooks that emphasized "nationalist, patriarchal, and sexist values."[66] They subsequently protested against discrimination against lesbians and gay men, against sexist behavior on the part of Serbian MPs, and against sexist language in Serbia's independent media.

A small group of activists called Women in Black has operated independently of the Women's Party and the Arkadia Lobby but for similar goals. They have placed at the center of their critique of the Belgrade regime the patriarchal character of nationalism and war, protesting, *inter alia,* against the killing of civilians, against "ethnic cleansing," and against compulsory mobilization.[67]

But in Serbia, as in Croatia, feminists found it hard to function, and by 1993 the (Serbian) Women's Party was dead. Meanwhile, in Croatia, the small feminist community was fragmented, as several members left for foreign soil (the United States, France, or elsewhere) and as those who remained in Croatia began to attack both each other and those who had left.[68] In essence, the war has so transformed politics in both Serbia and Croatia that antifeminist sentiments have been inflamed and feminists demonized— a result that has only been accentuated by feminists' embrace of pacifism as an integral element in their programs. The reasons for this are not at all specific to South Slav societies but are characteristic of all human societies. For one thing, as Jean Howard has noted, "in times of general social dislocation"—such as is associated with a war—"fears about change are often displaced onto women."[69] Or, to put it differently, when men feel threatened, they take it out on "their" women. Second, war feeds on nationalism and, as I have noted elsewhere, "glorifying the nation always ends up meaning that women's interests should be subordinated to men's and that women should accept, as their principal purpose in life, the 'duty' to bear children" for the nation.[70] Third, to those leading the struggle, the waging of war usually seems to require a simplification of the agenda and often a postponement of programs that might otherwise enjoy higher priority in times of peace. This desire for "simplification" leads directly to the marginalization of any dialogue directed toward women's equality and to calls for focusing all national energies on war and survival. Interestingly enough, by construing the nation as "victim"—something Serbia, Croatia, and Bosnia have all done, with varying degrees of legitimacy—regimes and their media lose sight of the fact that women are themselves victimized by patriarchal society. A very clear example of this comes from Croatia, where in May 1992 a law was drafted that exempted violence within the family from prosecution.[71] Indeed, among the five Yugoslav successor states, only Slovenia recognizes that a woman might be raped by her husband.[72]

In spite of the intensification of chauvinist rhetoric and the creation of a climate hostile to feminism, feminist groups have continued to be active. Some women's groups, such as Women of Bosnia-Herzegovina and Pearl, have taken an interest specifically in Muslim women refugees, while others, such as Bulwark of Love and Cherry Tree, have devoted themselves to working with Croatian women. But there have also been a number of women's groups in the region that have worked for women's rights without regard for the nationality of the women, such as the Autonomous Women's House in Zagreb, the Center for Women Victims of the War, and the Women's Lobby in Belgrade.[73] In Belgrade, a phone-in organization called SOS Telephone for Women and Children Victims of Violence has been active since 1991 and provided assistance to some 770 persons in the first three years of its existence.[74] Similar organizations have been operating in Kraljevo (since June 1990) and Kruševac (since November 1993).[75]

Then there is rape as a weapon of war. I have already noted (in Chapter 6) research by Nancy Chodorow that interpreted machismo as a violent reaction against maternal authority, underpinned by fear of women. Robert Stoller has confirmed this finding, tracing male aggression against women, and indeed all behavior that degrades women, including, for example, coprolalia (the indulgence in dirty language for the sake of sexual titillation), to the male's uncertainty about his own "manliness."[76] Deprived of close contact with a male role model in early childhood and exposed to exaggerated notions of what "manliness" entails, men in macho societies could be expected, if Stoller's ideas are any guide, to be more apt than men in less macho societies to resort to rape as a weapon of warfare.

Be that as it may, Bosnian Serbs forces have not only set up "rape camps," in which systematic and repeated rape of women has been organized,[77] but have also disseminated reports about the alleged rape of Serbian women by Muslims and about supposed "Muslim-Croatian brothels" to which captured Serbian women were said to be confined.[78] What is so staggering about all of these accounts, both those that have been and those that cannot be documented (for whatever reason), is that the act of rape, an act of violence and power by the male against the female, is given a specifically *national* content: it is the rape of a *Muslim* woman by a *Serbian* man, or of a *Serbian* woman by a *Muslim* man. Rape is thus used to act out, in symbolic terms, the subjection of one nation by another, transmuted to the level of the subjection of one sex by another. At the same time, rape affirms the subordination of gender issues (such as respect for the equality of the other sex) to nationalist concerns.[79]

Even in Slovenia, which escaped with comparatively less damage from the brief hostilities of June–July 1991, the subordination of gender issues to nationalist concerns makes itself manifest. Take, for example, the Slovenian Alliance, organized by Aleš Žužek in early 1993. Modeling itself on the French National Front of the 1970s, this radical-right party quickly drew up a program, placing "ethnic purity" at the center of its concerns. But how to assure "ethnic purity"? The Slovenian Alliance proposed to expel all residents not of Slovene descent and offered the following guidelines to determine who is and is not a *bona fide* Slovene:

> A mixed marriage is considered to be Slovene only in the case of a marriage between a Slovene man and a non-Slovene woman, and the descendants of that marriage are also considered to be Slovene. Such families are exempt from being [expelled]. A marriage between a non-Slovene man and a Slovene woman is considered to be a non-Slovene marriage, the descendants of such a marriage are non-Slovenes, and those families must also be returned to the homeland of the non-Slovene spouse.[80]

Thus, although sociological studies of interethnic marriage have shown that children of such marriages are far more apt to identify with the national identity of the mother,[81] Žužek's party prefers to give priority to the nationality of the father as determinative of the nationality of the offspring.

In Communist times, women filled 22 percent of elective posts in Slovenia (in 1986). But after the multiparty elections of 1990, only 10 percent of those elected to the Slovenian Assembly were women.[82] Moreover, as Meznarić and Ule comment, "As a result of financial difficulties and the media's loss of interest in independent women's movements [in Slovenia] since the mid-1980s, women's initiatives in almost all fields lack support and have difficulty attracting public recognition."[83]

It should be clear, thus, that it is not just the war that is reviving patriarchy in the Balkans. Otherwise, how is one to explain the fact that all across Eastern Europe people have witnessed a deepening of patriarchal values and forms, a shelving of women's issues and women's concerns, and a far-reaching removal of women from positions of prominence? Obviously, other factors are at work. Among these one might note the profound reaction against everything associated with socialism (hence, all talk of women's equality) that set in as soon as people realized that communism was finished. Perhaps even more important here has been the dedication with which the Christian Churches, now freed of the constraints imposed by the Communist parties, have set about dismantling some of the prerogatives enjoyed by women (most especially access to abortion) and affirming the "naturalness" of what is rather self-servingly called the traditional role of women. Yet another factor that has contributed to this result is that men already enjoyed an advantaged position under socialism, and with the relaxation of the strictures imposed by socialism and the expansion of possibilities for free enterprise, men have been better situated than women and

have thus quickly widened the gap in their incomes. Finally, given the economic duress under which not just the Yugoslav successor states but almost
all of the East European states have labored, all too many women have
been driven to take jobs as prostitutes and topless dancers, taking "advantage" of the new positions opened up by "free enterprise." This phenomenon has been especially striking in Serbia,[84] Macedonia,[85] and Albania.[86]

The problem, as Rada Iveković has pointed out, is how to transform
women from being *objects* of history into being *subjects* of history, on an
equal basis with men. "Just how precarious women's rights are," Iveković
writes,

> is now shown by the development[s], in exsocialist countries: [such rights] are
> historically never safe, they can be threatened and done away with by the arbi-
> trary decision of men (males). The law is, after all, not divine or neutral. There
> is, behind it, a human subject and author: historically, he is masculine. Women
> and minorities appear only as the objects of law, *in* the framework construed by
> the historically dominant subject. Unless we develop and put into action a con-
> cept of plural co-subjectivity, that is, unless we dismantle and reconstruct the
> framework of the law itself (with all the practical, political, social, and other im-
> plications), women (or others in an analogous situation) will remain subordi-
> nated to men.[87]

THE CULTURAL SECTOR

Culture has most transparently figured, in this war, as an arena in which
political ambitions have been projected. To conquer a territory in the fullest
sense entails also the conquest of its history, an "annexation" of the history
of the region to one's own nation. This is also why the victors in wars for
territorial gain typically rewrite the history books upon the conclusion of
their wars, in order to justify their conquests. It is also why, in the Yugoslav
ethnic war, the Bosnian Serbs have taken such care to destroy not only the
mosques and Catholic churches in areas into which they move but also
other buildings of historical, aesthetic, and cultural importance.

A correspondent for the *Boston Globe* captured this thinking all too well
in recollections published in July 1994: "In September 1992," he recalled,
"a reporter covering the Bosnian conflict for the BBC asked a Serb artillery
commander why his men were shelling a Holiday Inn in Sarajevo that
housed foreign journalists. The commander apologized. It was only the
National Museum behind the hotel that his men were trying to blow up, he
said. The error was promptly corrected, and the shells reached their intended target."[88]

In Croatia, Serbs damaged or destroyed more than 500 monuments and
historical buildings and more than 370 museums, libraries, and archives in
the short period between July 1991 and January 1992. Among the targets

damaged or destroyed were the eleventh-century Church of the Trinity in Split, a newly excavated fourth-century ancient Roman palace (also in Split), the fifteenth-century Church of St. John Capistran (in Ilok), along with its richly furnished monastery, historical sections of Dubrovnik and Karlovac (the latter dating from the sixteenth century), and the entire city of Vukovar, including some beautiful and ornate buildings dating likewise from the sixteenth century. These buildings had survived the Turkish occupation, the turmoil of 1875–1878, and World Wars I and II, including Nazi occupation. That they have been shelled now is the result of a deliberate Serbian policy of targeting other peoples' cultural treasures, on the formula, "the more precious the site, the more vulnerable it is to attack."[89] Self-styled "Chetniks" even entered Catholic churches in Dubrovnik in order to destroy valuable works of art hanging inside.[90]

Both Serbian and Croatian forces have targeted mosques in Bosnia-Herzegovina. In November 1993, Croats blew up the famous arched bridge in Mostar, which had spanned the Neretva River for more than 400 years, and Croatia also demolished the sixteenth-century Serb Orthodox Zitomislic monastery in Herzegovina. Serbian forces reduced the National Library in Sarajevo to rubble, sending many irreplaceable manuscripts and books up in flames, and destroyed Sarajevo's Oriental Institute, along with its 22,000 manuscripts. The Muslims, in retaliation, have destroyed or damaged a number of Serbian Orthodox churches, particularly in the Tuzla region.[91]

In a moving gesture of solidarity with the people of Sarajevo, internationally renowned conductor Zubin Mehta, a former conductor of the Los Angeles and New York philharmonic orchestras, journeyed to Sarajevo in June 1994 to lead the Sarajevo Symphony Orchestra and chorus in a televised performance of Mozart's *Requiem*.[92] Held in the charred ruins of the National Library, the concert was a poignant recognition of the intense suffering that the people of Sarajevo and all of Bosnia have endured.

Efforts to erase all signs of the culture of the "enemy" have extended even to pop music. Thus, in September 1994, the host of a Sarajevo radio show, Mimo Sahinpašić, who had been playing *antiwar* songs by Djordje Balašević and other Serbian singers, was ordered by Bosnian Minister of Culture Enes Karić to stop playing "aggressor music." Sahinpašić, however, promised to defy the proscription.[93]

Thus it is when culture is an *object* of attack. Culture has also figured as a *subject*, refracting political messages, reflecting on the war, and sometimes serving simply to raise spirits.

In fact, culture is one of the mediums in which politics may manifest itself, and it is often (especially in times of social stress) permeated with political meanings, influences, and symbols. Just as politics is culturally grounded and reflects the assumptions and values of a society, so too is culture grounded in politics. It is for these reasons that changes in politics tend to be accompanied by and even adumbrated in changes in the cultural sector. Hence too—to borrow a line from von Clausewitz—cultural products may figure at times as "a continuation of politics by other means." Susan Sontag, the American novelist, was most certainly conscious of this use for culture when she staged Samuel Beckett's play, *Waiting for Godot*, in Sarajevo in August 1993.[94]

The Artists

Artists have told the story of the war in paintings, graphics, and sculptures that have been displayed worldwide. New York's Kunsthalle, for example, played host to an exhibit of works in sundry mediums by a group of Sarajevo artists in March 1994. The setting was apt: the Kunsthalle had been devastated by a fire two years earlier, which had left a hole in the ceiling and the floors scuffed.[95] The art on exhibit in New York was composed from such materials as the artists had found in the ruins of Sarajevo. The works on display showed images of the cramped conditions of Sarajevans, of graves, of people changed, even physically distorted, by war. A sculpture by Mustafa Skopljak showed small heads peaking out from a grave. Another sculpture, the work of forty-three-year-old Nusret Pašić, placed distended, twisted figurines on bricks lined up in a row. With one figurine to a brick, the fantasy evoked a scene of the claustrophobia and isolation experienced by Sarajevans under siege. Multimedia artist Sanjin Jukić used his artistry to indict Western diplomats and politicians for their failure to respond effectively. As Jukić notes,

> For Western Europe and the U.S., . . . Sarajevo is no more than a media sound bite produced with Hollywood melodrama. *Sarajevo Ghetto Spectacle*—which the artist calls an "anti-video clip" . . . is a collage of media coverage of the Bosnian war taken from CNN and various European television stations. The video was projected on the bare brick wall. Below it, illuminated by black lights, a glowing white sign, reminiscent of the Hollywood sign that looks down over Los Angeles, spelled out "Sarajevo."[96]

A similar exhibition was organized by Dunja Stjepanović and Robert Ness and staged in the Seattle Convention Center, April–July 1994. Bringing together paintings and sketches by seventeen artists, created between June and September 1992 during the siege of Sarajevo, the exhibit also featured documentary photographs by Milena Soree-Džamonja.[97] The artists, all professors or graduates from the School of Fine Arts at the University of Sarajevo or local professional artists, rendered their impressions of the war.

As Dunja Blažević noted in an article for *art press*, "With every sudden shift of society, especially in times of collective trauma, the question of political involvement [of] the artist is once again thrown into the spotlight. Under such circumstances, it is morally imperative to take a stand."[98]

Playwrights and Poets

Macedonian playwright Goran Stefanovski's play about the siege of Sarajevo, *Sara's Story*, represents one effort to make the tragedy concrete. Written in 1992, it opened at the International Theater Festival in Antwerp, Belgium, in 1993.[99] In Sarajevo itself, the Bosnian rock musicians—Srdjan 'Gino' Jevdjević and Amir 'Lazy' Beso—staged the legendary musical *Hair* in Sarajevo's Kameni Theater in November 1992. *Hair*'s pacifist message provided powerful commentary both on the Serbian siege of Sarajevo and on the slowness of the West to react. Admission was free, and the show, which played at least three days a week for weeks on end, was publicized by word of mouth only.[100] In 1995, by which time Jevdjević and Beso had made their way to Seattle, Washington, the two veteran musicians teamed up with local playwright Talvin Wilks to mount a multimedia music-theatrical event entitled "Sarajevo: Behind God's Back."[101] The piece avoids politics, concentrating instead on conveying the experience of living under siege. Some scenes deal with hunger and snipers. Others deal with "café society," showing Sarajevans' desperate attempt to hold onto civilized life and at least a few of its perquisites. In one particularly striking scene, Srdjan (a character more or less modeled on Jevdjević) gives vent to rather transparent xenophobia, brought on by the war:

> *Srdjan:* Are you a Serb? You see him next to you. He's a Serb, you can tell, can't you? Did you know that when you sat down? Would you like to move? You must be a Serb, did they seat you there on purpose?
> *Mama:* Srdjan . . .
> *Srdjan:* Their seats are better than yours. Did your ticket say no Jews, Serbs or dogs?
> *Mama:* Srdjan!
> *Srdjan:* Will all Serbs please stand up![102]

The poets have likewise responded to the destruction and carnage. In Serbia, Croatia, and Bosnia, newspapers print poems that appeal to nationalist sentiments and talk of homeland, defense, hope, even revenge. Other poets, whether in former Yugoslavia or abroad, have aspired to be sounding boards for the world's conscience. Still others retrace paths of history and try to take stock of the uses that politicians have made of myth or record the images and emotions associated with the war. Two examples will serve.

The first example is an excerpt from "Child's Play" by an American poet living in London named Judi Benson. It is one of 114 poems, mostly by Americans and West Europeans, collected in a small book, *Klaonica: Poems for Bosnia*. The poem begins by asking how people who had been friends and neighbors for 40 years could suddenly kill and rape each other. It then looks at how the siege affected one adolescent:

Yesterday I was a little girl, wondering will I be pretty?
will the boys notice me? Today I chop off my hair,
disguise myself as my dead brother. I take on his swagger,
wear his mean look, hope the men don't see me
pick up his weapon. Little brother, such a big gun.[103]

Now armed with a gun, the girl plays hopscotch "with the dead." The poem closes on a touchingly childlike note:

One potato two potato three potato four.
Mother used to say I talked too much. Now I don't talk at all.
Five potato six potato seven potato more. Wish I could take all this hate
turn it into water, take a long drink of forgetfulness. There's no end.
Stack hands, tit for tat, tag—you're it—the games we play.[104]

The second example is taken from one of four poems about Yugoslavia, composed by P. H. Liotta in 1994. Entitled "How It Must End," the poem tries to separate insight from illusion:

. . . I see Dubrovnik
and Sarajevo burn, the roar of the shell
and spent lives . . .
What will it take, my friend?
Sofia, Tiranë, Skopje—these will be next
say those who know nothing at all.
They smile and nod the way one speaks
to a child who has never behaved.
We knew this would happen!
Perhaps they are the ones I would think
to kill first. Perhaps they are no one.
Perhaps it is only my rage at knowing
the angel of death and the angel of life
have nothing to do with this, no part
in the unfolding betrayal. Only
ourselves alone with the world.[105]

The Musicians

Vadran Smailović, a cellist in the Sarajevo Symphony, outraged by the massacre of innocent civilians in front of a bakery, went out to the site of the battue every day for twenty-four days to play Albinoni. It was an inspiring demonstration of the power of music to console, to inspire, to commemorate. Others have done likewise, whether one thinks of a group of Seattle cellists who honored Smailović by replicating his gesture, likewise for twenty-four days, or of British composer Nigel Osborne's chamber-opera *Sarajevo*, a work driven by empathy with the people of that city and by anger at a world which has remained impassive in the face of Bosnia's on-going agony.[106] "Musicians," said Angelina Papp, a pianist at the Sarajevo Conservatory of Music, "are people who see war as something very strange to them. All musicians of the world speak the same language: the language of their scores. Moreover, music has no limits and so it constantly poses the question, why must we live in this cage?"[107]

A Seattle composer, David Hahn, composed a quiet, brooding piece for two cellos and crickets to honor a journalist classmate from Stanford who had been killed by Croatian Serbs in 1991 while covering the war; Hahn's selection of the cello as his medium was guided by his desire simultane-ously to honor Smailović of Sarajevo. Later, on 5 and 6 September 1995, Hahn collaborated with Zagreb musicians Davorka and Damir Horvat to perform an evening of highly charged music, featuring pieces with names such as "World Circus News," "Death Within Death," "On the Border with the War Zone," and "Dona Nobis Pacem."[108]

Among the rock musicians of Serbia and Croatia, there have been both pacifists (such as Zagreb's Steamroller and Belgrade's Rambo Amadeus), who have performed in concerts for peace, and bards of bellicose nation-alism (such as Zagreb's Psihomodo pop[109] and Belgrade's Oliver Mandić), who have recorded songs about victory and serenaded the troops in the field.[110] Rijeka's popular band, Let 3 (Flight No. 3), which had made its name with its apolitical 1989 album, *Two Dogs Fuckin* (title in English), turned political in 1994 with an album bearing the simple title "Peace."[111]

War has politicized rock in other ways. In Croatia, for example, radio sta-tions have observed a quiet embargo against rock albums by Serbian mu-sicians,[112] while in Bosnia some Muslim imams have condemned *all* rock music as the work of "Satan."[113] Some rock musicians have reacted by tak-ing flight from politics. Jasenko Houra and his band Dirty Theater are a good example. At a time when politicians talk of national causes and na-tional survival and call on the nation to concentrate on the great tasks at hand, Dirty Theater has taken to emphasizing romantic songs. Says Houra, "I think that a time of romanticism is coming, when small things become important."[114]

Other rock musicians have redefined their "opposition." Bora Djordjević, who provided a *nationalist* alternative when Ivan Stambolić was Serbian party boss, was starting to sound more and more like the official rock bard of the Republic of Serbia once Milošević came to power. But by 1992 Bora was once again striking out on his own. Later, in *Zbogom Srbijo*, a rock album released in summer 1994, Bora sang against the war and its sav-agery, even while asserting his own brand of pacifist nationalism.[115] The title song evokes both the ultimate pointlessness of violence and the sadness it instills.

> *I'm going to die,*
> *To take the head of a stranger,*
> *Go with God, Serbia.*[116]

Elsewhere on that same album, Bora makes a play on the ruling party's slogan ("That's the way it should be") to offer the following suggestion,

> *Today there's no milk,*
> *Today there's no bread,*
> *Because of that, eat shit.*
> *That's the way it should be.*[117]

Still others have been sucked into the very tidepools of war. Here was Simonida Stanković, decked out in miniskirt and black leather jacket, singing to troops in the field about their "glory":

> *They're protecting Serb glory,*
> *They're defending Serb lands,*
> *Arkan's Tigers,*
> *They're heroes without a flaw.*[118]

While Stanković's rock panegyrics have propelled her to fame, another would-be rock warrior, Sonja Karadžić (Radovan's daughter) had less success in this regard. Described by friends as "a good Serbian woman, complete with moustache,"[119] thirtyish Sonja Karadžić released her first rock video in 1992, singing, not too tactfully, about the "degenerate, materialistic, obsessive Serbs in Belgrade who owe everything to the real Serbs in Bosnia."[120] As a result, Belgrade Television circumspectly decided not to broadcast her video. Her first rock album, *Warrior from Paradise*, did not fare much better, and by August 1994 she had taken the post of chief of the press office in Pale, the Bosnian Serbs' political headquarters.

But it is the Slovenian group Laibach that has perhaps best captured the sheer senselessness and irrationality of the war. In the group's 1994 album, *NATO*,[121] the title "song" is a wordless hard-driving piece that starts out with the sound of bombs dropping and then shifts into a rock beat overlay on "Mars" from Gustav Holst's *The Planets*. "In the Army Now" includes the mournful but ambiguous comment,

> *Vacation in the far-off land*
> *Uncle Sam does the best he can.*[122]

In yet another song, "Dogs of War" (written by David Gilmour and Anthony Moore and originally performed by Pink Floyd), Laibach takes up the hopelessness of war:

Dogs of war and men of hate,
with no cause, we don't discriminate
discovery is to be disowned,
our currency is flesh and bone . . .

Even our masters don't know the webs we weave
one world, it's a battleground
one world, and we will smash it down . . .

The dogs of war don't negotiate
the dogs of war won't capitulate
they will take and you will give . . .

And you must die so that they may live . . .

You can knock at any door, but wherever you go,
you know they've been before . . .

One world, it's a battleground
one world, and we will smash it down.[123]

NOTES

1. See Mark Juergensmeyer, *The New Cold War? Religious Nationalism Confronts the Secular State* (Berkeley: University of California Press, 1993), pp. 33–34.

2. For details, see Sabrina Petra Ramet, "The Serbian Church and the Serbian Nation," in Sabrina Petra Ramet and Ljubiša S. Adamovich, eds., *Beyond Yugoslavia: Politics, Economics, and Culture in a Shattered Community* (Boulder, Colo.: Westview Press, 1995), pp. 112–113.

3. Details in ibid., pp. 113–115.

4. Tanjug (28 March 1990), trans. in *Foreign Broadcast Information Service (FBIS), Daily Report* (Eastern Europe), 29 March 1990, p. 56.

5. Vladimir Dedijer, *Vatikan i Jasenovac: Dokumenti* (Belgrade: Izdavačka Radna Organizacija, 1987). The English edition is Vladimir Dedijer, *The Yugoslav Auschwitz and the Vatican: The Croatian Massacre of the Serbs During World War II*, trans. from the German translation by Harvey L. Kendall (Buffalo, N.Y.: Prometheus Books, 1992).

6. Jure Kristo, "The Catholic Church in a Time of Crisis," in Ramet and Adamovich, *Beyond Yugoslavia*, p. 441.

7. Ibid., p. 442.

8. Quoted in ibid., p. 443.

9. Quoted in *Danas* (Zagreb) (17 March 1992), p. 27.

10. *Glas koncila* (Zagreb) (8 March 1992), p. 3.

11. See the official Church translation of the Memorandum of the Holy Synod of Bishops of the Serbian Orthodox Church, 28 May 1992.

12. Recounted in David A. Steele, "Former Yugoslavia: Religion as a Fount of Ethnic Hostility or an Agent of Reconciliation?" *Religion in Eastern Europe*, Vol. 14, No. 2 (October 1994), p. 5.

13. E.g., Catholic Archbishop France Perko of Belgrade, in interview with *NIN* (Belgrade), No. 2235 (29 October 1993), p. 31.

14. Interview with Hadži Hafiz Halil efendi Mehtić, mufti of Zenica, in *Globus* (Zagreb) (2 September 1994), p. 42.

15. *Kana* (Zagreb) (March 1992), p. 37; *Novi vjesnik* (Zagreb) (28 September 1992), p. 4A; and *Slobodna Dalmacija* (Split) (29 September 1994), p. 6.

16. *Borba* (Belgrade) (17 February 1993), p. 8; confirmed in *Nedjeljna Dalmacija* (Split) (25 November 1994), p. 7.

17. *Ljiljan* (Sarajevo–Ljubljana) (5 October 1994), p. 8.

18. *Süddeutsche Zeitung* (Munich) (13–15 August 1994), p. 6.

19. *Glas Slavonije* (Osijek) (8 June 1994), pp. 26–27.

20. *Vreme* (Belgrade) (13 June 1994), p. 22.

21. *Süddeutsche Zeitung* (29–30 October 1994), p. 4. See also *Globus* (11 November 1994), pp. 44–45.

22. *Philadelphia Inquirer* (18 November 1994), p. A39.

23. *Glas Istre* (Pula) (11 June 1994), p. 14.

24. Ibid. See also *Verčernji list* (Zagreb) (21 March 1992), p. 4.

25. *New York Times* (8 May 1993), p. 1.

26. AFP (Paris) (9 September 1993), in *FBIS, Daily Report* (Eastern Europe), 14 September 1993, p. 35.

27. *National Catholic Reporter* (26 August 1994), p. 11.

28. *NIN*, No. 2235 (29 October 1993), p. 30.

29. See, for example, *NIN* (9 October 1992), pp. 26–28; and *Politika* (29 October 1992), p. 14.

30. Trudy Rubin, "Bosnian Serbs Have Helped Create a Muslim State Right Next Door," *Philadelphia Inquirer* (18 November 1994), p. A39.

31. *Ljiljan* (21 December 1994), p. 23.

32. *Globus* (23 September 1994), p. 11.

33. In an earlier *Globus* poll, reported on 10 December 1993, as cited in Wolf Oschlies, "Zur politischen Rolle orthodoxer Kirchen auf dem Balkan," *Südost Europa*, Vol. 42, No. 10 (October 1993), p. 587.

34. Details in *Evropske novosti* (Belgrade–Frankfurt) (26 November 1994), p. 6.

35. Oral presentation by Obrad Kesić, American Association for the Advancement of Slavic Studies, Philadelphia, 18 November 1994.

36. *Delo* (Ljubljana) (27 February 1993), p. 27, excerpt trans. in *FBIS, Daily Report* (Eastern Europe), 17 March 1993, p. 56.

37. Radio Tirana Network (Tirana) (8 December 1992), trans. in *FBIS, Daily Report* (Eastern Europe), 10 December 1992, pp. 57–58.

38. For background, see Stevan K. Pavlowitch, "The Orthodox Church in Yugoslavia, I: The Problem of the Macedonian Church," *Eastern Churches Review*, Vol. 1, No. 4 (1967); and Pedro Ramet, "The Serbian Orthodox Church," in Pedro Ramet, ed., *Eastern Christianity and Politics in the Twentieth Century* (Durham, N.C.: Duke University Press, 1988), pp. 242–244, 245, 247.

39. Quoted in *Politika* (Belgrade) (18 December 1992), p. 9, trans. in *FBIS, Daily Report* (Eastern Europe), 15 January 1993, p. 67.

40. *Evropske novosti* (19 November 1994), p. 6.

41. *Evropske novosti* (10 December 1994), p. 5.

42. *Politika* (7 June 1994), p. 14.

43. *Borba* (7 April 1993), p. 1.

44. Tanjug (2 February 1994), trans. in *FBIS, Daily Report* (Eastern Europe), 3 February 1994, p. 36.

45. Tanjug (2 April 1993), trans. in *FBIS, Daily Report* (Eastern Europe), 5 April 1993, p. 53.

46. Tanjug (10 August 1994), trans. in *FBIS, Daily Report* (Eastern Europe), 11 August 1994, p. 44; *The European* (London) (19–25 August 1994), p. 2; and *The Sunday Times* (London) (21 August 1994), p. 19. Regarding the waxing amity between Karadžić and Patriarch Pavle, see *Ljiljan* (30 November 1994), p. 9.

47. *Oslobodjenje* (European ed.) (21 January 1994), trans. into English in *Oslobodjenje* (Sarajevo–Washington, D.C., English ed.) (April 1994), p. 12.

48. *Evropske novosti* (24–26 December 1994), p. 10.

49. *Globus* (Zagreb) (19 August 1994), p. 6.

50. *Neue Zürcher Zeitung* (9 September 1994), p. 3.

51. *La Repubblica* (Rome) (18 August 1994), p. 3.

52. *Sunday Times* (London) (4 September 1994), p. 14. See also *Sunday Telegraph* (London) (4 September 1994), p. 20.

53. *New York Times* (8 September 1994), p. A8.

54. *Neue Zürcher Zeitung* (26 August 1994), p. 2.

55. *Danas* (Zagreb), new series (20 September 1994), p. 4. See also *Neue Zürcher Zeitung* (5 August 1994), p. 3; and *Vreme* (12 September 1994), p. 8.

56. Quoted in *Boston Sunday Globe* (11 September 1994), p. 11.

57. Quoted in *National Catholic Reporter* (23 September 1994), p. 7.

58. Quoted in ibid. See also *The European* (16–22 September 1994), p. 7.

59. Quoted in *New York Times* (9 September 1994), p. A7.

60. *Bosnjački avaz* (Sarajevo) (1–15 October 1994), p. 3.

61. Sefko Omerbašić, in interview with *Delo* (6 February 1993), p. 22, trans. in *FBIS, Daily Report* (Eastern Europe), 4 March 1993, p. 55.

62. *Boston Sunday Globe* (27 November 1994), p. 14; and *Neue Zürcher Zeitung* (29 November 1994), p. 3. See also the cover story about Puljić's elevation to the College of Cardinals in *Arena* (Zagreb) (19 November 1994).

63. Quoted in Lepa Mladjenović and Vera Litričin, transcribed by Tanya Renne, "Belgrade Feminists 1992: Separation, Guilt and Identity Crisis," in *Feminist Review*, No. 45 (autumn 1993), p. 115. See also "Protest Arkadije i Beogradskog Ženskog lobija: žene, homoseksualci i lezbejke," in *Žene za Žene* (Belgrade: Žene u crnom, 1994), p. 60.

64. Quoted in Mladjenović and Litričin, "Belgrade Feminists 1992," p. 115.

65. Cynthia Cockburn, "A Women's Political Party for Yugoslavia: Introduction to the Serbian Feminist Manifesto," *Feminist Review*, No. 39 (winter 1991), pp. 155, 157.

66. Mladjenović and Litričin, "Belgrade Feminists 1992," p. 116. See also Ružica Rosandić, "Patriotic Education," in Ružica Rosandić and Vesna Pešić, eds., *Warfare, Patriotism, Patriarchy: The Analysis of Elementary School Textbooks* (Belgrade: Centre for Anti-War Action Association MOST, 1994), pp. 41–57.

67. "Reakcije prolaznica/prolaznika na protest Žena u crnom," in *Žene za žene,* p. 15. See also Bojan Aleksov and Staša Zajović, "O mobilizaciji i antimobilizaciji" (pp. 36–40) and "Protest protiv opšte mobilizacije u republići Srpskoj i protiv formiranja Ženskih jedinica" (pp. 46–47), in the same volume.

68. For one reflection of this, see Asja Armanda and Natalie Nenadić, "Activists Warn Do Not Be Fooled by Genocide/Rape Revisionists," *Northwest Ethnic News* (Seattle) (November 1994), pp. 2, 7.

69. Jean E. Howard, "Cross-dressing, the Theater, and Gender Struggle in Early Modern England," in Lesley Ferris, ed., *Crossing the Stage: Controversies on Cross-Dressing* (London and New York: Routledge, 1993), p. 28.

70. Sabrina Petra Ramet, *Social Currents in Eastern Europe: The Sources and Consequences of the Great Transformation,* 2d ed. (Durham, N.C.: Duke University Press, 1995), p. 443.

71. Rada Iveković, "The New Democracy—With Women or Without Them?" in Ramet and Adamovich, *Beyond Yugoslavia,* p. 406.

72. Ibid., 403.

73. Lepa Mladjenović, "Ženska prava i rat u Bosni," *SOS bilten* (Belgrade), Nos. 6–7 (December 1993), p. 44.

74. Zorica Mršević, "Istraživanje 'tri godine rada SOS telefona za žene i decu žrtve nasilja,'" *Feminističke sveške* (Belgrade), No. 2 (1994), p. 43. See also *Žene za žene: Protesti, apeli, izjave, informacije autonomnih ženskih inicijativa* (Belgrade: Žene i društvo, November 1993), pp. 7–10.

75. Svetlana Stanić, "Iskustva SOS-a," p. 63; and "Izveštaj o radu SOS-a u Kruševcu," p. 55, both in *Feminističke sveške,* No. 2 (1994).

76. Robert J. Stoller, *Presentations of Gender* (New Haven, Conn.: Yale University Press, 1985), p. 18.

77. Theodor Meron, "Rape as a Crime Under International Humanitarian Law," *American Journal of International Law,* Vol. 87, No. 3 (July 1993), p. 425; confirmed in Adam Jones, "Gender and Ethnic Conflict in Ex-Yugoslavia," *Ethnic and Racial Studies,* Vol. 17, No. 1 (January 1994); also *The Times* (London) (23 December 1992), p. 6. See Zorica Mršević, *Ženska prava su ljudska prava* (Belgrade: STEP, 1994), pp. 125–148.

78. *Vojska* (Belgrade) (7 January 1993), pp. 12–13, trans. in *FBIS, Daily Report* (Eastern Europe), 26 February 1993, pp. 35–38.

79. Regarding the role of rape in "ethnic cleansing," see Nadežda Cetković, "Feministička alternativa nacionalizmu i ratu," *SOS bilten,* Nos. 6–7 (December 1993), p. 71.

80. Quoted in *Dnevnik* (Ljubljana) (9 February 1993), p. 3, trans. in *FBIS, Daily Report* (Eastern Europe), 4 March 1993, p. 52.

81. See, for example, Brian Silver, "Social Mobilization and the Russification of Soviet Nationalities," *American Political Science Review,* Vol. 68, No. 1 (March 1974).

82. Silva Meznarić and Mirjana Ule, "Women in Croatia and Slovenia: A Case of Delayed Modernization," in Marilyn Rueschemeyer, ed., *Women in the Politics of Postcommunist Eastern Europe* (Armonk, N.Y.: M. E. Sharpe, 1994), p. 161.

83. Ibid., pp. 161–162.

84. *Vjesnik* (8 June 1993), p. 25.

85. *Sunday Times* (London) (29 May 1994), p. 17.

86. *Welt am Sonntag* (4 December 1994), p. 3.

87. Iveković, "The New Democracy," p. 398.

88. *Boston Sunday Globe* (31 July 1994), p. 7.

89. Alexandra Tuttle, "Croatia's Art and Architecture Buried in Rubble," *Wall Street Journal* (16 January 1992), p. A8.

90. Details in *Novi vjesnik* (Zagreb) (16 June 1992), p. 24A.

91. *RFE/RL News Briefs* (8–12 November 1993), p. 13; *RFE/RL News Briefs* (22–26 November 1993), p. 15; and *New York Times, Weekly review* (International ed.) (27 February 1994), p. 4.

92. *New York Times* (20 June 1994), p. A7.

93. *New York Times* (10 October 1994), p. A3.

94. The people of Sarajevo had been waiting for NATO to come to their rescue by conducting aerial strikes against Bosnian Serbs positions.

95. Jamey Gambrell, "Sarajevo: Art in Extremis," *Art in America* (May 1994), p. 102.

96. Ibid.

97. Interview with Dunja Stjepanović, Seattle, 8 December 1994.

98. Dunja Blažević, "Destruction of the Image—Image of Destruction," *art press*, No. 192 (June 1994), p. 49.

99. *MILS NEWS, Dnevni vesti* (18 March 1993).

100. "Bosnian Blues," *The Stranger* (Seattle), 22–28 November 1994.

101. Mike Romano, "Art during wartime," *Seattle Weekly* (16 August 1995), p. 29.

102. *Sarajevo: Behind God's Back,* music by Amir Beso and Srdjan Jevdjević; text by Amir Beso, Srdjan Jevdjević, and Talvin Wilks, 3rd draft (7 September 1995), p. 40.

103. Judi Benson, "Child's Play," in Ken Smith and Judi Benson, eds., *Klaonica: Poems for Bosnia* (Newcastle upon Tyne: Bloodaxe Books, 1993), p. 104.

104. Ibid., p. 105.

105. P. H. Liotta, "How It Must End," *The Antioch Review,* Vol. 52, No. 2 (spring 1994), special issue on War, pp. 318, 320.

106. *The European—élan* (London) (19–25 August 1994), p. 10; and *Globus* (Zagreb) (30 September 1994), pp. 23, 25.

107. Quoted in *New York Times* (23 October 1994), p. 3.

108. David Hahn, interview by the author, Seattle, 15 July 1995 and concert program Connexions: Seattle-Zagreb (Zagreb, 5–6 September 1995).

109. See their song, "Hrvatska mora pobijediti" [Croatia must win], on their album, *Maxi Single za Gardiste,* Croatia Records MS-D 2 03553 3 (1991); and article in *Verčernji list* (24 June 1994), p. 15.

110. For elaboration regarding these and other performers since the war began, see Sabrina Petra Ramet, "Shake, Rattle, and Self-Management: Making the Scene in Yugoslavia," in Sabrina Petra Ramet, ed., *Rocking the State: Rock Music and Politics in Eastern Europe and Russia* (Boulder, Colo.: Westview Press, 1994), pp. 125–126; and Sabrina Petra Ramet, *Social Currents in Eastern Europe: The Sources and Consequences of the Great Transformation,* 2d ed. (Durham, N.C.: Duke University Press, 1995), p. 261. See also "B92: Struggling for Air," *Uncaptive Minds,* Vol. 6, No. 3 (fall 1993), pp. 101–102. See also *Nedjeljna Dalmacija* (6 January 1995), p. 36.

111. See *Nedjeljna Dalmacija* (23 December 1994), pp. 36–37.

112. *Vreme* (Belgrade) (5 September 1994), p. 37.

113. *Der Spiegel* (Hamburg) (24 October 1994), p. 160.

114. Quoted in *Vjesnik* (Zagreb) (15 April 1993), p. 14.

115. For a recent, short article about him, see *Vreme* (30 May 1994), p. 34.

116. I am grateful to Obrad Kesić for providing me with the English translation of the song. I have neither seen nor heard the album myself.

117. Ibid.

118. Quoted in *The European* (London) (4–10 July 1993). See also *Vreme* (13 June 1994), p. 34.

119. As quoted in *Daily Telegraph* (London) (12 August 1994), p. 15.

120. Quoted in ibid.

121. For two recent articles about this album, see *Globus* (7 October 1994), pp. 30–31, and (21 October 1994), p. 33. For an early article about Laibach, see N. L. Centrum, "Neue Slowenische Kunst," *Art Forum* (November 1984), pp. 151–152.

122. Song "In the Army Now," on Laibach, *NATO*, Mute Records, 61714–2 (1994).

123. Song "Dogs of War," on Laibach, *NATO*.

Epilogue

Socialist Yugoslavia was always a Tower of Babel, with its builders not only speaking different languages but talking past each other. In many ways, the diverse peoples of socialist Yugoslavia failed to comprehend each other's cultures. Disintegration seemed to be sewn into the very fabric of the state.

There were, of course, signs of trouble even before the socialists took power, indeed from the very beginning. When Serbian armies entered Dubrovnik at the end of World War I, for example, they hoisted Cyrillic banners to celebrate the event—even though local Croats could not read Cyrillic and viewed that alphabet as completely foreign. The Belgrade government followed this up by imposing Cyrillic throughout Croatia and Bosnia. This was a sign of things to come.

In the post-World War II period, the real troubles began around 1980 when the economy started to fall apart. Coincidentally, 1980 was also the year in which Tito died.

By the early 1980s, the gathering economic, ethnic, political, and moral crisis was already pushing the country toward disintegration. Historian Milovan Dželebdžić had a foreboding of this as early as January 1982 when he fretted "lest we experience some new trauma, some new civil war, some new massacre."[1] In October the following year, Slovenian historian Dušan Biber told a group of historians in Zagreb that if the trends then prevailing should continue, "we will turn into a second Lebanon."[2] I echoed these warnings a month later, writing that, as a result of the mishandling of liberal currents in 1971 and the ensuing political line, "it is probably only a matter of time before another bloodbath occurs between Serbs and Croats."[3]

It would be a tricky business and, in part, no doubt, artificial, to try to pinpoint any single event as a turning point in the disintegration of Yugoslavia. Certainly, the rise of Slobodan Milošević provided a strong push toward civil war. But he did not create the hatreds in Yugoslavia. He catered to them, manipulated them, and amplified them.

Three factors contributed to the eventual outbreak of ethnic war between the Yugoslav republics: (1) the aforementioned economic deterioration, creating rising tides of discontent; (2) the decentralized, ethnic-based federal system that Tito had created, which channeled discontent along ethnic lines and guaranteed that programs to remedy the situation would be addressed to the ethnic audience associated with each given republic; and (3) the appearance of Milošević, a politician willing to set a match to this tinderbox by endeavoring to stoke and exploit ethnic hatreds for his own purposes.

Nineteen eighty-nine and 1990 were years of clear disintegration and by early 1991, it was clear to many scholars that the country was seriously threatened by civil war. Milan Andreyevich, Marko Milivojević, and I were among those who understood that by January of that year, interethnic war was, at best, only a matter of months away. As I wrote at the time, "As of late February 1991, it appears that within a matter of weeks, Yugoslavia could be in the grip of a full-scale civil war centered in Croatia, Bosnia, southern Serbia (specifically, [the] Sandžak of Novi Pazar), and Kosovo. The most dangerous of these flashpoints has been Croatia. . . . "[4]

Yet, until the explosion came on 26 June 1991, the sheer complexity of the situation, with diverse political groupings within each republic and province, factions within each grouping, and sometimes factions within factions, left part of the picture in the shadows and seemed to leave open the possibility of a sudden change of the scenario. For example, when the Serbian opposition took to the streets of Belgrade in March 1991 to protest the drift toward war and economic catastrophe, the possibility that Milošević might be forced to retire and that the political deck in Serbia might be reshuffled seemed to have been opened. And coloring *everything*, as ever in Yugoslavia, was the national question, that prickly and seemingly insoluble dilemma.

THE FAILURE OF DIPLOMACY

More than four years later, there are probably 300,000 to 500,000 persons dead (making this conflict more sanguinary than any recent conflict other than that in Sudan) and some 3.7 million refugees (more than the numbers of refugees from Rwanda-Burundi, Liberia, and Somalia combined).[5] Moreover, the latter figure does not count the 300,000 to 400,000 Albanians forced out of Kosovo[6] and the 170,000 or more non-Serbs expelled by Serbian authorities from Vojvodina and the Sandžak.[7] The fighting in Yugoslavia in World War II lasted four years and three months, lasting from April 1941 to July 1945. At this writing, it appears likely that the war unleashed by Milošević, which began in Slovenia in June 1991, will break the records set by the earlier war in terms of sheer duration; as of September 1995, the current war has already clearly outdistanced World War II in terms of property destruction and most especially when one talks of the destruction of churches, cemeteries, libraries and archives, museums, historic buildings of artistic significance, schools, and hospitals—all favorite targets of Serbian gunners.

The West imposed an arms embargo on all Yugoslav successor republics in September 1991 only to realize later that the embargo was the single greatest help that the West could have given to the Serbs in their effort to annex large portions of Croatia and Bosnia. By early 1993, Germany and the United States were trying to persuade Britain and France to agree to support a lifting of the arms embargo, but the British and the French persistently blocked such endeavors, ostensibly for domestic political reasons.

Meanwhile, the U.N.- and E.C.-sponsored mediation effort quickly proved to be a theater of the absurd. Internationally appointed mediators David Lord Owen (for the European Community) and Cyrus Vance (for the U.N.) were instructed to devise a peace plan but were provided with neither tangible incentives with which to entice the warring parties to lend their assent, nor coercive instruments with which to compel the assent of recalcitrant combatants. Vance and Owen tried, nonetheless, to bring the warring sides to an agreement and failing that, unilaterally devised their own plan, the ill-fated "Vance-Owen Plan," rejected by the Bosnian Serbs in January 1993, again in March 1993, yet again in April 1993, and for the final time in May 1993. Interestingly enough, from January until May, Lord Owen continued to express optimism that the Bosnian Serbs would eventually accept the plan, despite the absence of any reassuring evidence that might have suggested that such a conclusion was warranted. The E.C. admitted on 20 June that their peace plan was dead but asked Lord Owen to begin negotiating a new peace plan, still failing to equip him with either "carrots" or "sticks." By then Vance had retired from his role as international mediator, and Norwegian diplomat Thorvald Stoltenberg had taken his place.

The subsequent "Owen-Stoltenberg Plan" (August 1993), based largely on ideas developed by Milošević and Tudjman, seemed, on the basis of the cynicism of its derivation, to have some prospect of "success" (that term seeming to refer not to achieving justice or self-determination or stability but merely to obtaining some sort of treaty). But it was the Bosnian Serbs who eventually gutted the plan; Karadžić's ambitions, it seemed, were by that point greater than Milošević's.

With the collapse of the Owen-Stoltenberg Plan, the United States went to work to bring about a reconciliation between the Croats and the Muslims. This bore fruit in early 1994, when the two sides signed a truce and began to treat each other as partners. In February 1994, the Bosnian Muslims and Bosnian Croats agreed to merge their armies and began work on establishing a common federal framework. In June 1994, the resultant Croatian-Bosnian federal parliament (uniting Bosnia's Croats and Muslims) elected Bosnian Prime Minister Haris Silajdžić to serve as prime minister of the new federation.[8] Moreover, by that time, Iranian arms supplies were beginning to reach the Croats and Muslims, giving their now-combined forces an additional strength.[9] By the end of May, Bosnian-government troops, supplied with tanks and heavy artillery, had undertaken a major offensive against Serbian forces west of Tesanj in northern Bosnia.

While the tides of war shifted, U.N. and European mediators continued to work on possible maps for the area. In June, supported by the United States and Russia, they produced yet another plan (Plan 3), this time assigning 51 percent of Bosnian territory to the Croat-Muslim federation and 49 percent to the Bosnian Serbs.[10] The Croats and Muslims accepted the plan, although not entirely enthusiastically, but on 21 July, the Bosnian Serbs rejected this proposal too, at the same time calling for further negotiations.[11] The Western powers had threatened the Serbs with aerial attacks and a tightening of the embargo unless they accepted the plan.[12] But the Serbs rejected the plan, and the West did nothing. The Serbs' rejection had only confirmed that the West had little credibility remaining, in Serbian eyes.[13]

Undeterred by the consistent failure of diplomatic efforts not backed up by force, a contact group consisting of U.S. Ambassador to Croatia Peter Galbraith, Russian Ambassador to Croatia Leonid Kerestedijanc, and two officials from the International Conference on the Former Yugoslavia (one representing the U.N., the other representing the E.C.) set about drawing up a plan for peace in Croatia. The resultant "Z-4" plan (named for Zagreb where most of the negotiations took place), to which Ambassador Galbraith made a significant contribution and lent his solid support, proposed to sanction permanent Serb self-government in all portions of Croatia in which Serbs had constituted a majority before June 1991.[14] Croatia was to receive nominal suzerainty over these two areas, but in every other respect, it was the Serbs who were to have exercised sovereignty in those areas with authority over education, currency, local legislation, and an autonomous parliament and police force.[15] The plan, which closely followed the pattern of Austria's 1878 occupation of Bosnia-Herzegovina (which nominally respected Ottoman suzerainty), aroused profound disgust at all levels of the Croatian government and society.[16] Ambassador Galbraith, a Middle East specialist with no previous experience in Balkan affairs, attempted to browbeat Tudjman into accepting the plan. He not only failed in this endeavor but soon found himself publicly branded, in the Croatian press, as an enemy of Croatia.[17] Ultimately, both the Croatian government and the

Croatian Serbs rejected the plan which, quite obviously, did not emerge as a compromise between the relevant parties, but as the product of the ideas of the mediators.[18] In January 1995, Ambassador Galbraith had assured a Seattle audience that he fully expected the Z-4 plan to be accepted by both sides.[19] But when, to his surprise, the plan was rejected, he tried to put the best face on this setback to his policy approach and asserted, "I consider the rejection of the Z-4 Plan by both sides as a sign [that] the mediators accomplished what we set out to do."[20]

About the same time that the Z-4 plan was collapsing, yet another Western-backed peace proposal for Bosnia was snubbed by the Bosnian Serbs.[21] Devised by a "contact group" consisting of representatives of the United States, Russia, Great Britain, France, and Germany, this plan, like Plan 3, would have recognized Bosnian Serb rule in 49 percent of Bosnia. Hoping to mobilize Belgrade against Pale (Karadžić's makeshift capital), officials of the five-nation contact group offered to suspend most of the U.N. sanctions against Serbia (including all trade sanctions) if Serbia would merely extend diplomatic recognition to the governments of Croatia and Bosnia-Herzegovina. Milošević, however, refused the offer, demanding that the sanctions be lifted first *before* he would take up the question of Serbian recognition of these governments.[22] The offer died on the table.[23]

Despite continued Serbian rejection of any and all peace plans, continued Serbian policies of genocide not only in war zones but also in Bosnian Serb towns such as Banja Luka, Bijeljina, Rogatica, and Bosanska Gradiška[24] as well as in several regions of the Republic of Serbia (specifically, Kosovo, Vojvodina, and the Sandžak); transparent Serbian intentions of annexing large portions of Croatian and Bosnian territory;[25] and even repeated Serb confinement or chaining up of U.N. soldiers,[26] the U.N. and NATO declined to translate repeated threats of significant military action into the real thing. In a typical expression of the thinking underlying the mild posture adopted by the U.N. and NATO in response to repeated Serbian aggression, one North American scholar argued (without either offering evidence or confronting countervailing evidence),

> air strikes would likely have only a very limited and futile impact [on the Serbs]. . . . For example, air strikes could not effectively and permanently roll back Serbian victories or the results of "ethnic cleansing," could not punish those responsible for atrocities, and thus would not be much of an object lesson deterring others from committing similar acts in other localities outside the Balkan region. Moreover, only delicate political negotiations, not air strikes, would potentially establish a viable system of governance in Bosnia-Hercegovina or its constituent parts. . . .[27]

Leaving aside Lenard Cohen's suggestion that aerial strikes against Bosnian Serb positions might be intended, in part, to deter tyrants "outside the

Balkan region"—say, in the southern tip of Latin America or in West Africa—there are some obvious (I believe) problems with his argument that the Serbs would be unimpressed by any and all aerial strikes (i.e., regardless of the payload delivered or the amount of destruction inflicted), as with his assumption that the wholesale destruction of Bosnian Serb military and economic resources could not "roll back Serbian victories," as with his supposition that political negotiations are best served by swearing off the use of force to enforce adherence to internationally mediated agreements. If military force is so useless to achieve political change, then how does Cohen suppose the Bosnian Serbs came into possession of 70 percent of Bosnia's land in the first place?

But Cohen was not expressing an isolated opinion here. On the contrary, his (mis)understanding of the situation represents, at least, the standard ideological justification for inaction and perpetual mollification of Serbs offered by the hesitant governments of Britain, France, and the United States, some of their military commanders, and at least some U.N. and NATO spokespersons. An example is Lt.-Gen. Sir Michael Rose, Commander of the U.N. Forces in Bosnia until January 1995, who, in an interview with *Oslobodjenje* the preceding September, "warned against the dangers of [NATO's] using excessive force [in Bosnia], which he said could plunge the U.N. operation here into a Somalia-type debacle."[28] And while no one is going to advocate or defend the use of "excessive" force, Rose's intention was not to state a tautology but to criticize advocates of a hard line against Serbian aggression.

Misha Glenny, the distinguished *Times* correspondent with well-known pro-Serbian tendencies, lent his support to this counsel of perpetual patience:

> If the world accepted the advice of Senator Bob Dole and former Prime Minister Margaret Thatcher [advocates of aerial strikes against Serbs], [dire] consequences would be likely to close in on us like a garrote. To offer large-scale military support to the Bosnian Government would trigger a ferocious response from Belgrade, bringing the unbridled might of the Serbian and Bosnian Serb armies into play.[29]

In this brief, translucent paragraph, Glenny has stated explicitly the governing assumption of those who abjure counterforce in the face of genocide and prefer to rely on reason alone[30]: viz., that the combined strength of the Serbian and Bosnian Serb armies is so great that, if "unbridled," it would give NATO a "ferocious" battle, inflicting unacceptable losses on NATO forces. But, as Herbert Okun, Cyrus Vance's deputy during his engagement as Bosnian peace negotiator, once quipped, "Diplomacy without the threat of force is like baseball without a bat."[31]

Yet even as some Western commentators were declaring the Serbs for all practical purposes "invincible," with more than a few even declaring that the war was "over" and that the Serbs had "won," a rather different picture of Serb and Bosnian Serb military strength began to emerge in news reports and military analyses. A detailed analysis of Bosnian Serb strength published in *Ljiljan* in November 1994 revealed that the Bosnian Serb military budget was exhausted and that salaries to Mladić's soldiers were, depending on the area, anywhere from three to eighteen months in arrears; in attempting to cope with the situation, the demoralized Bosnian Serb soldiers resorted to thefts from each other or to going AWOL and looking for a more remunerative job.[32] The internal command system was also said to have broken down to the extent that, in Mladić's own words, Serbian soldiers had become "incapable of acting and performing combat activities on their own."[33] The Bosnian Serb army was also said to be plagued by poor intelligence, widespread apathy, and bad discipline, and Mladić's soldiers, like soldiers in the Krajina Serb army, were said to be spending much of their time drunk.[34] A report in *Slobodna Dalmacija*, published in February 1995, indicated that the Krajina Serbs were seriously outmanned and outgunned by the Croatian armed forces, and that, although possessing large stocks of heavy artillery, they were relying on missiles and tanks technologically inferior to what the Croats had succeeded in obtaining.[35] And in July 1995, the London daily newspaper *The Independent* indicated that the same analysis might well be extended to the Yugoslav Army (of the FRY) itself. Sapped of its earlier strengh by a steadily tightening budget, by Milošević's frequent political purges of qualified generals, and by the wholesale flight of qualified physicians, engineers, and other persons with university degrees from the army, seeking to take up new residences abroad, the army was said to be spending part of its time courting the small private sector in Serbia, in search of private firms willing to "sponsor" army bases.[36] Yugoslav Army General Borivoje Jovanović even admitted, in a 1995 article for *Vojska* (the Yugoslav Army official journal) that "the army's inability to pay its bills has caused the state electrical company to threaten to cut electricity supplies to bases and installations."[37] Added to that were the prospects for rising unemployment in the munitions industry (resulting in a significant decline in Serbian arms and ammunition production) and further cuts in the FRY/Serbian military budget.[38]

While Serbian military strength declined, Croatian and Bosnian Muslim military strength has increased. By February 1995, the Croatian Army was said to reported to have, at its disposal, some 100,000 troops on active duty with another 180,000 troops in reserve, 36 fighter aircraft, 320 battle tanks, 2,000 artillery batteries, and 3,000 antitank weapons. This high-morale army (which had benefitted from training by qualified Western officers[39]) enjoyed, thus, a clear advantage over the Krajina Serbs, who possessed at that time, 28 fighter aircraft, 250 battle tanks, something over 1,000 artillery batteries, and 62 missile batteries, with only 50,000 men under arms.[40]

As for the Bosnian Army loyal to the government headed by Alija Izetbegović and Haris Silajdzić, *Jane's Defence Weekly* had reported already in November 1994 that it had doubled in size within the previous 12 months and now stood at 164,000 troops, "all in uniform and equipped."[41] Moreover, thanks to more or less clandestine supply flights, the Bosnian Army had, by March 1995, a growing arsenal of heavy weaponry, including mortars and middle-range artillery. General Rasim Delić, chief of the General Staff of the Bosnian Army, admitted, however, that thanks to the arms embargo, his army remained short of long-range artillery, tanks, and aircraft.[42]

THE CROATIAN CAMPAIGNS OF MAY–AUGUST 1995

By January, rumors were afloat that Croatia would soon put its new military strength to the test.[43] As spring arrived and the weather warmed, tensions began to mount along the frontier between the Republic of Croatia and Serb-occupied Croatia. The Serbs expected an attack but were unsure which enclave the Croats would target first—the so-called Krajina, western Slavonia, or eastern Slavonia. Then, on 1 May, the Croatian Army struck with force against western Slavonia, crossing effortlessly through U.N. ceasefire lines. More than 2,500 Croatian troops participated in the initial attack, backed by tanks and heavy artillery. Serbs attempted to retaliate by shelling Zagreb and in the process, killed six people and wounded another 185.[44] But by the end of 2 May, Croatian leaders were able to claim victory in western Slavonia. Between 8,000 and 13,000 Serbs fled the area in the following days, leaving only, at most, 1,500 Serbs behind in western Slavonia as of late June.[45] While Croatia celebrated the reconquest of one of the three areas seized by rebel Serbs, dissension and recrimination ripped through Serbian ranks. One high-ranking general in the so-called Krajina Army (Milan Celeketić) resigned his commission, blaming the reversal on the failure of Milošević and Karadžić to render assistance.[46]

Some Western observers interpreted such recriminations rather literal-mindedly. The prestigious London daily newspaper *Financial Times*, for example, reported that "Belgrade has so far remained on the sidelines," and offered as evidence the observation that "Milošević has been restrained in his comments on the latest fighting in Croatia."[47] The facts tell a different story. According to evidence assembled by Croatian authorities, Belgrade had directly participated in the occupation of Croatia all along: by assigning one of its own officers, Lt.-Gen. Mile Mrkšić, hitherto Assistant Chief of the General Staff of the Yugoslav (i.e., Serbian) Army, to assume command of the Serb paramilitary forces in Croatia; by assigning other Yugoslav Army officers to direct occupation forces in the three sectors; by paying the salaries of these officers as well as of other Croatian Serb military and governmental personnel (albeit, behind schedule); and by sending military supplies and other materiel to Serb occupation forces in occupied Croatia.[48] The Croatian government offered some telling details:

> On June 13, 1995, two Yugoslav army tank units totalling 26 M-84 MBTs operated by the Yugoslav Army's 211th Armored Brigade were sent from Nis, Serbia, across the border with Bosnia and Herzegovina, and deployed in Slunj, in the occupied territories of Croatia in sector Glina. In addition, on June 12, 1995, one unit of armored personnel carriers (APCs) consisting of 10 vehicles operated by the Yugoslav Army Second Motorized Brigade was sent from Valjevo, Serbia, across the border with Bosnia and Herzegovina, and deployed in the same region in Croatia, at Banovina. Furthermore, on June 19, 1995, the Yugoslav army supplied equipment for two MI–8 rotary-wing aircraft located at the Udbina airport in the occupied territories, sector Knin, through the territory of Bosnia and Herzegovina.[49]

The U.N. did not have to rely on the Croatian authorities, however, for evidence of FRY involvement in the occupation of the Krajina and parts of Slavonia. The London weekly newspaper *The European* had created a stir already in early April by reporting that Major General Aleksandr Perelyakin, commander of the Russian and Belgian U.N. troops in the so-called Krajina region, had ordered the troops under his command to allow a Serbian convoy of six M-36 tanks, six howitzers, six 100 mm. guns, and a busload of Serb soldiers to cross U.N. lines into Krajina to reinforce Serbian occupation forces there.[50] The Belgian soldiers complained bitterly, and the senior-ranking Belgian officer, Colonel Francois Thonon, protested that these orders were contrary to U.N. guidelines. The convoy went through, but shortly thereafter, Perelyakin was dismissed by the U.N. for "severe shortcomings."[51]

In the weeks following the Croatian reconquest of western Slavonia, Serbian occupation authorities in the so-called Krajina forcibly recruited as many able-bodied Serbs as they could, including recent refugees from western Slavonia.[52] On 28 July, Croatian forces overran the towns of Glamoč and Bosansko Grahovo, thereby choking off the Serbs' supply route to Knin. Then, on 4 August, the Croatian Army, its morale enormously boosted after its recent victory in western Slavonia, trained its guns on the Krajina. The Croatian Serb capital at Knin was bombarded by Croatian heavy artillery, and about 120,000 Croatian troops moved into the Krajina in a massive, multipronged attack. Within 36 hours, the Croats had retaken Knin, and within another 12 hours, the Croatian Army had liberated about 80 percent of the so-called Serbian Krajina.[53] Some 4,000 Serb fighters south of Zagreb surrendered to the Croats, while 150,000 other "Krajina" Serbs fled to Serb-occupied western Bosnia, abandoning their homes, their belongings, and their heavy weapons.[54] The operation also relieved the long Serbian siege of the Bihac enclave, where some 180,000 people (mainly Muslims) had endured hunger and privation for months. General Ivan Tolj, a Croatian Defense Ministry spokesperson, triumphantly proclaimed, "Nothing is going to be the same again after this. Any dreams about a 'greater Serbia' are past." As for Croatian Serb forces in the "Krajina," their fighting capacity was now, he declared, "totally destroyed."[55]

The British,[56] French, and Russian governments—all unsympathetic to the Croatian and Bosnian governments—condemned the Croatian offensive. The U.S. and Germany restricted themselves to expressing the opinion that a peaceful solution would have been preferable—in effect applauding the successful and virtually bloodless Croatian offensive. By the end of a week, the Croatian Army had established its control throughout what the Serbs had called the "Krajina" or, as the region has been called historically, central Dalmatia.[57] Moreover, as a result of this campaign, the Serbian presence in Croatia, which had accounted for 11.6 percent of the republic's population in 1991, was reduced to a mere 3 percent.[58]

Serbian refugees from the Krajina streamed into Bosnian Serb territory and into Serbia proper, some reduced to begging on the streets of Belgrade. The Holy Synod of the Serbian Orthodox Church now spoke out against Milošević, on 8 August, in its sharpest criticism since June 1992. "The shortsighted policy of the Yugoslav, Serbian, and Montenegrin leadership," the statement said, "has brought the Serbian people into a deadend, from which there is no escape."[59] Asserting that the Milošević regime had shown itself "incapable of continuing to lead this people," the Synod demanded Milosevic's resignation and the establishment of a "government of trust."[60]

HAMLET IN BOSNIA

To strike or not to strike, that is the question. It has always been the question. But like Shakespeare's Hamlet, the U.N. has seemed to require almost indefinite time to reflect on the essential question, even then not coming up with a clear answer. For the U.N., it seemed easier to postpone the point of decision, and so the decision was postponed and postponed and postponed again.

In fact, the UN's endless dithering about "what to do" may well lead one to conclude, as David Rieff has suggested, that "U.N. peacekeeping was an entirely unsuitable instrument for dealing with an ongoing conflict of the kind taking place in Bosnia."[61] Indeed, as Rieff conceded, there are sufficient grounds to speculate "that the great powers did not in fact want anything to be done [about the genocide in Bosnia], but rather wanted to give the appearance of doing something as a way of mollifying domestic public opinion in their respective countries."[62] And insofar as that may have been their chief motivation, cheap and easy measures are infinitely preferable to the more ambitious measures required to work toward self-determination, justice, and regional stability in the Balkans. This is why the U.N. and NATO have been generous with threats and proclamations and statements of intent and stingy when it comes to action. Former U.S. Secretary of State George P. Schultz spoke to precisely this issue in testimony before Congress in October 1994, telling those present, "You can't just snap your fingers. We don't need more statements, because we have got statements. The Universal Declaration on Human Rights says it all. What we need is operational capability. And I think the U.N. should try to do that."[63]

Aerial strikes could be employed to serve any of three distinct purposes—punitive, tactical, and strategic. *Punitive air strikes* are designed as purely retaliatory measures and have the objective of changing the targeted party's attitude and behavior. Punitive air strikes do not, by definition, change the balance of power, either locally or throughout the theater of operations. NATO aerial strikes conducted against Bosnian Serbs between 1993 and mid-September 1995 were strictly punitive in nature (although by no means without military and diplomatic significance). *Tactical air strikes*, by contrast, are designed to weaken the targeted party's capabilities locally and usually only temporarily. They are, therefore, useful in connection with specific battles or campaigns or in support of the realization of limited objectives. They usually involve targets such as weapons emplacements, radar sites, and communications facilities. The NATO air strikes against the Bosnian Serbs which began on 30 August 1995, had the potential to make a tactical difference, but Western governments chose to limit it to achieving largely "punitive" aims.[64] *Strategic air strikes,* finally, are designed to weaken the targeted party's capabilities throughout the theater of operations, preparatory to imposing a dictated peace.

Advocates of aerial strikes against Serbian and Bosnian Serb positions have generally had in mind *strategic air strikes* on the supposition that practitioners of genocide and mass rape should be considered "unreasonable" men, not readily restored to rational thinking. Yet as of this writing (17 September 1995), NATO has declined to launch strategic air strikes against the Bosnian Serbs, thus failing to change the balance of power in such a way as to bring about peace. This is why advocates of aerial strikes resented claims that aerial strikes had been tried and shown to be ineffective against the Serbs; such claims missed the point. It is true that some sort of peace might be obtained in this way; what may be doubted is whether a just or stabilizing peace could be obtained without first impacting the Serbs' capacity for offensive war and pushing the Serbs out of much of their Bosnian conquests.

But the point was not lost on the Bosnian government which, by 1995, treated the U.N. and NATO with increasing disdain and prepared its forces for counteroffensives against Bosnian Serb positions. Former U.S. President Jimmy Carter visited the region in December 1994 and negotiated a four-month ceasefire amid unrealistic expressions of optimism that the ceasefire might lead directly to peace in Bosnia.[65] The ceasefire was a convenience to both sides, given the inconveniences associated with Bosnia's winter. The most concrete result of the ceasefire was an exchange of prisoners, on which the Bosnian government and Bosnian Serbs agreed in mid-January.[66] The Bosnian government used the ceasefire to prepare its military for a spring offensive. During these months, there were repeated flights of C-130 transport aircraft into Bosnia, landing on a Bosnian government–controlled airstrip outside Tuzla. Among the weaponry delivered were Stinger antiaircraft missiles. The identity of the supplier remained undisclosed, although it was speculated that Turkey, Iran, and perhaps the U.S. might be responsible for the flights.[67] The Serbian side took advantage of the lull to complete the construction of a new detour road for use in Belgrade's continued supply of Karadzic's forces, by-passing international observers monitoring the main highway.[68] Serbs also denied U.N. monitors access to their radar equipment for a period of four days in early February 1995, during which "unexplained helicopter flights" were reported by U.N. ground troops.[69] In August 1995, the *Wall Street Journal* reported that, over the course of the preceding 12 months (i.e., since Milošević's promise to terminate all military supplies and support to the Bosnian Serbs—a promise for which Milošević had been rewarded with an easing of U.N. sanctions), Milošević had "rotated something like 108,000 troops in and out of Bosnia and supplied Bosnian Serbs with 512 tanks, 506 armored personnel carriers, some 250 mortars, howitzers and other types of artillery, 10 high-performance military jets, 18 transport helicopters and 8,700 tons of fuel."[70]

On 2 March, in flagrant disregard of the terms of the still-valid ceasefire accord, Bosnian Serbs revoked permission for food shipments to continue to be sent into besieged Bihać in northwest Bosnia, even though international aid workers "warned that civilians could starve to death."[71] Within three weeks, heavy fighting resumed in central and northeastern Bosnia, with battles around Tuzla and Travnik. Just north of Tuzla lay the strategic Posavina Corridor, a narrow strip of land that served Bosnian Serbs as a vital lifeline for supplies from Serbia.[72] Bosnian Serbs now raided the U.N.-supervised heavy weapons depot at Lukavica, southeast of Sarajevo, ignoring the fact that a Security Council resolution had threatened to unleash air strikes in such an eventuality.[73] The ensuing confrontations between government forces and Bosnian Serbs were described as the bloodiest battles since the beginning of the war three years earlier, prompting German journalist Carl Gustav Ströhm to speculate that the Bosnian government's struggle to overcome Serbian aggression may have reached a turning point.[74]

Thrown on the defensive, Bosnian Serb leader Karadžić responded by ordering artillery bombardment of Sarajevo, Tuzla, Bihać, and Goražde (all of them U.N.-declared "safe havens"), by announcing a general mobilization, and by calling for immediate peace talks and the return to the battle lines of 23 December.[75] In early April, Bosnian government forces captured Mount Vlasić from the Serbs; overlooking the town of Travnik, Mount Vlasić represented an important strategic stronghold.[76] Bosnian government forces also fought their way into the Majevica mountain range north of Tuzla. Representatives of the internatioanl "contact group" held talks in Belgrade and Zagreb, although they had nothing new to offer. These discussions took place amid renewed Serbian shelling of U.N. "safe havens" at Sarajevo, Bihać, and Tuzla. But while fighting in Bosnia intensified, NATO commanders talked not of enforcement of the "safe havens," but of withdrawal.[77]

The Bosnian Serbs launched a counteroffensive in early May, supported by massive artillery fire and tank forces. Unable to make any headway against the Bosnian government forces, the Bosnian Serbs took out their frustration on populations already under their jurisdiction, by blowing up at least six Catholic churches in Banja Luka and its immediate vicinity in the course of May alone, killing a Catholic priest and a nun, placing the Bishop of Banja Luka under house arrest, and driving other Catholic priests, monks, nuns, and lay persons from the area.[78] The Serbs had blown up all 16 of Banja Luka's mosques two years earlier.[79]

Belatedly responding to the Bosnian Serb seizure of heavy weapons from Lukavica, the U.N. demanded that the weapons be returned by noon on 25 May, threatening air strikes if the Serbs failed to comply. Bosnian Serbs rebuffed the U.N., issuing counterthreats of their own. The U.N. therefore authorized NATO warplanes to bomb a Bosnian Serb munitions depot outside Pale.[80] Bosnian Serbs, in turn, shelled all six U.N. "safe havens," killing more than 70 persons in Tuzla alone. NATO aircraft once again attacked Serb positions, bombarding the munitions depot a second time and destroying six bunkers. The same day Bosnian Serbs rounded up more than 370 U.N. troops and chained them up in front of an ammunition depot and at other sites, using them as human shields.[81] On 29 May, Bosnian Serb leader "Radovan Karadžić and his army's supreme command voted . . . to cancel all U.N. resolutions to which they had been a party because the United Nations 'interfered in the war and allied with our enemies.'"[82] Interestingly enough, this Serbian claim to be exempt from international law and from the decisions of international bodies came within two weeks of a decision by the U.N. War Crimes Tribunal in The Hague to name Karadžić, Bosnian Serb General Ratko Mladić, and Karadžić's secret police chief, Mico Stanišić, as war criminals.[83]

Although the U.N. shortly negotiated the release of its peacekeepers, the humiliation was an object lesson to many advocates of the "soft touch." The immediate impact was the prompt policy-makers in Britain, France, and other countries to agree to establish a mobile rapid reaction force consisting of 4,000 troops and to move more military equipment into the area. In connection with this new force, U.S. Defense Secretary William J. Perry announced on 4 June that the United States would establish a secret intelligence-gathering unit to assist in monitoring Bosnian Serb movements of troops and military hardware.[84] The United States also agreed to provide close air support for operations of the rapid reaction force, including AC-130 gunships.[85]

In mid-June, the Bosnian government massed between 15,000 and 30,000 troops north and northwest of Sarajevo around the towns of Breza and Visoko in what was described as an unprecedented concentration of forces. In the ensuing offensive, government troops made territorial gains at the Serbs' expense. In the course of the June offensive, Bosnian government forces captured Mt. Treškavica, south of Sarajevo and temporarily cut off a key access road to Pale. The Serbs replied by shelling Sarajevo's main hospital and other civilian targets in the Bosnian capital.[86] This merely replicated what has become a *Leitmotif* of the Bosnian war: Bosnian government offensives have been directed largely against military objectives, inflicting casualties primarily on Bosnian Serb *soldiers*, while Bosnian Serb campaigns have been directed principally against civilian centers and unarmed civilians, repeatedly killing women, children, the elderly, patients in hospitals, schoolchildren at school, priests, and nuns.

As civilian casualties in Sarajevo continued to mount and responding, more specifically, to a violation of the "no fly" zone by two Serb warplanes, NATO requested authorization to destroy the main Bosnian Serb air base. But as had happened so often in the past, the request was denied.[87] In a potentially portentous development, the U.N. "withdrew all of its peacekeepers who were manning weapons collections points around Sarajevo, in effect acknowledging [its] inability to stop the Serbs from shelling the city," and simultaneously denied a request from Lt.-Gen. Rupert Smith, U.N. Commander in Bosnia, for permission to use force to secure a corridor for food supplies to be brought into Sarajevo.[88]

General Smith's request was indicative. Indeed, since assuming command of U.N. forces in Bosnia in January 1995, the general had repeatedly demanded that the U.N. and NATO get tough with the Serbs.[89] But even as Britain, France, and Russia continued to prevent the U.N. and NATO from even providing an effective defense of Bosnian civilians, British Prime Minister John Major told the G-7 leaders at a June meeting in Halifax, Nova

Scotia, that all of them collectively were "at a loss [as to] how to end the bloodshed" in Bosnia[90]—ignoring the fact that President Clinton and German Chancellor Kohl, not to mention former British Prime Minister Margaret Thatcher, did not consider themselves "at a loss," but merely road-blocked . . . by Major, among others. As General John Shalikashvili, Chairman of the U.S. Joint Chiefs of Staff, admitted, "The problem has not been with my colleagues in this Administration. The problem has been in the inability to convince our international partners."[91]

Ironically, it was the Bosnian Serbs themselves who would soon help to convince Britain of the necessity of military action. Having lost land in central Bosnia, the Bosnian Serbs decided to seek compensation in the east, specifically by overrunning the government-held towns of Srebrenica and Žepa, both U.N.-declared "safe havens." The first "safe haven" to fall to the Serbs was Srebrenica (where 42,000 persons were housed), which fell to a 1,500-man force on 11 July. Bosnian Serb forces immediately began rounding up women and children, putting them on buses; the men were taken away, allegedly to be "screened for war crimes." Eventually, some 30,000 refugees from Srebrenica made it to Tuzla, another "safe haven." But up to 10,000 persons, mainly young men, remained unaccounted for. The U.N. was soon able to document that the Serbs had liquidated them en masse and buried them in a mass grave. Refugees tearfully described scenes of intense cruelty and brutality, including rapes, physical degredation, and outright slaughter of unarmed civilians.[92] The U.N. made no response, however. A U.N. official explained: "To reclaim Srebrenica, you'd have to be prepared to fight . . . and there is no political will to do that."[93]

Disgusted with the U.N.'s evident weakness, Bosnian government troops surrounded U.N. bases and observation posts in Žepa and Goražde and confiscated the U.N. forces' weapons. In Žepa, the 70 Ukrainian soldiers who comprised the U.N. "peacekeeping" force there at first refused to surrender their arms. But after Bosnian government troops surrounded their base and mined the entrance, the Ukrainians reconsidered and turned over their weapons. The Bosnian government troops then took the Ukrainians into custody and moved them to the frontlines to serve as human shields against the expected Serb attack.[94] The Serbs overran Žepa a few days later, all the same, allegedly using poison gas to subdue resistance.[95] The Bosnian commander of Žepa, Colonel Avdo Palić, attempted to negotiate a surrender, but the Serbs ignored the tradition of safe passage and executed Palić on the spot.[96] The ill-fated Ukrainians now fell into Bosnian Serb hands and were once agan put to use as "human shields"—this time to ward off NATO air strikes. Some of Žepa's 16,000 inhabitants were shot by the Serbs, though at least 3,000 escaped into the hills around Žepa. After taking the town, the Serbs looted Žepa, then torched it, firing shots into the woods in hopes of killing any civilians who might be hiding there.[97]

As the Powers took stock of these developments, Radovan Karadžić defiantly warned that Bosnian Serb gunners would shoot down any NATO warplanes that might attempt to salvage either of these two fallen "safe havens." The White House now drew up a proposal for intensive NATO bombing of Bosnian Serb positions and began lobbying with the British and French. The French readily agreed, and on 20 July, the British finally gave their assent. The result was a rather unbelievable warning to the Serbs that any Serbian assault on the Bosnian-government enclave of Goražde would meet with a "substantial and decisive response" by the international community.[98] Russian Defense Minister Pavel Grachev registered Moscow's opposition to the resolution, but U.S. Secretary of State Warren Christopher dismissed Russia's objections, observing, "The Russians do not have a veto" over NATO decisions.[99] On 1 August, ignoring Russian objections, the NATO allies extended their guarantee of air strike retaliation to the other three remaining "safe havens," Sarajevo included.

A TURNING POINT?

Over the preceding two and a half years, the presence of U.N. "peacekeepers" had repeatedly been cited by U.N. and E.C. spokespersons as a reason for not bombing the Serbs; on their argument, any such bombardment would risk retaliation against the "peacekeepers." Gradually, however, a consensus emerged in NATO and E.C. councils that if the presence of "peacekeepers" obstructed actions necessary to enforce peace, then they were not peacekeepers at all, but *peace-obstructers*. It was with this realization that the U.N. began moving its so-called "peacekeepers" out of Goražde in mid-August.[100] Even so, it took two further incidents to bring NATO to the moment of decision. The first was a fatal attack on three high-ranking diplomats, who were driving along the Mount Igman road into Sarajevo.[101] After initial hesitations, the Western states eventually blamed the Bosnian Serbs for the attack. The second incident occurred on 28 August when Bosnian Serbs fired a 120-mm. mortar into downtown Sarajevo, killing at least 39 persons and wounding more than 80.[102] The Bosnian Serb attack was probably inspired by military reverses that the significantly better-armed Bosnian Serb forces had experienced in the field since the latest Croat-Muslim joint offensive.[103] Western leaders expressed outrage, and the United States now pressed its NATO partners to agree to a strong response.

NATO's response came two days later when more than 60 NATO aircraft began bombing Bosnian Serb missile sites, radar sites, communications facilities, artillery positions, ammunition dumps, and other military objects. After several hours of bombing, NATO spokespersons claimed that the air strikes had already achieved their "preliminary objectives" and that "a substantial number of targets were damaged or destroyed" as a result of the first day's strikes.[104]

NATO air strikes continued over the next two days, hitting army barracks, weapons depots, artillery batteries, and other military targets. The Bosnian Serbs fired back at NATO aircraft, but in three days of aerial strikes, succeeded in downing only one French jet.

NATO called a temporary halt to air strikes on 1 September in order to give the Serbs the opportunity to signal their willingness to cooperate. When such signals failed to materialize, NATO resumed bombing on 5 September.[105] As NATO continued to destroy radar sites, barracks, communications centers, and ammunition dumps, not only around Sarajevo and Pale, but also at other locations throughout Bosnia, Bosnian Serb General Mladić struck a bizarre note, accusing NATO of having been "more brutal than . . . Hitler."[106] But despite the ostensible toughness, NATO was in fact carefully circumscribing its attacks. As the *Washington Post* noted, "Few airstrikes have been directed against frontline units . . . including the artillery ringing Sarajevo. NATO has specifically placed those targets off-limits so as not to be seen as trying to strategically affect the outcome of the war."[107]

But as the strikes continued, Russian President Boris Yeltsin protested and warned that Moscow would reassess its relationship with the West unless the air strikes ended quickly.[108] Equally unsurprising was the Greek government's expressions of "strong reservations" about the strikes, even though Athens had been required to render its assent before the strikes could begin.[109]

The air strikes continued for more than a week; the Serbs remained defiant at first, and even fired two missiles on a NATO reconnaissance jet near Goražde on 15 September.[110] Eventually the Serbs gave in to U.N. pressure and began to pull their heavy guns out of the U.N. weapons exclusion zone. By nightfall, 16 September, the Bosnian Serbs had moved some 43 heavy weapons away from Sarajevo.[111] But as the Serbs gradually complied with an extended U.N. deadline, Bosnian and Croatian troops rolled back the Serbs in western Bosnia, mopping up Jajce and moving, by 17 September, to within striking distance of Banja Luka, the Serbs biggest prize in western Bosnia.[112]

Even as the NATO allies threatened to continue aerial strikes until the Serbian threat to "safe havens" had been removed and the Serbs showed signs of abiding by U.N. decisions, U.S. Assistant Secretary of State Richard Holbrooke continued to press the Serbs to agree to a peace plan that would give the Serbs—31.46 percent of Bosnia's population in the April 1991 census—49 percent of Bosnia's land.[113] That this plan amounts to rewarding Serbian aggression does not seem to have occurred to Western diplomats, any more than they have grasped the irony of branding Karadžić a "war criminal" and then negotiating with him or with his sponsor Milošević as if they were legitimate heads of state. But the air strikes were not designed to serve in the pursuit of justice, but merely to compel the Serbs to agree to what is, by any objective standard, an appeasement constitutive of gross injustice. Two former State Department officials put their fingers on the nub of the problem: "Serbia's genocidal assault . . . is a military, not a political, problem; it will have to be dealt with militarily before negotiations can bear fruit."[114] But at this writing, the air strikes of 30 August–16 September notwithstanding, it does not appear that either NATO or the Western powers (those being equivalent) have the will to persist in military measures until a just and stable solution can be achieved. What the West seems to want is to recapitulate the kind of folly it realized at previous peace conferences in 1878 and 1913.[115] The West is fond of grumbling about the headaches that it must suffer on account of the Balkans. It would be well for the West to remember that some of these headaches are of Western manufacture.[116]

CONSEQUENCES OF THE WAR

From the beginning of Latin American stirrings for independence from Spain in the early nineteenth century until the outbreak of war in Bosnia in 1992, the international community had largely recognized the principle of *uti possedetis*, which held that in the event of the breakup of colonial empires or preexisting states alike, internal administrative boundaries should be accepted as the boundaries of new states. This principle had been explicitly reaffirmed by the International Court of Justice in 1986 and by the Arbitration Commission on Yugoslavia in January 1992.[117] It may well be that Bosnia was a special exception that required a different approach. But by making an exception of Bosnia, the West has paid a high diplomatic price, scuttling a principle of international law designed to reward negotiation not aggression. The scuttling of the principle of *uti possedetis* is the first consequence of the sluggishness of Western response in the Balkan war.

A second consequence is to have demonstrated that there is no Europe. In the late 1980s, Soviet General Secretary Mikhail Gorbachev popularized the notion of "our Common European Home," and after the collapse of communism in Europe, the notion of a single Europe grew even though many of the converts to this new myth were not entirely sure what it was that they believed. But if London and Paris can experience difficulty in understanding why an armed response is necessary to combat genocide and mass rape in the Balkans until the number of dead reaches half a million, then it is clear that there is no sense of a common Europe. Moreover, the internal bickering among the West European states (principally Britain and

France against Germany) indicated that a truly united Europe is still far from being realized.

A third consequence is to have raised serious doubts about NATO, an organization created to guarantee peace and security in Europe (but not everywhere in the world as A. M. Rosenthal, among others, seems to think[118]). The air strikes of 30 August–1 September and 5–16 September 1995 notwithstanding, NATO has failed its first serious test. Confronted with massive genocide and mass rape, with *apartheid*, and with repeated violations of U.N. dictates and resolutions by the Serbs, NATO proved slow and indecisive. Turkey has already raised the question why it should remain in NATO, given its appalling record in the Bosnian crisis.[119] If Britain had been attacked and subjected to genocide on a massive scale, rather than Bosnia, it would not have required three years of bombardment and massacre, until the death toll reached more than 300,000, for Whitehall to conclude that NATO might play some role in defending the civilian population. This is generally understood, and this general understanding only contributes to the growing disillusionment in NATO.

A fourth consequence relates to the U.N. Up to now, it has generally been accepted that the victors of World War II had a right to permanent seats in the U.N. Security Council and to veto powers. Yet it is British, French, and Russian brandishing of their vetos that prevented the ill-conceived arms embargo against the Bosnian Muslims from being lifted. What may be necessary—as Jonathan Steele has suggested—if the U.N. is to have any efficacy in the future and any control over its own resolutions, is to *eliminate* the veto privilege of these powers.[120] Decisions by majority vote would be the logical alternative.

Fifth, the West's illusions about having created a collaborative relationship with Russia have been shown to be largely folly. Not only has Russia not respected the U.N. embargo, but it has literally flaunted its violations, ostentatiously signing economic agreements with the FRY (Serbia) in September 1994 and February and May 1995,[121] as well as a military agreement in March 1995.[122] The West yearns for what Francis Fukuyama has called an "end of history," but the Bosnian war has provided ample evidence that the adversarial relationship between Russia and the West continues, suggesting that policies framed on the assumption of collaboration will be apt to have unintended consequences.

Sixth, there is the domestic impact of the war on the states directly concerned, viz., Bosnia, Croatia, and the FRY. Aside from the casualties (estimated variably at 200,000–300,000 dead in early 1994, but probably closer to 500,000 today), the refugees (3.7 million as of mid–1995), the maimed (estimated at 58,000 in Croatia and Bosnia as of early 1994[123]), and the missing, there has also been wholesale damage to infrastructure in all three states—in Bosnia and Croatia as a direct product of the war, in Serbia and

Montenegro as a by-product of the financially unwise diversion of vital resources from internal consumption to the war effort. Lebanon is still rebuilding, some 10 years after its own civil war wound down. The Yugoslav successor states, which may have endured a bloodier and more destructive war than that experienced in Lebanon, stand to require even more time.

Bosnia-Herzegovina has been the hardest hit by the war. In 1993, industrial production in that republic was estimated at just 4.8 percent of the level of 1992.[124] As of October 1994, there were about one million persons unemployed in those parts of Bosnia still controlled by the Bosnian government.[125] At least seven railway bridges have been destroyed, cutting off Sarajevo from both Mostar and Ploce. The cost of rebuilding the railway system alone has been estimated at $150 million.[126] The health care and educational systems have been totally disrupted, with the universities functioning only on a nominal basis.[127]

The Croatian economy was functioning at only 50 percent of its 1989 level in 1993, having suffered staggering declines in industrial production since 1990.[128] Croatia's shipbuilding and tourist industries, two mainstays of the Croatian economy, have also been hard hit—the former due to shortages of raw materials. The Croatian railway and road network has also been severely damaged. Burke and Macdonald estimate that some 6,500 kilometers of roads in Croatia were rendered unusable as a result of the fighting in 1991, and cited, in particular, the destruction of 33 bridges. They further estimate that some 30 percent of the railway system was put out of operation and note heavy damage to the airports at Zadar, Dubrovnik, and Osijek, as well as damage to the port at šibenik.[129] There has also been war damage to major touristic sites, such as the 500-year-old arboretum in Trsteno (near Dubrovnik) which was destroyed by Serbian artillery fire, the Plitvice Lakes National Park (which had been classified a World Heritage Site), and much of the historic town of Dubrovnik. Agriculture in Croatia has also been hurt. Moreover, even with the expulsion of the Serbian occupation forces from western Slavonia, the presence of large numbers of land mines, planted by Serbian forces, "will ensure that farming is a dangerous business in some areas for years to come."[130]

Although there has been no combat in Serbia or Montenegro as of this writing, the economy of the FRY has been severely impacted by the war, both because of the diversion of manpower and resources and because of the U.N. economic sanctions. In April 1995, economic output in the FRY was estimated at 49.3 percent of the level of April 1991.[131] As of January 1994, some 600,000 persons were registered as unemployed in the FRY, while another 2 million were classified has having been "temporarily" laid off.[132] The quality of healthcare, education, media, and food supplies has declined dramatically. As Burke and Macdonald note, "Not only has [Serbia's] pre-war economy essentially ceased to exist, [but] its relatively advanced welfare state has all but disappeared as a result of the channelling of resources into the war effort."[133]

Seventh, while the war may be traced directly to Serbia's embrace of nationalism and authoritarianism, Croatia might have fared better, in political terms, but for the war. By giving stimulus and free rein to deep hatred of Serbs—as aggressors but also simply as Serbs—the war has reinforced a tendency toward authoritarianism that already inhered in the CDC and has muted political opposition. Nepotism has reared its head in Croatia, the *Sabor* (Assembly) has been marginalized, key media outlets have been taken over, and there have been confirmed pressures on Serbs to convert to Catholicism, alongside other human rights abuses of Serbs.[134] Žarko Puhovski, a University of Zagreb professor much respected in opposition circles, drew attention, in a 1995 article for the British journal, *Red Pepper*, to the promotion of an *ad hoc* body known as the Security Council to the "real center of power," concluding that the Croatian state under Tudjman "is more like an imitation of 18th century absolutism than any modern regime."[135]

An eighth consequence of the war as to do with the psychological scars of the war. In Bosnia, most of the 300,000 civilians still living in Sarajevo are said to exhibit paranoid symptoms reminiscent of concentration camp victims in World War II. A UNICEF survey of children in East Mostar found that there was a high incidence of traumatic flashbacks, sleeplessness, and indigestion among the children of Mostar; moreover, 85 percent of the children surveyed no longer had families, either because of deaths or because they had fled their homes.[136] Dr. Soren Jennsen, a Danish psychiatrist who took leave from his position at Aalborg, Denmark, to help with psychiatric care in Sarajevo, says, "Some 20,000 full-time experts would be needed to cope with this number [of psychiatric disorders]. . . . But there are only 100 top professionals available, so we can cope with only one or two percent of the real needs."[137] In Croatia, psychologists report "extraordinary rates of divorce, alcoholism, drug abuse, suicide, and domestic and public violence," since 1991.[138] Post-traumatic stress, exaggerated feelings of guilt, and sudden emotionality have all become far more common in Croatia. And in the FRY, broken marriages, domestic and public and violence, alcoholism, and post-traumatic stress have also become rampant. Belgrade anthropologist Petar Vlahović has estimated that altogether some 9 million people in the three states concerned have been directly affected by the war.[139] There is, therefore, a special irony in the fact that three of the Serbs' leaders all have backgrounds in psychology or psychiatry: Biljana Plavšić, renowned as one of Pale's most extreme "hawks," once taught psychoanalysis; Jovan Rašković, the leading ideologue of Serbian nationalism in the late 1980s, had training in psychiatry and was fond of talking about the Croats' alleged "castration complex" and the alleged "rectal frustrations" of the Muslims;

and Karadžić himself was working, before 1990, as a psychologist for a local soccer team.[140]

REFLECTIONS

This book has argued that political dynamics are reflected in, and even adumbrated by, changes in the cultural sphere and that the religious sphere underpins and legitimizes actions and decisions taken in the political sphere. The political, cultural, and religious spheres do not exist apart from each other; they are, rather, organic parts of a religio-politico-cultural system, in which activity in one part has intentions, reflections, and consequences in other parts. Hence, the Serbian Orthodox Church's endorsement of the Serbian military campaign in 1991[141] heightened the political profile of that Church, deepened and cemented its growing alliance with the Serbian government of Slobodan Milošević, and distorted the Church's Gospel itself. Yet so involved did the Serbian Church become in the Serbian nationalist revival and in support for the military campaign that the Vatican, which was overtly sympathetic to the Croatian aspirations for independence,[142] sent its Secretary for Foreign Relations, Jean-Louis Toran, to Belgrade on 7 August 1991, to confer with Patriarch Pavle about the crisis.[143]

More broadly, the disintegration of the political fabric in Yugoslavia was presaged by an unremitting fixation, on the part of Serbian writers, on war and war-induced suffering[144] and by a deterioration of interethnic relations in various spheres, including ecumenical contacts, the media, and even, as outlined earlier in this book, rock music. Later, the rise of nationalist movements in Serbia, Croatia, and Slovenia was reflected in sundry spheres: including rock music, where the strident tones of Laibach served as a warning (with Bora Djordjević as the self-appointed rock bard of Serbian nationalism), and in the sphere of gender relations, where the new chauvinists expressed disdain for feminists and impatience with demands that women be treated with dignity. More recently, the psychological scarring that the war has produced in Serbian society has been reflected in the names of some of the newest rock bands. These include bands such as Acroholia, Bloodbath, Bomba za system (A Bomb for the System), Boneblast, Corpus Delicti, Dead Ideas, Ekstremisti, Hands in Ashes, Malfunctions, Mortuary, Napred u Prošlost (Forward into the Past), Pogibija (Catastrophe), Purgatory, and Scaffold. One of Serbia's new breed of "turbo-rock" bands offered this bleak alternative: "We are going to Mars. Life is better there."[145]

Some cultural figures sought to assail the very cultural underpinnings of each other's nation. For example, *Politika* reported claims made by certain Serbian figures at Croats' expense. Milan Paroški, a deputy in the Serbian parliament, told that body that "Croats did not have any literature except for Serbian literature," while Serbian writer Antonije Isaković declared, "Seeing that they could not constitute a nation on the cakavian and kajkavian dialects (spoken in Croatia), Croats got the idea to take our language (Serbian)."[146] The denigration of the culture of the "enemy" nation may even extend to disparagement of specific songs. For example, the Serbian daily *Politika* claimed, in August 1991, that Croats were singing patriotic songs honoring wartime fascist leader Ante Pavelić.[147] The denigration of the other's culture is, thus, one side of the politicocultural coin.

The other side of the coin is that political atavism invariably entails cultural atavism. And hence, calls in Serbia in the course of 1991 for a restoration of the alleged glory of the interwar Kingdom of Serbs, Croats, and Slovenes—including the restoration of its laws—were accompanied not merely by renewed interest in the Karadjordjević dynasty, and especially Crown Prince Alexander, but also by calls for the restoration of the old Serbian coat of arms and anthem.[148]

In fact, intercommunal political conflict necessarily has a cultural dimension. And victory or defeat in the political sphere may entail as well corresponding victory or defeat in the cultural and religious spheres.

The Titoists had some sense of this, and this is why they argued back and forth in the 1950s and early 1960s, as to whether they should aspire to create a new culture, a Yugoslav culture, which would melt down and assimilate the "partial" cultures of the component peoples of this country, or whether they should rather extend toleration to all component cultures, while promoting a thin overlay of "Yugoslav culture," based ultimately on Partisan mythology from World War II and notions of self-management. In 1964, at its Eighth Party Congress, the League of Communists opted for the second strategy: toleration while promoting a thin overlay of "Yugoslavism." The internal contradiction here, not noticed at the time, was that in tying this Yugoslavism to the Partisan mythology, this strategy entailed constant reminders of the inter-communal internecine strife of that war. Hence, even while trying to build a concept of "Yugoslavism," Yugoslavia's communists constantly stirred up the old fires of intergroup hatred. Viewed in this way, civil war was the logical outcome of this strategy.

Could the alternative approach—energetic homogenization—have worked? Successful instances of this approach in Europe tend to involve cases where unification and adoption of this policy occurred much earlier (e.g., England, France, Spain). Twentieth-century European attempts to pursue such a policy (the USSR, interwar Czechoslovakia, interwar and early postwar Yugoslavia, and Romanian Transylvania) have all run up against serious difficulties.

A 1991 article by Andrei Simić sheds additional light on the dynamics of these processes. Describing the concept of a "moral field" (defined as "an interactional sphere where those engaged typically behave towards each other with reference to ethically perceived imperatives, that is, rules that are accepted as being 'good,' 'God-given,' 'natural,' 'proper,' and so forth,"[149]) Simić argues that the membership of a moral field depends on criteria of recruitment that generally are functions of kinship, tribe, or nation. "Within a moral field," Simić points out, "members are expected to act towards each other with reference to a common set of shared ideas by which behavior is structured and evaluated. In contrast, behavior outside the moral field can be said to be *amoral* in that it is primarily idiosyncratic and as such may be purely instrumental or exploitative without being subject to sanctions. Thus, for the individual, those belonging to other moral fields can be said to form part of his or her *amoral* sphere."[150] And hence, actions which might be deemed morally reprehensible when committed against a fellow member of the moral field (such as murder, torture, rape, confiscation of goods) may be seen as morally commendable when committed against persons not included in the group's moral field.

Viewing the issue in this way, it is apparent that the Titoists failed to create a common moral field in which all Yugoslavs would be included. Instead, moral fields remained coincident with ethnic communities, heightening the risks and dangers of political disintegration. Morality, molded and manipulated by politics, culture, and religion alike, ultimately has lain at the heart of the breakdown of the Yugoslav system and the breakup of Yugoslavia itself.

NOTES

1. Quoted in Ivo Banac, "The Dissolution of Yugoslav Historiography," in Sabrina Petra Ramet and Ljubiša S. Adamovich, eds., *Beyond Yugoslavia: Politics, Economics, and Culture in a Shattered Community* (Boulder, Colo.: Westview Press, 1994), p. 60n.

2. Quoted in *Radio Free Europe Research* (25 November 1983), p. 2.

3. Pedro Ramet, "Yugoslavia and the Threat of Internal and External Discontents," in *Orbis*, Vol. 28, No. 1 (Spring 1984), p. 114. (The article was written in November 1983).

4. Sabrina P. Ramet, "The Breakup of Yugoslavia," *Global Affairs*, Vol. 6, No. 2 (Spring 1991), p. 97.

5. *New York Times* (5 March 1995), p. 3.

6. *Rilindja* (Zofingen) (22 February 1995), p. 5, trans. in *(FBIS), Daily Report* (Eastern Europe), 24 February 1995, p. 43; confirmed in *Neue Zürcher Zeitung* (6 March 1995), p. 14.

7. According to Human Rights Watch, the Serbs expelled some 69,000 Muslims from the Sandžak between 1991 and summer 1993 and some 60,000 ethnic Hungarians and 40,000 Croats from Vojvodina between 1991 and spring 1994. See "Abuses Continue in the Former Yugoslavia: Serbia, Montenegro, and Bosnia-Hercegovina," *Human Rights Watch Helsinki*, Vol. 5, Issue 11 (July 1993), pp. 6–7, 13; Commission on Security and Cooperation in Europe, *Sandžak and the CSCE*

(Washington, D.C.: A Report prepared by the staff of the CSCE, April 1993), pp. 1, 6; "Human Rights Abuses of Non-Serbs in Kosovo, Sandzak and Vojvodina," *Human Rights Watch Helsinki,* Vol. 6, Issue 6 (May 1994), p. 7; and *MTI* (Budapest), 9 September 1993, in *FBIS, Daily Report* (Eastern Europe), 10 September 1993, p. 12. For compatible but earlier estimates of the numbers being driven out of Vojvodina and the Sandžak, see *MTI* (10 November 1991), *Nexis* and *Washington Post* (11 November 1992), p. A1.

8. Croats and Bosnian Muslims remained divided on salient issues and on the first anniversary of the federation, West European newspapers suggested that the federation still existed largely only on paper. See *Večernji list* (Zagreb) (24 June 1994), p. 7; *Frankfurter Allgemeine* (24 June 1994), p. 6; *Neue Zürcher Zeitung* (17 March 1995), p. 6; and *Die Welt* (Bonn) (21 March 1995), p. 4. See also *Oslobodjenje,* European ed. (Sarajevo/Ljubljana) (26 January–2 February 1995), p. 2, and 24–31 August 1995, p. 3.

9. *Seattle Times* (13 May 1994), p. A3; and *The Sunday Times* (London) (15 May 1994), p. 17.

10. *Boston Sunday Globe* (19 June 1994), p. 6; *Večernji list* (Zagreb) (21/22 June 1994), p. 8; and *La Repubblica* (Rome) (1 July 1994), p. 13.

11. *The Globe and Mail* (Toronto) (22 July 1994), p. A8.

12. *Daily Telegraph* (London) (21 July 1994), p. 13.

13. For a discussion of the limp Western response to the Bosnian crisis, see Sabrina Petra Ramet, "The Yugoslav Crisis and the West: Avoiding 'Vietnam' and Blundering into 'Abyssinia,' " in *East European Politics and Societies,* Vol. 8, No. 1 (Winter 1994).

14. *Slobodna Dalmacija* (Split) (2 February 1995), p. 2; *Frankfurter Allgemeine* (4 February 1995), p. 3; *Feral Tribune—Glede i unatoč* (Split) (6 February 1995), pp. 6–7; *Večernji list* (16 February 1995), p. 3, 20 February 1995, p. 2, and 21 February 1995, p. 9; and *Nedjeljna Dalmacija* (Split) (24 March 1995), pp. 22–23.

15. *New York Times* (30 January 1995), p. A3.

16. A poll conducted by *Večernji list* in the first week of February 1995 among 450 Croats from all of Croatia's counties found that 72.2 percent of those polled considered the Z-4 Plan "unacceptable," while only 10.8 percent approved of it. See *Večernji list* (9 February 1995), p. 2, trans. in *FBIS, Daily Report* (Eastern Europe), 9 February 1995, p. 26.

17. See Darko Vukorepa, "Galbraith radi protiv Hrvatske interese," *Nedjeljna Dalmacija* (30 December 1994), pp. 5–6. Regarding subsequent Croatian criticism of Galbraith in connection with his expressions of sympathy with Serbs fleeing the Krajina in August 1995, see *Globus* (18 August 1995), pp. 3–5.

18. Regarding rejection by the Croatian government, see *New York Times* (31 January 1995), p. A3. Regarding rejection by the Croatian Serbs, see *Süddeutsche Zeitung* (Munich) (1 February 1995), p. 1; and *Evropske novosti* (4 February 1995), p. 5.

19. Public talk by Ambassador Peter Galbraith at the University of Washington, Seattle, Washington, January 1995. On the same occasion, Ambassador Galbraith expressed the view that peaceful population exchanges were an "inhumane" way of resolving intense border conflicts and indicated that, in the Bosnian situation, the actual developments, in which roughly half a million persons have lost their lives,

are—in his view—*preferable* to population exchanges, even if they could have saved lives. Regrettably, Ambassador Galbraith did not explain how he had reached this conclusion.

20. Ambassador Peter W. Galbraith, "Diplomacy Helps Contain the Bosnian Conflict", *SAIS Review*, Vol. 15, No. 2 (Summer-Fall 1995), p. 117.

21. *Süddeutsche Zeitung* (14 February 1995), p. 6; and *Neue Zürcher Zeitung* (16 February 1995), p. 1.

22. *New York Times* (15 February 1995), p. A4; *Süddeutsche Zeitung* (16 February 1995), pp. 1, 4; *Večernji list* (16 February 1995), p. 32; *Neue Zürcher Zeitung* (21 February 1995), p. 1, and (23 February 1995), p. 3; *Balkan News International & East European Report* (Athens) (5–11 March 1995), p. 28; *Naša borba* (Belgrade), 23 March 1995, p. 1; and *Vjesnik* (Zagreb), 24 March 1995, p. 8.

23. In fact, the Belgrade government reiterated its refusal to recognize the Bosnian government's authority even within the existing borders in late May 1995. See *Welt am Sonntag* (Hamburg), 28 May 1995, p. 7.

24. For documentation on Serb "ethnic cleansing" in these areas 1994–1995, see *New York Times* (30 August 1994), pp. A1, A5; *Vreme* (Belgrade) (12 September 1994), pp. 18–19, trans. in *FBIS, Daily Report* (Eastern Europe), 5 October 1994, pp. 35–37; Radio Croatia Network (Zagreb) (6 February 1995), trans. in *FBIS, Daily Report* (Eastern Europe), 7 February 1995, p. 45; *Welt am Sonntag* (26 February 1995), p. 2; AFP (Paris), 1 March 1995, in *FBIS, Daily Report* (Eastern Europe), 2 March 1995, pp. 30–31; and *Reuters World Service* (2 June 1995), *Nexis*.

25. Manifested, for example, in the announcement in February 1994 that the Bosnian Serb "Republic" was joining the FRY monetary and financial system. See Srpski Radio-Televizija Studio (Pale), 28 February 1994, trans. in *FBIS, Daily Report* (Eastern Europe), 1 March 1994, p. 32.

26. For some examples of confinement and chaining, see *AFP* (Paris) (19 September 1994), in *FBIS, Daily Report* (Eastern Europe), 19 September 1994, p. 25; *Neue Zürcher Zeitung* (5 April 1995), p. 2; *Frankfurter Allgemeine* (8 April 1995), p. 6; *New York Times* (30 May 1995), p. A1; and *Focus* (Munich) (3 June 1995), p. 228.

27. Lenard J. Cohen, *Broken Bonds: Yugoslavia's Disintegration and Balkan Politics in Transition*, 2nd ed. (Boulder, Colo.: Westview Press, 1995), p. 293.

28. *AFP* (Paris) (29 September 1994), in *FBIS, Daily Report* (Eastern Europe), 30 September 1994, p. 19.

29. Misha Glenny, "Council of Despair", in *New York Times* (6 December 1994), p. A15.

30. Cf. Lt.-Gen. Sir Michael Rose: "We are pro-reason. And I don't think anyone can criticize us for that." Quoted in *New York Times* (29 January 1995), p. 6.

31. Quoted in David Rieff, "The Lessons of Bosnia: Morality and Power", *World Policy Journal*, Vol. 12, No. 1 (Spring 1995), p. 84.

32. *Ljiljan* (9 November 1994), p. 15, trans. in *FBIS, Daily Report* (Eastern Europe), 23 November 1994, p. 36.

33. Quoted in ibid., p. 36.

34. Ibid., p. 37.

35. *Slobodna Dalmacija* (25 February 1995), p. 8, trans. in *FBIS, Daily Report* (Eastern Europe), 7 March 1995, pp. 40–41.

36. *The Independent* (London) (10 July 1995), p. 8.

37. Ibid.

38. *Globus* (Zagreb) (17 February 1995), pp. 12–13, trans. in *FBIS, Daily Report* (Eastern Europe), 23 February 1995, p. 62.

39. Reports as to who actually provided the training have differed. *Evropske novosti* (29 July 1995), p. 4, claimed that U.S. officers and instructors provided training at the Petar Zrinski military school in Zagreb.

40. The figure for the number of troops in the Krajina Serb Army comes from *Slobodna Dalmacija* (25 February 1995), p. 8, trans. in *FBIS, Daily Report* (Eastern Europe), 7 March 1995, p. 40. All other figures reported here come from *Die Welt* (28 February 1995), p. 4. Regarding Croatia's new military strength, see also *Balkan News International & East European Report* (4–10 June 1995), p. 15.

41. Quoted in *The Sun* (Baltimore) (6 November 1994), p. 11A.

42. *Večernji list* (8 March 1995), p. 7, trans. in *FBIS, Daily Report* (Eastern Europe), 10 March 1995, p. 18. For further discussion, see *Ljiljan* (19 July 1995), pp. 5–6.

43. See reports in *Welt am Sonntag* (29 January 1995), p. 2; *New York Times* (10 February 1995), p. 4; and *Naša borba* (20 March 1995), p. 2.

44. *Financial Times* (5 May 1995), p. 3.

45. *Neue Zürcher Zeitung* (22 June 1995), p. 5. See also *Stern* (Hamburg), 11 May 1995, pp. 200–202.

46. *The Economist* (London) (20 May 1995), p. 51.

47. *Financial Times* (5 May 1995), p. 3.

48. Ambassador Sarčević's "Memorandum to the Members of Congress", *Croatia Today: Newsletter of the Embassy of the Republic of Croatia*, No. 7 (July 1995), p. 2. Milošević's personal responsibility for placing General Mrkšić in command in the so-called Krajina is confirmed in *Christian Science Monitor* (5 July 1995), p. 6.

49. "Memorandum to the Members" (note 46).

50. *The European* (London) (7–13 April 1995), p. 1.

51. *Daily Telegraph* (12 April 1995), p. 13. See also *The European* (14–20 April 1995), pp. 1—2.

52. *Neue Zürcher Zeitung* (20 June 1995), p. 1.

53. *Süddeutsche Zeitung* (5/6 August 1995), p. 1; *Salt Lake Tribune* (6 August 1995), pp. A1, A10; and *Der Spiegel* (Hamburg) (7 August 1995), pp. 112–113.

54. *The Globe and Mail* (9 August 1995), p. A1; and *The Economist* (12 August 1995), p. 13.

55. Quoted in *Salt Lake Tribune* (6 August 1995), p. A1.

56. The ruling Conservative Party led by Prime Minister John Major pursued what amounted, de facto, to a pro-Serb policy. However, the opposition Labour Party showed itself to be not only critical of this policy orientation, but favorably disposed toward the Bosnian and Croatian governments.

57. *Neue Zürcher Zeitung* (12/13 August 1995), p. 1; also *Evropske novosti* (26 August 1995), p. 4. For details of subsequent fighting between the Croatian Army and Serbian forces in western Bosnia (in mid-August), see *Globus* (25 August 1995), pp. 5–6.

58. This figure was reported in *New York Times* (10 August 1995), p. A4.

59. Quoted in *Neue Zürcher Zeitung* (9 August 1995), p. 1.

60. Ibid.

61. Rieff, "Lessons of Bosnia", p. 80.

62. Ibid., p. 81.

63. *Hearing before the Subcommittee on International Security, International Organizations and Human Rights of the Committee on Foreign Affairs, House of Representatives*, 103rd Congress, 2nd Session, October 24, 1994 (Washington D.C.: U. S. Government Printing Office, 1994), p. 11.

64. *CNN World News* (29 August 1995), evening. It was already 30 August in Sarajevo at the time of broadcast.

65. For the text of the ceasefire, see *Neue Zürcher Zeitung* (4 January 1995), p. 5.

66. *The Weekend Australian* (Sydney), 14/15 January 1995, p. 19.

67. *Der Spiegel* (6 March 1995), p. 158. See also *New York Times* (1 March 1995), p. A6; *The European* (3–9 March 1995), p. 2; and *The Sunday Times* (5 March 1995), p. 16.

68. Radio Bosnia-Herzegovina (Sarajevo), 9 February 1995, trans. in *FBIS, Daily Report* (Eastern Europe), 10 February 1995, p. 26.

69. *New York Times* (9 February 1995), p. A6. See also *Slobodna Dalmacija* (14 February 1995), p. 32.

70. *Wall Street Journal* (31 August 1995), p. A10.

71. *New York Times* (3 March 1995), p. A5.

72. *The Times* (London) (21 March 1995), p. 9; and *Neue Zürcher Zeitung* (21 March 1995), p. 1.

73. *The Times* (22 March 1995), p. 8; and *Süddeutsche Zeitung* (22 March 1995), p. 9.

74. *Die Welt* (Bonn) (25/26 March 1995), pp. 1, 3, and 27 March 1995, p. 6. See also *Slobodna Dalmacija* (23 March 1995), p. 32.

75. *Boston Sunday Globe* (26 March 1995), p. 26; *Die Welt* (27 March 1995), p. 4, and (28 March 1995), p. 4, and (29 March 1995), p. 3.

76. *The Times* (5 April 1995), p. 10.

77. *Neue Zürcher Zeitung* (6 April 1995), p. 2; *Frankfurter Allgemeine* (12 April 1995), p. 6; *Neue Zürcher Zeitung* (26 April 1995), p. 2; and *The Times* (26 April 1995), p. 11.

78. *Süddeutsche Zeitung* (15 May 1995), p. 2, and (16 May 1995), p. 9; *National Catholic Reporter* (19 May 1995), p. 11; *Reuter—German language service* (19 May 1995), on *Nexis*; *The Toronto Star* (20 May 1995), p. A26; and *Slobodna Dalmacija* (23 May 1995), p. 3, and (24 May 1995), p. 2. For further discussion of the repression of non-Serbs in Banja Luka, see *Neue Zürcher Zeitung* (15 August 1995), p. 2; *Oslobodjenje*, European ed. (24–31 August 1995), p. 21; and sources cited in note 7.

79. As reported in *New York Times* (16 August 1995), p. A4. For in-depth discussion of Serbian "ethnic cleansing" in Banja Luka, see David Rieff, *Slaughterhouse: Bosnia and the Failure of the West* (New York: Simon & Schuster, 1995), Chapter 4. The Serbs expelled about 30,000 Croats and Muslims from Banja Luka between 1992 and summer 1995. Regarding Serb expulsions of yet another 5,000 Croats and Muslims from Banja Luka in the first half of August 1995, see *Christian Science Monitor* (14 August 1995), p. 5.

80. *Lloyds List* (26 May 1995) and *AFP* (26 May 1995)—both on *Nexis*.

81. *Los Angeles Times* (26 May 1995), p. A1; *Süddeutsche Zeitung* (27/28 May 1995), p. 1; and *New York Times* (27 May 1995), p. 1.

82. *Los Angeles Times* (30 May 1995), p. A8.

83. See *Die Welt* (16 May 1995), p. 4.

84. *Los Angeles Times* (5 June 1995), p. A1.

85. *Los Angeles Times* (4 June 1995), p. A1.

86. *The European* (16–22 June 1995), p. 1; *Irish Times* (Dublin) (17 June 1995), p. 1; and *Neue Zürcher Zeitung* (19 June 1995), p. 1.

87. It was denied by the U.N. Commander of U.N. Forces in the Former Yugoslavia, Gen. Bernard Janvier. See *Washington Post* (22 June 1995), p. A25.

88. *Washington Post* (22 June 1995), p. A25.

89. *Christian Science Monitor* (8 June 1995), p. 7.

90. *Reuters World Service* (18 June 1995), *Nexis*.

91. Quoted in *New York Times* (29 June 1995), p. 4.

92. *Christian Science Monitor* (10 July 1995), p. 2; *New York Times* (13 July 1995), p. A1, and (14 July 1995), pp. A1, A4, A10; *The Economist* (15 July 1995), p. 31; "Pad Srebrenice," in *Vreme International* (Belgrade), 17 July 1995, pp. 8–10; *Neue Zürcher Zeitung* (26 July 1995), p. 2; *New York Times* (10 August 1995), pp. A1, A4; and *Christian Science Monitor* (25 August 1995), pp. 1, 7.

93. Quoted in *Christian Science Monitor* (14 July 1995), p. 18.

94. *Christian Science Monitor* (17 July 1995), p. 6; and *Neue Zürcher Zeitung* (19 July 1995), p. 1.

95. *Los Angeles Times* (18 July 1995), p. A1; and *Evening Standard* (28 July 1995), p. 22.

96. *Boston Sunday Globe* (30 July 1995), p. 1.

97. Ibid. See also *Balkan News & East European Report* (30 July–5 August 1995), p. 3; *Ljiljan* (23 August 1995), pp. 12–13; and *Oslobodjenje*, European ed. (24–31 August 1995), p. 23.

98. *New York Times* (21 July 1995), p. A1; and *The Guardian—International* (22 July 1995), p. 1.

99. Quoted in *The Guardian—International* (22 July 1995), p. 1.

100. *New York Times* (19 August 1995), p. 4; *Neue Zürcher Zeitung* (26/27 August 1995), p. 2; and *Welt am Sonntag* (27 August 1995), p. 1. Regarding Bosnian government concerns about the withdrawal of U.N. forces from Gorazde, see *New Zealand Herald* (Auckland) (26 August 1995), p. 9.

101. Details in *Christian Science Monitor* (21 August 1995), pp. 1, 18.

102. *New York Times* (29 August 1995), p. A1.

103. On this, see *Welt am Sonntag* (13 August 1995), pp. 1, 6–7.

104. *CNN Headline News*, 30 August 1995 (11:00 a.m.).; and *Financial Times* (31 August 1995), p. 1. The time of broadcast reported for CNN Headline News in this and all subsequent notes is the time of reception in Seattle.

105. *Süddeutsche Zeitung* (2/3 September 1995), p. 1; and *Neue Zürcher Zeitung* (6 September 1995), p. 1.

106. Mladić's own words, in a letter to Lt.-Gen. Bernard Janvier, commander of U.N. Forces in the Former Yugoslavia, as quoted in *New York Times* (8 September 1995), p. A1.

107. *Washington Post*, as reprinted in *Seattle Times* (13 September 1995), Morning ed., p. A3. (The evening edition of that day did not carry the story.)

108. *Reuters World Service* (6 September 1995), *TASS* (7 September 1995), and *Deutsche Presse-Agentur* (7 September 1995)—all on *Nexis*.

109. *Xinhau News Agency* (6 September 1995), on *Nexis*.

110. The Serbs missed. *CNN Headline News*, 15 September 1995 (10:36 p.m.) and 16 September 1995 (9:39 a.m.).

111. *CNN Headline News*, 16 September 1995 (10:41 p.m.).

112. *CNN Headline News*, 17 September 1995 (11:00 p.m.).

113. The Serbs were reported to have accepted this plan as of 1 September. *CNN Headline News*, 31 August 1995 (10:36 p.m.).

114. Marshall Freeman Harris and Stephen W. Walker, "Will the U.S. Sell Out the Bosnians?" *New York Times* (23 August 1995), p. A15.

115. I am thinking here of the Congress of Berlin (1878) which prevented Macedonia from uniting with Bulgaria and divided Bulgaria in two, and the London Conference (1913) which compelled Albania to cede Kosovo to Serbia and Montenegro.

116. For documentation of this claim and an analysis of the flaws of the Western plan promoted by Holbrooke, see Sabrina P. Ramet, "Balkan History Haunts Peace Plan," *Seattle Times* (17 September 1995), p. B5.

117. Rein Mullerson, "The Continuity and Succession of States, by Reference to the Former USSR and Yugoslavia," *International and Comparative Law Quarterly*, Vol. 42, Pt. 3 (July 1993), p. 486.

118. See A. M. Rosenthal, "Why Only Bosnia?," in *New York Times* (30 May 1995), p. A13. In this editorial, Rosenthal confesses himself unable to understand why, if NATO gets involved in Bosnia, it does not also involve itself "in Iraq, Turkey, in Sri Lanka, the Sudan, Algeria, Kashmir, [and] Mexico." If taken literally, Rosenthal's ideas would require fundamental changes to NATO's charter and a complete reworking of the entire world security system.

119. *Ljiljan* (19 July 1995), p. 16.

120. Jonathan Steele, "Gridlock," in *Red Pepper* (London), September 1995, pp. 10–11.

121. Tanjug (Belgrade), 14 September 1994, in *FBIS, Daily Report* (Eastern Europe), 16 September 1994, p. 40; *Politika* (7 February 1995), p. 11; and *Evropske novosti* (20 May 1995), p. 36.

122. The military agreement was signed by Russian Defense Minister Pavel Grachev and FRY Defense Minister Pavle Bulatović on 1 March on the occasion of the latter's visit to Moscow. See *Die Welt* (2 March 1995), p. 4.

123. Angela Burke and Gordon Macdonald, "The Former Yugoslavia Conflict," in Michael Cranna, ed., *The True Cost of Conflict: Seven Recent Wars and Their Effects on Society* (New York: New Press, 1994), pp. 162, 173.

124. Radio Bosnia-Herzegovina (Sarajevo), 23 August 1993, trans. in *FBIS, Daily Report* (Eastern Europe), 24 August 1993, p. 31.

125. *Ljiljan* (26 October 1994), p. 8.

126. Burke and Macdonald, "Former Yugoslavia Conflict" (note 114), p. 166.

127. Ibid., p. 161.

128. Ibid., pp. 174–175; also details in Sabrina Petra Ramet, *Social Currents in Eastern Europe: The Sources and Consequences of the Great Transformation*, 2nd ed. (Durham, N.C.: Duke University Press, 1995), pp. 414, 416.

129. Burke and Macdonald, "Former Yugoslavia Conflict," pp. 174, 176.

130. Ibid., p. 175.

131. *Balkan News & East European Report* (21–27 May 1995), p. 19.

132. Burke and Macdonald, "Former Yugoslavia Conflict," citing Tanjug (27 January 1994).

133. Burke and Macdonald, "Former Yugoslavia Conflict," p. 168.

134. See *The Independent* (London) (13 February 1995), p. 8.

135. Žarko Puhovski, "Croatian complicity", *Red Pepper* (October 1995), p. 28.

136. *Daily Telegraph* (3 March 1995), p. 15; and Burke and Macdonald, "Former Yugoslavia Conflict", p. 161.

137. Quoted in *Daily Telegraph* (3 March 1995), p. 15.

138. *New York Times* (9 January 1995), p. A4.

139. *DPA* (23 July 1995), on *Nexis*.

140. *Irish Times* (17 June 1995), p. 11. The information about Karadžić's career with the soccer team was related to me by Peter F. Sugar on 25 August 1995.

141. See any issue of *Pravoslavlje* in 1991 for documentation and confirmation; also *Politika—International Weekly* (22–28 June 1991), p. 6.

142. See *Politika* (Belgrade), 18 August 1991, p. 3.

143. *Politika* (8 August 1991), p. 5.

144. See especially Vasa D. Mihailovich, "War in the Works of Dobrica Ćosić," *Serbian Studies*, Vol. 3, Nos. 1/2 (fall/spring 1984/85) and Heiko Flottau, "Alle Geschichten, giftige Hetze, verblasene Hetze," in *Süddeutsche Zeitung, Wochenende* supplement (Munich), 2/3 September 1995, p. 37.

145. Quoted in *Wall Street Journal* (27 June 1995), p. A1. See also *Sunday Times* (London), 2 July 1995, *Nexis*.

146. Both quoted in *Politika—International Weekly* (3–16 August 1991), p. 7.

147. *Politika* (17 August 1991), p. 3.

148. *Politika—International Weekly* (27 July–2 August 1991), p. 1.

149. Andrei Simić, "Obstacles to the Development of a Yugoslav National Consciousness: Ethnic Identity and Folk Culture in the Balkans," in *Journal of Mediterranean Studies*, Vol. 1 (1991), No. 1, p. 31.

150. Ibid. Along the same lines, see the comments by Dušan Kecmanović, as cited in "Grupni portret nacionalizma," *Vreme International* (22 May 1995), especially p. 28.

For Further Reading

FOR A COUNTRY OF JUST OVER 20 million people, Yugoslavia has attracted a great deal of attention. Needless to say, among the various books that have addressed themselves to the scrutiny of this polyglot country, there have been some truly splendid books and some utterly wretched and profoundly misleading books. I do not propose hereunder to weigh the merits of all the books that have received attention in recent years but will merely highlight some of the books and other writings, appearing in English, that I consider to be among the best and the most useful.

GENERAL STUDIES, HISTORIES

Among books of a more general nature, Duško Doder's *The Yugoslavs* (Random House, 1978) still stands as one of the most readable accounts of modern-day Yugoslavia. Its age is no fault, and it has weathered the years well. As a general introduction to this country, especially for someone with no previous knowledge of Yugoslavia, it is without equal.

Two other works of an introductory nature are Fred Singleton's *A Short History of the Yugoslav Peoples* (Cambridge University Press, 1983), and his *Twentieth Century Yugoslavia* (Columbia University Press, 1976). Singleton's scholarship is solid, albeit marred by a pro-Serbian slant.

Three outstanding works of history should also be mentioned. Ivo Banac's *The National Question in Yugoslavia* (Cornell University Press, 1984) won the Wayne Vucinich Prize for that year. Its subject is the formation of the Yugoslav state in 1918 and the experiences of the various parties in the subsequent two decades. Banac highlights especially well the reasons for Croatian disillusionment with the Serbian-dominated state apparatus. Jozo Tomasevich's *The Chetniks: War and Revolution in Yugoslavia, 1941–1945* (Stanford University Press, 1975) is a painstakingly researched account of the war years and well deserves its reputation as the single most reliable source for its subject. Finally, a newer book, by Aleksa Djilas, *The Contested Country: Yugoslav Unity and Communist Revolution, 1919–1953* (Harvard University Press, 1991), covers the evolution of the Yugoslav Communist Party from its founding through its first eight years in power.

Finally, a general book for a more advanced reader is *Yugoslavia in the 1980s*, edited by Pedro Ramet in 1985. This book brings together writings by a variety of authors on such subjects as politics, economics, foreign policy, the environment, the military, women's status, the media, and religion.

POSTWAR POLITICS

The classic treatment of the early postwar period is Dennison I. Rusinow's *The Yugoslav Experiment, 1948–1974* (University of California Press, 1977). Generally sympathetic to Tito, Rusinow sketches the major crises of this period, both in internal politics and in foreign relations, starting with the expulsion of Yugoslavia from the Cominform and ending with the adoption of a new constitution in 1974.

For the more recent period, I would refer the reader to my own book, *Nationalism and Federalism in Yugoslavia, 1962–1991,* 2d ed. (Indiana University Press, 1992). In its second edition, the book traces the role that nationalism played in producing political crises and in finally plunging the country into civil war in summer 1991. The book also highlights the cultural aspects of the attendant political problems. A third edition, covering the years 1941–1996, is in preparation.

Among the several biographies of Tito, my own favorite is Milovan Djilas's *Tito,* (Harcourt Brace Jovanovich, 1980). Djilas has a keen mind, and the book contains many insights into Tito's character and strategies.

Aside from these three books, I might add that I continue to be impressed by the argument offered by Gary K. Bertsch and M. George Zaninovich in their 1974 article for *Comparative Politics*: "A Factor-Analytic Method of Identifying Different Political Cultures: The Multinational Yugoslav Case."

THE MEDIA

For many years the only book available about the media in Yugoslavia was Gertrude Joch Robinson's *Tito's Maverick Media: The Politics of Mass Communications in Yugoslavia* (University of Illinois Press, 1977), although Paul Lendvai's *The Bureaucracy of Truth: How Communist Governments Manage the News* (Westview Press, 1981) also contains material germane to the Yugoslav case. Of the two books, the Lendvai book is the more useful. Recently, there is a fascinating new book: Tom Gjelten's *Sarajevo Daily: A City and Its Newspaper Under Siege* (New York: HarperCollins, 1995). Further information about the Yugoslav media may also be obtained from my earlier essay, "The Yugoslav Press in Flux," published as Chapter 5 in my *Yugoslavia in the 1980s*, and from Jasmina Kuzmanović's essay, "Media: The Extension of Politics by Other Means," published as Chapter 4 in *Beyond Yugoslavia: Politics, Economics, and Culture in a Shattered Community*, edited by Sabrina Petra Ramet and Ljubiša S. Adamovich (Boulder, Colo.: Westview Press, 1995). For separate essays on the media in Slovenia, Croatia, and Serbia, see the special issue of *Uncaptive Minds* on "Media in Eastern Europe," Vol. 6, No. 2 (Summer 1993).

ROCK MUSIC

There is almost no scholarly literature devoted to rock music in Yugoslavia. I am responsible for what English-language material exists. Here the chief sources are my interview article, "Bora Djordjević: Vanguard of Rock Protest (An Interview with Pedro Ramet)," published in *South Slav Journal* (winter 1987–88), and my essay, "Shake, Rattle, and Self-Management: Making the Scene in Yugoslavia," published as Chapter 6 in my book, *Rocking the State: Rock Music and Politics in Eastern Europe and Russia* (Boulder, Colo.: Westview Press, 1994). I have included some additional material about the Yugoslav rock scene in my introductory essay to *Yugoslavia in the 1980s* (Westview Press, 1985). "Apocalypse Culture and Social Change," in my essay "Yugoslavia 1987: Stirrings from Below," for *South Slav Journal* (autumn 1987), and, within the context of a broader discussion of rock music in Eastern Europe generally, in Chapter 10 of my book, *Social Currents in Eastern Europe: The Sources and Consequences of the Great Transformation*, 2d ed. (Durhan, N.C.: Duke University Press, 1995).

WOMEN

The only book-length treatment of Yugoslav women of which I am aware is Vida Tomšić's fine book, *Women in the Development of Socialist Self-Managing Yugoslavia*. Published in Belgrade in 1980 by Radnička štampa, the book traces the fortunes of Yugoslav women from their experiences in the partisan war to their gains under the self-management system and contains ample statistical data. Barbara Wolfe Jancar's *Women Under Communism* (Johns Hopkins University Press, 1978), although covering all of Eastern Europe and the Soviet Union, is also useful in this regard.

Among shorter studies one might mention Bette S. Denich's "Sex and Power in the Balkans," which was included in the collection, *Woman, Culture, and Society* (1974), edited by Michelle Zimbalist Rosaldo and Louise Lamphere; Barbara Jancar's sensitive treatment in "The New Feminism in Yugoslavia," included in the collection, *Yugoslavia in the 1980s* (Westview Press, 1985); my own discussion of "Feminism in Yugoslavia," included as Chapter 8 in my *Social Currents in Eastern Europe*; Obrad Kesic's "Women and Revolution in Yugoslavia (1945–1989)," in *Women and Revolution in Africa, Asia, and the New World* (University of South Carolina Press, 1994), edited by Mary Ann Tetreault; and several chapters in the collection, *Women, State, and Party in Eastern Europe* (Duke University Press, 1985), edited by Sharon L. Wolchik and Alfred G. Meyer.

RELIGION

Stella Alexander's *Church and State in Yugoslavia Since 1945* (Cambridge University Press, 1979) is a highly detailed and immensely useful discussion of the Catholic Church and the Serbian Orthodox Church during the years 1945–1970. The same author subsequently wrote a biography of Stepinac that is as good as any other in English: *The Triple Myth: A Life of Archbishop Alojzije Stepinac* (East European Monographs, 1987). Also useful is my essay, "Religion and Nationalism in Yugoslavia," included in the collection, *Religion and Nationalism in Soviet and East European Politics*, edited by Pedro Ramet, revised and expanded ed. (Duke University Press, 1989). That collection also includes a useful essay by Zachary T. Irwin on Muslims of the Balkans. For information about Yugoslav Protestants, see the essay by Paul Mojzes and N. Gerald Shenk, "Protestantism in Bulgaria and Yugoslavia Since 1945," published as Chapter 7 in *Protestantism and Politics in Eastern Europe and Russia: The Communist and Post-Communist Eras*, edited by S.

P. Ramet (Duke University Press, 1992). Aside from those sources, the reader will be best served by consulting the journal, *Religion, State, and Society: The Keston Journal* (formerly known as *Religion in Communist Lands*).

THE ECONOMY

There are a number of excellent treatments of the Yugoslav economy. Among the best known are: Deborah D. Milenkovitch, *Plan and Market in Yugoslav Economic Thought* (Yale University Press, 1971); Svetozar Pejovich, *The Market-Planned Economy of Yugoslavia* (University of Minnesota Press, 1966); Fred Singleton and Bernard Carter, *The Economy of Yugoslavia* (St. Martin's Press, 1982); and Branko Horvat, *The Political Economy of Socialism: A Marxist Social Theory* (M. E. Sharpe, 1984). Among recent books, Dijana Pleština's *Regional Development in Communist Yugoslavia* (Westview Press, 1992) is worthy of note. For post-Yugoslav economics, see the essays by Ljubiša Adamovich ("Economic Transformation in Former Yugoslavia with Special Regard to Privatization") and Oskar Kovač ("Foreign Economic Relations"), published as Chapters 11 and 12, respectively, in *Beyond Yugoslavia: Politics, Economics, and Culture in a Shattered Community*, edited by Sabrina Petra Ramet and Ljubiša S. Adamovich (Westview Press, 1995).

BOSNIA

The best introduction to the history of Bosnia-Herzegovina in any language is Noel Malcolm's *Bosnia: A Short History* (New York University Press, 1994). This book should be supplemented with the extremely fine book by Robert J. Donia and John V.A. Fine, Jr., *Bosnia and Hercegovina: A Tradition Betrayed* (Columbia University Press, 1994). An interesting edited collection is *Why Bosnia?* (Pamphleteer's Press, 1993), edited by Rabia Ali and Lawrence Lifschultz, which contains essays by journalists, academics, several poets, and even a former chief justice of the Constitutional Court of Bosnia-Herzegovina. Dževad Karahasan's *Sarajevo: Exodus of a City* (Kodansha International, 1994) is a very sensitive, personal treatment of the experience of coping with life under siege in Sarajevo since 1992.

THE WAR, KOSOVO

New titles dealing with the Yugoslav war appear each month. Few are entirely worthless, but many are shallow and have difficulty rising above the sundry misconceptions that have floated around in the heads of nonspecialists. Probably the single best treatment of the subject is Misha Glenny's *The Fall of Yugoslavia: The Third Balkan War* (Penguin, 1992), which covers the course of the war up to May 1992 and mixes historical background with tales of the author's personal adventures. The book at times has a bit of the flair (and charm) of Baron Münchhausen's tales.

There is not much in-depth work on Kosovo in English. The best work here has been done by Elez Biberaj. Among his publications on this subject is his monograph, *Kosova: The Balkan Powder Keg*, published in the "Conflict Studies" series in February 1993. Those seeking an understanding of human rights problems in the region should read *Open Wounds: Human Rights Abuses in Kosovo*, published by Human Rights Watch/Helsinki in March 1993.

About the Book and Author

In this thoroughly updated and revised edition, which includes four new chapters and a new epilogue, a veteran observer of the Yugoslav scene describes the forces that have fragmented the country. Arguing that cultural and religious values underpin political behavior, Sabrina Ramet traces the steady deterioration of Yugoslavia's social and political fabric over the past decade. This decline, she maintains, is deeply rooted in historical trauma and memory and was foreshadowed in the cultural sphere.

Ramet lays the groundwork for understanding the current crisis by exploring the unfolding political debates from 1980–1986, the gathering crisis triggered by the ascent of Slobodan Milošević to power in Serbia, and the dramatic collapse of the existing political order beginning in 1989. She ties these events to the often overlooked religious and cultural elements of society that have influenced political change. She then examines the political dynamics within Serbia and Croatia since 1991, the domestic and foreign challenges faced by independent Slovenia and Macedonia, the grinding conflict in Bosnia, and the repercussions of the war on gender relations and on cultural and religious life.

With her detailed and graphic knowledge of the inescapable links between politics, culture, and religion, Ramet paints a strikingly original picture of the disintegration of Yugoslavia and the emergence of the Yugoslav successor states.

Sabrina Petra Ramet is professor of international studies at the University of Washington. She is the author of four previous books including *Nationalism and Federalism in Yugoslavia, 1962–1991*, second edition (1992), and *Social Currents in Eastern Europe: The Sources and Consequences of the Great Transformation*, second edition (1995).

Index

Abdić, Fikret, 253, 262
Abortion, 126, 128, 158, 228, 285
Absurdities of Historical Reality
    (Tudjman), 41
Abu Abbas, 66
Adultery, 124
Adžić (General), 50
Afghanistan, 256
"After Tito, Tito" (song), 95–96
Agnostics, 154
Agriculturist societies, 120, 123–124
Agrokomerc scandal, 39, 77, 104
Air strikes, 53, 250, 253, 255, 256, 257,
    260, 263, 264, 302, 303–304, 308,
    310, 311, 314–315, 316, 317
    purposes/types, 309
Akashi, Yasushi, 253, 263, 281
Albania, 54, 105, 254, 328(n115). *See*
    also Albanians
Albanians, 1, 40, 41, 121, 185
    women, 191–192, 286
    See also under Kosovo; Macedonia
Alexander (Serbian Crown
    Prince/King), 30–31, 168, 201,
    203, 321
Alexander, Stella, 173
Ali drugog puta nema (Šagi-Bunić),
    155–156
"Anarchy All Over Bascarsija" (song),
    109
Aporea, 29, 101
Arabic, 278
Arkadia lobby, 282
Arms embargo, 244–245, 247, 251, 252,
    254, 255, 256, 257, 261–267,

270(n50), 301, 302, 306. *See also*
    Weapons
Art, 29, 287, 288
Artuković, Andrija, 137
Arzešnek, Vladimir, 13
Association of Journalists, 66
Atheism, 147, 148, 149, 151, 153(table),
    153, 154, 172
Atrocities, 50, 258, 277, 313. *See also*
    Genocide
Australia, 165, 188
Austria, 1, 51, 54, 123, 166, 188, 226,
    227, 247, 302
Authoritarianism, 209, 212, 319
Autonomism/autonomy, 8, 15, 48, 213,
    214, 235
Autonomous provinces, 21, 27, 41. *See*
    also Kosovo; Vojvodina
Avramović, Dragoslav, 206

Baby Doll, 98
Bahtijarević, Stefica, 154
Bakarić, Vladimir, 138, 139
Baker, James, 37, 51
Bakočević, Aleksandar, 53
Bakrac, Drago, 205
Balašević, Djordje, 96, 99
Baljak, Momčilo, 68
Banac, Ivo, 210, 211
Banja Luka, 252, 262, 277, 278, 303,
    311, 315, 326(n79)
Bankruptcies, 45
Banks, 227
Baranja, 213
Bardin, Tomislav, 77

Bastards (rock group), 106
Beatles, 94
Bebek, Željko, 94, 96
Belgrade, 34, 97, 111, 119, 122, 123,
    127, 154, 180, 188, 200, 201, 282,
    283, 300
    Belgrade Television, 80, 110, 204,
        292
    Catholics in, 278
    Metropolitan of Belgrade, 166
    Radio-Television Belgrade, 207
    Theological Faculty in, 174
Belgrade, University of, 179
Benson, Judi, 289–290
Berisha, Sali, 235, 254
Beso, Amir "Lazy," 289
Bhutto, Benazir, 256
Biber, Dušan, 299
Bibliography of Croatian Writiers of
    Bosnia-Herzegovina Between the
    Two Wars, 192
Bihać enclave, 253, 262, 264, 308, 310,
    311
Bilić, Jure, 16, 66
Bilirakis, Michael, 232
Blackbourn, David, 157
Black markets, 9
Blažević, Dunja, 288
Blažević, Jakov, 141, 142, 143
Blue Orchestra, 99–100, 111
Boardwalk, 110–111
Boban, Mate, 249
Bogdanović, Radmilo, 49
Bogoslovlje, 174
Bolsheviks, 53
Borba, 16, 69, 70, 72, 78, 81, 83,
    88(n47), 143, 173, 207
Borders, 34, 48, 210–211, 226, 231, 233,
    245, 249, 254, 267
    AVNOJ borders, 213
Borovo Selo, 50
Bosanska Srpska Republic, 279
Bosnia-Herzegovina, 3, 7, 10, 11, 21,
    22, 25, 29, 31, 33, 39, 41, 42, 44,
    46, 53, 82, 83, 103, 105, 144, 147,
    149, 151, 152, 156, 185, 230,
    243–268
    cabinet in, 248
    Croats in, 186, 244, 247, 248,
        264(table)
    elections in, 243–244
    elite discord in, 54
    independence of, 38, 54, 246
    Muslim army in, 252, 262, 264,
        264(table), 302, 305–306, 313
    Muslims in, 186, 190, 193, 199, 243,
        244, 248, 277, 291
    nationalities in, 186, 187(table)
    and Orthodox Church, 166, 167
    partition of, 244, 246, 248, 251, 257,
        302, 315
    Prijedor district, 259
    recognition of, 245, 256, 303,
        324(n23)
    Serb controlled areas in, 246, 277,
        278
    Serb military budget in, 305
    Serbs in, 43, 44, 186, 193, 243, 245,
        246, 248, 249, 250, 252, 254–255,
        257, 262, 264(table), 281, 284
    troop strengths of rival forces in,
        264(table), 305, 306, 310
    women in, 129
    See also under Croatia; Serbia; United
        States
Bošnjak, Branko, 154
Boston Globe, 286
Boutros-Ghali, Boutros, 247, 253, 264
Bozović, Radoman, 201
Bratstvo factory, 252
Brcin, Dragutin, 207
Bread and Salt, 97, 98
Bregović, Goran, 91–92, 96, 99, 102,
    105
Brkić, Milovan, 75–76
Buble, Marin, 32
Budak, Mile, 170
Budiša, Dražen, 212, 279
Bukatko, Gabrijel, 150
Bukčević, Risto, 53
Bulatović, Momir, 53, 203
Bulgaria/Bulgarians, 48, 170, 172, 225,
    230, 233, 255, 261, 328(n115)
    Orthodox Church, 175

Bulldozer, 97
Burke, 318–319
Bush administration, 51, 247
Byzantium, 29, 101

Čaldarević, M., 12
Canada, 188, 253
Cantonization, 246
Capitalism, 203
Car, Pavel, 74
Carter, Hodding, 260–261
Carter, Jimmy, 310
Casualties, 37, 50, 53, 140, 170, 171,
    201, 208, 248, 257, 264, 267, 277,
    300, 306, 311, 312, 313, 314, 317
Catholic Church, 12, 24, 40–41, 54, 79,
    123, 128, 135–159, 168, 179
  church-state relations, 145–149, 150,
    156, 157, 178, 190
  concordat for, 168–169
  destruction of churches, 278, 287,
    300, 311
  internal divisions in, 150–153
  Old Catholic Church, 138
  priests' associations, 143–145, 151
  See also Education, religious; Press,
    Catholic press; Vatican; *under*
    Croatia; Serbian Orthodox Church;
    Slovenia
Čavoški, Kosta, 74
CDC. *See* Croatia, Croatian Democratic
    Community
Cease-fires, 53, 226, 245, 248, 261, 310
Čekada, Smiljan, 136, 150, 151
Censorship, 64, 66, 81, 85, 104–108
Central Conference of Methodist
    Churches, 255
Central Intelligence Agency (CIA), 265
Centralization/recentralization, 10, 11,
    12–13, 16, 17, 18, 21, 26, 32, 39,
    176
Change, 283, 320. *See also* Political
    change; Social change
Chauvinism, 31, 118, 121, 127, 320
Chetniks, 287
Children, 148, 155, 173, 188, 285, 313,
    319. *See also* Education; Schools

"Child's Play" (poem), 289–290
China, 51, 55, 227
Chodorow, Nancy, 121
Christianity Today Theological Society,
    136, 149, 150, 151–152, 191
Christmas, 157–158, 180, 189
Christopher, Warren, 314
Church of St. Sava, 179, 279
Churkin, Vitaly, 254
CIA. *See* Central Intelligence Agency
Čicak, Ranka, 78
Civic turmoil, 42–44
Civil war, 34, 42, 52–53, 85, 193, 200–
    201, 202, 212, 229, 300–301, 321
  consequences of, 316–319
Class issues, 118, 126, 171
Clinton, Bill, 232, 247, 250, 261, 313
  administration, 253, 254
Clothes. *See* Dress
Codex, 94
Cohen, Lenard, 303–304
Collective presidency, 50, 52
Communism, 137–138, 238, 285. *See
    also* League of Communists of
    Yugoslavia; Marxism
Communist Party of Yugoslavia (CPY),
    138, 171–172
Community, sense of, 34
Conference of European Churches, 255
Conference on Security and
    Cooperation in Europe (CSCE),
    247
Confiscations, 40, 139, 172, 173, 179,
    181, 228–229
Congress of Berlin (1878), 328(n115)
Conservatives, 11, 39, 117
Constitution(s). *See under* Yugoslavia;
    individual republics
Contact groups, 212, 257, 302, 303, 311
Convoys, 248, 263, 307
Coprolalia, 2845
Corruption, 8, 31, 104
Ćosić, Dobrica, 68, 199–200, 203
Cot, Jean, 253
Courts, 71–72, 79
CPY. *See* Communist Party of
    Yugoslavia

Crime, 23
hate crimes, 204
Crises, 10–11, 15, 23, 38, 39, 72, 77,
226, 299, 320
Crkva u svijetu, 149
Crkveni život, 30
Croatia, 3, 7, 10, 11, 15, 18, 19(n2),
21–22, 25, 27, 30, 31–32, 42, 44,
46, 47, 50, 51, 66, 81, 208–213,
230, 245, 265, 291, 319
armed forces, 305–306, 306–308
and Bosnia-Herzegovina, 192–193,
210–211, 212, 214, 246, 262,
301–302, 314, 323(n8). *See also*
Croats, and Bosnian Serbs
and Catholic Church, 135, 137, 138,
145, 147, 149, 151, 157, 158, 180,
276, 277
constitution, 276
Croatian Association of Press
Reporters, 211–212
Croatian-Bosnian federation, 302,
314, 323(n8)
Croatian Democratic Community
(CDC), 209, 210
economy, 208, 215, 318
elections in, 209, 276
independence of, 37, 38, 49, 267
military offensive of 1995, 306–308,
314
most respected/hated persons in, 279
names in, 210
nationalism in, 209–210, 320
and Orthodox Church, 175, 179, 181,
276, 279–280
parliament, 209
press in, 82, 85, 141, 211–212, 213,
302
Privatization Fund in, 211
recognition of, 280, 303
Serb occupation in, 209, 212,
254–255, 262, 278, 307. *See also*
Krajina
Serbs in, 42–43, 44, 47, 49, 50, 52,
53, 199, 210, 211, 212, 219(n89),
220(n110), 265, 276, 291, 302–303,
308
Society of Catholic Priests, 145

Society of Journalists, 80
Supreme Court, 72
Ustasha fascists in, 40, 41, 79, 135,
137, 140, 141, 157, 170, 210
women in, 120, 123–124, 128, 129,
283
See also Croats; *under* Germany;
Serbia; Slovenia; United States
Croats, 1, 41, 50, 153, 185, 251,
322(n7), 326(n79)
and Bosnian Serbs, 251, 256–257
and Muslims, 251, 256, 257
See also under Bosnia-Herzegovina
Cryillic, 299
CSCE. *See* Conference on Security and
Cooperation in Europe
Cukvaš, Veselin, 178
Culture, 2–3, 7, 10, 21, 42–43, 108–109,
112, 117, 128–129, 204, 254, 320
buildings destroyed, 286–287, 301.
See also Catholic Church, destruction of churches; Mosques, de-
struction of
and civil war, 286–293
cultural atavism, 321
cultural underground, 29
gender culture, 117, 118
and politics, 287–288, 321
Serbian vs. Croatian, 320–321
traditionalism, 126, 127, 128, 129
urban/rural, 118
See also Art; Music; Playwrights;
Poets; Serbia, writers in
Currency, 45, 54, 210
hard currency, 208
Cvitković, Ivan, 32
Czechoslovakia, 321
Orthodox Church in, 175

Dabčević-Kučar, Savka, 41, 42
Dalmatia, 48, 123, 153, 157, 212, 308
Danas, 77, 79, 83, 211
Dapčević, Peko, 13
Dark Is the Night (Popović), 206
Daughters, 120
Death to Fascism! 99–100
Decentralization, 10, 12, 17, 18, 22, 63,
77, 103, 176, 190, 300

Decisionmaking, 23, 26, 123, 126
Dedijer, Vladimir, 276
Dee Dee Mellow, 98, 100
De Lapresle, Bertrand, 264, 273(n139)
Delić, Rasim, 306
Delo, 72, 76, 83, 226, 279
Democracy, 10, 28, 31, 32, 41, 42, 75,
    158, 207, 215, 230, 237, 267–268
Demonstrations, 24, 40, 48–49, 202,
    235, 237
Denich, Bette, 119, 120, 124
Dervish order, 191
Diplomacy, 300–306
Diplomatic service, 126
Dirty Theatre, 112, 291
Djakovo diocese, 144
Djilas, Milovan, 27, 72, 74, 92, 143
Djindjić, Zoran, 55, 207
Djogo, Gojko, 22, 28, 198
Djordjević, Bora, 28, 96, 102, 105, 107,
    291–292, 320
Djordjević, Irinej, 172
Djordjević, Jovan, 16
Djurdjević-Lukić, Svetlana, 204–205
Dmitrović, Ratko, 76
Dnevnik, 68, 79, 81, 82
Dobrečić, Nikola, 143, 160(n41)
Dobri pastir, 144, 145
"Dogs of War" (song), 293
Dolanc, Stane, 14
Dole, Robert, 304
Dragosavac, Dušan, 16
Drašković, Vuk, 199, 201, 202, 203–204
Drašković, Danica, 203–204
Dress, 108, 109, 114(n57)
Drnovšek, Janez, 242(n92)
Družina, 148
Dual subordination, 224
Dubrovnik, 54, 281, 287, 299, 318
Duga, 77–78, 79, 85
Dželebdžić, Milovan, 299

Eagleburger, Lawrence, 258
EC. *See* European Community
Economy, 9, 34, 38, 39, 42, 44–45, 92,
    112, 223, 299
    and political systems, 23, 32, 125, 126
    reforms, 33, 44–45, 125

See also under individual republics
Ecumenical Council of Churches, 255
Education, 118, 125, 147, 213, 231, 236,
    318
    religious, 179, 180, 187, 188, 190,
        191, 228, 276, 277
    textbooks, 204, 217(n39), 283
    See also Schools; Universities
EFTA. *See* European Free Trade
    Association
Elections, 13, 25, 31, 42, 45, 74, 75,
    158, 215
    See also under Macedonia; Serbia
Electricity, 23, 54, 206
Electric Orgasm, 97, 98, 111
Elites, 33, 54, 209
Embargos. *See* Arms embargo; *under*
    Trade
Episcopal Conference of Yugoslavia,
    148, 151–152, 158
Etatism, 92
Ethnic cleansing, 193, 214, 249, 262,
    268, 277, 281, 283, 322(n7),
    326(n79). *See also* Genocide;
    Refugees
Ethnic issues, 18, 22, 31, 34, 40, 127,
    129, 171, 177, 190, 263(table),
    267–268, 268(n6), 320
    ethnic peripheries, 213–214
    ethnic purity, 285
    mixed marriages, 285
    in rock music, 99–101
    in Serbia, 202
    See also Civil war; Ethnic cleansing;
        Kosovo, Serb-Albanian frictions in
European, The, 307
European Community (EC), 37, 51, 52,
    53, 212, 227, 228, 231, 232, 246,
    247, 248, 249, 301, 314
    Badinter Commission, 245
    Declaration on Former Yugoslavia,
        250
European Court of Justice, 233
European Free Trade Association
    (EFTA), 228, 244
European Union, 227, 233, 244
    European Union Plan of June 1994,
        256–258, 262, 302

Europe as united, 316–317

Fall of Byzantium, 101
Fall of Rock 'n' Roll, The (film), 111
Families, 118, 120, 123, 283–284, 319
Fascism, 79, 99–100, 102, 142,223–224.
    See also Croatia, Ustasha fascists in
Fear, 121, 122, 185, 186, 283
Federalism, issues of, 33, 34, 48, 67,
    158, 181, 193, 300, 302
Federal Republic of Yugoslavia (FRY),
    3, 203, 217(n42)
    Army, 305, 306–307. *See also* Serbia,
        military purges in
    Federal Assembly, 277. *See also*
        Yugoslavia, Federal Assembly
    See also Serbia; Montenegro
Feminism, 7, 118, 119, 122, 126,
    128–129, 282–283, 320
    groups, 284
    political parties, 127
Fiery Kiss, 99
Financial Times, 306
Fish Soup, 97, 102, 105, 107, 111
Folk music, 92, 99, 100, 109, 204
Food, 266, 310, 312, 318
Foreign debt, 44, 66, 126
Foreign investments, 45
France, 51, 55, 227, 232, 233, 247, 250,
    253–254, 255, 265, 303, 308, 312,
    314, 316–317, 321
    and arms embargo, 251, 252, 261,
        267, 301, 317
    as pro-Serbian, 259, 263, 266–267,
        304
Franciscans, 141–142, 144, 145, 147,
    150, 152, 156, 158
Franić, Frane, 136, 145, 146, 150–151
FRY. *See* Federal Republic of
    Yugoslavia
Fuel, 257–258, 266, 310
Galbraith, Peter, 302–303, 323(n19)
Galija, 115(n73)
Galvin, John, 265
Garden, Ashes (Kiš), 197–198
GATT. *See* General Agreement on
    Tariffs and Trade

Gavrić, Svetozar, 81
Gay men, 282, 283
Gender issues, 117–129, 284–285, 320.
    See also Feminism; Machismo;
    Patriarchy; Women
General Agreement on Tariffs and
    Trade (GATT), 227
Geneva Peace Conference (1992), 248
Genocide, 22, 53, 247, 259, 260, 275,
    303, 304, 313, 317. *See also* Ethnic
    cleansing
Georgia, 226
Georgievski, Ljupčo, 237
German (Serbian Patriarch), 178, 179
Germany, 51, 52, 188, 227, 232, 233,
    247, 251, 255, 261, 301, 303, 317
    and Croatia, 259, 308
    See also Naziism
Gilligan, Carol, 121
Glas crkve, 28
Glas koncila, 64, 79, 147, 148–149, 189,
    276
Glasnik, 174
Glenny, Misha, 304
Gligorov, Kiro, 42, 230, 236, 237
Globus, 212, 279
Goati, Vladimir, 13
Goli Otok prison, 11, 63, 198
Goljevšček, Alenka, 69
Goražde, 261, 311, 313, 314
Gore, Al, 232
Gošev, Petar, 237
Goulding, Marrack, 2476
Grachev, Pavel, 314
Grbić, Čedo, 13, 14
Great Britain, 55, 93, 97, 211, 247, 250,
    253–254, 265, 303, 308, 312, 314,
    316–317, 321
    and arms embarago, 251, 252, 261,
        267, 301, 317
    Labour Party in, 325(n56)
    as pro-Serbian, 259, 263, 266–267,
        304, 325(n56)
Greece, 55, 224, 231–233, 255, 315
    military strength of, 232(table)
Grličkov, 14, 16
Gypsies, 1, 233(table)

Hahn, David, 291
Hair, 289
Halili, Nevzet, 235
"Hard Blood Shock" (song), 112
Haxhi-Shehu, Jemaly, 191
Health care, 318
Heavy metal music, 97–98
Helsinki Act, 34, 48, 249, 267
Helsinki Watch, 48
Herceg-Bosna, Republic of, 211, 247–248
Herzegovina, 43, 44, 148, 150, 156–157, 158, 211, 247, 248. *See also* Bosnia-Herzegovina
Historical issues, 40–41, 101, 286
Hitler, Adolph, 103
Hofman, Branko, 199
Holbrooke, Richard, 315
Homelessness, 208, 248
Horvat, Branko, 13
Horvat, Davorka and Damir, 291
Houra, Jasenko, 291
House, Karen Elliott, 260
Houses of Belgrade, The (Pekić), 197
Howard, Jean, 283
"How It Must End" (poem), 290
Hribar, Tine, 69
Hrvatski tjednik, 86(n9)
Human rights, 148, 189
Human Rights Watch, 322(n7)
Human shields, 311, 313
Hungary/Hungarians, 1, 52, 68, 100, 166, 206, 213, 214, 227, 322(n7)
Hurd, Douglas, 252, 259

Iakovos (Archbishop), 232
Ideology, 8, 76, 78, 154
IDP. *See* Istria, Istrian Democratic Party
Ilirida Republic, 235
Illiteracy, 125, 126
Ilustrovana politika, 78
INA petrochemical company, 45
Indeksi, 95, 97
Independent, The (London) 305
Independent State of Croatia (NDH), 170
Industry, 27, 41, 53, 229

production, 44, 54, 208, 227, 228, 236, 318
Inflation, 9, 23, 44–45, 100, 126, 205, 206, 208, 228
Infrastructures, 317–318
Intellectuals, 7, 18, 69, 73, 213
Interest groups, 34
International law, 316. *See also Uti possidetis, ita possidetis*
Intervju, 54, 81, 85
Iran, 255–256, 257, 261, 302, 310
Iraq, 185, 189, 244
Irinej (Bishop), 173
Irredentism, 197, 225, 276
Isaković, Antonije, 23, 198, 321
Islam, 185–193
administrative regions, 186–187
Islamic states, 247, 251, 252, 255–256, 261, 266
publications, 188
religious instruction, 277
Supreme Assembly, 193
See also Muslims
Ismaili, Isa, 192
Istria, 48, 57(n46), 139, 143, 144, 227
Istrian Democratic Party (IDP), 213, 214
Italy/Italians, 51, 54, 71, 139, 170, 213, 214, 226, 227
Ivanković, Nenad, 251
Ivanović, Predrag, 93
Iveković, Rada, 286
Izetbegović, Alija, 42, 43, 47, 54, 243, 246, 266, 281

Jacobsen, Carl, 259–260
Jancar, Barbara, 127
Jančar, Drago, 229
Jane's Defence Weekly, 306
Janic, Vojislav, 167
Janša, Janez, 24, 25, 229
Japan, 232
Jazz music, 92
Jedinstvo, 68
Jelačić, Ban Josip, 30
Jelić, Ratko, 177
Jennsen, Soren, 319

Jesuits, 151
Jevdjević, "Gino," 289
JNA. *See* Yugoslav National Army
John Paul II, 280–282
Josef II (Emperor), 32
Journalists, 76–77, 158. *See also* Press
Jovan (Metropolitan), 279
Jovanović, Borivoje, 305
Jovanović, Dušan, 10, 198
Jovanović, Jovan, 166
Jovič, Borislav, 50
Judiciary, 158. *See also* Courts
Jugoton record company, 93, 94
Jukić, 288
Juppe, Alain, 262

Kadijević, Veljko, 44
Karadjordjević, Jelena (Princess), 30
Karadžić, Radovan, 47, 198, 244, 246,
    257, 258, 301, 312, 316, 320
    poetry collection of, 254
    See also under Milošević, Slobodan
Karadžić, Sonja, 292
Karajlić, Nele, 102, 108–109, 114(n57)
Karamazovs, The (Jovanović), 10–11,
    198–199
Kardelj, Edvard, 39, 95, 176
Karić, Enes, 287
Karlovac, 167
Kasandra, 98
Katedra, 74
Katolički list, 137
Kavčič, Stane, 42
Kerestedijanc, Leonid, 302
Keresteianets, Leonid, 212–213
Kingdom of Serbs, Croats, and
    Slovenes, 167, 321
Kiš, Danilo, 197–198
Klaonica: Poems for Bosnia, 289
Klapper, Joseph, 85
Knin, 307
Književne novine, 70, 78, 80
Kohl, Helmut, 313
Kojić, Dušan Koja, 111
Komunist, 66, 67, 71, 77, 80
Končar, Rade, 12, 19(n15)
Korni Group, 94–95

Kosovo, 1, 8, 10, 11, 15, 26, 28, 34, 40,
    46–47, 71, 77, 105, 109, 194(n19),
    300, 303, 328(n115)
    Albanian-language press in, 67–68
    Albanians in, 10, 11, 16–17, 18, 21,
        29, 39, 46, 47, 54, 85, 106, 118,
        179, 191–192, 193, 213, 214
    Orthodox Church in, 179, 279
    Serb-Albanian frictions in, 16–17, 21,
        39, 47, 66, 85, 190
    women in, 118, 119, 120, 124, 125
Kosovo Polje, Battle of, 180, 189
Kovač, Josip, 94
Kovačh, Kornell, 94, 96
Kožja, Luka, 243
Kraigher Commission for the Reform of
    the Economic System, 9
Krajina, 47, 49, 52, 207, 212, 305, 306,
    307–308
    army in, 306, 308, 325(n48)
    ethnic composition of, 263(table)
Krajišnik, Momčilo, 54
Krško nuclear plant, 227
Kučan, Milan, 25, 49, 225
Kuharić, Franjo, 79, 147, 149, 158, 181,
    189, 277, 279
Kumanovo, 192
Kunsthalle (New York), 288
Kurtović, Elvis J., 107, 108, 109,
    114(n57)
Kuwait, 189, 244
Kvaternik, Slavko, 140, 141

Labor force. *See under* Women
Lach, Josip, 138
Laibach, 29, 98, 102–104, 292–293, 320
Lake, Anthony, 232
Land mines, 318
Language, 24, 25, 26, 32, 40, 43, 70, 77,
    97, 102, 209–210, 213, 225, 231,
    236, 278, 284, 299, 321
Latvia, 226
Law on Agrarian Reform and
    Colonization, 173
Law on Religious Communities, 173
Law on the Legal Status of Religious
    Communities, 146, 173

LCY. *See* League of Communists of
   Yugoslavia
League of Communists of Yugoslavia
   (LCY), 7, 14, 67, 147, 321
   Central Committee, 9, 11, 12, 13, 15,
      16, 17, 65
   Information Commission, 65, 68
   Party Congresses, 12, 16, 17, 18
   regional party organizations, 8, 9, 10,
      11, 12, 14–15, 16, 17
   and religious belief, 148, 155
   women leaders in, 124(table)
Lebanon, 34, 318
Legitimacy, 215
Leković, Zdravko, 66
Leninism, 13
Leo XIII, 139
Lesbianism, 127, 282
Liberalization, 10, 11, 23, 63, 126, 147,
      190
Liberals/liberalism, 7, 31, 39, 41–42,
      135, 150, 158
Libya, 185, 189
Licht, Sonja, 128
Life expectancy, 124–125
"Life Is Life" (song), 103
Lilith, 127
Liotta, P. H., 290
Lisac, Josipa, 98
Lisica, Goran "Fox," 109
Listica, 50
Literary revivals, 28–29
Lithuania, 226, 230
Ljiljan, 305
Ljubljana, 34, 73, 97, 119, 123, 127
   Theological Faculty, 144, 158
Localism, 70
London Conferences
   1913, 328(n115)
   1992, 248
Losić, Saša, 100
L'Osservatore Romano, 141, 142–143
Lukač, Sergij, 96
Lukavica, 310, 311
Lumbarda, Vojislav, 199

Macdonald, 318–319

Macedonia, 3, 7, 10, 21, 22, 27, 29, 31,
      32, 33, 38, 39, 42, 44, 46, 48, 70,
      82, 85, 92, 100, 101, 110, 165, 170,
      171, 224–225, 230–237, 328(n115)
   Albanians in, 224, 234–236
   censuses in, 234
   constitution, 230, 231
   economy, 233, 236
   elections in, 237
   and Greece, 231–233
   independence of, 54, 230, 231
   Internal Macedonian Revolutionary
      Organization–Democratic Party for
      Macedonian National Unity,
      47–48, 49
   military of, 232(table), 233
   Movement for All-Macedonian
      Action, 47
   Muslims in, 191
   name of, 231, 232
   nationalities in, 233(table)
   Orthodox Church, 175–177, 178, 179,
      181, 279
   parliament, 234, 237
   Party for Democratic Prosperity
      (PDP), 234, 235, 237
   peacekeeping forces in, 254
   political parties in, 237
   recognition of, 230–232
   Serbs in, 234, 236, 279
   Veterans Association, 105, 107
   women in, 120, 121, 286
   Yugoslav National Army in, 230
   See also Macedonians
Macedonians, 1, 40, 41, 153, 185
Maček, Vlatko, 141, 168
Machismo, 120–121, 122, 284
Magyar Szó, 68
Major, John, 259, 312–313, 325(n56)
Mamula, Branko, 44, 74–75
Managers, 126
Manatos, Andrew, 233
Mančevski, Veljo, 175
Mandić, Oliver, 99
"Maniac" (video), 104
Manolić, Josip, 246
Marcone, Ramiro, 138

Marinc, Andrej, 15
Marković, Ante, 22, 42
Marković, Dragoslav, 15
Markus, Zlatko, 136
Martić, Milan, 207
Marxism, 150, 154(table), 180. *See also*
    Communism; Socialism
Mass graves, 313
Mastnak, Tomaž, 207
Materialism, 166, 172
Mead, Margaret, 121
Media, 10, 11, 110, 127, 148, 179, 203,
    211, 229, 257, 260, 318, 320. *See
    also* Press; Radio; Television;
    under Serbia
Medjugorje, miracle at, 156–157
Mehta, Zubin, 287
Memory (rock group), 112
Mesič, Stipe, 50, 52, 209, 210, 211
Metikoš, Karlo, 903
Meznarić, Silva, 285
Middle East, 185, 189
Mihailo (Belgrade Metropolitan), 166,
    167
Mihailović, Draža, 22, 28, 172, 204
Mikulić, Branko, 39, 74
Milanović, Božo, 143
Milivojević, Dionisije, 175
Milošević, Mirjana, 44
Milošević, Sladjana Aleksandra, 96
Milošević, Slobodan, 15, 21, 22, 26–28,
    31, 32, 37, 39, 42, 43, 45, 46, 47,
    50, 53, 105, 106, 111, 127, 200,
    214, 258, 279, 299–300, 303, 306
  and Karadžić, 207, 245, 249, 250,
    257, 262
  and military, 207, 325(n48). *See also*
    Serbia, military purges in
  oppostition to, 48–49, 55, 122,
    194(n19), 201, 202–203,
    203–204, 300, 308
  and press, 69, 78, 80, 81
  and Serbian Orthodox Church, 180,
    279, 280, 308
  and Tudjman, 251
  wife of, 44
Milošević, Vladimir, 51

Mirić, Jovan, 16
Misetić, Bosiljko, 210
Mitterrand, Danielle, 204
Mizar, 101
Mladenović, Tanasije, 181
Mladić, Ratko, 258, 305, 312, 315
Mladina, 71, 72–75, 103, 110, 148
Mladost, 71
Mlinarec, Drago, 94
Mojzes, Paul, 146
Monarchies, 30–31, 40, 168
Montano, Tonny, 99
Montenegro, 3, 10, 11, 17, 21, 23, 25,
    30, 31, 39, 40, 41, 42, 44, 46, 48,
    49, 76, 80, 91, 144, 166, 175, 203,
    205
  Association of Catholic Priests, 145
  Movement for the Unification of
    Serbia and Montenegro, 47
  women in, 120, 121, 124
  See also Federal Republic of
    Yugoslavia; Montenegrins
Montenegrins, 1, 27, 82, 153, 185
Moral fields, 321–322
Mosques, 185, 186, 187, 191, 192, 223,
    277
  destruction of, 278, 287, 311
Mosse, George, 128
Mostar, 156, 278, 287, 319
Mothers, 120, 121, 128
Mount Treškavica, 312
Mount Vlasić, 311
Mrkšić, Mile, 306, 325(n48)
Mullerson, Rein, 249
Multiparty system. *See under* Political
    parties
Music, 28, 29, 92–93, 290–293, 321. *See
    also* Folk music; Rock music
Muslims, 1, 2, 22, 40, 41, 46, 123, 153,
    178, 185, 211, 213, 214, 322(n7),
    326(n79)
  and Catholic Church, 281–282
  populations, 186
  See also Islam; Women, Muslim;
    under Bosnia-Herzegovina;
    Croats; Kosovo; Macedonia
Mutilations, 50

Naši dani, 75–76
Nationalism, 15, 18, 21, 26, 27, 39, 45,
    47, 67–70, 105, 111, 127, 128, 135,
    170, 171, 179–180, 190, 201, 208,
    209–210, 215, 231, 276, 291, 320
    novels and plays about, 199
    and patriarchy, 283
Nationalization, 146, 173
National question, 185, 300
NATO. *See* North Atlantic Treaty
    Organization
Naziism, 102, 165, 200, 276
NDH. *See* Independent State of Croatia
Nedić, 276
Nedjeljna Dalmacija, 72, 80, 147, 149
Nektarije (Bishop), 173
Netherlands, 247
Neue Slowenische Kunst, 29, 102–103
Neue Zürcher Zeitung, 45
New primitivism, 108–109
New York Times, 265
Nikolaj (Bishop), 173
Nikolić, Tomislav, 205
NIN, 11, 77, 79, 80, 81, 83, 85, 96, 204
No fly zone, 312
North Atlantic Treaty Organization
    (NATO), 253, 261, 263, 264, 265,
    266, 267, 303, 304, 309, 310, 311,
    312, 314–315, 317, 328(n118)
Nova Makedonija, 82
Nova revija, 24, 69–70, 74
Novels, 197–200
Novi list, 211–212
Novi Pazar, 46, 194(n19), 300
Novi Sad, 81, 111
Nož (Drašković), 199

Oil, 39, 54, 227. *See also* Fuel
Okun, Herbert, 304
Olbina, Živana, 69
Omerbašić, Sefko, 281–282
Omladinska Iskra, 72
Opačić, Jovo, 22, 42, 43
Opinion polls, 30, 57(n46), 75, 81,
    82–83(tables), 154, 203, 205, 212,
    225, 226, 278–279, 323(n16)

Organization of the Islamic Conference,
    256
Osborne, Nigel, 291
Oslobodjenje, 76, 79, 108, 280
Owen, Lord David, 248, 249–251, 301
Owen-Stotenberg Plan, 251, 252, 301
Oznanilo, 145

Pacifism, 282, 283, 291
Pakistan, 256, 261
Paldum, Hanka, 99
Palić, Avdo, 313
Panić, Milan, 203, 244
Panić, Života, 204
Pantič, Miroslav, 54
Papandreou, Andreas, 232
Papić, Žarana, 282
Papp, Angelina, 291
Paraga, Dobroslav, 148, 189
Paroški, Milan, 320–321
Partisan mythology, 321
Pašić, Nusret, 288
Pastoralism, 119–122, 123, 124
Patriarchy, 118, 119, 120, 121, 122, 124,
    125, 128, 282–286
Pavelić, Ante, 140, 141, 321
Pavić, Milorad, 197, 275
Pavičević, Miso, 77–78
Pavle (Orthodox patriarch), 181, 202,
    207, 277, 279, 280, 281, 320
PDP. *See* Macedonia, Party for
    Democratic Prosperity
Pekić, Borislav, 197
Perelyakin, Aleksandr, 307
Perezić, Marina, 98
Perić, Ratko, 157
Perišic, Momčilo, 207
Perry, Duncan, 235–236
Perry, William J., 263, 264, 265,
    273(n139), 312
Peterle (Slovenian prime minister), 225,
    226
Petešić, Ćiril, 137
Petrović, Milutin, 178
Petrovski, Metodi, 70
PGP RTB record company, 93, 109
Phallocracy, 128–129

Philippines, 230
Pichler, Alfred, 150
Pigeonhole (Radulović), 10–11, 199
Pius XII, 137
Planinc, Milka, 66
Plavšić, Biljana, 319
Playwrights, 199, 289
Plitvice National Park, 47, 49, 318
Pluralism/pluralization, 7, 22–23, 28,
    31, 33–34, 80, 81, 112, 158, 193,
    224, 229
Poets, 289–290
Poland, 261
Polarization, 10–11, 151
Police, 168, 210. *See also under* Serbia
Political change, 7, 17–18, 68, 200, 268,
    287–288, 304
Political fragmentation, 31–32
Political parties, 7, 18, 24, 25, 31,
    33–34, 127, 202–203, 224, 229, 234
    multiparty system, 22, 32, 42, 75, 190
Politika, 68, 69, 70, 77, 80, 81, 82, 83,
    85, 180, 320, 321
Politika ekspres, 81, 85, 110
Politika Publishing House, 69, 70, 80,
    81, 207
Popit, France, 16
Popović, Aleksandar, 206
Popović, Danko, 200
Popovič, Davorin, 95
Popović, Dušan, 16
Popović, Mihailo, 14
Popović-Perišić, Nada, 204
Pop Rock, 110
Populations, 1, 124, 186, 233(table),
    244, 263(table), 268(n6), 308
    peaceful exchanges of, 323(n19)
Posavina Corridor, 310
Positivism, 166
Poverty line, 217(n42)
Pozderac, Hamdija, 16
Pravoslavlje, 65, 174, 177, 179, 180,
    181, 189, 276
Pravoslavna misao, 174
Pravoslavni misionar, 174
Preporod, 188, 189, 192
Press, 10, 11, 15, 26, 29, 40, 47, 63–85,
    190, 202

Albanian-language, 220(n114). *See
    also Rilindja*
bannings, 65, 66, 71, 73, 74, 80. *See
    also* Censorship
Catholic press, 141, 142–143, 144,
    145, 147, 148–149
Communist, 165
as critical, 77–80
freedom of, 211–212
highest circulation newspapers,
    84(table), 85
Islamic, 188
new laws on, 70–72, 81
newspaper copies sold, 84(table)
periodical most respected/frequently
    read, 82–83(tables)
publication statistics, 63
republicanization of, 67–70, 81, 83
and rock music, 96, 110
Serbian Church press, 174, 177
Ustasha press, 141
youth press, 63, 64, 66–67, 71,
    72–76, 79, 85, 103
See also under Croatia; Serbia;
    Serbian Orthodox Church;
    Slovenia; Vojvodina
Priests' associations. *See under* Catholic
    Church; Serbian Orthodox Church
Priština, 187, 188, 279
Priština, University of, 213
Privatization, 42, 208, 215, 226, 228. *See
    also* Reprivatization
Prostitution, 122–123, 123(table), 286
Protestants, 2, 153
Protocols of the Elders of Zion, 198
Prušina, Ivan, 152
Psychological disorders, 319, 320
Public meetings, participation in,
    155(table 7.3)
Public opinion, 309. *See also* Opinion
    polls
Puhovski, Žarko, 319
Puljić, Vinko, 282
Punk music, 97, 100, 102
Pusić, Vesna, 215

Rabzelj, Vladimir, 23
Račan, Ivica, 212

Radaković, Milan, 244
Radin, Furio, 214
Radio, 64, 110, 149, 157, 256, 291
  Radio Luxemburg, 93
  Radio Mileva, 22
  Radio Student, 73
  Radio-Television Belgrade, 207
  Radio-Television Slovenia, 228
Radulović, Jovan, 10, 199
Railways, 318
Ralph, Regan, 258
Rambo Amadeus, 99, 291
RAM operation, 43
Ranković, Aleksandar, 41, 176
Rape, 129, 258–259, 262, 267,
      274(n160), 284, 313
  as weapon, 284
Rapid reaction force, 312
Rasić, Mihailo, 66
Rašković, Jovan, 185, 319
Ratković, Radoslav, 13
Raznjatović, Željko, 205, 258
Record companies, 93, 94, 109
Referenda, 43, 47, 54, 230, 235,
      245–246, 250, 257
Reforms, 139, 214. *See also under*
      Economic issues
Refugees, 53, 205, 208, 214, 229, 249,
      267, 300, 308, 313, 317
Reis-ul-ulema, 186, 193, 277
Religion, 1–2, 2–3, 10, 11, 118, 179,
      181, 321
  believers/nonbelievers, 153(table),
      153–156, 155(tables), 280. *See also*
      Atheism
  conversions, 141, 160(n31), 170, 319
  interconfessional relations, 276–282
  leaders, 189
  religious laws, 146, 149, 173
  See also Catholic Church; Education,
      religious; Islam; Serbian Orthodox
      Church
Reporter, 78, 79
Reprivatization, 33, 34, 45, 224. *See also*
      Privatization
Ribičič, Čiril, 16, 23, 25
Ribičič, Mitja, 158
Rieff, David, 308

Rijeka, 123
Rilindja, 39, 68, 213
Riots, 10, 18, 34, 39, 66, 200, 201
Ristić, Bora, 236
Ristić, Ljubiša, 78
Rittig, Svetozar, 137, 138
Rizman, Rudi, 229
Rock music, 91–112, 291–293, 320
  American/British influence, 93, 94,
      97
  early years, 92–95
  ethnicity in, 99–101
  festivals, 94, 97, 111
  groups in 1990, 98
  managers for, 109–110
  names of new bands, 320
  pacifist, 291
  and political authority, 101–104
  pro-Tito, 95–96, 107–108
  Šogar rock, 100
  vocalists, 98–99
Romania, 50, 55, 172, 255, 261
  Orthodox Church, 175
Rose, Sir Michael, 263, 304, 324(n30)
Rosenthal, A. M., 317, 328(n118)
Roter, Zdenko, 135
Rupel, Dimitrij, 225
Russia, 55, 115(n73), 204, 212, 213,
      227, 230–231, 232, 247, 249, 252,
      257, 265, 302, 303, 308, 314, 315,
      317
  and Serbian forces, 254–255, 258,
      261

Safe havens, 251, 311, 313, 314, 315
Šagi-Bunić, Tomislav, 155–156
Sahinpašić, Mimo, 287
Sališ-Seewis, Franjo, 238
Sandžak, 40, 213, 214, 300, 303,
      322(n7)
Sarajevo, 94, 97, 98, 186, 248, 253, 255,
      261, 278, 281, 288, 289, 311, 312,
      314, 319
  airport, 247
  Center for the Social Activities of
      Youth, 104, 110
  Islamic Theological Faculty in, 188,
      192

National Library in, 287
State Commission for the
    Investigation of War Crimes,
    274(n160)
Sarajevo (chamber-opera), 291
"Sarajevo: Behind God's Back," 289
Sara's Story (Stefanovski), 289
Sarbanes, Paul, 232
Šarić, Ivan, 137
Satan Panonski, 112
Saudi Arabia, 255, 256
SAWPY. *See* Socialist Alliance of
    Working People of Yugoslavia
Schools, 126, 139, 146, 158, 168. *See
    also* Education; Universities
Scientific institutes, 17, 126
Seattle Convention Center, 288
Secessions, 23, 24, 25, 34, 38, 43, 46,
    49, 51, 55, 194(n19), 213, 225,
    246, 259
Secularism, 153, 166, 229
Šeks, Vladimir, 73
Self-managing communities (SIZ), 9, 33
Šeligo, Rudi, 229
Selimoški, Jakub, 193, 277
Seni diocese, 144
Separatism, 15, 190. *See also* Secessions
Šeper, Franjo, 146–147, 150
Serbia, 3, 25, 26–31, 40, 44, 45, 46, 54,
    127, 138, 144, 148
    Academy of Sciences and Arts,
        Memorandum of (1986), 198, 200
    anthem of, 26–27
    and Bosnia-Herzegovina, 32, 42,
        192–193, 202, 204
    Constitutional Court, 16
    constitutions, 27, 28, 167, 181
    and Croatia, 22, 32, 42, 44, 48, 50,
        85, 157, 170, 180, 201, 244, 246,
        320–321
    Democratic Party, 202
    DEPOS coalition, 202–203
    economy, 204, 205, 206, 215,
        318–319
    elections in, 202, 203, 207, 282
    hatred of non-Serbs, 198, 200, 282
    internal conflicts, 202–204. *See also*
        Milošević, Slobodan, opposition to

Kingdom of Serbia, 30, 166, 167
media in, 85, 283
military purges in, 202, 204, 305. *See
    also* Federal Republic of
    Yugoslavia, Army
parliament, 282
party organization in, 10, 14–15, 21,
    26
Philosophical Society, 78
police, 48, 207, 213
press in, 69, 76, 219(n89)
prostitution in, 123(table)
Radical Party, 201, 205
Renaissance Party, 201, 202
Republic Committee for Information,
    68
and Russia, 317. *See also* Russia, and
    Serbian forces
sanctions against, 236, 247, 250, 255,
    257, 262, 310, 318
Socialist Party of Serbia, 25, 201–202,
    207, 280
and Slovenia, 32, 42, 44, 48, 85, 228
women in, 119–122, 123, 124, 128,
    129, 282–283, 286
Writers' Association, 28
writers in, 28, 197–200, 320
See also Federal Republic of
    Yulgoslavia; Milošević, Slobodan;
    Serbian Orthodox Church; Serbs
Serbian Orthodox Church, 1–2, 11, 21,
    26, 28, 30, 65, 79, 123, 153,
    165–181, 225, 243, 276, 287, 320
    and Catholic Church, 168–169,
        180–181, 276, 277
    church-state relations, 167–168,
        171–173, 176, 177–180, 190
    construction programs, 173–174, 178,
        179, 180, 279
    nationalism of, 179–180
    opposition within, 177, 178
    politics of, 279–280
    press of, 174, 177
    priests' associations, 172–173,
        175–176, 177, 178
    vilification of, 165
    and World War II, 170–171
    See also under Milošević, Slobodan

Serbian Republic of Bosnia-
  Herzegovina, 245, 246
Serbian Socialist Youth Foundation, 179
Serbs, 1, 82, 153, 185. *See also under*
  individual republics
Šešelj, Vojislav, 74, 201, 205, 258
Sex and Character (Weininger), 122
Sexuality, 117, 124, 127, 129
Shadows, 93–94
Shalikashvili, John, 313
Shoup, Paul, 202
Shultz, George P., 309
Šiber, Ivan, 209
Silajdžić, Haris, 257, 302
Simić, Andrei, 120, 321–322
Široki Brijeg, 141–142
SIZ. *See* Self-managing commnunities
Skopje, 123, 187, 192, 235
Skopje, University of, 235
Slavonia, 212, 213, 306, 307, 318
Slavonski Brod, 50
Slavs, 1, 68, 119
Slijepčević, Djoko, 171
Slobodna Dalmacija, 83, 85, 211, 305
Slovenia, 3, 7, 10, 11, 14, 15, 17, 21,
  27, 31, 34, 42, 44, 45–46, 102, 127,
  189, 225–230, 320
  and Catholic Church, 135, 138, 143,
    144, 149, 157, 158, 228, 229
  Committee for the Protection of
    Human Rights, 24
  Communist Party in, 25
  constitution, 24, 228
  and Croatia, 39, 44, 48, 52, 54, 227
  economy, 226, 227–228, 229
  elections in, 237, 242(n92), 285
  Foreign Ministry, 224
  foreign relations of, 226–228
  independence of, 37, 38, 43, 49, 51,
    69, 225–226, 267
  Journalists' Association, 76
  Liberal Democratic Party, 228, 237,
    242(n92)
  military in, 225
  mobilization of, 24–26
  press in, 69–70, 81, 82. *See also*
    Slovenia, youth press
  recognition of, 227, 280

Republican Party, 226
Socialist Youth Organization, 73
Slovenian Alliance, 285
Slovenian Peasant Union, 24
Supreme Court, 73
  women in, 119–120, 123–124, 125,
    128, 284–285
  writers in, 28–29
  youth organization, 24–25
  youth press, 66–67, 71, 72–75, 103
  See also Slovenes; *under* Serbia
Slovenes, 1, 71, 82, 153
Smailović, Vadran, 290–291
Smiljković, Radoš, 13–14
Smith, Rupert, 312
Smoking Forbidden, 102, 104, 107–108,
  109
Smole, Jože, 69
Social change, 128–129, 268
Socialism, 223–224, 236, 285
Socialist Alliance of Slovenia, 24–25
Socialist Alliance of Working People of
  Yugoslavia (SAWPY), 9, 12, 13–14,
  25, 65, 71, 72, 78, 144, 148, 154,
  188, 189–190, 224
Socialist Youth Federation, 71
Society of Catholic Priests, 145
Society of Journalists, 158
Socijalizam, 8, 13
Sontag, Susan, 288
SOS Telephone for Women and
  Children Victims of Violence, 284
Soviet Union, 51, 101, 137, 172. *See*
  also Russia
Spain, 227, 321
Sporazum, 8, 19(n2)
Srebrenica, 313
Srem, 41
Srškić, Milan, 167
Stambolić, Ivan, 21, 26, 39, 106, 180,
  291
Stanišić, Mico, 312
Stanković, Milić, 199
Stanković, Simonida, 292
Start, 79, 80, 83, 85, 211
Stav, 68
Steele, Jonathan, 317
Stefanovski, Goran, 289

Stepinac, Alojzije, 41, 79, 135, 136, 137,
    139, 147, 157, 168, 189, 204, 281
  trial of, 140–143
Stojadinović, Milan, 168, 169
Stojanović, Ivan, 69
Stojanović, Lazar, 206
Stojanović, Svetozar, 13, 14
Stoller, Robert, 284
Stoltenberg, Thorvald, 251, 301
Ströhm, Carl Gustav, 311
Strossmayer, Josip Juraj, 135, 136, 144,
    157, 210
Student, 75
Stupar, Slobodan, 206
Stvarno i moguće (Ćosić), 68
Subsidies, 144, 168
Sudan, 256
Sušak, Gojko, 261
Šuštar (Archbishop), 157–158
Svetosavsko zvonce, 174
Switzerland, 227
Symbols, 135–136, 254
Syria, 185

Tadić, Dušan, 259
"Tamo daleko," (song) 26–27
Tanjug, 16, 43, 148, 217(n42)
Taxation, 45, 128, 151
Tehran Radio, 256
Telephone tapping, 207
Television, 64, 80, 81, 107, 110, 149,
    204, 207, 228, 229, 292
Terzić, Dragan, 181
Thatcher, Margaret, 304, 313
Thomas, Dorothy, 258
Thonon, Francois, 307
*Tito: For the Second Time Among the
    Serbs* (film), 206
Tito, Josip Broz, 2, 7, 10, 23, 27, 32, 38,
    39, 41–42, 85, 92, 93, 95–96, 102,
    104, 106, 107–108, 206, 299, 300,
    321, 322
  and Catholic Church, 138–140, 143,
    146, 147, 158
  and Stalin, 198
Tito, Jovanka, 97
Titograd, 187

Tolj, Ivan, 308
Tomac, Zdravko, 23
Toran, Jean-Louis, 320
Totalitarianism, 29, 103
Tourism, 208
  tourist sites damaged, 318
Trade, 44, 227–228
  embargos, 232, 233, 236. *See also*
    Serbia, sanctions against
Trailović, Dragoljub, 68
Trajkovski, Goran, 101
Transylvania, 321
Travnik, 310, 311
Tren 2 (Isaković), 198
Trifunović, Ljuba, 96
Tri-named people, theory of, 40
Tripalo, Miko, 27, 41, 42
Tudjman, Franjo, 41, 42, 50, 52, 135,
    209, 210, 211, 212, 214, 219(n89),
    279, 281, 319
Tunisia, 256
Tupurkovski, Vasil, 31
Turkey/Turks, 1, 28, 188, 230, 233, 236,
    256, 310, 317
Tuzla, 310, 311
TV Politika, 81

Ukraden, Neda, 98
Ukraine, 256, 265, 313
Ule, Mirjana, 285
Unemployment, 44, 125, 126, 205, 208,
    218(n71), 228, 236, 305, 318
Union of Yugoslav Journalists, 72
Unitarism, 26, 68
United Nations, 212, 232, 233, 236, 267,
    313
  General Assembly, 252
  peacekeeping forces, 245, 247, 253,
    257, 261, 263, 264, 265, 307, 308,
    312, 314. *See also* United Nations,
    Protection Force
  Protection Force (UNPROFOR), 247,
    256, 263, 265–266, 266(table). *See
    also* United Nations, peacekeeping
    forces
  Security Council, 244, 247, 250, 258,
    310

soldiers retained by Serbs, 303, 311

vetos in, 317

United States, 37, 51, 93, 102, 104, 165, 175, 188, 211, 226, 227, 304, 314

and arms embargo, 251, 252, 254, 257, 261, 265, 301

and Bosnia-Herzegovina, 247, 250, 253–254, 260–261, 263, 302, 303, 310

and Croatia, 265, 308

Franciscan Center in, 156

and Macedonia, 231, 232–233

Serbian advocacy in, 259–260

Universities, 10, 125, 146, 235, 318

UNPROFOR. *See* United Nations, Protection Force

Urban areas, 118, 119, 153, 178, 278

Ustasha fascists. *See under* Croatia

Uti possidetis, ita possidetis, 249–250, 267, 316

Valentić, Nikica, 208, 279

Values, 2, 29. *See also* Culture, traditionalism

Vance, Cyrus, 245, 248, 249–251, 301

Vance-Owen Plan, 249–251, 301

Van Heuven, Marten, 260

Vasić, Miloš, 55

Vatican, 147, 157, 276, 320

Vatican II Council, 135, 136, 150–151

See also Catholic Church; John Paul II

Vatikan i Jasenovac (Dedijer), 276

Večernje novosti, 69, 79, 83

Večernji list, 211

Vego, Ivica, 152

Velimirović, Nikolaj, 171, 172

Veselinov, Dragan, 55

Vesić, Dušan, 95, 106

Vesnik, 173, 177, 178

Veto system, 27, 38

Victim psychology, 197, 198, 199, 277, 283

Victorija, Snežana Mišković, 98

Vidik, 75

Vietnam War, 244

Vjesnik, 18, 70, 71, 72, 158, 211, 251

Vlahović, Petar, 319

Vlahović, Veljko, 126

Vlaškalić Commission, 16

Vojno delo, 244

Vojska, 305

Vojvodina, 8, 10, 11, 15, 21, 26, 28, 39, 45, 49, 71, 91, 100, 123, 124, 138, 170, 213, 214, 300, 303, 322(n7)

press in, 68, 76, 80

Serbs in, 48

Vrcan, Srdjan, 147

Vreme, 55, 81, 207

Vreme smrti (Ćosić), 199–200

Vrhovec, Josip, 17

Vučković, Dušan, 259

Vukasinović, Milić, 99

Vukov, Vice, 105

Vukovar, 287

Vušković, Lina, 282

Wall Street Journal, 310

War crimes, 258–259, 311–312, 316. *See also* Atrocities; Ethnic cleansing; Genocide; Rape

Washington Post, 315

Weapons, 43, 47, 52, 204, 213, 235, 245, 246, 250, 252, 256, 259, 302, 310, 311, 313

of combatants in Bosnian war, 265(table), 305–306, 307

exclusion zones for, 261, 315

Russian arms for Bosnian Serbs, 254–255, 261

Serbian arms for Bosnian Serbs, 257–258, 310

See also Arms embargo

Weber, Vinko, 145

Weininger, Otto, 122

Western Europe, 247, 316–317. *See also* European Community; *individual countries*

White Button, 91, 96, 98, 99, 102, 105, 106, 107, 111

Wilks, Talvin, 289

Women, 83, 124(table), 188, 228, 280, 313

fear of, 121, 122, 284

in labor force, 124, 125, 126, 128
Muslim, 191–192, 274(n160), 278
names of, 121
Women in Black, 283
Women's Party, 282, 283
See also Abortion; Feminism; Gender
issues; Lesbianism; Patriarchy;
Rape; *under individual republics*
Workers' councils, 126
World Bank, 208
World War II, 23, 40, 79, 135, 136–137,
157, 165, 170–171, 181, 197, 198,
243, 276, 300, 321
veterans, 154

Xenophobia, 205
Xhaferi, Arben, 235

Yeltsin, Boris, 315
Yugoslavia, 1–2, 34, 49
budgets, 38, 44, 45–46, 54
Constitution, 16, 25, 38, 68, 146, 149,
181
establishment of, 1, 37
Federal Assembly, 32, 81, 277
Federal Executive Council, 46
Kingdom of Yugoslavia, 279
military forces, 50, 52, 149, 168, 169.
See also Yugoslav National Army
Office of the State Prosecutor, 64–65
relations among republics in, 38, 48,
49, 190, 225, 321

State Secretariat for Information, 66
See also League of Communists of
Yugoslavia; Tito, Josip Broz;
Yugoslavism
Yugoslavism, 321
organic vs. integral, 176
Yugoslav League of Journalists, 71
Yugoslav National Army (JNA), 8, 37,
43, 44, 46, 48, 49–50, 50–51, 52,
54, 63, 226, 228–229, 243, 244,
245, 246, 252
and press, 66–67, 75
purges, 202, 204
YU-Group, 100
YU-Madonna, 98

Zagreb, 34, 97, 119, 127, 186, 208, 281
Z–4 plan, 302–303, 323(n16)
Zakaria, Fareed, 260
Žanić, Pavao, 152, 156–157
Zavrl, Franci, 75
Zbogom Srbijo, 291–292
Žepa, 313
Zeri i Rinise, 47, 75
Z–4 plan. *See under* Zagreb
Žilnik, Želimir, 206
Živković, Miroslav, 13
Žužek, Aleš, 285
Žvan, Antun, 12, 13
Žuroslav, 13
Žužek, Aleš, 285
Žvan, A